D1606595

THE ROLE OF THEORY
IN SEX RESEARCH

THE KINSEY INSTITUTE SERIES

John Bancroft, *General Editor*

Volume I
MASCULINITY/FEMININITY: Basic Perspectives
Edited by
June Machover Reinisch, Leonard A. Rosenblum,
and Stephanie A. Sanders

Volume II
HOMOSEXUALITY/HETEROSEXUALITY:
Concepts of Sexual Orientation
Edited by
David P. McWhirter, Stephanie A. Sanders,
and June Machover Reinisch

Volume III
ADOLESCENCE AND PUBERTY
Edited by
John Bancroft and June Machover Reinisch

Volume IV
AIDS AND SEX:
An Integrated Biomedical and Biobehavioral Approach
Edited by
Bruce Voeller, June Machover Reinisch,
and Michael Gottlieb

Volume V
RESEARCHING SEXUAL BEHAVIOR:
Methodological Issues
Edited by
John Bancroft

Volume VI
THE ROLE OF THEORY IN SEX RESEARCH
Edited by
John Bancroft

THE ROLE OF
THEORY IN
SEX RESEARCH

Edited by John Bancroft

Indiana University Press
Bloomington • Indianapolis

This book is a publication of
Indiana University Press
601 North Morton Street
Bloomington, IN 47404-3797 USA

http://www.indiana.edu/~iupress
Telephone orders 800-842-6796
Fax orders 812-855-7931
Orders by e-mail iuporder@indiana.edu

The paper used in this publication meets the minimum requirements of American National Standard for Information Sciences—
Permanence of Paper for Printed Library Materials, ANSI Z39.48-
1984.

Manufactured in the United States of America

Library of Congress Cataloging-in-Publication Data

The Role of theory in sex research / John Bancroft, editor.
    p. cm.—(The Kinsey Institute series; v. 6)
Proceedings from a conference held at the Kinsey Institute on
    May 14–17, 1998, in Bloomington, Indiana.
Includes bibliographical references and index.
ISBN 0-253-33706-2 (cloth)
    1. Sexology—Research—Congresses. 2. Sex—Congresses.
I. Bancroft, John. II. Kinsey Institute for Research in Sex,
Gender, and Reproduction. III. Series.

HQ60 .R65 2000
306.7'072—dc21
                                        99-056971

1   2   3   4   5   05   04   03   02   01   00

Contents

Introduction

Researchers into human sexuality are currently grappling with issues of major importance to the human race. The field of sex research, however, is fragmented, partly by discipline and partly by contrasting epistemological approaches. Typically, we see research by the medical and psychological sciences that is relatively atheoretical in approach and guided principally by the application of "scientific method" (in particular the testing of ostensibly refutable hypotheses). Increasingly in the social sciences we see research from a different epistemological background, using methods of inquiry (e.g., qualitative research) which are not easily combined or integrated into those of the conventional medical/psychological school. Furthermore, these differences also result in difficulty in meaningful communication across approaches.

Yet the field urgently needs interdisciplinary research which crosses this epistemological gap. At its simplest, any comprehensive understanding of human sexuality requires that we take both biological and cultural determinants into account, even if the relative importance of each may vary from issue to issue.

This book is the outcome of a workshop entitled "The Role of Theory in Sex Research," held at the Kinsey Institute on May 14 to 17, 1998. The principal objective of the workshop, and of this book, is to seek useful discourse among researchers from different epistemological backgrounds which would facilitate interdisciplinary research in the future. Obviously, we had to be selective about what topics we covered. Four themes were chosen, "Sexuality through the Life Cycle," "Sexual Orientation," "Individual Differences in Sexual Risk Taking," and "Adolescent Sexuality." In each case two presenters were chosen who were known to use different theoretical perspectives, so that a contrast in the use of theory would be evident and open for discussion. For each theme two or three people, again coming from varying theoretical backgrounds, were invited discussants. The format for the workshop was much the same as that used for the last volume in the Kinsey Symposium Series, *Researching Sexual Behavior* (edited by John Bancroft, Indiana University Press, 1997). Each presenter prepared a preconference manuscript which was circulated to all participants. They were then asked to present the gist of their paper briefly at the workshop, taking no more than 10 minutes. The invited discussants were given around 15 minutes to present their responses, and the bulk of the program time was given to general discussion, all of which was recorded, transcribed and subsequently edited. The presenters and the invited discussants had the opportunity to polish or develop their papers after the conference for the purpose of this volume. In some cases, the presenter's or discussant's final papers were substantially different from their original contribution. In such cases, any obvious inconsistency with the published discussion will be commented on as an editorial footnote. To a considerable extent the general discussion stands on its own.

Each presenter was asked to keep in mind the potential policy implications of their approach, and for the fourth session, on adolescent sexuality, particular emphasis on policy was requested from both the presenters and discussants.

An underlying assumption in the planning of this workshop was that the human sexual condition, like most aspects of the human condition, is too complex to be grasped in reality by the human intellect, and that the best we can do is to develop models which are simplified versions of the reality. By virtue of this simplification, the models are comprehensible. Their worth, on the other hand, will depend on their value in helping to formulate strategies for tackling important problems. Hence part of this value will be measured by their usefulness in influencing policy makers. The differences that will undoubtedly remain will be in the criteria used for judging the value of the model. Such differences, defined in that way, are probably more resolvable than the basic differences in formulating the models in the first place. The challenge of the workshop was to discuss these alternative approaches—not to see which produced the best models, but to see how they might usefully work together in producing even better models. The reader will discover the extent to which we achieved that objective. Indeed, it will become apparent that participants varied in their preparedness to share the above assumption. To some extent, we had to change our themes as we tackled the process of finding suitable participants. We wanted participants who would differ in their approach but who would be genuinely interested in looking for common ground or building bridges between the different approaches. It would have been easy to select participants who would have quickly locked into intellectual warfare of an unproductive nature, and for the most part we succeeded in avoiding that. Perhaps the closest earlier example of such a meeting was held in Cascais, Portugal, in 1993, entitled "Theorizing Sexuality: Evolution, Culture and Development." I had the opportunity to discuss this meeting at some length with Paul Abramson and Gil Herdt, who were both organizers of that meeting funded by the Wenner Gren Foundation. This meeting was beset with problems, mainly because of the confrontation between irreconcilably different approaches of the participants (although a useful book resulted—*Sexual Nature, Sexual Culture,* edited by P. R. Abramson and S. D. Pinkerton (University of Chicago Press, 1995).

We had to make some late changes because people dropped out for one reason or another, and this did lead to some loss of balance in our program. This of course was not the fault of the participants, each of whom did what she or he said they would do, but of the organization.

In the final session, two participants were asked to summarize their impressions of the meeting: first Richard Parker, with a particular emphasis on cultural aspects and second Robert Michael, on policy. Using the editor's prerogative, I have added a third post-workshop summary as the final chapter, entitled "Some Conclusions and a Few Afterthoughts," which I have formulated as I worked on the editing of the volume.

—John Bancroft

Part 1

Sexuality across the Life Cycle

Gender, Sexuality, and Human Development

ANKE A. EHRHARDT

Introduction

The major goal of this paper is to propose a multidisciplinary approach toward our understanding of the development of human sexuality throughout the life course, with a particular emphasis on gender and the differences between women and men. I want to argue for a biopsychosocial theoretical perspective which will enrich our understanding and move us beyond our traditionally polarized viewpoints of biomedical viewpoints, on the one hand, and social constructionist viewpoints on the other. We have learned important lessons from both perspectives; the so-called essentialists have kept us abreast of shared behavior patterns and so-called social constructionists have illuminated our thinking about the diversity of behavior and encouraged us to be critical about our assumptions.

However, we urgently need more complex explanatory models that can encompass advances from different disciplines and might ultimately be integrated rather than leading to parallel investigations and discussions.

To provoke discussions of integrated theoretical approaches toward gender, sexuality, and the life course, I will draw on specific examples which seem to be crucial for the debate. These examples will focus on the development of gender differences and their importance for the understanding of sexual behavior between women and men.

For this paper, I am particularly drawing on writings by Alice Rossi and the work of the contributors to the book *Sexuality across the life course* (1994); Eleanor Maccoby's two important reviews on the development of gender—"Gender as a social category" (1988) and "Gender and relationships" (1990)—and her book *The two sexes: Growing up apart, coming together* (1998); John Gagnon's paper "Sexuality across the life course in the United States" (1989); and some of my own writings and presentations (for example, "The psychobiology of gender" [1984];

"Age, gender, and sexual risk behavior for sexually transmitted diseases in the United States" [with Wasserheit, 1992]).

Biopsychosocial Models

A biopsychosocial perspective emphasizes an integrative approach that includes biological, psychological and socio-environmental factors. To quote Alice Rossi (1994):

> Human beings are embodied creatures; our thoughts and feelings find expression through physical and chemical processes internal to our bodies, and despite enormous cultural diversity across all known societies in the human record, all societies accommodate key characteristics of the human species. . . . Any approach to the study of human sexuality that sets biology and social behavior in competition or that stresses only one dimension to the neglect of the other, is counterproductive. It is futile to study human behavioral systems without integrating all significant levels of causation. Hence our goal ought to be an integration of all relevant systems and all relevant disciplines involved in sexual and reproductive functioning. (p. 4)

It seems to me that the difficulty with integrating these different sets of influences is related to our passionate search for explanations that are too simple that take us into sharply divided fields of research and lead us back and forth between the discovery of a biological marker and a social constellation, which strips the mind from the brain and the rest of the body.

The model most often applied is the *main-effect model,* which postulates that *one* factor determines or predominantly influences a particular behavioral outcome. For instance, a constitutional defect, such as an abnormality in the prenatal or postnatal hormonal makeup of a person, produces a specific sexual orientation, irrespective of the social environment in which the individual grows up. Conversely, a specific environment will produce a sexual orientation, no matter what the individual's genes, hormones, and sex organs are. The model has the advantage of being simple, practical for the researcher, and conclusive. Researchers typically hone in on *one* event that is taken to be the most important determinant of the behavior, and they are often ready to discard all knowledge of other relevant factors. The problem with the main-effect model is that many cases do not fit a one-factor model. Therefore, we are particularly vulnerable to going from one new discovery to the next in hope of finding a better explanation of the behavior under study.

The second model is the *interactional model.* This model considers a variety of constitutional and social environmental factors to explain and, more important, to predict an individual's behavior. For a number of years some of us have been arguing for an *interactional* or *transactional* model that is based on a dynamic concept of development which posits a continual and progressive interplay between the organism and its environment. But we have not made sufficient progress in conceptualization or methodology to truly apply new approaches. Instead, we have split into essentialists and social constructionists.

Other areas of human development have moved forward and applied such an interactional approach and are defining theory and method. For instance, in his excellent Op-Ed piece on the bell curve in the *New York Times* (December 26, 1994), Myron Hofer points out that static biological main-effect models have become totally outdated. Hofer points out that "fetal and infant brains in a wide range of species have been found to organize the structure of their own cell networks on the basis of feedback from the sensory environments of early life and from the stimulation provided by their own behavior. Individual genes in the cells of the developing brain are in effect turned on and off in a complex pattern by signals from their immediate and distant environments. Genes in the action, we have learned, are more like an information network than the static blueprints they were once likened to" (p. A19).

In an article about postnatal brain development in the *Science Times* (August 29, 1995), Sandra Blakeslee presents evidence from both animal and human brain development and suggests that the newborn brain comes equipped with a set of genetically based rules for how learning takes place and then is literally shaped by experience. For instance, it has, of course, been known for a long time that hearing and language are abilities that develop during critical time periods. A Japanese baby can distinguish an "R" from an "L" but loses the ability to do so at age three, since Japanese does not have an "L" sound. After ten, most people cannot learn to speak a second language without an accent. In recent years, the search for other critical windows of development has extended to other biological systems of the brain. There is evidence that many animal and human infants develop a control point in early infancy for how much of various stress hormones they will release in particular conditions.

My colleague Myron Hofer at the New York State Psychiatric Institute has been directing research on development with different animal species and human infants and has shown the profound and long-term effect of maternal-infant interactions on regulation of the infant's neural development (Hofer, 1994; Hofer, 1996). Of course, we have known for some time that early human development is very important, but now the evidence is mounting that there are demonstrable brain changes based on social-environmental experiences.

Bill Greenough, who has been a pioneer in this field, has shown the changes of synaptic and neuronal density for rats reared after weaning in environmentally different cages for thirty days (Greenough & Sirevaag, 1991). There is now direct evidence for analogous changes in brain development in human infants. Studies by Harry Chugani (1998) at the University of Michigan and Peter Huttenlocher (Huttenlocher & Dabholkar, 1997) at the University of Chicago based on anatomical measurements of the brains of children killed in car accidents and on infant PET scans suggest that humans are not too different from other species. Newborn brains have fewer connections between neural cells, synapses, than adult brains. Indeed, the number of synapses reaches adult level by age two and continues to increase; it surpasses the adult level from age four to ten and then begins to drop to the adult level by age eighteen. Similar patterns seem to hold for the complexity of dendrites or branches (Blakeslee, 1995).

Many questions remain, but the evidence certainly suggests an ongoing interplay between the genome and learning that has direct effects on the wiring of the brain. Modulated by experience, the process seems to create human brains similar in overall structure and interconnections but unique in terms of fine connections. The concept of a critical period for different kinds of learning needs to be determined and so does the extent of brain plasticity beyond early stages of development.

As Greenough and Sirevaag (1991) point out, this kind of evidence has revolutionized the conceptualization of brain development since the 1960s but has had very little influence on developmental theory in psychology, where we are still stuck on the identical twin paradigm, which we have made more static than it ever was before.

I would strongly suggest that we need to move beyond the debate whether, for instance, gender identity or sexual orientation is inborn or learned. We need to apply a more complex model to our understanding of human development and assess and determine the specific chains of events which integrate different kinds of determinants.

The Development of Gender

A life course perspective can be a heuristic framework from which to examine patterns of sexuality from birth to death and to tie behavior patterns to age, to major social transitions, or to major physical transitions, such as puberty, reproductive events, menopause, and decline of health. Whatever approach they use, most theories attribute major importance to gender as a structuring principle.

My discussion will specifically address the critical importance of gender in the unfolding of sexuality between women and men. In this context, I will not deal with sexual orientation in any detail since that is the topic of other papers in this volume.

My argument will be that development of gender during the first decade of life is of crucial importance for the unfolding of sexuality and sexual interactions between women and men. I will attempt a bio-psychosocial approach without attributing any weighted importance to any one factor, whether its origin is genetic, hormonal, or social-environmental. In this context, three crucial aspects of gender involve gender identity, gender behavior differences, and gender interactions.

When it comes to *gender identity* as a person's own sense of belonging to one sex or the other, our theoretical positions have varied dramatically from a biological deterministic one to an integrative one and, most recently, to an interesting split into two camps that attribute major deterministic power to biology, on the one hand, and to gender as a social construction on the other. The paradigm of children born with intersexuality has been at the center of this debate.

A brief historical overview of our shifting theoretical points of view is illustrative in this context. Until about 50 years ago, scientists and clinicians did not use the term *gender* but spoke of *sex*. Sex was determined by biology, and at that time biology meant the structure of the gonads, which were either testicular or ovarian. If a person's sex was in doubt, as in babies with ambiguous genitalia, an exploratory laparotomy and a histologic examination of the gonads determined the sex of rearing. The underlying assumption was that the gonads represented the *true* sex and that they also determined a person's feelings of identity. Several examples exist of people who lived tragic lives of obscurity because they could not identify with their declared gonadal sex and were not allowed to get a valid birth certificate or to get married because no physician would verify their gender identity if it differed from their gonadal sex. In particular, this applied to genetic males with an extreme degree of microphallus who identified as females or to genetic females totally virilized during pre- and postnatal development who identified as males.

In 1945, Albert Ellis published a review article based on 84 cases of hermaphrodites, stating that the sex role in such cases "accords primarily not with his or her internal or external somatic characteristics, but rather with his or her masculine or feminine up bringing" (p. 120). The breakthrough, however, came in 1955 when John Money, in co-authorship with Joan and John Hampson (Money, Hampson, & Hampson 1955a; Money, Hampson, & Hampson 1955b) formulated a new theory of the determinants of sex, using for the first time the terms *gender role* and *gender identity*. The introduction of gender role and gender identity as new terms was critical because it meant having a term not bound to biological sex that included behaviors related to masculinity and femininity other than sexual behaviors. The most important scientific advance of the proposed theory, though, was that sex was determined by a number of variables rather than one, including psychological and social sex. This was a major contribution to our knowledge of psychosexual differentiation. For a while, the theory that gender is determined by a number of variables interacting with each other seemed to be on solid ground.

Recently, this theory has been challenged and has been labeled as "not biological" enough, because of examples of patients who did not identify with their assigned gender at birth or thereafter and who changed their gender later in life. If these changes are concordant with a prenatal biological variable, such as the chromosomes, significant influence is attributed to biology; this has led to the questioning of the importance of postnatal social environmental effects of gender identity development.

Another criticism of the application of Money's theory to the management of intersex babies comes from a different camp, namely from patient groups and some social scientists, who argue against assignment to the female or male gender at birth and lobby for personal freedom of the affected child to give him or her the freedom to choose his or her own gender at a later point in life (Meyer-Bahlburg, 1998).

Gender Differences and Gender Negotiation

Most people do not question that their primary identification is to one or the other gender. Gender identity, thus, may not be the most interesting aspect of gender in our discussion of women's and men's sexual behavior. However, the expression of one's gender identity is reflected in *gender-role behavior* and *gender-specific behavior,* often referred to as masculine and feminine behavior. Sex differences in behavior are more variable than gender identity; they may change with one's age, social contacts, or cultural norms. Maccoby (1988) examined the profound effect of gender on girls' and boys' play behavior and encounters with each other during the pre-pubertal years. Maccoby examined the significance of gender in the children's social groupings. From preschool years until puberty, children prefer same-gender groups. Maccoby and Jacklin (1987) described a longitudinal study in which they were able to document that among nursery school children of 4.5 years of age, children spent three times as much time with peers of the same gender. By age 6.5 years, the ratio of same-gender to opposite-gender play time had increased to 11 to 1.

One of the likely explanations for this striking phenomenon is the difference in play behavior between boys and girls; boys tend to engage in more rough-and-tumble, body-contact play than girls. This difference in play style has profound effects on many different social contexts. Maccoby (1988) reviewed the observation by Charlesworth and Dzur (1987) of children who needed to set up a cooperative system to view a movie through a movie viewer with a one-eyed eyepiece. There were four children in each group, and only one child could view the movie at a time. Both boys' and girls' groups managed to achieve cooperation. However, the techniques used were different. In both cases, one child emerged as the dominant one. In boys' groups, dominant boys more often used the technique of shouldering other boys out of the way, while dominant girls used verbal persuasion. It is probably important that the physical dominance behavior of boys was not hostile behavior but was, rather, connected with expressed fun and pleasure. The same experiment on mixed groups of two boys and two girls resulted in the boys achieving the dominant role and the girls occupying helping positions. The verbal persuasion that worked for girls with other girls was not effective with boys.

Jacklin and Maccoby (1978) also found that girls' attempts to influence boys were not very effective even at the early age of 33 months. In mixed-gender groups, if one child expressed an undesirable behavior toward another child such as taking a toy away, a girl would respond to a boy's verbal request and stop, while the opposite interaction, a girl's vocal prohibition, would have no effect on the boy's behavior.

In her recent book, Maccoby (1998) strongly argues that the development of gender differences in childhood are of critical importance for the sexual interaction between adolescent girls and boys and, subsequently, between women and men. These long-term patterns of gender differences lend themselves to a biopsychosocial perspective.

The investigation of the potential role of prenatal hormones on gender differences in play behavior is relevant in this context. The series of studies that our own group has conducted with diverse groups of girls and boys who were exposed to prenatal hormonal anomalies illuminates the potential effect of estrogen and androgen on the expression of gender-related behavior (e.g., review by Ehrhardt & Meyer-Bahlburg, 1981). Our observations are generally consistent with those of other investigators. The most important finding in this context is perhaps the finding that girls exposed to unusually high levels of androgen during their prenatal development were found to show high levels of physically energetic outdoor play behavior and low levels of nurturant behavior in terms of parenting rehearsal. They were significantly different in these respects from matched normal controls. The behavior was long term and could not be solely explained by the various social and environmental factors assessed. In a number of separate studies, prenatal exposure to pharmacological doses of estrogen and progesterone was assessed, and it was found that those sex hormones were associated with the expected opposite effect, namely, relatively less physically energetic play behavior and an increase in more nurturant behavior as exhibited in doll play and infant care in girls and in less aggressive play behavior in boys. This finding could be interpreted as an antiandrogenic effect of some of the estrogen/progesterone compounds, analogous to some of the actions of these hormones demonstrated in animal experiments. The behavior variation *within* one gender is often wider than *between* the genders. Therefore, it may well be that the studies of clinical populations may ultimately point to more interesting relationships between levels of sex hormones and temperamental differences within rather than between genders.

Rather than examine in more detail the evidence on psychoendocrine relations in the development of human gender differences, I want to suggest the ways in which hormones might interact with social and environmental stimuli. For instance, if high levels of prenatal androgens are indeed associated with physical, energetic, rough-and-tumble play in normal children, what conclusion can be drawn from such a contingency? It certainly does not mean that prenatal androgens determine this particular play behavior independent of the social environment in which a child grows up. Rather, it may mean a predisposition to learn certain behaviors more readily.

I would suggest that the potential role of prenatal hormones may affect temperamental predisposition between boys and girls and variations within a gender. Within the context of a biopsychosocial approach, the actual expression of the behavior is dependent on a network of factors. Again, I am not attributing primacy or immutability to the hormonal variables—rather I would suggest that they may be an important link in a chain of events. Gender differences in play behavior of boys and girls in our society are typically described as the propensity of boys rather than girls to engage in rough-and-tumble play. Comparative studies have shown similar patterns in many other societies (Edwards & Whiting, 1988.) In spite of overlapping curves between girls and boys, this is thus a fairly stable difference.

However, as Maccoby argues, measuring individual differences of this type may not be as illuminating as differences in social groupings. Maccoby's 1990 article is of particular importance here. From the preschool years on, girls and boys differ in type and style of social interaction. In fact, Maccoby suggests that gender-typical differences in relationships with same-gender and opposite-gender peers signal differences in sexual interactions which remain seminal throughout many women's and men's lives (Maccoby, 1998).

Maccoby believes that the strong preference of girls for same-gender peers from early development on is attributable to the fact that the play behavior of boys is often characterized by rough-and-tumble interactions and by their orientation toward dominance and competition. Girls seem somewhat averse to these male-to-male interactions. The second reason for girls to prefer same-gender interactions may be that they find it difficult to influence boys. It is less clear why boys prefer other boys throughout childhood. Indeed, developmental studies suggest that girls leave boys' groupings at an earlier age. The important fact is that boys and girls develop distinctive styles of interaction which become firmly established and reinforced in their predominantly same-gender play groups throughout the first decade of life.

A number of studies have attempted to observe and analyze these distinctive patterns of interaction. For boys, issues of dominance are much more prevalent. For girls, conversation and verbal interaction are more socially binding processes, i.e., girls express agreement, pause, more readily give other girls room to speak, etc. There are other important examples of the different styles between boys and girls. Boys use more physical threats and girls use more "conflict-mitigating" strategies, more persuasion and attempts to keep group cohesion.

After children have developed their distinctive interactive styles in same-gender peer groups, there is very little play interaction with the opposite gender except during children's learning experiences in co-educational classrooms.

Girls and boys begin to have increased contact in adolescence under new parameters of physical attraction. They must adapt to cross-gender interactions with very little experience and very little guidance by adults, especially in our society where sex and gender education is at best sporadic. Boys and girls also come to these cross-gender interactions with expectations that they will encounter the same patterns of behavior they have experienced in their same-gender peer groups. Young women expect more reciprocal agreement; instead they are confronted with masculine patterns that are focused to a greater degree on performance, dominance, and competition.

As Maccoby (1998) argues, these established patterns of interactive styles among girls and boys may have a strong influence on gender-specific differences in sexual behavior throughout the life cycle, e.g., women's greater need for intimacy and men's emphasis on sexual performance.

Gender Sexuality Scripts

To understand women's and men's styles of interaction around sexual behavior, the script concept is particularly useful. It focuses on mutually dependent expectations and interactions, i.e., "the script as the organization of mutually shared conventions that allows two or more actors to participate in a complete act involving mutual dependence" (Gagnon & Simon, 1973, p. 20).

Issues of control, initiation, and dominance continue to play a crucial role in women's and men's gender scripts of sexual behavior. My colleagues and I have been conducting a series of qualitative studies with several hundred women and men in order to explore up-to-date gender scripts between women and men; we have become keenly aware of gender differences between women and men in their expectations, behaviors, and styles of interaction (Seal et al., 1995; Seal, Wagner-Raphael, & Ehrhardt, in press). In the 1990s men are still very much in a dominant position of controlling the interaction, and both women and men expect men to be the initiators most of the time.

Women's and men's sexual scripts have been the focus in research on sexual negotiation, e.g., around issues of family planning and HIV/STD prevention. Gender scripts also have received increased attention regarding decision making around wanted or unwanted sexual encounters and have resulted in heated debates about what constitutes date rape and sexual harassment.

Central issues of the sexual script include who initiates and who sets the boundaries. The traditional gender script is that men initiate and women set the boundaries. Many studies suggest that there is evidence that social changes have led to variability in both women's and men's gender roles in this respect. In other words, we found that many men readily acknowledge that traditional gender scripts exist and understand that they are expected to initiate romantic and sexual encounters. However, while men are aware of the norm, many feel burdened by that expectation.

On the other hand, men's attitude toward women making the first move is complex. Many men feel positive about women taking the initiative in romance but couldn't think of many examples that had ever happened to them. However, men are more ambivalent about women taking the initiative in sexual encounters.

Of course, there is variability; some men are positive, others definitely ambivalent, and others clearly negative about women being the initiator of sexual encounters. It appeared to us that the more stereotypic norm is still very present although there is movement in attitude leading to greater diversity of the interactive style between women and men around sexual issues.

What about women? In our qualitative interviews (Ortiz-Torres, Ehrhardt, Seal, Williams, & Clement, 1995), we found an indication of softening of the traditional scripts; some women now believe that initiation should be shared. While it is still the expected norm that men will initiate sexual encounters, there is evidence that subgroups of both women and men wish for more equal participation. At the same time, we do not have strong evidence that women are equal partners and can feel free and comfortable to initiate sexual interaction as much as men. Both women and men like the idea and some of them are already very comfortable in taking the lead; others are ambivalent or are uncomfortable. In western societies today, women are more determined that it is their prerogative to insist, to give permission, and to change their mind.

In spite of these changes and the movement toward a more egalitarian script, the threat of violence remains a critical gender difference; it is a much greater threat for women than for men. Clement's work on gender differences in sexual scripts in a sample of young German women and men (Clement, Hilffert & Schrey, 1995) reflects the threat of violence for women in an impressive way. In the female narratives in Clement's sample, the male partners are often described as abusive and exploitative. Particularly impressive is that none of the men in Clement's sample reported ever being afraid in a sexual encounter with a woman. The experience and the threat of violence undoubtedly profoundly effects women's behavior in sexual encounters, especially to the degree to which they will take action that will go beyond currently accepted normative gender scripts.

Overall it appears that the gender scripts of sexual encounters for both women and men are still strongly affected by traditional norms, although some evidence shows that women and men both desire and have made actual changes toward more equal participation among the genders. Many women are more insistent on wanting control. So far, we do not have a new gender script that guides both women and men. Rather, it appears that rules and guidelines of conduct are less clear and often confusing.

Of course, sexual encounters go beyond sexual negotiation. Not only do we often ignore the script aspect and focus on women only when we want to effect change, we also disregard the aspect of sexual arousal. It appears that we deal with sexual encounters as an affirmative action issue to bring about rational, correct, and egalitarian participation.

Gunter Schmidt (1995) wrote a seminal article, "Emancipation and the change of heterosexual relationships," for a book devoted to the state of heterosexual relations. Schmidt cites the debate in 1993 at Antioch College among male and female students on sexual correctness which resulted in strict rules about the appropriate rules of sexual interactions. The new principle that each partner explicitly and verbally agree to any sexual move guided these rules. Schmidt raises the issue that verbal negotiation may possibly become the antidote to sexual attraction and passion and points to the fact that the conditioning of sexual arousal is a part of a person's development and a person's learning and that it is not necessarily under rational control.

This point is well taken. While we have made progress in understanding the long-term effects of childhood negotiation patterns on adult interaction around sexual matters, we know much less about the development of specific patterns and triggers of sexual arousal and desire. The issue of sexual desire within the developmental context would be particularly appropriate for multidisciplinary investigation.

Conclusion

In this paper I have argued for a more integrative, multidisciplinary approach to the study of gender differences relevant to our understanding of long-term patterns of sexual negotiation.

As Gagnon (1989) points out, in our society many of these images expose pre-pubertal children to contradictory messages about explicitness, censorship, and unrealistic stereotypes. Certainly, children are not exposed to women and men who are equal in power, who negotiate sexuality, or who share responsibility for contraception and disease prevention in desirable, romantic, and sexually arousing contexts. Thus, adolescent girls and boys come to their sexual encounters with each other with very different needs, expectations, and interactive styles.

I would suggest that gender-specific interactive styles as expressed and established in childhood find their echo in women's and men's sexuality throughout the life cycle. I have given the example of gender scripts of sexual negotiation. Other examples are women's greater focus on intimacy rather than sexual performance, gender differences in marital patterns of divorce and remarriage, and different expressions of sexual orientation. I would suggest that these gender differences of sexuality lend themselves to examination from a biopsychosocial perspective that includes the role of gender-specific styles of interaction that has its roots in girls' and boys' behavior in childhood.

Acknowledgment

The author acknowledges support from grant P50-MH43520 from the National Institute of Mental Health.

REFERENCES

Blakeslee, S. (1995, August 29). In brain's early growth, timetable may be crucial. *The New York Times,* pp. B5–B6.

Charlesworth, W. R., & Dzur, C. (1987). Gender comparisons of preschoolers' behavior and resource utilization in group problem-solving. *Child Development, 58,* 191–200.

Chugani, H. (1998). A critical period of brain development: Studies of cerebral glucose utilization with PET. *Preventive Medicine, 27* (2), 184–188.

Clement, U., Hilffert, S., & Schrey, C. (1995, September). Gender differences in sexual scripts. Abstracts. Twenty-First Annual Meeting of the International Academy of Sex Research, Provincetown, MA.

Edwards, C. P., & Whiting, B. B. (1988). *Children of different worlds.* Cambridge, MA: Harvard University Press.

Ehrhardt, A. A. (1984). The psychobiology of gender. In A. S. Rossi (Ed.), *Gender and the life course* (pp. 81–95). Hawthorne, NY: Aldine Publishing Co.

Ehrhardt, A. A., & Meyer-Bahlburg, H. F. L. (1981). Effects of prenatal sex hormones on gender-related behavior. *Science, 211,* 1312–1318.

Ehrhardt, A. A., & Wasserheit, J. N. (1992). Age, gender, and sexual risk behaviors for sexually transmitted diseases in the United States. In J. N. Wasserheit, S. O. Aral, K. K. Holmes, & P. J. Hitchcock (Eds.), *Research issues in human behavior and sexually transmitted diseases in the AIDS era* (pp. 97–121). Washington, DC: American Society for Microbiology.

Ellis, A. (1945). The sexual psychology of human hermaphrodites. *Psychosomatic Medicine, 7,* 108–125.

Gagnon, J. H. (1989). Sexuality across the life course in the United States. In C. F. Turner, H. G. Miller, & L. E. Moses (Eds.), *AIDS, sexual behavior, and intravenous drug use* (pp. 501–536). Report of the National Research Council Committee on AIDS Research and the Behavioral, Social, and Statistical Sciences. Washington, D.C.: National Academy Press.

Gagnon, J. H., & Simon, J. (1973). *Sexual conduct: The social origins of human sexuality.* Chicago: Aldine Publishing Co.

Greenough, W. T., & Sirevaag, A. M. (1991). A neuroanatomical approach to substrates of behavioral plasticity. In H. N. Shair, G. A. Barr, and Myron Hofer (Eds.), *Developmental psychobiology: New methods and changing concepts* (pp. 255–271). New York: Oxford University Press.

Herrnstein, R. J., and Murray, C. (1994). *The bell curve: Intelligence and class structure in American life.* New York: Free Press.

Hofer, M. A. (1994, December 26). Behind the curve. *New York Times,* Op-Ed page.

Hofer, M. A. (1994). Early relationships as regulators of infant physiology and behavior. *Acta Paediatrica, 397* (Supplement), 9–18.

Hofer, M. A. (1996). On the nature and consequences of early loss. *Psychosomatic Medicine, 58,* 570–581.

Huttenlocher, P. R., and Dabholkar, A. S. (1997). Regional differences in synaptogenesis in human cerebral cortex. *Journal of Comparative Neurology, 387* (2): 167–178.

Jacklin, C. N., & Maccoby, E. E. (1978). Social behavior at 33 months in same-sex and mixed-sex dyads. *Child Development, 49,* 557–569.

Maccoby, E. E. (1988). Gender as a social category. *Developmental Psychology, 24,* 755–765.

Maccoby, E. E. (1990). Gender and relationships: A developmental account. *American Psychologist, 45,* 513–520.

Maccoby, E. E. (1998). *The two sexes: Growing up apart, coming together.* Cambridge, MA: Harvard University Press.

Maccoby, E. E., & Jacklin, C. N. (1987). Gender segregation in childhood. In E. H. Reese (Ed.), *Advances in child development and behavior* (pp. 239–288). New York: Academic Press.

Meyer-Bahlburg, H. F. L. (1998). Gender assignment in intersexuality. *Journal of Psychology & Human Sexuality, 10,* 1–21.

Money, J., Hampson, J. G., & Hampson, J. L. (1955a). Hermaphroditism: Recommendations concerning assignment of sex, change of sex, and psychologic management. *Bulletin of The Johns Hopkins Hospital, 97,* 284–300.

Money, J., Hampson, J. G., & Hampson, J. L. (1995b). An examination of some basic sexual concepts: The evidence of human hermaphroditism. *Bulletin of The Johns Hopkins Hospital, 97,* 301–319.

Ortiz-Torres, B., Ehrhardt, A. A., Seal, D. W., Williams, S., & Clement, U. (1995, September). Women's perceived gender scripts in heterosexual romantic interactions. Abstracts. Twenty-First Annual Meeting of the International Academy of Sex Research, Provincetown, MA.

Rossi, A. S. (Ed.). (1994). *Sexuality across the life course.* Chicago: University of Chicago Press.

Schmidt, G. (1995). Emanzipation und der Wandel heterosexueller Beziehungen. (Emancipation and the change of heterosexual relationships.) In S. Düring & M. Hauch (Eds.), *Heterosexuelle Verhältnisse* (pp. 1–13). Stuttgart: Ferdinand Enke Verlag.

Seal, D. W., Ehrhardt, A. A., Dunne, E., Ortiz-Torres, B., Schönnesson, L., & Clement, U. (1995, September). Men's perceived gender roles and scripts for romantic and sexual situations. Abstracts. Twenty-First Annual Meeting of the International Academy of Sex Research, Provincetown, MA.

Seal, D. W., Wagner-Raphael, L. I., & Ehrhardt, A. A. (in press). Sex, intimacy, and HIV: An ethno-graphic study of a Puerto Rican social group in New York City. *Journal of Psychology & Human Sexuality.*

Human Reproductive Strategies and Life History Theory

ANTHONY WALSH

The only scientifically valid theory of *basic* behavioral design for both sexes of any animal species is evolution by natural selection. (The only alternative is purposeful design by a divine creator, and that is not science). An understanding of the basic behavioral differences between the sexes within species requires the additional guidance of the theories of sexual selection and parental investment, although it is not always apparent which sexually dimorphic behaviors are attributable to which process, nor is it possible to always clearly differentiate between the processes themselves (Mayr, 1972). Through the operation of these evolutionary processes, all sexually reproducing organisms, including humans, possess a suite of traits that determine how they will apportion mating effort and parental investment in order to assure maximum viability of their genetic material. The incredibly complex nature of human sexual behavior requires yet another layer of theory to render it coherent because any evolved genetic propensities to behave in one way or another are necessarily mediated by neurohormonal, developmental, and contextual variables. Life history theory is a strong candidate for providing this additional theoretical layer. Life history theory (which began over 30 years ago in quantitative genetics [Bonner, 1965]), while fully consistent with evolutionary theory, stresses and takes seriously the position that genes regulating evolved strategies are expressed facultatively (see Chisholm [1996] for an excellent overview of evolutionary life history theory).

Because of the requirements imposed by sexually dimorphic anatomy and physiology, female investment of physiological energy in gestating, feeding, and guarding offspring is both obligatory and enormous. On the other hand, the only *necessary* male investment is the provision of stud service, a negligible expenditure of energy. Endowed with cheap and plentiful sperm which could be shed almost at will, our ancestral hominid males could best assure the representation of their genes in subsequent generations by maximizing the number of their offspring, which is only possible by copulating with as many females as their abilities and good fortune allowed. Sexual selection provided males with the necessary mechanisms (testosterone-driven strength, aggression, and sex drive) to compete with other males for access to sexual partners. Our ancestral females, on the other hand, meagerly endowed with ova which are shed only periodically, could best assure their genetic survival by being discriminating about their mating choices, thereby maximizing the viability of a limited number of offspring. A male who copulated with a different female each night would increase his genetic fitness tremendously, but a female who copulated with a different male every night would not increase her fitness one iota. Indeed, any female in our ancestral environments who adopted such a mating strategy would be putting herself at grave risk of abandonment by her paramours given the risk of cuckoldry they all would have faced. Her likely abandonment also endangered the viability of her offspring and put her at risk for becoming a genetic "dead end."

It is for this reason that any genes inclining females to adopt an unrestricted sexual strategy should have been culled from the gene pool long ago. But we know that some women do engage in promiscuous mating despite the evolutionary prediction that they should not, just as many men do not relentlessly pursue multiple sex partners, despite the evolutionary prediction that they should. We observe many departures from general evolutionary expectations because humans have not been locked into a single gender-specific reproductive strategy by a history of relentless sexual selection the way many other species have. Sexual selection operates most vigorously in species characterized by polygynous mating; it operates much less so on pair-bonding species such as our own (Clutton-Brock, 1991). Nevertheless, we do observe considerable gender differences in human sexuality worldwide—such as in masturbation frequency and in interest in casual sex and pornography—(see Oliver & Hyde, 1993, for a meta-analysis of 177 studies) which indicates that we have evolved gender-typical (not gender-specific) sexual strategies.

It has been observed that throughout history males have divided females into discrete "whore" or "Madonna" categories, and it has been proposed that the behaviors described by this dichotomy may be alternative evolutionary reproductive strategies females have used to acquire resources from males (Fisher, 1992, p. 94). Males enhance paternal certainty, and hence their fitness, by committing to females whose sexual reticence offers cues to future fidelity and males have evolved cognitive algorithms that have led them to abandon sexually unrestricted women with whom they had copulated (Barkow, 1991). However, a uniform reproductive strategy of sexual restriction may not have always served the fitness needs of ancestral females. If the environmental situation were such that some females were not able to secure commitment from a single male (say a situation in which the sex ratio was significantly skewed), less restricted females could garner at least temporary investment from a number of males in exchange for sexual favors. Research has shown that while males consider a promiscuous reputation to be the least desirable attribute in a woman in terms of a long-term relationship, it is viewed fairly positively when seeking a short-term relationship because it signals sexual accessibility (Buss & Schmitt, 1993). Similarly, males must also rein in their promiscuous tendencies when seeking a long-term mate because such behavior signals an unwillingness to invest resources in offspring. In some evolutionary environments, long-term pair bonding may have had greater fitness consequences for males as well as females in that it maximized the viability of the few offspring a bonded couple could raise to reproductive age (Lancaster & Lancaster, 1987; Lovejoy, 1981; Wilson, 1980). There is thus no insurmountable evolutionary barrier to the survival of any genes that might incline some females to pursue an unrestricted reproductive strategy.

The current evidence seems not to support the position that there are two different genotypes defining discrete, alternative morphs following separate obligate reproductive strategies, although the possibility cannot be ruled out. Gangestad and Simpson (1990), for instance, suggest that two types of reproductive strategies (restricted and unrestricted) have evolved among women via frequency-dependent selection and show that personality traits associated with female sexual behavior are bimodally distributed consistent with these two types. However, in an adaptively plastic species such as ours it would be more efficient to have genes switched on and off in response to environmental cues rather than to have discrete morphs with reproductive strategies determined at conception regardless of the environments in which they find themselves (Tooby & Cosmides, 1990). This is the mechanism proposed by life history theory, which attempts to understand differences in reproductive strategies as a function of both the evolutionary history of the species and the developmental history of the individual and is thus more nuanced than other evolutionary theories, such as sociobiology, which tend to ignore the more proximate causes of behavior.

Basically, life history theory proposes that sensitive developmental periods of childhood nudge children along a path that "sets" the reproductive strategy that they will probably follow as sexually mature adults (Belsky, Steinberg, & Draper, 1991; Cashdan, 1993; Chisholm, 1993). Of course, neither the mating effort or the parental effort strategy is consciously chosen or articulated, but rather flows from differential expectations of the stability of interpersonal relationships based on early experiences. Men and women who have experienced the breakup of the parental home and have witnessed parents engaging in one short-term relationship after another may enter the mating game earlier and with decreased expectations of obtaining a lasting relationship and may be more willing to emphasize their sexuality (mating effort) than their fidelity, chastity, and willingness to invest in parenting (Cashdan, 1993; Gangestad & Simpson, 1990). If children learn that interpersonal relationships are ephemeral and undependable, they are less likely to expect commitment (parental investment) from the opposite sex later in life and will probably adopt a strategy of relatively unrestricted sexuality (requiring weaker attachment and less time before engaging in sex with a partner). Cashdan's (1993) study supports this proposition: It found that women with high expectations of male parental investment emphasized their fidelity and chastity (restrictive sexuality) whereas women who indicated that they were unlikely to receive male parental investment emphasized their sexuality.

Attachment to parents is a further predictor of adult sexual strategies. Parental attachment is viewed as a strong affective bond between caregiver and child that affords the child a sense of security that lays a foundation for future attachment behavior. According to attachment and life history theories, children develop internal working models of how affective relationships "should be" based on the quality of their early attachments (Chisholm, 1993, 1996; Shaver, Hazan, & Bradshaw, 1988). Belsky, Steinberg, and Draper (1991) point to several highly significant correlations among variables such as offspring sexual behavior, positive spousal and parent/offspring relationships, timing of puberty, and level of parental investment. The absence of a father in the home apparently triggers an early increase in gonadal and adrenal hormones facilitating early sexual activity among girls (Rossi, 1997). Walsh (1995a) found that parental attachment was negatively related to number of sex partners and to masculinity among both males and females (the lower the parental attachment the greater the number of sexual partners and the higher the masculinity score on the Bem Sex Role Inventory).

Some theorists see a possible disjunction between genetic and environmental explanations for the emergence of restricted and unrestricted sexual strategies. Cashdan (1993) writes that Gangestad and Simpson (1990) present evidence showing that the personality traits underlying socio-sexual behaviors (extroversion, disinhibition, aggressiveness, etc.) are highly heritable. Other researchers have shown that socio-sexual behavior is influenced by the type of fathering received when young (Draper & Harpending, 1982). McDonald (1997) also shows that variables related to reproductive strategies (he relates warmth/

nurturance, impulsivity, likelihood of divorce, and intelligence) have heritable components. However, human phenotypical traits result from both genetic and environmental factors just as do the traits of all living things. Children receive both a set of genes and an environment from their parents which mutually incline them in certain directions; that is, genotypes and the environments they find themselves in are not random with respect to one another. Just as parents with high IQs provide their children with genes favoring a high IQ and an environment in which intellectual activities are modeled and reinforced, parents provide their children with genes and environments biasing their sexual behavior one way or the other. In other words, sexual strategies tend to be self-perpetuating from generation to generation for both genetic and environmental reasons. Traits, behaviors, characteristics, and lifestyles as functions of the covariation of genes and environments develop in passive, reactive, and active ways.

Passive gene/environment (G/E) correlation places an individual on a life history trajectory independently (passively) of anything he or she has done. This does not mean that the child does not actively engage with the environment, it only means that the child has simply been *exposed* to it and has not been instrumental in forming it. Regardless of the connotation of the term "passive" with feebleness or weakness, McDonald (1997, p. 332) points out that "parents and their children are a co-evolving system in which passive genotype-environment correlations are of great importance. The influence of passive G/E correlation declines from infancy to adolescence and adulthood as the scope of environmental interaction widens and the person is confronted with and engages a wider variety of other people and behavioral options" (Scarr, 1992; Plomin, 1995).

Reactive G/E correlation picks up the developmental trajectory as children begin to respond more actively to an expanding number of people and situations in their environments. Reactive G/E correlation refers to the way others react to the phenotypical characteristics and traits individuals bring with them to interpersonal situations. Those who have come to view interpersonal relationships as undependable and as opportunities to exploit others will evoke negative responses from others which will tend to reinforce such views. Those who have come to consider other people reliable and valuable will evoke positive responses from them that also serve to bolster their views that people are decent and reliable. Reactive G/E correlation thus serves to further amplify phenotypical differences.

Active G/E correlation is about what Scarr and McCartney (1983) call "niche-picking"; that is, seeking out environments compatible with their genotypes in which the person feels fully comfortable. People with genes that code for different traits, characteristics, and temperaments will seek out different kinds of environments when they are able (genes and environments will covary positively). Because of the influences of passive and reactive G/E correlation, sexually mature adults will enter the mating game with expectations that will lead them to seek out mating environments consistent with those expectations. Women who have come to view men as "dads" rather than "cads" (Cashdan, 1993) arrange their environments in such a way as to advertise their chastity and fidelity, and feel perfectly "at home" psychologically in such environments; women who view men as "cads" will feel just as natural advertising their sexuality. This does not preclude that women may follow the opposite strategy if or when the appropriate situation arises. However, the opposite strategy will feel "unnatural" (negative G/E correlation) and the pretense will become obvious and the person will revert to type sooner or later. This will also be true of men inclined to promiscuity who temporarily abandon their mating effort strategy in favor of parenting effort.

An Illustrative Example

Following is the description of a study which aims to test some of the predictions of life history theory.

Subjects were 109 white female (*M* age = 26.9) and 83 white male (*M* age = 24.2) university undergraduates who participated in the study for extra credit points. All students asked to participate did so in a classroom setting after being informed of the purpose of the study. The data described here are part of a larger study exploring many aspects of psychosocial development.

The variables of major interest relating to sexuality were: (1) their lifetime number of sex partners, (2) their age at first intercourse, (3) their desire to be sexually promiscuous, (4) masculinity, and (5) femininity. Variable 3 asked respondents to assess themselves on a scale of zero to 100: "To what degree do you feel that you want to be sexually promiscuous?" and variables 4 and 5 asked them to assess their masculinity/femininity on a scale of zero to 100.

We utilized four measures designed to tap the affective dimensions of life history theory: Two were experiential/behavioral and two assessed interpersonal relationships. The experiential/behavioral variables were *parental divorce* and *respondent's divorce*. Whether or not a respondent's parents were divorced is consistent with life history theory's emphasis on the role of early experience in setting later reproductive strategies, and the respondent's own divorce may be considered a reflection of ephemeral expectations about relationships.

The interpersonal relationship variables utilized in this study were *positive affect* and *parental attachment*. The positive affect scale is a six-item Likert scale which asks respondents to check the number of people with whom they have "fairly regular and frequent contact" who make them feel valued, appreciated, respected, admired, liked, loved, and understood. This is designed to assess their current relationships with others. The scale has a reported alpha reliability coefficient of .91 (Walsh & Balazs, 1990).

Parental attachment. The parental attachment scale is a six-item Likert scale designed to tap the amount of love, caring, value, trust, respect, and happiness respondents perceived themselves to have received from their parents during their childhood. While the positive affect scale relates to all relationships currently being experienced, the parental attachment scale is specific to parental relationships experienced in the past. This scale has a reported alpha reliability coefficient of .86 (Walsh, 1995a). Age was the only other variable included in this study.

Findings. Table 1 reports a series of t-tests for female subjects, broken down by intactness of parental home. Females whose parents were divorced were significantly younger at first intercourse, had significantly more sex partners, and self-assessed their desire to be significantly more promiscuous than females whose parents were not divorced. They also defined their attachment to their parents significantly lower and rated the positive affect they were currently receiving from others significantly lower. Additionally, they self-assessed their masculinity higher and their femininity lower than females from intact homes.

Because age naturally increases opportunities to acquire additional sex partners, it is obviously a variable that should be taken into consideration when assessing the relationship between parental divorce and number of sexual partners. Women whose parents were divorced were significantly younger than women whose parents were not (means of 24.7 and 28.1 years, respectively: $t = -2.36$, $p = .021$). This finding indicates that age functions as a suppressor variable masking the "true" relationship between parental divorce and number of sexual partners among women in this sample. The zero-order correlation between parental divorce and number of sexual partners was $-.334$; as expected, controlling for age increased the correlation slightly to $-.344$.

An additional marker of lack of attachment and commitment is the respondent's own marital status. We examined the women who were ever married to determine if their parent's marital status predicted theirs. Of the 56 women who were or had ever been married (51.4% of the total number of women in the sample), 40 percent of those whose parents were divorced were themselves divorced, while only 11 percent of those whose parents' marriage remained intact were divorced ($\chi^2 = 6.37$, $p < .02$, $\phi = .337$).

Table 1
Variables Relevant to Life-History Theory for Females Whose Parents Were and Were Not Divorced

	Parents Divorced	$\bar{N}$	X	S	T	*Sig.*
AGE AT FIRST INTERCOURSE	YES	41	16.19	1.94	-3.99	<.0001
	No	52	18.19	2.70		
NUMBER OF SEX PARTNERS	YES	43	8.65	10.59	3.53	<.0001
	No	58	3.38	3.56		
PARENTAL ATTACHMENT	YES	43	23.72	4.78	-2.09	.039
	No	58	25.73	5.17		
POSITIVE AFFECT	YES	43	38.23	6.41	-4.28	<.0001
	No	58	43.31	5.49		
DEGREE TO WHICH WOULD LIKE TO BE PROMISCUOUS	YES	43	27.34	20.11	2.25	.002
	No	58	14.55	18.87		
MASCULINITY SCORE	YES	43	28.83	24.71	2.28	.011
	No	56	17.68	18.31		
FEMININITY SCORE	YES	43	63.91	21.76	-2.62	.010
	No	58	73.90	16.61		

Table 2 repeats the above exercise for males. The differences between the two conditions were not as dramatic for males as they were for females; two tests were non-significant and one (masculinity) was significant in the direction opposite to what we might have predicted. Parental attachment was the only variable in which the difference between the two conditions of parental divorce was greater in the male sample than in the female sample. We do observe significant differences in age at first intercourse and number of sex partners, but not on self-assessed desire to be promiscuous. Nevertheless, the same general pattern emerged vis-à-vis actual sexual behavior and the age at which it commenced.

Table 2
Variables Relevant to Life-History Theory for Males Whose
Parents Were and Were Not Divorced

	Parents Divorced	N	$\bar{X}$	S	T	Sig.
AGE AT FIRST INTERCOURSE	YES	32	15.75	2.34	−3.01	<.0001
	No	38	17.52	2.55		
NUMBER OF SEX PARTNERS	YES	36	19.83	13.42	2.82	.006
	No	47	11.53	13.17		
PARENTAL ATTACHMENT	YES	36	24.67	3.28	−2.87	.005
	No	47	26.89	3.66		
POSITIVE AFFECT	YES	36	37.94	5.41	−1.92	.059
	No	47	40.30	5.64		
DEGREE TO WHICH WOULD LIKE TO BE PROMISCUOUS	YES	36	51.05	24.64	1.15	NS
	No	47	44.55	26.19		
MASCULINITY SCORE	YES	36	70.33	19.42	−3.09	.003
	No	47	81.59	13.82		
FEMININITY SCORE	YES	36	18.82	18.22	0.45	NS
	No	47	16.80	20.20		

Age also acted as a suppressor variable for males, masking the strength of the relationship between parental divorce and number of sexual partners; the zero-order correlation was −.299 and the first-order correlation was −.313. We could not perform a chi-square test to assess the impact of parental divorce on respondents' own divorces among the males since only 20 of the 89 males (22.5%) were or were ever married, and only two of those were divorced (both had divorced parents).

The purpose of this study has been to provide a limited test of evolutionary life history theory which posits that childhood attachment experiences "set" individuals on a particular developmental trajectory leading to the adoption of a restrictive or unrestrictive mating strategy in adulthood. Individuals whose experiences might lead them to define relationships as undependable become biased in the direction of following an unrestricted strategy. We hypothesized that parental divorce would lessen general feelings of attachment to others, including potential mating partners, and that it would signal a relatively unrestricted mating strategy.

As previously indicated, life history theory is more nuanced than straightforward evolutionary theories in that it takes into account developmental and contextual variables. It proposes that females are genetically "prepared" to follow either strategy facultatively; the "choice" is made based on environmental contingencies, particularly early attachment experiences. As explained earlier, females may opt to follow one of two reproductive strategies, one emphasizing fidelity and chastity, the other emphasizing sexuality. The strategy "chosen" is said to depend to a large extent on expectations of male parental investment; that is, whether she views men in general as either "cads" or "dads" (Cashdan, 1993). If she views men primarily as "cads" she will not expect long-term parental investment and will emphasize sexuality to procure short-term investment from a variety of males; if she views them as "dads" she will emphasize chastity and fidelity. The female view of males as "cads" or "dads" is assumed to be largely a function of the quality of early attachment experiences. Positive attachment experiences provide the message that relationships are dependable, trustworthy, and long lasting; negative attachments send the opposite message. The finding that females from divorced homes were less likely to be married and, if ever married, significantly more likely to be divorced and that they reported significantly less parental attachment and positive affect provides support for this hypothesis.

The findings for the male sample were somewhat more ambiguous. Males from broken homes had significantly lower scores on positive affect and parental attachment than males from intact homes and reported significantly more sexual partners and an earlier age of onset of sexual behavior. However, there were no significant differences between the two conditions in their desire to be promiscuous or in their femininity score (although scores were in the predicted direction), and their masculinity scores were significant in the *non-predicted* direction. The smaller effect of parental divorce on male sexual behavior may be consistent with the contention that environmental events *should* have more of an impact on female sexuality than on male sexuality given the huge disparity in parental investment between the sexes. In other words, because of the tremendous investment in time and resources a female must make, she should be more sensitive to environmental cues relevant to the potential resource investment of prospective mates and adjust her strategy accordingly. The reproductive consequences of being less sensitive to environmental cues would have been no more costly to our ancestral males, with the result that males have faced considerably less pressure to select for such sensitivity.

Consistent with the above findings, we should also find greater variability and heritability for the propensity to engage in casual sex among females than among males. Walsh (1995b, p. 167) points out that when coefficients of skewness are reported in studies comparing males and females on the number of sex partners they have experienced, the female coefficient is always considerably larger than the male coefficient. This indicates that atypically sexually active females pull the female mean further to the tail of a positively skewed distribution than do atypically active males.

Gangestad and Simpson (1990) report a heritability coefficient of .76 for their socio-sexuality scale for women, indicating strong genetic input. Unfortunately, they did not include males in their study. However, based on the Australian Twin Registry and using a similar scale, Bailey (1997) reports heritability coefficients of .20 and .60 for males and females, respectively. From an evolutionary point of view, this indicates that males have almost reached genetic fixity in terms of reproductive strategies, but that females retain considerable genetic variation. This is entirely consistent with the idea that because females have more to lose by adopting the "wrong" reproductive strategy, natural selection would have retained (facultatively expressed) genes for at least two alternative (restrictive vs. unrestrictive) strategies.

Although the sample used here is small and was not randomly chosen, most propositions suggested by life history theory were supported. That is, females from broken homes were more likely to have experienced the breakup of their own marriages if ever married and to report a lower level of parental attachment and a lower level of positive affect. These experiences are linked to the adoption of a sexually unrestricted lifestyle by their self-reported responses to the sexuality-related variables listed in Table 1. The findings among the male sample were in the same general direction, but were somewhat more ambiguous.

Because of sampling limitations and the non-experimental nature of this study, no cause/effect statements can be made. We are also of the opinion that our rather crude demographic measures (parental divorce, respondent's divorce) should be supplemented by individual-level measures that may reveal important evidence of differential responses to those situations hidden within the crude umbrella measures. For instance, the age of the respondents when their parents divorced, the quality of the parental marriage, whether parental divorce was responded to with relief or sadness, and so forth, may provide several interesting elaborations of the data we have presented here. Further, the self-reported variables were not defined for respondents, thus allowing for subjective definitions and idiosyncratic interpretations. Nevertheless, the overall pattern of associations of behavioral, demographic, and attitudinal variables in the directions predicted by life history theory indicates considerable consistency in the respondents' interpretations across many variables. However, if subjects were provided more specific definitions perhaps a somewhat different pattern of findings might emerge.

To the extent that these data are useful, they provide further evidence for the centrality of love and attachment to the healthy development of human beings. Those who perceive themselves as less attached (both to parents and to their peers) tend to behave in a manner that is not conducive to either physical or psychological health. The tendency appears to be that they drift in and out of short-term relationships which provide neither themselves nor any future offspring with secure foundations.

The evolutionarily species-expected environment of rearing is, at the very least, an environment that includes a mother and a father (Berger & Berger, 1984; Lancaster & Lancaster, 1987; Rossi, 1977; Walsh, 1995b). When some critical mass of children lack such a firm foundation, "insecurity becomes embedded and acquires a cultural history" (Marris, 1991, p. 87). In these days of ever-rising rates of illegitimacy and sexually transmitted diseases, the importance of parental investment has never been more clear.

References

Bailey, J. M. (1997). Are genetically based individual differences compatible with species-wide adaptations? In N. Segal, G. Weisfeld, & C. Weisfeld (Eds.), *Uniting psychology and biology* (pp. 81–106). Washington, DC: American Psychological Association.

Barkow, J. (1991). *Darwin, sex, and status: Biological approaches to mind and culture.* Toronto: University of Toronto Press.

Belsky, J., Steinberg, L., & Draper, P. (1991). Childhood experience, interpersonal development, and reproductive strategies: An evolutionary theory of socialization. *Child Development, 62,* 647–660.

Berger, B., & Berger, P. (1984). *The war over the family: Capturing the middle ground.* Garden City, NY: Anchor Press.

Bonner, J. (1965). *Size and cycle.* Princeton: Princeton University Press.

Buss, D., & Schmitt, D. (1993). Sexual strategies theory: An evolutionary perspective on human mating. *Psychological Review, 100,* 204–232.

Cashdan, E. (1993). Attracting mates: Effects of paternal investment on mate attraction strategies. *Ethology and Sociobiology, 14,* 1–23.

Chisholm, J. (1993). Death, hope, and sex: Life history theory and the development of reproductive strategies. *Current Anthropology, 34,* 3–24.

Chisholm, J. (1996). The evolutionary ecology of attachment organization. *Human Nature, 7,* 1–38.

Clutton-Brock, T. (1991). *The evolution of parental care.* Princeton: Princeton University Press.

Draper, P., & Harpending, H. (1982). Father absence and reproductive strategy: An evolutionary perspective. *Journal of Anthropological Research, 38,* 255–273.

Fisher, H. (1992). *Anatomy of love: The natural history of monogamy, adultery, and divorce.* New York: W.W. Norton.

Gangestad, S., & Simpson, J. (1990). Toward an evolutionary history of female sociosexual variation. *Journal of Personality, 58,* 70–96.

Lancaster, A., & Lancaster C. (1987). The watershed: Changes in parental investment and family formation strategies in the course of human evolution. In J. Lancaster, J. Altman, A. Rossi, & L. Sherrod (Eds.), *Parenting across the life span: Biosocial perspectives* (pp. 187–205). New York: Aldine de Gruyter.

Lovejoy, C. (1981). The origin of man. *Science, 211,* 341–350.

Marris, P. (1991). The social construction of uncertainty. In C. Parkes, J. Stevenson-Hinde, & P. Marris (Eds.), *Attachment across the life cycle* (pp. 77–90). London: Routledge.

Mayr, E. (1972). Sexual selection and natural selection. In B. Campbell (Ed.), *Sexual selection and the descent of man* (pp. 87–104). Chicago: Aldine Publishing Co.

McDonald, K. (1997). Life history theory and human reproductive behavior: Environmental/contextual influences and heritable variation. *Human Nature, 8,* 327–359.

Oliver, M., & Hyde, J. (1993). Gender differences in sexuality: A meta-analysis. *Psychological Bulletin, 14,* 29–51.

Plomin, R. (1995). Genetics and children's experiences in the family. *Journal of Child Psychology and Psychiatry, 36,* 33–68.

Rossi, A. (1977). A biosocial perspective on parenting. *Daedalus, 106,* 1–31.

Rossi, A. (1997). The impact of family structure and social change on adolescent sexual behavior. *Child and Youth Services Review, 19,* 369–400.

Scarr, S. (1992). Developmental theories for the 1990s: Development and individual differences. *Child Development, 63,* 1–19.

Scarr, S., & McCartney, K. (1983). How people make their own environments: A theory of genotype→environment effects. *Child Development, 54,* 424–435.

Shaver, P., Hazan, C., & Bradshaw, D. (1988). Love and attachment: The integration of three behavioral systems. In R. Sternberg & M. Barnes (Eds.), *The psychology of love* (pp. 68–99). New Haven: Yale University Press.

Tooby, J., & Cosmides, L. (1990). On the universality of human nature and the uniqueness of the individual: The role of genetics and adaptation. *Journal of Personality, 58,* 17–68.

Walsh, A. (1995a). Parental attachment, drug use, and facultative sexual strategies. *Social Biology, 42,* 95–107.

Walsh, A. (1995b). *Biosociology: An emerging paradigm.* Westport, CT: Praeger.

Walsh, A., & Balazs, G. (1990). Love, sex, and self-esteem. *Free Inquiry in Creative Sociology, 18,* 37–41.

Wilson, P. (1980). *Man: The promising primate.* New Haven: Yale University Press.

DISCUSSION

Edward Laumann: I was wondering if you could elaborate a bit on the sample that this table is based on because the average number of sex partners being reported presumably for college students of up to about age 22 is 19, if I'm reading this correctly. That seems to be extraordinarily high and atypical.

Anthony Walsh: It seems high for the males?

Edward Laumann: The median for the adult population is about six for males and two or three for females.

Anthony Walsh: The average age for males in this sample was 26. It's a nontraditional urban university. The students tend to be older than you get in many other universities.

Edward Laumann: What was the title of the course?

Anthony Walsh: There were a variety of classes, primarily in criminal justice.

Edward Laumann: Training to be policemen? Police officers, probation and parole officers, and that kind of thing may be a little more macho than average. These are self-reports then?

Anthony Walsh: Yes, self-reports.

Edward Laumann: Did you look at the median as opposed to the average? Did you have some suggestion that this is a very atypical distribution, and that an average is very much affected by extreme outliers?

Anthony Walsh: Absolutely. I haven't published this particular data, but others that I have published in a similar vein tend to look at the skew because there's a lot of criticism that male and female averages should be equal, and mathematically, I suppose, that logic is unassailable. I tend to look at the coefficient of skewness, and the female coefficient was always considerably higher than the male coefficient of skewness, meaning that very atypically sexually active females were pulling that mean toward a high end. Females who decide that they're going to emphasize their sexuality rather than chastity have an easier time of it than males who make the same decision. So every sample I've taken like that of the skewness of females is a lot higher than the skewness of males. Median modes are always higher for males than females.

John Bancroft: I'd like to ask Anke and Tony to comment on the extent to which their approaches are similar or different.

Anke Ehrhardt: I see myself thinking less about a predetermined system and more about how we can identify a chain of events. These chains of events can be enormously changed by the different kind of variables we all think about and the difference is probably in the degree of predictability. I think of the predictability as much less than is typical in evolutionary thinking.

Gary Dowsett: There's a line in your paper which I would like you to expand on and that's in relation to differences within gender rather than between genders. Could you say more about that?

Anke Ehrhardt: If we assume and accept that exposure to androgens before birth has something to do with the propensity to behave aggressively, then the enormous difference between androgen levels in boys and girls prenatally is likely to account for some of the difference in aggressive behavior between boys and girls; that is a logical assumption. But there are also variations of androgens among girls and among boys and that could be one variable accounting for diversity in behavior within gender. However, that's only one simple way of looking at it. Androgens could play a part, but it then depends on rearing, both within gender and between gender, how the behavior unfolds. So I think that if we accept the differences between genders it is attractive to think also how such factors might explain diversity within genders. In all gender differences, as we all know, we have a huge overlap.

Connie Nathanson: As a sociologist I guess I'm troubled about both of these papers because although you're talking about a wide range of outcomes, aggressiveness and interaction patterns, parenting and mating, there is an absence of consideration of the enormous cultural and social-structural variations in these behaviors. I realize that these are in part disciplinary differences and you're interested in different things. On the other hand, to make generalizations without attention to these differences is liable to lead to difficulties.

Anke Ehrhardt: My point was not to make a generalization about the particular behavior pattern, but to propose the theory of approach or perspective which might explain behavior and those variables in a different society. I deliberately said in the introduction that all of those variables have to be integrated in that kind of socio-cultural perspective. But, to take one behavior, differences in aggression between boys and girls are very profound in many societies. But that doesn't mean that such gender differences aren't larger or smaller, or showing more or less overlap across different societies. I don't see this as a closed system or a predetermined chain of events.

Rafael Diaz: I'm a little troubled, after so many years, to be still talking about what's biology and what's environment. We cannot talk about any biological variable that is not impacted and affected by context and environment and similarly we cannot get away from the fact that genes really do affect environments. Can we take the stand that in explaining human development it is impossible to separate biology from environment? I'm looking for a paradigm, a language that can help us understand human development without making this separation of biology and environment.

Anke Ehrhardt: I think that is exactly my point, but I think we need to learn how to talk about it. I don't think the solution is to say it's inseparable and therefore we cannot talk about biology; that's typically what happens. We don't have language and models for how to talk about it so therefore we ignore either the biology or the environment. I suggest that we have to find new ways and a new language for examining the interaction between biology and environment.

Discussion Paper

SARAH BLAFFER HRDY

I share with Anke Ehrhardt and Anthony Walsh their fundamental assumptions concerning the existence of what Anke terms "key characteristics of the human species." But even when we can identify basic attributes (as in the example of higher androgen levels in males) these don't take us all that far in explaining "diversity of behavior" (Ehrhardt, 2000). Anke reviewed open-ended biopsychosocial attempts to reconcile essentialist and social constructionist positions, while Anthony explored ways that life history theory could be incorporated into models for explaining specific biopsychosocial phenomena such as the timing of sexual maturation in girls. Both are valuable approaches.

Before proceeding to discuss Anke's more general propositions and Anthony's specific case study, I need to clarify what we mean by the word "biology." To embark on the search for what Anke aptly terms a "new language," we need to agree on a working vocabulary. As a sociobiologist and evolutionary anthropologist, I do not use the word "biological" to mean "genetic."

Genetic ≠ Biological. What genes do is code for proteins. In and of themselves, then, they do not interact with the environment. Genes do not interact with the environment, only phenotypes—which are the observable properties of individuals—do. Phenotypes already represent outcomes of multiple developmental events, many of which are independent of genes. By the time a phenotype is detectable in any way that would permit natural selection to either favor it or weed it out, intervening accommodations have already taken place. These accommodations have to do with life and are as such "biological." They are not necessarily genetic.

When natural selection leads to differential survival or reproduction of traits, the traits selected for are those expressed in a phenotype. Neither the environment nor natural selection has access to genes, only phenotypes which are influenced by, but are not necessarily determined by genes.

Not long ago, the biologist and entomologist Mary Jane West Eberhard (who has been articulating such views since the late 1970s) gave a lecture which made her point clearer to me than it ever had been before. She asked her audience to consider a frog in the earliest stages of development. Hours after fertilization, in the fast-dividing blastula of a frog embryo already 4,000 cells strong, none of the embryonic frog's own genes are yet activated. The only instructions to be had are from hormones and proteins circulating in cytoplasm which the mother contributed to the egg. Far from genetically "determined," initial development of this new individual with its "hand-me-down" phenotype is influenced by the mother's condition, her nutritional status, minerals that she may have or may lack, toxins she may have imbibed, and so forth.

The expression of genes, then, is always contingent on context, and that context is provided by the egg-producing mother. In mammals of course, maternal effects (defined as nongenetic traits that are transmitted from mother to offspring)[1] are critical, lasting for months or years, with sometimes lifelong consequences. In the case of humans, where other group members have always been critical to help the mother provide for her young, her social status, cultural milieu, and general family situation have critical repercussions at every phase of fetal-infant-child development.

Sexual identities are not determined by genes alone, but neither are they culturally constructed. This kind of interactional view of development has been around for a long time. It is not new. Alfred Kinsey certainly would have been aware of it, because long before he was a sexologist, he was an entomologist. By the nineteenth century for example, people knew a great deal about honeybees and how they developed. If a honeybee grub is fed ordinary pollen by the nurses in the first hours or days of development, that organism grows up to be a worker bee that most likely will spend its life as a nonreproductive organism, never engaging in sex and devoting her life to rearing her sister's progeny. If, however, that same organism (identical genotype) is fed royal jelly, she grows to be a different size, a different shape, and spends her life pollinating eggs, reproducing at an extraordinary rate.

In the case of the bee, it takes few neurons and no culture for genetically identical organisms to develop two very different reproductive profiles: a female who is reproductive versus a female with the same genotype who is celibate and nonreproductive. (I thought about referring to these as two different "genders," but decided against it because gender has so much to do with being able to verbalize and conceptualize, with worrying about how others see us and what they think of us, and only humans do these things. But clearly these are different sexual roles.)

There is a genetic blueprint here, but it is anything but static, and not particularly deterministic. Even at fairly simple nonhuman organismal levels dichotomies between "essentialism" and "environmentalism" have no use other than as extreme metaphors for what in the natural world are more nearly nuances. This way of thinking was axiomatic, built into the worldviews of such sociobiological pioneers as Edward O. Wilson, Richard Alexander, or Mary Jane West Eberhard, who were all first and foremost entomologists familiar with examples like the honeybee. When they use a term like "sociobiology," they do so with an awareness of how much flexibility is built into the word "biology." They didn't call what they did "sociogenetics," for example; they called it sociobiology because that assumed considerable flexibility was already built in.

Biology and genetics are not identical, and among practicing biologists, I don't know any "genetic determinist" in the pejorative sense in which that phrase is flung around. Clearly genes play a role. Different researchers weight their input differently. So, for example, Wilson stresses the role of genes more; others like West Eberhard (and I fall in her camp) stress development and context more. But for all of us, "genetic determinism" is a misnomer. It exists in the mental constructs of critics of sociobiology or among essentialists (wherever they are) who may live up to the label. But you don't find these people out in the field studying the behavior of real animals in their natural environments. (The anthropologist William Irons calls these "environments of evolutionary relevance.") We have no traffic with genes. All we ever see are phenotypes and whole organisms, with all the known and unknown intervening steps that that entails. If this is true for insects, it is even more true for primates, and even more complexly true for humans among whom, as Anke puts it, "development of gender during the first decade of life is crucially important for the unfolding of sexuality."

What about when the theory is fine but we need a more scientific method? Most of what I am saying has been known for a long time, except that more attention is being paid today to maternal effects than in the past. The point is, though, that when I read (as I did in Anthony's paper) about genes controlling evolved strategies, or genes switched on and off in response to the environment, or read that the absence of the father in the home triggers early increase in gonadal hormones facilitating early sexual activity, I yearn to have some of the intervening developmental steps between genotype and phenotype filled in, which is where Anke's biopsychosocial approach comes in.

Is early menarche an evolved strategy to cope with the kinds of social environments that in the past would have characterized a family where the father is absent? This is a very provocative hypothesis. But what kind of evidence supports it? Set the standard of evidence too high, and we make it impossible to even explore some of the most fascinating questions about ourselves. So how do we stay in the game and still practice science? We design alternate competing hypotheses that actually help us winnow out wrong claims. Much of the recent research in evolutionary psychology is set up so that the alternative to accepting a particular hypothesis is rejecting evolutionary theory itself (i.e., if you don't accept my evolutionary interpretation that means you reject Darwinian logic regarding natural selection).

Anthony's paper is a case in point. A model derived from evolutionary theory is used to generate predictions, and when those predictions are confirmed, it is concluded that the theory is correct. But that is not enough.

Life history theory is a branch of evolutionary thinking that examines how organisms allocate resources between somatic growth and reproduction, etc. over the course of its lifetime. But which aspects, if any, of these very broad theories are relevant to the fascinating correlation between early menarche and the absence of the father in the household?[2]

By mammalian life history standards, all apes take a long time to mature to breeding age. But humans are off the scale. Within the age range possible for different ape species, however, individuals mature at different times. In general, better-nourished females reach menarche sooner, conceive earlier, and reach full body size sooner (in that order). Typically, a wild chimp at Jane Goodall's study site at Gombe gives birth for the first time around age fourteen, reaching menarche anywhere from six months to three years earlier than that. A chimp on a particularly productive territory, however, blessed with supportive and influential kin (Flo's eldest daughter Fifi, the wild chimp record holder for early menarche and lifetime reproductive success, comes to mind) reached menarche as early as age eight.

In the 1970s, nutritionist Rose Frisch confirmed nineteenth-century suspicions that there was a connection between nutritional status and age of menarche and that women resembled apes and other primates in this respect. Since then, Peter Ellison (in press) and others have done much to fine-tune what we know about "the ecology of the ovaries."

With the accumulation of reproductive fat in the months and years after puberty begins, some of the fat cells secrete the hormone leptin. Soon the girl's hypothalamus will release regular pulses of gonadotropin-releasing hormones every ninety minutes. These pulses are the critical event in puberty, stimulating the pituitary gland to secrete hormones addressed to long-dormant ovarian follicles—follicle-stimulating hormones and luteinizing hormones that essentially tell this egg-incubating organ to switch on. No matter how well fed a female is, average age of menarche does not fall below eight for chimpanzees or twelve for humans. Life history theory as employed by Eric Charnov (1993), Paul Harvey, Bob Martin, and Tim Clutton-Brock (1987), and others has had marked success at predicting the timing of different life stages for mammals generally using data on body size, mortality schedules, and other attributes of these species, although by these standards, age of menarche in humans is very late, and the reasons why hotly debated.

So far as explaining individual variation between girls, I think Anthony Walsh's basic model, derived from Patrica Draper and Henry Harpending, is a useful one (Draper & Harpending, 1982).[3] According to the Draper-Harpending model, young girls grow up in complex social environments. They look out at the world and learn to classify adult men as either "dads" (progenitors who will invest in their families) or "cads" (progenitors who will default or be unable to invest in their families) and adjust their expectations accordingly. That is, girls who see a world of "cads" supposedly respond to stress in their environment by reaching menarche earlier so as to use sexual relations with men as an adaptive way to make their way in the world. It seems plausible, even likely, that these girls' sexual *behavior* is shaped by these perceptions. But do these subliminal assessments affect age of menarche? Do they, for example, affect the rate at which fat cells convert to leptin? Or responses at the ovarian level?

There is some comparative data from chimpanzee sexual behavior *consistent* with Anthony's interpretations in that young female apes do use their sexuality—rather like Nabokov's Lolita—in socially and materially advantageous ways. The sexual swellings of adolescent females are especially conspicuous. Young females apparently use them as "diplomatic passports" that permit safe passage through territories patrolled by strange males; they visit foreign communities to check out competitors and local resources before they decide where to settle and breed.[4] Protected from pregnancy by adolescent subfertility, a young female chimpanzee mates an estimated 3,600 times on average before her first conception.[5]

Since the Neolithic period, and especially in the last several centuries, better-nourished girls have begun to mature earlier and have become capable of conceiving earlier than ever before in human existence—closer to twelve than to twenty. However, any adolescent girl living as a forager who found herself in the unusual situation of being able to stockpile enough body fat to trigger menarche in her early teens would almost certainly also have been in an unusually productive habitat. She also, and more important, would have been surrounded by adults helping to provision her because unlike other primates it is rare for an adolescent female in a foraging complex to provide all her own calories.

In modern societies, however, adolescents can be terribly disadvantaged, lack all manner of social and economic support, and still be hypernourished. Far from allowing her to take advantage of especially good conditions by breeding early, the amount of fat a girl has on board has become a dangerously misleading signal telling this young mammal, currently very ill served by the fat-storing precautions her body has taken to avoid starvation, that it is a good time to go ahead and reproduce, when it is anything but that.

Current rhetoric about the Pleistocene Environment of Evolutionary Adaptedness to the contrary notwithstanding, the way the hypothalamus and the pituitary respond to signals secreted by fat cells is one of those domains where evolution most certainly did not end with the Pleistocene period or stop when our ancestors left Africa. Each girl's threshold for responding to the hormones that trigger menarche are set slightly differently so that age of menarche varies not only with a girl's immediate circumstances but with the history of the populations in which her ancestors lived. (It is not known what variables are most relevant or how these variables produce this effect. Climate, food availability, body type, height, and metabolic rates are obvious candidates.)

Even when they are fed the same diet of high-fat, high-carbohydrate foods—Big Mac equivalents, for example—daughters of mothers born in the warmer climes of southeastern Europe reach menarche earlier on average than daughters whose ancestors came from northwestern Europe. Just why this is so (cold winters? taller bodies? greater likelihood of famine?) is not known. Nevertheless, recent European migrants to Australia, all currently living in the same environment, start to menstruate at different ages depending on whether their mothers came from southern or northern Europe (Danker-Hopfe, 1986)—strong evidence that some genetic component influences age of menarche.

Why girls with absent fathers reach menarche early. In all primates, menarche can be speeded up or slowed down by various factors. Females respond to stressful circumstances, unpredictable resources, or a mother's low status by delaying puberty.[6] Hence if father absence is stimulating early menarche in human girls, the underlying physiology is working differently than is the case in other primates. Anthony points out that girls whose parents are separated engage in sex earlier and with more different partners (Walsh, 2000). The fact that they also reached menarche earlier (Surbey, 1990) is what led Jay Belsky, Anthony Walsh, and others to hypothesize that sexual maturation is speeded up perhaps by higher levels of social stress in the home that "triggers an early increase in gonadal and adrenal hormones facilitating early sexual activity among girls" (Rossi, 1997). Essentially, then, early menarche is assumed to be a maternal effect, brought about by socio-ecological circumstances that characterize the mother's niche, which her daughter shares. (In mammals, construction of this niche in which her offspring mature is a critical maternal effect.) The daughter's developmental response to this niche is assumed by Anthony Walsh to be an evolved reproductive strategy that is genetic in origin. This is the premise that I now seek to pit against competing explanations.

Early menarche is the opposite response to stress that we see in other primates. For example, daughters of stressed or low-ranking baboon or chimp mothers who are deprived of resources reach menarche later, not earlier. In all other primates, stressed females *delay* rather than speed up maturation, and the daughters of mothers who are stressed exhibit delayed, not accelerated, puberty. So there is no comparative evidence to support the interpretation being made. So what might be alternative explanations for the correlation between absent fathers and early menarche? Given the lack of comparative evidence, one obvious alternative is that the correlation we are seeing is an artifact of something else. One alternative hypothesis, then, would be to focus on the known heritable components to age of menarche. How would this work? If mothers who reach menarche earlier engage in sex earlier and become pregnant at an earlier age and are less likely to end up in a stable relationship as a result of this personal history, then their early maturing daughters would find themselves growing up in a household without a father. This would make early menarche more nearly an ancient adaptation to local geographical conditions evolved among the girl's ancestors. The correlation between early menarche and absent fathers would be more nearly an incidental correlation of an early maturing mother's unfortunate mate choices than her daughter's adaptation to cope with such choices.

If the theory is sound, the task is to prevent theory from becoming reified as dogma. Darwin's theory of natural selection is widely accepted, and evolutionary perspectives generate a wide range of explanatory hypotheses. We are blessed with robust theory that for most problems generates a series of alternate hypotheses, rarely just one "evolutionary explanation." The problem for evolutionists is not to come up with theory, but to avoid misapplying theory, or treating hypotheses generated by evolutionary theory as too sacred. There are times when those of us in fields of research with strong theory need to be less respectful of it.

References

Belsky, J., Steinberg, L., & Draper, P. (1991). Childhood experience, interpersonal development, and reproductive strategies: An evolutionary theory of socialization. *Child Development, 62,* 647–660.

Charnov, E. (1993). *Life history invariants.* Oxford: Oxford University Press.

Danker-Hopfe, H. (1986). Menarcheal age in Europe. *Yearbook of Physical Anthropology, 29,* 81–112.

Draper, P., & Harpending, H. (1982). Father absence and reproductive strategy: An evolutionary perspective. *Journal of Anthropological Research, 38,* 255–273.

Drickamer, L. (1974). A ten-year summary of reproductive data for free-ranging Macaca mulatta. *Folia Primatologica, 33,* 262–272.

Eberhard, M. J. W. (in press). *The flexible phenotype.* Oxford University Press.

Ehrhardt, A. (2000). Gender, sexuality, and human development. In J. Bancroft (Ed.), *The Role of Theory in Sex Research* (pp. 3–16). Bloomington: Indiana University Press.

Ellison, P. (in press). *On fertile ground.* Cambridge: Harvard University Press.

Fox, C. W., Thakar, M. S., & Mousseau, T. A. (1997). Egg size plasticity in a seed beetle: An adaptive maternal effect. *American Naturalist, 149*(1), 150–163.

French, J. (1997). Proximate regulation of singular breeding in callitrichid primates. In N. A. Solomon & J. French (Eds.), *Proximate regulation of singular breeding in Callitrichid primates* (pp. 34–75). Cambridge: Cambridge University Press.

Frisch, R. (1978). Populations, food intake, and fertility. Historical evidence for a direct effect of nutrition on reproductive ability. *Science, 199,* 22–29.

Harvey, P. H., Martin, R. D., & Clutton-Brock, T. H. (1987). Life histories in comparative perspective. In B. Smuts, D. Cheney, R. Seyfarth, R. Wrangham, & T. Struhsaker (Eds.), *Primate societies* (pp. 181–196). Chicago: University of Chicago Press.

Hrdy, S. B. (1999). *Mother Nature: A history of natural selection, mothers, and infants.* New York: Pantheon.

Kirkpatrick, M., & Lande, R. (1989). The evolution of maternal characters. *Evolution, 43*(3), 485–503.

Pennisi, E. (1996). Research news: A look at maternal guidance. *Science, 273,* 1334–1336.

Rossi, A. (1997). The impact of family structure and social change on adolescent sexual behavior. *Child and Youth Services Review, 19,* 369–400.

Rossiter, M. C. (1996). Incidence and consequences of inherited environmental effects. *Annual Review of Ecology and Systematics, 27,* 451–176.

Surbey, M. (1990). Family composition, stress and the timing of human menarche. In T. Zeigler & F. Bercovitch (Eds.), *Socioendocrinology of primate reproduction* (pp. 11–32). New York: Wiley Liss.

Tutin, C. (1975). *Sexual behavior and mating patterns in a community of wild chimpanzees (*Pan troglodytes schweinfurthii*).* Unpublished doctoral dissertation, University of Edinburgh.

Walsh, A. (2000). Human reproductive strategies and life history theory. In J. Bancroft (Ed.), *The role of theory in sex research* (pp. 17–32). Bloomington: Indiana University Press.

Weinrich, J. D. (1977). Human sociobiology: Pair-bonding and resource predictability (effects of social class and race). *Behavioral Ecology and Sociobiology, 2,* 91–118.

NOTES

1. For more on maternal effects, see, e.g., Pennisi (1996, p. 1334); Fox, Thakar, & Mousseau (1997); Kirkpatrick & Lande (1989); and especially Rossiter (1996) for a detailed overview. Mary Jane West Eberhard's book on *The flexible phenotype* will be published, perhaps in 2000 (and not necessarily with that title), by Oxford University Press. My own ideas on the role of maternal effects and phenotypic flexibility in humans appear in *Mother Nature: A history of mothers, infants and natural selection* (New York: Pantheon, 1999).

2. In his paper Anthony Walsh reviews the literature on the correlation between father absence and age of menarche.

3. For discussion of the developmental aspects of this hypothesis see Belsky, Steinberg, & Draper (1991). For the classic paper on the relationship between income predictability and promiscuity in humans, see Weinrich (1977).

4. This idea was first proposed by Tutin (1975).

5. This estimate was calculated by Richard Wrangham primarily from data collected at the Gombe Stream Reserve.

6. For example, delayed breeding by subordinate females among cercopithecine monkeys, first reported by Drickamer (1974); subordinate females in tamarins and marmosets and other cooperative breeders may delay reproduction indefinitely (French, 1997).

DISCUSSION

Heino Meyer-Bahlburg: I want to address one particular aspect, which was implied but not spelled out, namely, that progress in science in general and in neuroscience in particular—and, in my reading of science history, progress in the behavioral sciences as well—comes not only from theory but also specifically from advancements in measurement. What I have seen largely neglected in discussions between psychobiologists and social constructionists is the measurement aspect which is implied in your testability issue. Furthermore, the effects of family-context variables on developmental outcome are currently addressed in the developmental psychopathology of, for instance, conduct disorder (e.g., Loeber, Farrington, Stouthamer-Loeber, & Van Kammen, 1998). The latter can serve as a very good partial model of how to address what happens in the development of sexuality. Progress in developmental psychopathology is largely due to improvements of measurements with multivariate approaches applied to complex situations—methodology issues that are largely absent from much of the discussion about gender.

Anke Ehrhardt: I think your example of the age at menarche and the different effects on behavior is a good one to make clear what I'm striving for. In each case, while you're taking a different kind of approach, each of them still involves biological variables, social variables, and cultural variables. What you're saying is we can have a different kind of mix to explain that phenomenon. And to come back to Rafael's comment, rather than saying that this is all too complex and we just can't deal with it, I think we should struggle with how to define and then test them. But it doesn't mean that there need be only one approach.

Sarah Hrdy: The age of menarche issue may be somewhat separate from the young girl learning about what she can expect from males. You have a situation where males are making what could be thought of as a life historical trade-off. Where resources are poor and unpredictable, it behooves men to behave as "cads" rather than "dads." Women pick up on this. But it's complicated because the menarche factor may be quite separate. Yes, girls who have menarche earlier are very likely for obvious reasons to engage in sex earlier. Nothing about this age of menarche model makes sense in terms of what we know about animal life histories and factors speeding up or slowing down maturation.

If we consider life history theory in terms of a set body of resources, then the female animal's job is to allocate those resources over the course of her life in a way that is optimally adapted to her circumstances. In an organism that encounters stressful conditions, poor conditions, poor resources, the normal thing is to delay ovulation and to suppress breeding. So that if you're talking about social mongooses or tamarins where you have suppression of ovulation of the subordinate animals in the presence of a dominant female, it's the opposite effect. If you have situations, as Jeanne Altmann and colleagues (1988) have reported for baboons or Lee Drickamer (1974) for macaques, daughters born to low-ranking females reach menarche many months later than do daughters born to high-ranking females. So this is a very different kind of situation, and one that makes sense. It's a puzzle then, why an organism anticipating unpredictable resources would mature sooner. So we have the same life history models, based on the same evolutionary theory, making quite different predictions for rates of maturation in nonhuman and in human primates. This makes me uncomfortable. What's going on here? There's obviously some intervening variables having to do with the cognitive assessment of what's going on and I think the whole menarche issue may have a separate explanation.

John Bancroft: I think the menarche concept actually takes us to issues which are going to crop up in various points during this meeting. It's relevant to the session on adolescent sexuality, it's relevant to the session on sexual orientation, and it really confronts us in a very interesting way with the interaction between biology and environment. Thinking about what you were saying about the control over fertility, one interesting example comes from hunter-gatherers such as the !Kung where, from an evolutionary perspective, having children has a high cost for their lifestyle and where you see a delay in their fertility; a long period of adolescent infertility. We need to look at a variety of factors, and some of them have already been mentioned, such as diet, and there are some behavioral ones that have been clearly documented as affecting age of puberty. But you said that the girl with an earlier onset of puberty or menarche would be more likely to engage in sexual activity early.

Sarah Hrdy: In our society, I believe that is true. I'm assuming that a girl who was sexually cycling would be more interested in sex, and that a girl who was physically more mature (e.g., has breasts) would attract more sexual attention. You are right though that in traditional societies like the !Kung, sex play goes on prior to menarche. Does the frequency or intensity increase after menarche? I don't know.

John Bancroft: Yes, but I think that's possibly an oversimplification. Kinsey was very interested in the relationship of the age of the onset of puberty and sexual behavior, and 50 years ago he found a very striking relationship in boys and he found very little relationship in girls. Now that might have changed over the past 50 years. I understand Joe Rodger's paper is going to be suggesting evidence that age of puberty in girls played an important part in their model. So we may be dealing with an interaction again between biological and social factors within that particular context, social factors being more important for females than for males, who have perhaps a more robust relationship between age at puberty and onset of sexual activity.

Sarah Hrdy: Well, if this is true, and it hadn't occurred to me that the age of menarche and sexual activity in girls are not necessarily linked, it would make Tony Walsh's job easier because he could just throw out the menarche issue and look at the age of sexual interactions. But in defense of what Tony is saying here, yes, this has become dogma among evolutionary psychologists that age of menarche is earlier in families in which the father is absent.

Edward Laumann: We have been looking at the age of first intercourse in our national sample and we came up with a cluster of variables that we called "personal biography" that included age at menarche and sexual contacts between prepubescent children and adults (cf. Laumann, Gagnon, Michael, & Michaels, 1994.) This has not been very often looked at but we found about one in five women reporting such prepubescent sexual experiences. These two variables, plus intact family status at age 14, predict the age of first intercourse. However, it interacts in very complicated ways for white women; for that group these factors are not important for women who were 18 before 1970 but they are very important for those who reached 18 after 1970.

Gil Herdt: It might be worth making a contrast quite explicit in view of Sarah's remarks about the difference between age of menarche and the cultural permission or power given to the girl or to the girl's parents or some sort of agent who is responsible for the control of her sexuality. I think what we know in anthropology is in terms of the great diversity of social and cultural values and roles that we see. These, by the way, are certainly not unlimited; there is a range and I do think that within that range there are certain important general patterns, but I think the key variable here has to do with the social status and the relationship between social status and menarche. For the !Kung, as well as to a lesser extent the Australian Aborigines, what we know is that in those hunting and gathering societies there tends to be a fairly high level of approval of early sexual relationship with a great deal of agency given to the girl. Whereas with respect to societies that are more hierarchical, where property and social status is more hierarchical, less and less agency is given to the girl and more and more power is given to the persons who are regarded as the protectors or guardians or overseers of the girl, whether it's her parents or someone else. And obviously there is a very significant relationship between the social status of the girl, the social group to which she belongs, and the existence of social elites or hierarchies in these cultures. So there's a very important distinction to be made between recognizing in the local community or culture the difference between the age of menarche and what's regarded as the socially accepted or "normal" age of sexual intercourse, which usually is going to occur in a socially approved alliance, whether it's a marriage or something else in the community. With respect to that, there's a general tendency in anthropology to erase the relationship between the private and the public here, which we must not do. That is to say, the existence of the ideal norm does not mean that people don't transgress against that norm in private; there may be infractions. There may be, in fact, a very high percentage of cases of people who violate the norm and have casual sexual relations against the norm. However, that is not the recognized and or sanctioned social behavior and what matters in the social life of these communities is the political legitimacy given to a relationship between the girl and a socially acknowledged person who will have sexual relations with her, because it's the offspring of that socially acknowledged relationship which will be credited as the legitimate heirs.

REFERENCES

Altmann, J., Altmann, S. A., & Hausfater, G. (1988). Determinants of reproductive success in savannah baboons (*Papio cynocephalus*). In T. H. Clutton-Brock (Ed.), *Reproductive success: Studies of individual variation in contrasting systems* (pp. 403–418). Chicago: University of Chicago Press.

Drickamer, L. (1974). A ten-year summary of reproductive data for free-ranging *Macaca mulatta*. *Folia Primatologica, 33,* 262–272.

Laumann, E. O., Gagnon, G., Michael, R., & Michaels, S. (1994). *The social organization of sexuality.* Chicago: University of Chicago Press.

Loeber, R., Farrington, D. P., Stouthamer-Loeber, M., & Van Kammen, W. B. (1998). *Antisocial behavior and mental health problems.* Mahwah, NJ: Lawrence Erlbaum Associates.

Discussion Paper

LEONORE TIEFER

Let's Look at Contexts

The context of this conference. Let me take a step back from a focused discussion on these two papers and start with a surprising question. What is the meta-narrative of this conference on the role of theory in sex research? Just as sex does not take place without a context, so also conferences don't take place without a context, and we should take a moment to think about what our context might be.

The first aspect of context I draw your attention to is the explosive growth of sexuality theory in recent years in two brand-new areas—the academic humanities and the pharmaceutical industry. First, the humanities. English departments now have more courses in topics related to sexuality and gender than social science departments have ever been able to support. Studies in the history of sexuality, especially from the queer studies perspective, are growing exponentially. Sexuality theory is becoming more oriented toward texts and less focused on physical reality every day (e.g., Lancaster & diLeonardo, 1997; Nardi & Schneider, 1998).

At the same time, there is now an explosion of sexuality drug trials on erectile dysfunction and, just beginning, on women's sexual disorders. This explosion is driven by commercial interests (profit), which are in turn supported by shifts in demographics, cultural changes in the meaning of sexuality, and a political atmosphere which encourages collaboration between academe and industry (Tiefer, 1998). Biomedical sex researchers are attracted to the opportunity for financial support and legitimacy that they have not previously had.

Now, it is interesting that neither the world of historical and literary analysis nor the world of pharmaceuticals is represented at this conference, yet their specter hovers over us. They are where the action is in sexuality research today—although it is less clear that they are developing new theory. Perhaps we at this conference are trying to reclaim some vitality for the traditional psychobiosocial center of sexuality theory and research.

The other aspect of context I draw your attention to has to do with the contemporary politics of sexuality in America. We live in strange times for sexuality and strange times for sexuality scholarship. Instead of hearing that the Kinsey Institute is receiving strong financial support from public and private sources because of its long-standing sterling reputation and continuing productivity, we have heard just the opposite. The director of the Kinsey Institute must, on a weekly basis, respond to politicians who are themselves responding to complaints from political conservatives. He must take time to explain that his Institute receives not a farthing, not a shekel, of support from our government's vast array of scientific funding programs. If the Kinsey Institute were in the business of developing abstinence-only sex education curricula, it would presumably be drowning in federal money, at least at the moment.

So traditional sex research which takes a biopsychosocial view is being usurped by humanities research (which responds to political trends and doesn't seem to need much funding) and pharmaceutical industry–sponsored research (which is largely oblivious to academic developments and hears only the sound of the cash register).

The conference goal: A unified theory? Now, given such aspects of the contemporary context of sex research, what can this conference accomplish with regard to theory and sex research? One possibility is that we can strive to remain oblivious to external matters and pursue a "pure science" unified theory. We can attempt to create a theory along the lines of the old story about the blind men and the elephant. That's the story where each blind man feels the elephant. One says it's a rope, another says it's a snake, and the third says, "You're both wrong, it is a tree!" We can operate like blind men at an interdisciplinary conference on sexuality, with the blind man from medicine saying "Sexuality is like an organ which functions naturally" and the blind man from social science saying "No, sexuality is a system of interacting components" and the blind humanities scholar saying, "No, it's a domain of symbols!"

But this model won't work for one simple reason. In the case of the elephant, there can be different perceptions of the elephant, but, voila, in the end they all turn out to be wrong because the elephant is more than its trunk, its tail, and its leg—it is the totality of all these things—a unity which is greater than the parts. But is that true for sexuality? Many of us have been influenced by the new academic sexuality studies in literature and history and have begun to see that sexuality itself is constructed anew by each disciplinary point of view and the methodologies that we use to view it. How can we ever have a unified "it" when our different disciplines create an un-unifiable "it" (e.g., Simon, 1996; Plummer, 1995; Weeks, 1991)?

Recall one of the few existing books on sexuality theory (Geer & O'Donohue, 1987). There were 15 different "approaches," with no effort to find unity, only the goal of "facilitating comparisons" and "increasing interaction among perspectives" (p. 1). This collection antedated the claim that sexuality is "constructed." Instead, the editors claimed that "the study of sex is multidisciplinary" (p. 2) and the relationship of different disciplines is compatible, "in that the truth of the assertions of one approach does not entail the falsity of assertions made in another approach" (p. 4).

There was no effort in 1987 to create a grand theory, only to engage in respectful parallel play. But now, in the face of a growing chorus of academic claims that sexuality is a social construct, are we not in an even worse position for creating a unified theory? Why should we not continue to be content with the peaceful coexistence of an anthropological view, a feminist view, a theological view, a developmental view, a learning view, etc.?

I would suggest that we need to spend more time working on this issue of meta-narrative, since it seems to me that the effort to create a grand theory at this point in time is an effort to erect a bulwark against powerful new trends in sex research such as those in the humanities and the pharmaceutical industry. I am not indisposed to bulwarks, but we need to be clear about what our project is. Moreover, we must integrate any valuable insights of the new trends lest they undermine our very project.

Life cycle approach and gender schemas. The present symposium addresses sexuality across the life cycle, but I observe that life cycle theory rarely gets beyond childhood and rarely deals with more than gender. It seems to me that this limitation results from the nature of the biological variables under consideration and the covert agenda of the work. Biological variables are used to make claims about the etiology of aspects of sexuality which are laid down prenatally, rather than about aspects of sexuality which unfold over a lifetime. So, for example, able-bodiedness is a physical variable which contributes a great deal to a person's sexuality, and whether a disability occurs at age 3 or 20 or 60 will make a significant contribution to that effect.

In the present papers, however, discussion of genotypes and reproductive strategies bypasses effects of particular biological variables in the quest to find universal statements about human sexuality. Not accidentally, I would suggest, these universal statements speak largely to gender difference. Such a quest seems primarily to serve the covert agenda of gender polarization, which Sandra Bem (1993) defines as "the ubiquitous organization of social life around the distinction between male and female" (p. 80). Bem challenges us not to reproduce the "culturally constructed dichotomy between masculine and feminine" in our research, and to "look *at* the lenses of a culture rather than *through* them" (p. 127).

My impression is that attempts to show how gender differences predict the expression and experience of sexuality are full of sweeping essentialistic generalizations and assumptions. A cognitive–social learning approach emphasizing the self-perpetuating aspects of gender self-labeling and internalized beliefs along with the multitude of available social reinforcements is rarely considered by those studying biological variables (Fagot, 1993). Such an approach would have room for the *discontinuities* of gender identity and gender-role learning and would show how "gender is a constitutive element of social relationships based on *perceived* differences between the sexes" (Scott, 1988, p. 42, emphasis added).

Theory and social context. Finally, to return to the issue of context and the purpose of this conference, I suggest we look at the fact that we develop theories at particular historical points in relation to issues of the time. The meaning of gender is evolving rapidly along with changes in demographics, reproductive technology, and the nature of human work, but the meaning of these changes are aggressively contested by different political groups. As a feminist, I am concerned with how gender assignment and arguments about gender difference perpetuate relationships of power. Consequently, I am most interested in theories of sexuality which can empower individuals and help equalize social opportunity. If theories relate to gender as if it were unchanged since humans lived in caves, they cannot help us understand the limits and uses of sexuality in our time.

Science is a fully social process, and theory making is an important intellectual contribution to political debate. Academic challenges, political challenges, and covert agendas all need to be aired. Theories represent academic points of view, yes, but also political interests. As we dialogue about data and theory, let us not forget to dialogue about social and political context.

REFERENCES

Bem, S. L. (1993). *The lenses of gender: Transforming the debate on sexual inequality.* New Haven: Yale University Press.

Fagot, B. (1993, June). *Gender role development in early childhood: Environmental input, internal construction.* Address to International Academy of Sex Research, Pacific Grove, CA.

Geer, J. H., & O'Donohue, W. T. (Eds.). (1987). *Theories of human sexuality.* New York: Plenum Press.

Lancaster, R. N., & diLeonardo, M. (Eds.). (1997). *The gender/sexuality reader: Culture, history, political economy.* New York: Routledge.

Nardi, P. M., & Schneider, B. E. (Eds.). (1998). *Social perspectives in lesbian and gay studies: A reader.* New York: Routledge.

Plummer, K. (1995). *Telling sexual stories: Power, change, and social worlds.* New York: Routledge.

Scott, J. W. (1988). *Gender and the politics of history.* New York: Columbia University Press.

Simon, W. (1996). *Postmodern sexualities.* New York: Routledge.

Tiefer, L. (1998, June). *Sexology and the pharmaceutical industry: Cooptation.* Paper presented at the International Academy of Sex Research, Sirmione, Italy.

Weeks, J. (1991). *Against nature: Essays on history, sexuality, and identity.* London: Rivers Oram Press.

General Discussion

John Bancroft: There are two points that Leonore raised that I want to respond to. One is struggling with the "it"; what is this thing we're dealing with, what is sexuality and so on. It strikes me that part of the reason why we struggle with that is because of what I feel is an extraordinary tendency to separate sexuality from reproduction in our thinking. I think reproduction is an "it" which we don't have too much problem dealing with. I'm very conscious of the fact that a lot of sexual behavior is separated from reproduction, but it is that relationship, how to separate it and why to separate it, that I think we tend to lose sight of. To keep reproduction in the picture may help us to structure our theory more appropriately. The other point is her comment about being frustrated because the life cycle models focus on the developmental stages. I'm not sure that I necessarily agree with her. At least put it this way; there are some very important processes affecting our adaptation and development sexuality that have to do with aging rather than early stages of development, and aging is a biological process as well as a social one too. So whereas Anke and Tony may appropriately concentrate more on the early years, in fact there are biological factors to keep in mind throughout the life cycle. In women in particular you have this striking three-phased life cycle of being pre-reproductive, reproductive, and post-reproductive, which has profound biological and sociological implications.

Anke Ehrhardt: Actually childhood is usually neglected in life course consideration of sexual behavior. I think what is correct is that studies of sexual behavior are typically frequent during adolescence, they go on to the 40s, and then they typically drop off. But in the life course thinking of other disciplines, early development is often neglected. I wanted to use it as an example of how we might approach, with a biopsychosocial perspective, life course unfolding and the importance of gender. Not that that is the only thing and one could certainly go through the other phases with a similar approach. A couple of other answers to Leonore. What typically happens in an interdisciplinary conference is that we end up acknowledging that things are too complex and that we get overwhelmed and do not go on with the debate to try to integrate the different kinds of variables. One of the reasons is the difficulty to keep up with the different kind of disciplines involved when there are so many advances in so many different fields. The other point, the political one, is a really troubling one. How can theories be exploited and how does that shape our thinking? As you are, I'm a feminist. I'm keenly aware of how things can be, if you bring biology in, exploited and used and misused in order to bring those two things together; thinking about the political consequences might have stopped scientific pursuit. At the same time you cannot *not* think about the political consequences. So that's a real dilemma. Why should we have a theory at all? Why should we have an integrated theory like that? I think the deep frustration of going from one discovery to the next when we have these very simple models is the main reason. Within the space of 30 years, our explanations of homosexuality can go from family constellation to the discovery of a gene; at each stage we think that that is the one and only explanation. That is a very strong reason to advance knowledge by having better integrated models. But we need to step back and even have new language for that. Other disciplines do that and we live in a time of technological explosion. Maybe we need new computer models. A final point about transgenderism. Children can have a concept of transgenderism, so it doesn't need a great deal of cognitive development to think in those terms. Cognitive development undoubtedly influences how we think about gender, but children have the capacity to be transgendered.

John Gagnon: The way I think about the life course is an individual life located against the backdrop of history within a microenvironment within a specific culture. The question becomes, how is that organized? History is not a variable like the year 1931, it is the times in which people live. Individuals live in history and they make history as they live in it. To abstract out of these transient processes general principles that are "true forever" is not going to work. It hasn't worked in the past and it isn't going to work in the future. As a number of people have said, the social types alive now, meaning us, may not be alive at all as social types in 50 years. So we are transient historical creatures ourselves at this very moment. A second point about the life course question; it seems to me that very little weight is ever given to the new environment to which the individual must adapt. The weight in life history research is always given to the past of the individual rather than to the adaptational situation which reshapes an individual as she enters into new phases of the life course. If you join the Marines, becoming a "Marine", will reshape most of your activities no matter what brought you to the Marine Corps. There's very little attention paid to the independence of future events from past events, or the weakness of the past in predicting the future, particularly in highly diverse and changing societies. For instance, we live in a world of high rates of immigration, but don't consider the fact that most immigrants now live successfully in new worlds. This suggests that the degree to which their past influences their living in the United States (for instance) may be very modest. As a result of this prejudice, childhood tends to dominate our thinking about the life course.

Shirley Lindenbaum: I wanted to say something about the way in which anthropology looks at sexuality and gender. I am struck by the way in which gender and sexuality are key domains in which changes wrought by capitalism and Christianity in colonial and post-colonial settings are manifested. The anthropological record suggests that specific types of persons are created in specific types of ways in ritual processes. I'm thinking of Papua New Guinea at the moment, but you could generalize that statement. These ritual processes tend also to create persons with specific types of sexual behavior. It's been the case, and it's still the case in the post-colonial context, that gender and sexuality are key domains for transforming persons. I'll give you an example. There's some interesting material coming from the Southern Highlands now that Holly Wardlow (1998) talks about, in which in the past there was a communal house where sexual interactions occurred among men and women in a ritualized context—they sang songs about their ancestors and about the society; they addressed specific women in the group over a nighttime of singing, and at the end of it alliances were made. It was a way of choosing partners. So a lot of future marriage partners were identified in such "sexual" ritual processes. In the present day, it looks, superficially, that this communal house has been transformed into a brothel, but it hasn't really. This is an interesting and particularly instructive transitional moment, when you can catch the transformation of sexual behaviors up close, when the whole political economy is changing. People are involved in wage labor and are becoming autonomous persons trying to detach themselves from demands on their wages, trying to keep their wages to themselves. The reflection of these changes are occurring in this sexual ritualized encounter. Now a specific man, not the community of men, builds the house; he charges a gate fee to have people participate. Only certain types of women are allowed to come in, not wives and not unmarried women. They are frequently divorced women and older women. The men come in dressed in traditional clothes, they sing traditional songs; it is a ritual event. At the end of it they have an assignation with a woman and they pay the woman, so that there's a certain amount of commercialization going on. They pay to get in, they pay a woman, but they call it free sex. But in what way is it free sex? It's unencumbered by kinship attachments. Its autonomous sex. There are no accusations of adultery. There's no bride price to be paid. There are no commitments to your in-laws. So what we're looking at are changing subjectivities and changing sexualities, and the form of sex is also different. They perform oral sex, which they never did before. They'd be sickened if they saw a woman's vagina in the past, and they would literally vomit. But now that's not the case. So the participants are becoming modern persons with modern sex. Autonomous persons in an autonomous sexual context. The whole political economy changing around them is producing more autonomous persons and it's interesting that gender and sexuality are the key domains to experiment with becoming different types of persons. I'm just struck by the way in which that was true in the past, and it's certainly true at the moment.

Ken Plummer: I'd like to ponder what the questions of this conference actually are. The first question Leonore raised, which I think is an incredibly important one, is What is the object of theory? As I was listening to the first speakers, I have to say I was deeply perplexed because what I heard was reproduction, which John Bancroft believes is the most important aspect, from what he has said. I also heard about mating behaviors. What I didn't hear much about, in either of the papers, was sexualities—about masturbation, oral sex, fellatio, sado-masochism, call it what you like, but I mean the many, many different sexualities that people engage in. And I thought, are we here to have another theory of gender or are we here to have a theory of sexualities? But that leads to another problem: What kind of theory are we going for? Certainly in the academic circles I generally move in these days, the idea of any kind of unitary, integrative, monolithic theory that brings everything together is simply out of court. We just don't talk as if we can do that kind of thing. I'm talking about—I have to use this word because we have to use it at some point—those dreadful people who we call post-modern social theorists who simply say that the idea of the big unifying progressive world narrative is dead.[1] It's no longer around. Previously we could take particular sets of Eurocentric and North American theories and use them to generalize around the world; but we must now learn from the failures of all that over the past couple of centuries or so. The time has arrived for a multiplicity of much more localized specific theories. AIDS is a very good example of this. People in AIDS work generally don't like the big global theories. They go to particular cities, to particular circumstances, and use those environments to generate their particular theories. One question to keep constantly in sight is what is the object we're trying to theorize.

I'm not clear yet, and I'm certainly not clear whether it should be a unifying thing.

One further point is the question of disciplinary languages. It is the case when people move into conferences of a multidisciplinary nature that they are exposed to wildly different languages. So, for instance, I have never heard the phrase "life history theory" used before in the way it has been used today, and yet I am a life history theorist. So I am deeply perplexed that I come to a conference and I read about life history theory when the ideas and language that are my daily currency are so different.[2] The language that I use is around "identities as life stories," "how people construct their identities," "the narrative reconstructions of lives," "the career phases people move through life from birth to death," on the social contingencies that shape that right throughout life, and, what everybody's talking about now within the social sciences, the flexibility and the reorganization of life stages. Erikson's straightforward psychosocial model of people moving through a definite hierarchy is no longer popular; instead, we have a much more complex one, shaped by class, gender, race, and all the rest of it. So there are really serious problems there: We're all talking about "life history theory" and yet we use the term in very different ways. I think it's very useful that I've learned something about another theory that I can add into what I'm thinking about; but it's very odd to me that there's a whole world of other life history theorists out there talking a fundamentally different language.

Finally, unless we get clear about our epistemologies, our ontologies if you like, and all the other "ies", we won't get very far. Leonore talked about the nature of theory and we do have to think about what a theory is. Is it a model, is it a hypothesis? Is it just a general way of thinking? Is it a grand theory? What are we thinking about when we say theory and with that, what are the different conceptions of reality that we have behind that? Is it really real "out there" or is it just a "social construction"?—to use another fashionable phrase. And what are the different kinds of epistemologies that we could be open to? I hear at work here versions of positivism and versions of realism. I don't hear much yet on the level of say, interpretivism. I don't hear much yet on the level of critical theory. I don't hear much work yet on the notion of feminist standpoint. And I don't hear much at all yet on the level of post-modern social theory and post-modern skepticism about grand narratives. Now I don't want to stir up trouble, but I feel I've moved into another world. We live in different social worlds[3] and this is a scientific sexological world of which I've rarely been part of before.

Anthony Walsh: The fact that we both used the same term, "life history," and we don't know what the other person is talking about is the reason I think we do need an umbrella theory so we can encompass all of these specific theories that you're talking about. And I think that umbrella theory has to be evolutionary theory. The opening sentence in my paper was that the only viable scientific explanation for basic behavioral design is evolutionary theory. We are part of life sciences as far as I'm concerned, sociology, anthropology, psychology are life sciences, and the overarching theory of biology is evolutionary theory, evolution by natural selection. I feel that certainly the more advanced, the more fundamental sciences are looking for grand theories. I think that is a noble thing to strive for. It doesn't preclude all of these specific theories. We who have a biological orientation to our data certainly do not neglect the environment.

Gary Dowsett: As someone who works with "theorized life history," I find the concept of life history presented here quite problematic, because with theorized life history the last thing you would do would be to believe the life history that you were given as a starting point for your work. Having said that, the main point I want to make is about Leonore's paper. I think she has opened up the first of the big questions that are going to make the divide between us, theoretically and methodologically, at the conference. And that is her representation of what constitutes "gender" as a vast system and structure of power as the main working tool that she uses. This bears very little relationship to the concept of gender either as sex differences noted in biology or as noted in basic social practices for determining different behaviors between young people in early age. The distance between those two notions and gender as a structure of power is completely untheorized in our work. To take Ken's point about the difference between gender and sexuality, certainly in my area of post-structuralism contemporary sexuality theory doesn't look anything like the sexuality that I'm hearing coming out of papers this morning—and that's not because I'm in an English Department. As an AIDS researcher, I would recognize in Ken's work that the theories of sexuality we're working with on a local practical public health level bear very little resemblance to the psychosocial models that are, in fact, underpinned by the kind of work on gender that we've been hearing this morning. Which is not to say I'm not learning something, but I want to throw into the mix here the notion that the size of that divide, represented by the example of gender, is much more enormous than we're acknowledging. Similarly, Sarah's representation of "environment" and the way in which environment and context are currently represented here as a few variables in the background that the individual deals with is, to a sociologist working with something of the size of gender, an enormously complex thing that is not at all simply a variable in which we play. I'm trying to represent environment as more than just context. I want to argue for a notion of society and social structure that is a vastly larger array; and that distance between systems like gender as Leonore describes them and what we've been talking about this morning is sometimes very vast.

Sarah Hrdy: Context and environment are very complicated. It depends on what you're talking about. If you're talking about some internal discreet physiological developmental phenomenon (like menarche) that is unfolding within a very specific context of the organs that are already in place, the cells that are there, the neurons that are already in place, that's a pretty complicated context. But when you get to something like gender, I agree completely that chronologically and in terms of the variety of sensory input, social relationships, resources available, emotional reactions, yes, it's very complex. I want to get back to Ken's point and his consternation at the way life history theory is being used. Actually, Anthony Walsh and I don't use life history theory in the same way. I'm wondering whether it would be helpful or else too time-consuming to insist that when people invoke a theory, they specify what they mean. For one thing, I believe that biologists may use the word theory in a different way from those in the humanities. To me as a biological anthropologist, a theory is a hypothesis that has been tested, and the tests have been confirmed and replicated. It is a hypothesis so firmly grounded and supported that it becomes a theory. So, for example, evolutionary theory, that's just some kind of general perspective and the term feminist theory, that's general perspective. A theory that I can think of in my field that really deserves that name is "natural selection." Predictions generated by Darwin's model were tested, not in Darwin's lifetime, but since Darwin. It has been shown to be a correct theory. So natural selection is a theory. The notion of "kin selection," which is a special subset of natural selection theory, having to do with behaviors evolved when the cost to the altruist is less than the benefit to the recipient calibrated by degree of relatedness, that has been demonstrated now for a number of different animal species. Kin selection is a bona fide theory. Evolutionary theory in this general sense, unless you mean sexual selection or natural selection or kin selection, is not really proven; it's a perspective. And the same for life history theory; it's a perspective. Feminist theory is a perspective having to do with power relationships, I gather, but it means different things to different people. So when we talk about theories here today I think mostly we're talking about perspectives, not scientific theories. It might be too time-consuming, but maybe we should specify what theory we mean and whether we mean it as a general perspective or whether we mean it as something that has been tested and shown to be true.

Martin Weinberg: I'm a sociologist and I have two points related to what Sarah's been saying against Anthony's assumption that evolutionary theory is the basic overarching theory. As someone who does interdisciplinary work, I also feel that if the subject of a program is "theory," then social constructionism has to be the basic approach because that is what theory is—a construction. Furthermore, what we're seeing here is that many of us are constructing the word "theory" differently. Thus we are constructing the title of the conference "the role of theory in sex research," differently. I know when I heard the title I thought what we'd be talking about are some of the questions Ken and Leonore brought up, because of my construction of the term "theory." I think that instead of this battle between social constructionism and essentialism on the level of theory, though, we still do have to deal with constructionism. We have to deal with these issues of how we're constructing things so that we can share our ideas with each another; we can then orient the approach we should take. We keep getting questions that indicate there's confusion because of the fact that we're making different constructions of even the title of the program.

John Bancroft: I feel a certain responsibility in having gotten you all here, and you not knowing why you are here. I did try to give you some rationale in the program that I sent you and I would actually be interested to know if any of you would want to reject the approach to the topic that I actually outlined in the introduction to the program. I knew very well that we were going to have people here with different points of view, different way of looking at things, and it wasn't the purpose of the conference to point that out. We all know that. I was also very conscious in thinking whom we should ask. It would be quite easy to get people who would just bat each other around the head and go away again. I don't think any of us would think that would be a particularly useful exercise. Let us start with the assumption that we're going to have a variety of different epistemological approaches here. Different ways of using the term *theory*. Let's assume that; there's no need to point it out. But is there any way that we can discuss from our different perspectives that is creative, that enhances our understanding? And a particular theme of this meeting is to focus on the extent to which the way we model or theorize about things might have useful implications for policy matters. I know some of you are extremely skeptical about that and you're entitled to be skeptical, but that is part of the purpose of this meeting. In fact, we see this as a first step; next year we're planning another meeting which will have attached to it a workshop which will be focusing directly on the relationship between theory and policies. So maybe I can ask you at some stage to reread what I sent you.[4] I would be interested to know where this can be disputed or how it might be better formulated. I was fascinated by

Ken's comment on how he'd come from a background which had been characterized by global theoretical models and he's come to realize that there was a need for having much more particular theoretical models now, because I come from an entirely opposite situation—from a fairly typical essentialist position which has avoided the overarching global theoretical models and has focused on relatively specific models to deal with specific issues. Half of my motivation for this conference, as somebody with a large biological input into my thinking, is that the changes in biology as they relate to behavior over the last 15 years or so have been immense, and the consequence of this has been increasing and quite devastating fragmentation of knowledge. Increasingly it becomes difficult to relate one piece of knowledge to another in any meaningfully useful way. So I come from a background where we desperately need some way to integrate our fragmented knowledge into a more useful concept of the whole.

Jay Paul: In listening to the various points made so far, I was struck by the notion of what it is that we collectively represent in these meetings. The selection process that led to our invitations to this conference suggests a certain level of productivity within our own disciplines. Thus, we each come here with a fluency and familiarity with distinct conceptual frames. Professional experiences, individual disciplines, and personal histories have shaped and defined the organizing principles we use to examine the world. One could therefore treat this conference as a naturalistic experiment with outcomes to be determined. To what degree will each of us be influenced by some of the other ideas that come up over the next few days? We are unlikely to completely abandon the point of view reinforced by our discipline. However, to what degree will we at least stop, pause, and think a little bit differently about the work we're doing as a consequence of this convocation?

John Gagnon: The issue of how you do interdisciplinary research. The only way you can create interdisciplinary theory is by doing concrete interdisciplinary projects. You have to work with somebody else who's doing empirical research, measuring something else in a concrete way. There are no theoretical ways to construct interdisciplinary theories. All you get is talk about talk. That ends up being a sterile exercise. What we're doing here is not unimportant because in listening to other people talk you may think, "If I'd made those kinds of measurements, if I worked in the laboratory with someone who thought that way, maybe I would find something interesting." But neuroscience did not begin because neurologists talked to psychologists. Neuroscience emerged because psychologists and neurologists worked in the same laboratory on the same set of empirical questions. That becomes the critical issue; that interdisciplinary work is emergent, rather than something that happens because we say it would be virtuous if we were all interdisciplinary. Talking about interdisciplinarity may keep the idea on the agenda, but out of this talk has to come people who say "I'd like to work with an economist," or "I'd like to work with a somebody else who thinks about the world in different ways than I do, who tells me we ought to gather different kinds of data or says we ought to think about different kinds of experiments."

Anke Ehrhardt: I agree and I disagree with you. I think that's correct about how interdisciplinary work has to be done. I have fought for the last 20 years to do that kind of thing. But you cannot skip the step of having clear hypotheses. And the kind of "supertheory" which Ken Plummer commented on is not what I have in mind. We need a perspective of integration, so that specific theories can become integrated, rendering hypotheses which can be tested in an interdisciplinary way, involving different people who have different methodologies.

Bob Michael: I'm an economist and I'm pleased not only by the diversity in the points of view that we bring, but really the positive attitude of sharing them in a pleasant way. I hope that continues. To put what you would think of as my biases, and which I think of as truth, out there, the theory that I understand to be theory is "downward slope to demand curves"; that is, as prices fall, quantities rise, as incomes go up people want more. People are effective in their demand for more and that's the basic result of 200 years in economic theory. There's a good bit of evidence in support of that and so one stands by it and doubts evidence that it isn't so. The unease I felt in hearing the papers was well expressed in some of the discussion. It had to do with the fact that it seemed so general and so noncontroversial that I didn't know where to go with it, not that I disagreed with it, but I didn't know what to do with it. The issue that was then raised about what was the "it" in sexuality, or Ken's listing of specifics, strikes me as the right way to go. It's when we get down to a specific issue and, in particular, a real problem, that the multidisciplinary approach comes into being. I have my perspective on a problem and it works pretty well but only partway if I really want to understand the problem. So if my focus is the problem I then need a sociologist or I need a psychologist or I need someone else to work with me to better understand that problem. So it seems to me what we should be doing first off is answering the question of what's the "it." So let me put my "it" on the table. My first "it" is specific sexual behavior, remembering Ken Plummer's list: Is it masturbation, is it homosexuality, is it numbers of partners, is it frequency of sex, is it frequency of oral sex? Getting the specifics of sexual practices strikes me as one important interesting issue that requires data—a real-world evidence of that "it." The second "it" is disease, in particular AIDS but not exclusively AIDS. The risks that we face in terms of our health and particularly disease-related interactions are worthy of all of our efforts and we don't want to leave them off the list. A third is uncoupling, the disassociation of sex and fertility or procreation that has changed so much of our lives and is interesting intellectually and interesting from a policy perspective.

Daryl Bem: I'm a social psychologist. In spite of all these disagreements, I think we all tend to agree about the nature of the enterprise. I would like to respond to Sarah's comment about theory. Your notion of a theory wipes out what I think is my theory because I reserve the right to be absolutely wrong and yet I will call it theory and under your definition there's no such thing as a theory that is wrong.

Sarah Hrdy: I find your ideas fascinating and provocative. To me, they constitute a hypothesis, or hypothetical model. If it survives testing, then I'll call it Bem's theory.

Joe Rodgers: I'm a psychologist. I also had the same almost whimsical criticism of Sarah's definition of theory. The first thing I thought was that all those theories out there that are clearly wrong, by definition aren't theories.

Sarah Hrdy: There are very few proven theories; gravitational theory, natural selection theory. All the rest are perspectives or hypothetical models of wide scope waiting to be tested.

Joe Rodgers: I think that's absolutely wrong, because I think that there are millions of theories. The only requirement that I would have for it to be a theory is that it first of all be a simplification of reality and second that it has some component that really does match reality. Given that perspective, that implies that there can be thousands of theories that are simultaneously correct. This is something that always bothers me in an interdisciplinary context. It's as though we believe that our different theories have to be resolved. In fact, if we flatten in one direction and flatten in another direction and flatten in a third direction, we may be simplifying in three entirely legitimate and interesting ways, but in different manners. The best example I can think of is that a theory of sexuality that treats it as a physiological process is not wrong because it builds a different theory than a theory of sexuality that treats it as a social process. Those are two different simplifications of a very complex reality that includes not only genes and hormones but also social processes and individual differences and so on. So within disciplines it strikes me that a lot of theory confirmation and testing goes on, because our theories generate conflicting and interesting tensions that need to be resolved. Across disciplines, my sense is that we don't really have very many differences to be resolved. What we're doing is flattening the complicated reality in a whole bunch of different directions that will be never be resolved and shouldn't be resolved. I agree with Tony's sense that evolutionary theory sits above it all, but I'm not sure that evolutionary theory is even a very interesting theory because it is so facile at explaining everything. The world works the way it does because we got to this point through a process of evolution that is not falsifiable, not testable; it's a perspective that sits above it all and so it doesn't really advance our understanding. It also can't really in any formal sense be tested with Bob's idea of data. We need theories to be in tension with our data and it's hard to ask evolution to do that. So what brings us together is an interest in simplifying this complicated reality in ways that are useful and valuable, and I think John Bancroft's statement in his original letter to us says this very well.

Leonore Tiefer: I'm a student of the history of sexology and I see this conference as occurring at an interesting moment when sexology has really lost control of the subject matter. Maybe some effort could be made by the Kinsey Institute with this conference to regain some leadership in that area. Sexology has been dominated by the "psycho" and "bio" part of this psychobiosocial model, while social influence and religious influences have not been so integral. The leaders in sexology have been "psycho" and "bio" kinds of people, often starting with clinical interests. Animal research initially thrived because it was the only type of sex research that could be funded in an anti-sexual environment. Biological variables which were very prominent in animal research were in the forefront. But then we come to the post-war or post-Kinsey period, or even more recently, when two amazing things happened to sexology. One was the AIDS epidemic and the other was the "linguistic turn," as it's called, this interpretative groundswell. The AIDS epidemic brought into sex research people with new ideas and different points of view and many of them also brought a fundamentally social perspective. This has provided a great challenge to sexology, not only to be useful and have something to say about this terrible epidemic, but also to have something to say theoretically. And then the linguistic turn developed which, as I said at the beginning of my remarks, has seized a certain kind of academic credibility that many of us have longed for hopelessly for many years. We see departments and fellowships and chairs and all kinds of credentials with the word sexuality on them and yet what they're studying is quite different from what sexology has had to offer. And so if I see one thing coming out of this conference, which has begun to come out in this last discussion, it is a reconceptualization of the social part of the psychobiosocial design to somehow incorporate or deal with or come to terms with the many different ways that the social piece can be discussed by people whose tradition has been more fundamentally psychological and biological. The social piece has itself changed but it has never been adequately recognized within sexology.

Gilbert Herdt: I just want to add one thing about anthropology, but also about the social sciences in general, to refine what is the meaning of the space that the social holds, in constructing not a unified paradigm but paradigms that interestingly interact with each other. This has to do with John's point about the relationship between the reproductive and sexual practices that are purposely or unintentionally not reproductive. I think Carol Vance (1991) has pointed out in a very interesting article that has become almost a classic that anthropology's rediscovery of sexuality was the discovery that all of our treatment of sexuality had to do with reproduction. That when anthropologists such as Margaret Mead went to a simple society and studied sexuality, they studied marriage and kinship, and then assumed that the content of marriage and kinship accounted for the content of sexuality. This, of course, is absurd and they never would have made such an equation in their own society. And I think then in almost all of the cases where certain problematical phenomena had presented themselves, for instance, the berdache among the North American Indians, where you have a person who is biologically a female who takes on the social role of the male sex, all these phenomena in general were treated reductively as biological deviations that had to be explained by temperamental or developmental variation or as individual differences that depart from the norm. This was very peculiar for these people to do. They were all pure cultural relativists and they always invoked pure culture relativist theory or structural functional theory to explain the phenomena. So why in the world did they then resort in those cases of individual difference to biological reductionist inferences? The answer is they had no theory of sexuality to account for sexuality. So what I think is really quite important is to consider all the cases where we think about what defines the social and the cultural dimension. If we don't want to be reductive and we want to talk about what is of importance today, we need to rethink those interesting cases where there are anomalies or problems for which there are data, to try to think through what part has been left out in our disciplines' approach to this. For anthropology, this was often, in the case of simple societies or nonwestern societies, How do you explain individual differences that depart from the norm? Obviously that leads us right back into the central problem of what is sexual orientation? What is sexual identity? What is gender? What are gender differences in the context of societies that have highly typified norms?

REFERENCES

Atkinson, R. (1998). *The life story interview.* London: Sage.
Best, S., & Kellner, D. (1997). *Postmodern theory: Critical interrogations.* London: Macmillan.
Denzin, N. K. (1989). *Interpretive biography.* London: Sage.
Giele, J. Z., & Elder, G. H., Jr. (1998). *Methods of life course research: Qualitative and quantitative approaches.* London: Sage.
Harvey, D. (1989). *The condition of postmodernity.* Oxford: Blackwell.
Linde, C. (1993). *Life stories: The creation of coherence.* New York: Oxford University Press.
Plummer, K. (1983). *Documents of life: An introduction to the problems and literature of a humanistic method.* London: Allen and Unwin.
Plummer, K. (1995). *Telling sexual stories: Power, change, and social worlds.* London: Routledge.
Ritzer, G. (1997). *Postmodern social theory.* New York: McGraw-Hill.
Simon, W. (1996). *Postmodern sexuality.* New York: Routledge.
Strauss, A. (1993). *Continual permutations of action.* New York: Aldine de Gruyter.
Vance, C. S. (1991). Anthropology rediscovers sexuality: A theoretical comment. *Social Science and Medicine, 33,* 875–884.
Wardlow, H. (1998). *Changing sexuality, changing self: The Huli Dana Anda as contemporary male ritual.* Paper presented at the meeting of the Association of Social Anthropology.

NOTES

1. Two useful guides to the nature of post-modern social theory are Best and Kellner (1991) and Ritzer (1997). Post-modern theory needs to be distinguished from post-modern society—a good account of which may be found in Harvey (1989). On post-modern sexualities, see Simon (1996). Plummer (1995) provides an overview of much of this.

2. For some discussions on the life history within the social sciences, see Atkinson (1998); Denzin (1989); Giele and Elder (1998); Linde (1993); and Plummer (1983).

3. Within sociology, the concept "social worlds" has a specific meaning and it is used in this way here. See Strauss (1993), especially chapters 9 and 10.

4. See p. viii in this volume.

Part 2
Sexual Orientation

The Exotic-Becomes-Erotic Theory of Sexual Orientation

DARYL BEM

The "Exotic-Becomes-Erotic" theory of sexual orientation (Bem, 1996) attempts to integrate biological, experiential, and cultural variables into a single unified account of both opposite-sex and same-sex erotic desire. It proposes that biological variables do not code for sexual orientation per se, but for childhood temperaments that influence a child's preferences for sex-typical or sex-atypical activities. These preferences lead children to feel different from opposite-sex or same-sex peers—to perceive them as "exotic." This, in turn, produces heightened physiological arousal that subsequently gets eroticized to that same class of peers: Exotic becomes erotic.

Throughout the years, several disciplines have attempted to answer the question What causes homosexuality? But the question itself is scientifically misconceived because it presumes that heterosexuality is so well understood, so obviously the "natural" evolutionary consequence of reproductive advantage, that only deviations from it are theoretically problematic. Freud himself did not so presume: "[Heterosexuality] is also a problem that needs elucidation and is not a self-evident fact based upon an attraction that is ultimately of a chemical nature" (1905/1962, pp. 11–12).

I agree with Freud. In fact, I would go further and assert that even the use of biological sex as the basis for choosing a sexual partner is a problem that needs elucidation. Accordingly, my Exotic-Becomes-Erotic (EBE) theory of sexual orientation seeks to account for three major observations: First, most men and women in our culture have an exclusive and enduring erotic preference for either male or female persons; biological sex is, in fact, the overriding criterion for most people's erotic choices. Second, most men and women in our culture have an exclusive and enduring erotic preference for opposite-sex persons. And third, a substantial minority of men and women have an exclusive and enduring erotic preference for same-sex persons. In seeking to account for these observations, EBE theory proposes a single unitary explanation for both opposite-sex and same-sex desire—and for both men and women.

The theory also seeks to account for sex differences in sexual orientation and departures from the modal patterns, such as bisexuality, sexual orientations that are not enduring but are fluid and changeable, and sexual orientations that are not even based on the biological sex of potential partners. And finally, the theory seeks both to accommodate and to reconcile the empirical evidence of the biological essentialists—who can point to correlations between sexual orientation and biological variables—and the cultural relativism of the social constructionists—who can point to historical and anthropological evidence that the concept of sexual orientation is itself a social construction (De Cecco & Elia, 1993).

Experience-based theories of sexual orientation have not fared well empirically in recent years. The most telling data come from an intensive, large-scale interview study conducted in the San Francisco Bay Area by the Kinsey Institute for Sex Research (Bell, Weinberg, & Hammersmith, 1981a). By comparing approximately 1,000 gay men and lesbians with 500 heterosexual men and women, the investigators were able to test several hypotheses about the development of sexual orientation. The study (hereafter, the San Francisco study) yielded virtually no support for current experience-based theories of sexual orientation, including those based on processes of learning or conditioning or on family dynamics (e.g., classical psychoanalytic theory). In fact, family variables were not strongly implicated in the development of sexual orientation for either men or women.

But before we all became geneticists, biopsychologists, or neuroanatomists, it seemed to me worth another try. In particular, I believed that the theoretical and empirical building blocks for a coherent, experience-based developmental theory of sexual orientation were already scattered about in the literature. EBE theory is, then, an exercise in synthesis and construction.

Overview of the Theory

The central proposition of EBE theory is that individuals become erotically attracted to a class of individuals from whom they felt different during childhood. Figure 1 shows how this phenomenon is embedded into the overall sequence of events that, according to the theory, leads to an individual's sexual orientation. The sequence begins at the top of the figure with Biological Variables (labeled A) and ends at the bottom with Erotic Attraction (F).

A → B. According to the theory, biological variables such as genes or prenatal hormones do not code for sexual orientation per se but for childhood temperaments (e.g., aggression, activity level).

B → C. A child's temperaments predispose him or her to enjoy some activities more than others. One child will enjoy rough-and-tumble play and competitive team sports (male-typical activities); another will prefer to socialize quietly or play jacks or hopscotch (female-typical activities). Children will also prefer to play with peers who share their activity preferences; for example, the child who enjoys baseball or football will selectively seek out boys as playmates. Children who prefer sex-typical activities and same-sex playmates are referred to as gender conforming; children who prefer sex-atypical activities and opposite-sex playmates are referred to as gender nonconforming.

C → D. Gender-conforming children will feel different from opposite-sex peers, and gender-nonconforming children will feel different from same-sex peers.

D → E. These feelings of being different produce heightened physiological arousal.

E → F. Regardless of the specific source or affective tone of the childhood arousal, it is subsequently transformed into erotic attraction. Steps **D → E** and **E → F** thus encompass specific psychological mechanisms that transform exotic into erotic (**D → F**).

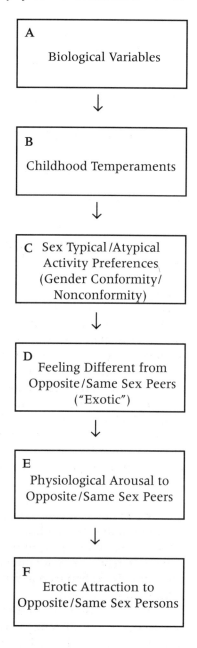

Figure 1. The temporal sequence of events leading to sexual orientation for most men and women in a gender-polarizing culture.

It is important to emphasize that Figure 1 is not intended to describe an inevitable, universal path to sexual orientation but the modal path followed by most men and women in a gender-polarizing culture like ours—a culture that emphasizes the differences between the sexes by pervasively organizing both the perceptions and realities of communal life around the male-female dichotomy (Bem, 1993).

Evidence for the Theory

Exotic Becomes Erotic (D→F)

The proposition that individuals can become erotically attracted to a class of individuals from whom they felt different during childhood is very general and transcends erotic orientations that are based on biological sex. For example, a light-skinned person could come to eroticize dark-skinned persons through one or more of the processes described by the theory. To produce a differential erotic attraction to one sex or the other, however, requires that the basis for feeling different must itself differentiate between the sexes; that is, to arrive at a sex-based erotic orientation, an individual must feel different for sex-based or gender-related reasons. Simply being lighter skinned, poorer, more intelligent, or more introverted than one's childhood peers does not produce the kind of feeling different that produces differential homoerotic or heteroerotic attraction.

Empirical support for this analysis comes from the San Francisco study, which found that 71% of the gay men and 70% of the lesbians in the sample had felt different from their same-sex peers during childhood. When asked in what ways they had felt different, they overwhelmingly cited gender-related reasons. Gay men were most likely to say that they had not liked boys' sports; lesbians were most likely to say that had been more masculine than other girls. In contrast, fewer than 8% of heterosexual men or women said that they had felt different from same-sex childhood peers for gender-related reasons. Those who had felt different from their peers tended to cite such reasons as having been poorer, more intelligent, or more introverted. (All statistical comparisons between gay and heterosexual respondents were significant at $p < .0005$.)

The study also showed that feelings of being different from same-sex peers was not a fleeting early experience for gay men and lesbians but a protracted and sustained feeling throughout childhood and adolescence. This is, I believe, why sexual orientations display such strong temporal stability across the life course for most men and women in our society.

Gender Conformity and Nonconformity:
The Antecedents of Feeling Different (C→D)

Feeling different from one's childhood peers can have any of several antecedents, some common, some idiosyncratic. The most common antecedent is gender polarization. Virtually all human societies polarize the sexes to some extent, setting up a sex-based division of labor and power, emphasizing or exaggerating sex differences, and, in general, superimposing the male-female dichotomy on virtually every aspect of communal life. These practices ensure that most boys and girls will grow up feeling different from opposite-sex peers and, hence, will come to be erotically attracted to them later in life. This, according to the theory, is why biological sex is the most common criterion for selecting sexual partners in the first place and why heteroeroticism is the modal preference across time and culture.

A less common occurrence is the child who comes to feel different from same-sex peers and who, according to the theory, will develop same-sex erotic attractions. As noted above, the most common reasons given by gay men and lesbians in the San Francisco study for having felt different from same-sex peers in childhood was gender nonconformity. In fact, childhood gender conformity or nonconformity was not only the strongest but the only significant childhood predictor of later sexual orientation for both men and women in the study (Bell, Weinberg, & Hammersmith, 1981a). As Table 1 shows, the effects are large and significant. For example, compared with heterosexual men, gay men were significantly less likely to have enjoyed boys' activities (e.g., baseball and football) during childhood, more likely to have enjoyed girls' activities (e.g., hopscotch, playing house, and jacks), and less likely to rate themselves as having been masculine. These were the three variables that defined gender nonconformity in the study.

Additionally, gay men were more likely than heterosexual men to have had girls as childhood friends. The corresponding comparisons between lesbian and heterosexual women are also large and significant.

It is also clear from the table that relatively more women than men had enjoyed sex-atypical activities and had had opposite-sex friends during childhood. As these data confirm, being a tomboy is common for a girl in our society, implying that it is probably not sufficient by itself to cause her to feel different from other girls. In fact, we see in the table that the difference between the percentages of lesbians and heterosexual women who enjoyed boys' activities during childhood (81% vs. 61%, respectively) is dwarfed by the difference in their child-

Table 1
**Percentage of Respondents Reporting Gender-Nonconform-
ing Preferences and Behaviors during Childhood**

	Men		Women	
	Gay	*Heterosexual*	*Lesbian*	*Heterosexual*
Response	*(n = 686)*	*(n = 337)*	*(n = 293)*	*(n = 140)*
Had not enjoyed sex-typical activities	63	10	63	15
Had enjoyed sex-atypical activities	48	11	81	61
Atypically sex-typed (masculinity/femininity)	56	8	80	24
Most childhood friends were opposite sex	42	13	60	40

Note. Percentages have been calculated from the data given in Bell, Weinberg, and Hammersmith (1981b, pp. 74–75, 77). All chi-square comparisons between gay and heterosexual subgroups are significant at $p < .0001$.

hood aversions to girls' activities (63% vs. 15%). Moreover, this latter difference is virtually identical to that between gay men and heterosexual men in their childhood aversions to boys' activities (63% vs. 10%).

The San Francisco study does not stand alone. A meta-analysis of 48 studies confirmed that gay men and lesbians are more likely than heterosexual men and women to recall gender-nonconforming behaviors and interests in childhood (Bailey & Zucker, 1995). As the authors observed, "these are among the largest effect sizes ever reported in the realm of sex-dimorphic behaviors" (p. 49). Prospective longitudinal studies come to the same conclusion. In the largest of these, 75% of gender-nonconforming boys became bisexual or homosexual in later years compared with only 4% of gender-conforming boys (Green, 1987). In six other prospective studies, 63% of gender-nonconforming boys later had homosexual orientations (Zucker, 1990). (At this time, there are no prospective studies of gender-nonconforming girls.)

How Does Exotic Become Erotic? (D→E→F)

EBE theory proposes that exotic becomes erotic because feeling different from a class of peers in childhood produces heightened non-specific physiological arousal (D→E) which is subsequently transformed into erotic attraction (E→F). To my knowledge, there is no direct evidence for the first step in this sequence beyond the well-documented observation that "exotic" stimuli produce heightened physiological arousal in many species, including our own (Mook, 1987); filling in this empirical gap in EBE theory must await future research. In contrast, there are at least three mechanisms that can potentially effect the second step, transforming generalized arousal into erotic attraction (Bem, 1996). Only one of these, the extrinsic arousal effect, is discussed here.

In his first-century Roman handbook, *The Art of Love,* Ovid advised any man who was interested in sexual seduction to take the woman in whom he was interested to a gladiatorial tournament, where she would more easily be aroused to passion. He did not say why this should be so, however. A contemporary version of Ovid's claim was introduced by Walster (1971; Berscheid & Walster, 1974), who suggested that it constitutes a special case of Schachter and Singer's (1962) two-factor theory of emotion. That theory states that the physiological arousal of our autonomic nervous system provides the cues for emotion, but that the more subtle judgment of *which* emotion we are feeling often depends on our cognitive appraisal of the surrounding circumstances. According to Walster, then, the experience of erotic desire results from the conjunction of physiological arousal and the cognitive causal attribution (or misattribution) that the arousal is elicited by a potential sexual partner.

And indeed, there is now extensive experimental evidence that an individual who has been physiologically aroused will show heightened sexual responsiveness to an appropriate target person. In one set of studies, male participants were physiologically aroused by running in place, by hearing an audiotape of a comedy routine, or by hearing an audiotape of a grisly killing (White, Fishbein, & Rutstein, 1981). No matter how they had been aroused, these men reported more erotic interest in a physically attractive woman than did men who had not been aroused. This effect has also been observed physiologically. In two studies, pre-exposure to a disturbing (nonsexual) videotape subsequently produced greater penile tumescence in men and greater vaginal blood volume increases in women when they watched an erotic videotape than did pre-exposure to a nondisturbing videotape (Hoon, Wincze, & Hoon, 1977; Wolchik et al., 1980).

In other words, generalized physiological arousal, regardless of its source or affective tone, can subsequently be experienced cognitively, emotionally, and physiologically as erotic desire. At that point, it *is* erotic desire. My proposal, then, is that an individual's protracted and sustained experience of feeling different from same- or opposite-sex peers throughout childhood and adolescence produces a correspondingly sustained physiological arousal that gets eroticized when the maturational, cognitive, and situational factors coalesce to provide the defining attributional moment.

The Biological Connection (A→F) versus (A→B)

In recent years, researchers, the mass media, and segments of the lesbian/gay/bisexual community have rushed to embrace the thesis that a homosexual orientation is coded in the genes or is determined by prenatal hormones and brain neuroanatomy. In contrast, EBE theory proposes that biological factors influence sexual orientation only indirectly, by intervening earlier in the chain of events to determine a child's temperaments and subsequent activity preferences.

Genes and homosexuality. The studies that have drawn the most public attention are those suggesting a correlation between an individual's genotype and his or her sexual orientation. For example, in a sample of 115 gay men who had male twins, 52% of identical twin brothers were also gay compared with only 22% of fraternal twin brothers and 11% of adopted brothers (Bailey & Pillard, 1991). In a comparable sample of 115 lesbians, 48% of identical twin sisters were also lesbians compared with only 16% of fraternal twin sisters and 6% of adopted sisters (Bailey, Pillard, Neale, & Agyei, 1993). A subsequent study of nearly 5,000 twins who had been systematically drawn from a twin registry confirmed the significant heritability of sexual orientation for men but not for women (Bailey & Martin, 1995). Finally, an analysis of families in which there were two gay brothers suggested a correlation between a homosexual orientation and the inheritance of genetic markers on the X chromosome (Hamer & Copeland, 1994; Hamer, Hu, Magnuson, Hu, & Pattatucci, 1993).

But these same studies also provided evidence for the link proposed by EBE theory between an individual's genotype and his or her childhood gender nonconformity. For example, in the 1991 study of male twins, the correlation on gender nonconformity between gay identical twins was .76 ($p < .0001$), compared with a nonsignificant correlation of only .43 between gay fraternal twins (Bailey & Pillard, 1991). This implies that even when sexual orientation is held constant, there is a significant correlation between the genotype and gender nonconformity. Similarly, the 1993 family study found that gay brothers who shared the same genetic markers on the X chromosome were more alike on gender nonconformity than were gay brothers who did not (Hamer & Copeland, 1994; Hamer et al., 1993). Finally, childhood gender nonconformity was significantly heritable for both men and women in the large twin registry study—even though sexual orientation itself was not heritable for the women (Bailey & Martin, 1995).

EBE theory further specifies that this link between the genotype and gender nonconformity (A→C) is composed of two parts: a link between the genotype and childhood temperaments (A→B) and a link between those temperaments and gender nonconformity (B→C). This implies that the mediating temperaments should possess three characteristics: First, they should be plausibly related to those childhood activities that define gender conformity and nonconformity. Second, because they manifest themselves in sex-typed preferences, they should show sex differences. And third, because they are hypothesized to derive from the genotype, they should have significant heritabilities.

One likely candidate is aggression and its benign cousin, rough-and-tumble play. Gay men score lower than heterosexual men on a measure of childhood aggression (Blanchard, McConkey, Roper, & Steiner, 1983), and parents of gender-nonconforming boys specifically rate them as having less interest in rough-and-tumble play than do parents of gender-conforming boys (Green, 1976). Second, the sex difference in aggression during childhood is one of the largest psychological sex differences known (Hyde, 1984). Rough-and-tumble play in particular is more common in boys than in girls (DiPietro, 1981; Fry, 1990; Moller, Hymel, & Rubin, 1992). And third, individual differences in aggression have a large heritable component (Rushton, Fulker, Neale, Nias, & Eysenck, 1986).

Another likely candidate is activity level, considered to be one of the basic childhood temperaments (Buss & Plomin, 1975, 1984). Like aggression, differences in activity level would also seem to characterize the differences between male-typical and female-typical play activities in childhood. Moreover, gender-nonconforming boys and girls are lower and higher in activity level, respectively, than are control children of the same sex (Bates, Bentler, & Thompson, 1973, 1979; Zucker & Green, 1993). Second, the sex difference in activity level is as large as it is for aggression. Even before birth, boys in utero are more active than girls (Eaton & Enns, 1986). And third, individual differences in activity level have a large heritable component (Plomin, 1986; Rowe, 1997).

Genes and heterosexuality. Perhaps EBE theory's most radical suggestion is that heterosexuality, too, is a consequence of childhood experience. As noted earlier, the theory implies that heterosexuality is the modal outcome across time and culture because virtually every human society ensures that most boys and girls will grow up seeing the other sex as exotic and, hence, erotic.

I am certainly willing to concede that heterosexual behavior is reproductively advantageous, but it does not follow that it must therefore be sustained through genetic transmission. As long as an environment supports or promotes a reproductively successful behavior sufficiently often, it will not necessarily get programmed into the genes by evolution. For example, it is presumably reproductively advantageous for ducks to mate with other ducks, but as long as most baby ducklings encounter other ducks before they encounter an ethologist, evolution can simply implant the imprinting process itself into the species rather than the specific content of what, reproductively speaking, needs to be imprinted. Analogously, because most cultures ensure that boys and girls will see each other as exotic, it would be sufficient for evolution to implant exotic-becomes-erotic processes into our species rather than heterosexuality per se. In fact, an exotic-becomes-erotic process is actually a built-in component of sexual imprinting in some species. For example, both male and female Japanese quail reared with their siblings later preferred their slightly different-appearing cousins to their own siblings (Bateson, 1978). This has been interpreted as a mechanism that prevents inbreeding—a biologically promoted incest taboo.

Other biological correlates. In addition to the genotype, prenatal hormones and brain neuroanatomy have also been shown to be correlated with sexual orientation (for summaries and reviews, see Bem, 1996; Byne & Parsons, 1993; Zucker & Bradley, 1995). But these correlations, too, do not necessarily controvert the EBE account. Any biological factor that correlates with one or more of the intervening processes proposed by EBE theory could also emerge as a correlate of sexual orientation. For example, any neuroanatomical feature of the brain that correlates with childhood aggression or activity level is likely to emerge as a difference between gay men and heterosexual men, between women and men, and between heterosexual women and lesbians. Even if EBE theory turns out to be wrong, the more general point—that a mediating personality variable could account for observed correlations between biological variables and sexual orientation—still holds.

Like all well-bred scientists, biologically oriented researchers in the field of sexual orientation dutifully murmur the mandatory mantra that correlation is not cause. But the reductive temptation of biological causation is so seductive that the caveat cannot possibly compete with the excitement of discovering yet another link between the anatomy of our brains and the anatomy of our lovers' genitalia. Unfortunately, the caveat vanishes completely as word of the latest discovery moves from *Science* to *Newsweek*. The public can be forgiven for believing that we are but one government grant away from pinpointing the penis-preference gene.

Sex Differences and the Fluidity of Sexual Orientation

There is now substantial evidence that men and women differ from one another in several aspects of sexuality, irrespective of their sexual orientations (Peplau, Garnets, Spalding, Conley, & Veniegas, 1998). As I tell my students, if you want to understand the sexuality of gay men, think of them as men; if you want to understand the sexuality of lesbians, think of them as women. But most of these differences have to do with the primacy or intensity of erotic desire, the relative emphasis on the physical attributes of potential partners, and the willingness to engage in impersonal sex without romantic involvement. Such differences are not pertinent to EBE theory's account of how erotic orientations develop (Bem, 1998).

There is, however, one sex difference that *is* pertinent to EBE theory: Women's sexual orientations are more fluid than men's. Many studies, including a national random survey of Americans (Laumann, Gagnon, Michael, & Michaels, 1994), have found that women are more likely to be bisexual than exclusively homosexual, whereas the reverse is true for men. Nonheterosexual women are also more likely to see their sexual orientations as flexible, even "chosen," whereas men are more likely to view their sexual orientations in essentialist terms, as inborn and unchangeable (Whisman, 1996). For example, men who come out as gay after leaving heterosexual marriages or relationships often describe themselves as having "finally realized" their "true" sexual orientations. Similarly situated lesbians, however, are more likely to reject the implication that their previous heterosexual relationships were inauthentic or at odds with who they really were: "That's who I was then, and this is who I am now."

The greater fluidity of women's sexual orientations is actually anticipated by EBE theory. As noted earlier, Figure 1 is not intended to describe an inevitable, universal path to sexual orientation but only the modal path followed by most men and women *in a gender-polarizing culture.* This qualification is key, because women in our society grow up in a phenomenologically less gender-polarized world than do men. Compared with boys, girls are punished less for being gender nonconforming, and, as the data in Table 1 reveal, they are more likely than boys to engage in both sex-typical and sex-atypical activities and are more likely to have childhood friends of both sexes. This implies that girls are less likely than boys to feel differentially different from opposite-sex and same-sex peers and, hence, are less likely to develop exclusively heteroerotic or homoerotic orientations.

Accordingly, many of today's nonheterosexual women may be giving us a preview of what sexual orientations might look like in a less gender-polarized future. It is possible that we might even begin to see more men and women who, instead of using biological sex as the overriding criterion for selecting a partner, might base their erotic and romantic choices on a more diverse and idiosyncratic variety of attributes. In the future some gentlemen (and ladies) might come to prefer blondes of any sex.

REFERENCES

Bailey, J. M., & Martin, N. G. (1995, September). *A twin registry study of sexual orientation.* Paper presented at the twenty-first annual meeting of the International Academy of Sex Research, Provincetown, MA.

Bailey, J. M., & Pillard, R. C. (1991). A genetic study of male sexual orientation. *Archives of General Psychiatry, 48,* 1089–1096.

Bailey, J. M., Pillard, R. C., Neale, M. C., & Agyei, Y. (1993). Heritable factors influence sexual orientation in women. *Archives of General Psychiatry, 50,* 217–223.

Bailey, J. M., & Zucker, K. J. (1995). Childhood sex-typed behavior and sexual orientation: A conceptual analysis and quantitative review. *Developmental Psychology, 31,* 43–55.

Bates, J. E., Bentler, P. M., & Thompson, S. K. (1973). Measurement of deviant gender development in boys. *Child Development, 44,* 591–598.

Bates, J. E., Bentler, P. M., & Thompson, S. K. (1979). Gender-deviant boys compared with normal and clinical controls boys. *Journal of Abnormal Child Psychology, 7,* 243–259.

Bateson, P. P. G. (1978). Sexual imprinting and optimal outbreeding. *Nature, 273,* 659–660.

Bell, A. P., Weinberg, M. S., & Hammersmith, S. K. (1981a). *Sexual preference: Its development in men and women.* Bloomington: Indiana University Press.

Bell, A. P., Weinberg, M. S., & Hammersmith, S. K. (1981b). *Sexual preference: Its development in men and women. Statistical appendix.* Bloomington: Indiana University Press.

Bem, D. J. (1996). Exotic becomes erotic: A developmental theory of sexual orientation. *Psychological Review, 103,* 320–335.

Bem, D. J. (1998). Is EBE theory supported by the evidence? Is it androcentric? A reply to Peplau et al. *Psychological Review, 105,* 395–398.

Bem, S. L. (1993). *The lenses of gender: Transforming the debate on sexual inequality.* New Haven, CT: Yale University Press.

Berscheid, E., & Walster, E. (1974). A little bit about love. In T. Huston (Ed.), *Foundations of interpersonal attraction* (pp. 355–381). New York: Academic Press.

Blanchard, R., McConkey, J. G., Roper, V., & Steiner, B. W. (1983). Measuring physical aggressiveness in heterosexual, homosexual, and transsexual males. *Archives of Sexual Behavior, 12,* 511–524.

Buss, A. H., & Plomin, R. (1975). *A temperament theory of personality development.* New York: Wiley.

Buss, A. H., & Plomin, R. (1984). *Temperament: Early developing personality traits.* Hillsdale, NJ: Erlbaum.

Byne, W., & Parsons, B. (1993). Human sexual orientation: The biologic theories reappraised. *Archives of General Psychiatry, 50,* 228–239.

De Cecco, J. P., & Elia, J. P. (1993). *If you seduce a straight person, can you make them gay? Issues in biological essentialism versus social constructionism in gay and lesbian identities.* Binghamton, NY: Harrington Park Press.

DiPietro, J. A. (1981). Rough-and-tumble play: A function of gender. *Developmental Psychology, 17,* 50–58.

Eaton, W. O., & Enns, L. R. (1986). Sex differences in human motor activity level. *Psychological Bulletin, 100,* 19–28.

Freud, S. (1962). *Three essays on the theory of sexuality.* New York: Basic Books. (Original work published 1905).

Fry, D. P. (1990). Play aggression among Zapotec children: Implications for the practice hypothesis. *Aggressive Behavior, 17,* 321–340.

Green, R. (1976). One-hundred ten feminine and masculine boys: Behavioral contrasts and demographic similarities. *Archives of Sexual Behavior, 5,* 425–426.

Green, R. (1987). *The "sissy boy syndrome" and the development of homosexuality.* New Haven, CT: Yale University Press.

Hamer, D., & Copeland, P. (1994). *The science of desire: The search for the gay gene and the biology of behavior.* New York: Simon & Schuster.

Hamer, D. H., Hu, S., Magnuson, V. L., Hu, N., & Pattatucci, A. M. L. (1993). A linkage between DNA markers on the X chromosome and male sexual orientation. *Science, 261,* 321–327.

Hoon, P. W., Wincze, J. P., & Hoon, E. F. (1977). A test of reciprocal inhibition: Are anxiety and sexual arousal in women mutually inhibitory? *Journal of Abnormal Psychology, 86,* 65–74.

Hyde, J. S. (1984). How large are gender differences in aggression? A developmental meta-analysis. *Developmental Psychology, 20,* 722–736.

Laumann, E. O., Gagnon, J. H., Michael, R. T., & Michaels, S. (1994). *The social organization of sexuality: Sexual practices in the United States.* Chicago: University of Chicago Press.

Moller, L. C., Hymel, S., & Rubin, K. H. (1992). Sex typing in play and popularity in middle childhood. *Sex Roles, 26,* 331–353.

Mook, D. B. (1987). *Motivation: The organization of action.* New York: Norton.

Peplau, L. A., Garnets, L. D., Spalding, L. R., Conley, T. D., & Veniegas, R. C. (1998). A critique of Bem's "Exotic Becomes Erotic" theory of sexual orientation. *Psychological Review, 105,* 387–394.

Plomin, R. (1986). *Development, genetics, and psychology.* Hillsdale, NJ: Erlbaum.

Rowe, D. C. (1997). Genetics, temperament, and personality. In R. Hogan, J. Johnson, & S. Briggs (Eds.), *Handbook of personality psychology* (pp. 367–386). San Diego, CA: Academic Press.

Rushton, J. P., Fulker, D. W., Neale, M. C., Nias, D. K. B., & Eysenck, H. J. (1986). Altruism and aggression: The heritability of individual differences. *Journal of Personality and Social Psychology, 50,* 1192–1198.

Schachter, S., & Singer, J. E. (1962). Cognitive, social, and physiological determinants of emotional state. *Psychological Review, 69,* 379–399.

Walster, E. (1971). Passionate love. In B. I. Murstein (Ed.), *Theories of attraction and love* (pp. 85–99). New York: Springer.

Whisman, V. (1996). *Queer by choice.* New York: Routledge.

White, G. L., Fishbein, S., & Rutstein, J. (1981). Passionate love and the misattribution of arousal. *Journal of Personality and Social Psychology, 41,* 56–62.

Wolchik, S. A., Beggs, V. E., Wincze, J. P., Sakheim, D. K., Barlow, D. H., & Mavissakalian, M. (1980). The effect of emotional arousal on subsequent sexual arousal in men. *Journal of Abnormal Psychology, 89,* 595–598.

Zucker, K. J. (Ed.). (1990). Gender identity disorders in children: Clinical descriptions and natural history. In R. Blanchard & B. W. Steiner (Eds.), *Clinical Management of gender identity disorders in children and adults.* Washington, DC: American Psychiatric Press.

Zucker, K. J., & Bradley, S. J. (1995). *Gender identity disorder and psychosexual problems in children and adolescents.* New York: Guilford Press.

Zucker, K. J., & Green, R. (1993). Psychological and familial aspects of gender identity disorder. *Child and Adolescent Psychiatric Clinics of North America, 2,* 513–542.

DISCUSSION

Bob Michael: There's a point that I don't understand. If you take the first two or three of these steps, the separation of the two groups creates the intrigue for the other one in terms of what you do and how you associate. If I thought of little people, middle people, and older people, little people are more separated in their play and their activities from older people than they are from people of the same size and different gender. Why then don't they develop their sexual arousals toward old folks?

Daryl Bem: This is a cognitive theory and my view is that it's the sex of people which is more important than the age difference. Society makes the difference between boys and girls more prominent than any other one. To be really exact about it, "the exotic becomes erotic" is actually "exotic but not too exotic become erotic." It's a U-shaped distribution. We know that from animal work and if it weren't for that we'd all be out with the beasts in the field. What we know about familiarity and arousal in animal work is that as soon as you get a little too far out, the animal becomes threatened, scared, repulsed. One can explain some variations, for example in cross-race attractions, on the basis that if you've never been with someone who is dark skinned in your life that's too far out; if you have some familiarity, that's a different matter. In Japanese quail, they don't choose to mate with their brothers and sisters, they prefer their cousins. There are some mathematical equations in sociobiology to indicate what is optimal, avoiding incest but indicating reproductive advantages to mate with your cousins.

Lucia O'Sullivan: The most intriguing part is the cognitive labeling of the sexual arousal and that's the hardest part. Physiological arousal in response to the exotic could be hate or a number of things. How could that be tested?

Daryl Bem: There are several explanations for the intrinsic arousal effect, and implicitly, without telling you, I adopted an attribution explanation. Attribution may not be the most relevant thing here, but it fits most easily. But how do you know it's not hate? Take the special case of sissy boys who are taunted by other boys. What is it that converts negative anger, hate, to a positive sexual thing and that requires a different mechanism and it's the opponent process theory? That's described in detail in my original article.

Leonore Tiefer: I was really surprised by your comment about Japanese quail. Are you recruiting animal mating behaviors studies to support various steps in your theory? You selectively recruit animal studies when it suits you and then move to the cognitive.

Daryl Bem: The most radical statement I make is that heterosexuality is also due to the same process. To support that I have to explain why heterosexuality does not appear to be coded genetically, and so I point to ducks. For ducks, presumably, it is reproductively advantageous for them to mate with ducks rather than with Konrad Lorens, for example. So all evolution has to program in is the imprinting process itself. It doesn't have to pay attention to what gets imprinted because the environment almost always cooperates. Rarely does a duck first see Lorens before seeing mama duck. Is there any reason to think that "exotic becomes erotic," a mechanism which I claim is universal, is actually built into or is "hard wired" into us? For that kind of data I look to animal mechanisms as analogues and it looks like in other species "exotic becomes erotic" is a way of essentially building an incest taboo. My theory is an exercise in construction and so I look everywhere I can for support, and when I come across a biological finding that I can't seem to assimilate I worry about it and work on it and in the longer article try to explain it away too.

Ed Laumann: How does your theory relate to homophobia?

Daryl Bem: You could say that gay men and lesbian women are too exotic for the run-of-the-mill straight person, but I think there are other mechanisms that can explain it more easily, including psychodynamic ones.

Why the Sambia Initiate Boys before Age 10

GILBERT HERDT

Introduction

The purpose of this chapter is to explain a phenomenon of Sambia (Papua New Guinea) male ritual practice that has puzzled me for 25 years: Why do the Sambia feel the urgent need to initiate boys *before age 10?* Put simply, the Sambia feel that the development of a boy's desires and sexual behavior are governed not by the intrinsic elements we would label "sexual orientation," but rather by cultural and material forces. While it is often assumed in western society that "sexual orientation" is driven from within the individual, whether by genes, hormones, brain symmetry, or some other intrinsic factor, the Sambia do not share in this view. Indeed, they lack a construct of "sexual orientation." They assume, instead, that it is possible through changes in the boy's social and material relationships to alter the boy's desires and hence to teach him new desires and direct subsequent developmental energy into these desires. Thus, the effort of ritual initiation is to forcibly alter the context of desire in order to change the outcomes of sexual and gender development. While a good deal of this claim has been substantiated in previous publications (Herdt, 1981, 1982a, 1987a, 1999; Herdt & Stoller, 1990; Stoller & Herdt, 1985), the question remains: Why age 10?

The Sambia express an intense belief that a boy must be initiated before he is "too old" or "too big" in order for the rite of passage to have its necessary and desired effect. That effect, in brief, is to (1) separate the boy from his mother, (2) to "defeminize" the boy through ritual practices such as blood-letting, (3) to "masculinize" the boy through other ritual practices such as insemination of the boy's body, and thus (4) to socialize him into the role of being a warrior/hunter in preparation for warfare and the perceived dangers of marriage. In fact, Sambia date the absolute threshold of this necessary and desired change at age 10.

Elders warn against the dangers of ignoring this "taboo"—both for the failure of the boy's successful development and the social failure that the opposition to the taboo will bring to society. What is remarkable about the distribution of these ritualized boy-inseminating practices throughout Melanesia is the persistence of the belief that the male body was "biologically" deficient in maturation and unable to masculinize the boy on its own: The rituals focus on the use of semen to genderize the physical body (Herdt, 1984; Strathern, 1988).

Notice that in these traditional soundings the personality of the boy, his conscious subjectivity and sexual identity, are never mentioned by the culture. The explicit ideology and folklore focus on the physical (not simply the symbolic) body of the boy, and the social and material circumstances of his care taking, not on his mind or dispositions. The meanings of desire, of identity, of attraction, are left implicit. The Sambia are like many other traditional peoples who reason that the physical body is the vessel for psychophysiological change in the person (Lloyd, 1979). By altering the routines and habits, the physical boundaries of the body, what goes in and comes out, and the sexual definition of these entities as well, they attempt to change the interiority of the novice (Turner, 1964). However, since the age of 10 is so critical to their theory of development, we can study the relational, emotional, and cognitive elements of the boy's life before this age to understand what the Sambia are trying to manipulate in this dramatic and harsh use of ritual well before puberty.

Readers familiar with my work, including the last essay which I published in a volume associated with the Kinsey Institute (Herdt, 1990), will be aware of these areas of prior study. While my view of the ethnography has not substantially changed from my theoretical view of 15 years ago (Stoller & Herdt, 1982), I no longer emphasize the mother/child bond as strongly as before; I now see other factors as vital in the sexual and gender development of the Sambia child (Herdt, 1999). Moreover, and most relevant for this chapter, what my prior work omits is specific attention to the sexual attractions of the boy, the development of his desires, and the basis for the expression of these desires by age 10. Only recently did I begin to realize the importance of explaining the cultural elaboration of the notion of the male as the preferred and idealized object of desire in Sambia culture (Herdt, 1999). But while I have now turned to understand early sexual development and erotic attraction, I do not assume that the general construct of sexual orientation is sufficient for the conceptual work of modeling these processes.

One of the aims of this chapter is to reconsider and deconstruct the concept of sexual orientation and its relationship to gender and sexual identity, especially the development of sexual attraction. The position I take in this essay is that the concept of "sexual orientation" is by default too "intrinsic" biologically and developmentally to account for the phenomenon to which it pertains in sexual and gender development (Adkins-Regan, 1984; Kinsey, Pomeroy, & Martin, 1948; Money & Ehrhardt, 1972; Pattatucci & Hamer, 1995; Storms, 1981; Bell, Weinberg, & Hammersmith, 1981). The construct covers greatly disparate areas of human development for which the sources of development differ, and these areas should not be conflated. A case study from a nonwestern culture helps us to rethink just why this claim might be so. The onset of sexual attraction at age 10 is uniquely suited for the task.

To understand why age 10 is critical requires an excursion into the three areas of my work: New Guinea anthropology and, in particular, the social and historical organization of boy-inseminating rituals practiced by the Sambia and the other 60 or so societies in Melanesia (Herdt, 1984, 1993; Knauft, 1993); sexual identity development in self-identified gay and lesbian teenagers (aged 14 to 20) studied in Chicago (Herdt, 1992; Herdt & Boxer, 1993, 1995); and the physiological and psychosexual significance of adrenarche and menarche, which suggests that beginning at age 6 and culminating at age 10 the awareness of sexual attraction grows and culminates in the first remembered attraction in child development (McClintock & Herdt, 1996). I will draw upon the threads of these studies in attempting to ascertain what is special for theories of sexuality and the development of attraction at about age 10.

Sambia Maturation and Sexual Development

The Sambia were a tribe of 2,000 people who lived in dense rain forest villages that were constantly at war. They married women imported from surrounding hostile villages; in New Guinea this practice was often referred to by the idiom "We marry our enemies." Every three or four years the villages would create a truce for the purpose of initiating a gathered cohort of age-graded boys from the nearby villages, a series of rites that today are no longer practiced. The account which follows describes the society as it was in the early 1980s. The boys range in age from 7 to 10. They are separated dramatically and placed in the men's house; for months the boys experience a series of ritual ordeals and events which gradually remove all traces of women and the profane world from their bodies—and hopefully from their psyches. This is all secret and hidden from the women. It is followed by five additional initiations in later years that lead up to young adulthood. This first initiation, however, has two key rituals of ritual rebirth: the nose-bleeding rituals, to remove the pollution of their mother's menstrual blood; followed by insemination by the older bachelors, who had themselves gone through the earlier ritual stage. The physical process is accompanied by many powerful ritual moods and emotions, and the separation from mother and the secular world is absolute and complete for years and years to come. This culminates, according to Sambia belief, in third-stage initiation, when the boy's body becomes biologically mature, he shows all the secondary sex traits, and his penis develops a mature glans penis.

Once the young boys (aged 7 to10) are initiated so as to remove through nose-bleeding rites and other painful ordeals their childhood "female" traces—the heritage of their mothers and of living in the women's world—the succession to phallic rites, especially because such rites depend upon and use the ritual sacred flutes (Herdt, 1982a), leads to advancement in the ranks of the men's society. The boys must prove their ability to withstand the ordeal of nose-bleeding, which the Sambia consider to be their most dangerous and repugnant ritual practice (Herdt, 1982b). Once the boy's body is emptied of femaleness (menstrual blood), then, and only then, can it be filled up with maleness (semen). In the cultural imagination of Sambia the two processes (letting blood and inseminating) are forever linked—the first a negation of femininity, the second an affirmation or at least an attempted virilization of the boy. Then the sexual hierarchy is ordered: The boys are inseminated by late-adolescent bachelors, only through oral intercourse, so the boys can grow strong and reproduce. Then the boys are initiated into the third stage and outgrow the phase of being semen recipients, after which they have to prove their manhood by serving as semen donors to the new crop of younger initiates. This exchange of semen between donor and recipient is the focus of many of the rituals and of the folklore of Sambia initiation.

In the precolonial world of the Sambia, at least before 1960,[1] the roles of men and women were highly polarized and politically opposed, in the condition proverbially described in the research literature as "sexual antagonism" (Langness, 1967). The women who came from other villages, invariably hostile and sometimes enemies of war, were forever regarded as alien and were mistrusted. The residential segregation of unmarried, vulnerable initiates in the men's clubhouse, while the women and children were tabooed and lived in the women's houses, symbolized this deep structure of perceived social and material difference in village life. The bond created between mothers and their children was an intense and anxious attachment that is difficult for us to imagine in the contemporary world (Herdt, 1981). I believe that this developmental condition was very special in its effects upon the inhibition of agency, and sexual subjectivity, in boys. While the early bonding/relational factor cannot explain the development of sexual orientation, it influenced in subtle ways the onset of sexual attraction and desire in the child, and the role that these developmental subjectivities

played in shaping the reality of the child—personality and cognition—
a point to which I shall return.

The offspring of Sambia couples were caught in a drama of conflicting roles: the sons to initiate as future warrior-comrades, and the
daughters to be available for future marriage exchanges for the sons of
other clansmen. These created complex and sometimes contradictory
religious and political alliances between village communities. The symbolism of the secret male initiation ceremonies was intentionally aimed
to merge the desires and developmental subjectivity of the growing
boy with the larger project of maintaining the warrior population of
these villages. At the early developmental stage of the pre-pubertal
boy, for example, the flute and penis ritual (which introduced the boys
to homoerotic practices [Herdt, 1981]) stressed the penis and compared it to mother's breast, thereby condensing the meanings of semen
and milk. At a more sophisticated level following maturation, however, the flutes signified the budding erotic relation between older adolescent warriors and their younger partners, initiated boys, whose insemination was supposed to make them big and strong too. These pairs
of pre-pubertal and post-pubertal unmarried males were referred to in
secret folklore as being "married." The secret mythology of the secret
ritual flutes further explains how an ancestor of the men's society was
once hermaphroditic and changed into a male through ritual practice
(Herdt, 1981). This myth ensured the need to hide the ritual practice
from the women and children, and thus perpetuated the elder men's
social control of younger males and all females.

In the Sambia initiation, the effect of the rites, typically begun for
an age cohort from a group of villages of many boys around age 7 or 8,
is to wean the boy from his mother, her body, and her cultural world
and to move him physically into the men's world. In fact, the Sambia
pinpointed this cut-off point at between the ages of 7 and 10 years old;
individual boys' ages average approximately 8.5 years. Sambia were
emphatic that the boy must never be more than 10.[2] He was inseminated, paving the way for the years-long exclusively homoerotic and
homosocial period of pre-adolescent and adolescent development, until his late teens or early twenties, depending upon the exact age at
which a particular boy marries and fathers a child (Herdt, 1981, 1987a).

I want to underline that the developmental change at issue for the
Sambia was restricted to males. Females, as far as we know, did not
engage in homoerotic relations in a customary fashion, nor was there
a female cult which paralleled that of the men (Gillison, 1993). Thus,
when I used to refer to these practices by the generic term "ritualized
homosexuality," I meant that this form of age-structured semen do-
norship, while typical of certain areas of Aboriginal Australia and Melanesia, was restricted to male development up to puberty. This cult of
the phallus is ancient, and indeed, it may hark back to an original

migrant protoculture, some 10,000 years old or more, which carried into the island of New Guinea the ritual complex of boy-inseminating rites to physically masculinize the body. If the existence of such an ancient ritual practice can be demarcated in the development of the child at age 10, then we obviously must pay attention to the significance of the age marker for generations. Gender differences in development are critical here. The fact that females do not have a comparable age marker in the Melanesian practice suggests that while the age of 10 has potential significance for the development of all sexuality and gender, the social stress on transforming the physical body of the boy, and thus his desires and behaviors, may be so large as to require gross change, while in females the stress may be less great and therefore less urgent to change (Herdt, 1987a, 1990).

"Puberty" (what I shall call "gonadal puberty") or the onset of secondary "sex characteristics" in adolescence, was very late in precolonial Melanesia (and well into the 1970s) in the Highlands of New Guinea. Boys did not achieve these "sex characteristics" until the ages of 13 to 14 years, while girls reached menarche as late as 19.2 years (Malcolm, 1968). This fact makes the importance of age 10 as affirmed by these New Guinea cultures all the more remarkable. Clearly, these tribal peoples are recognizing a change in the child's phenomenology, in his total being—physical and mental—that differs from the subsequent gonadal puberty. It may be the case that due to the lateness of gonadal puberty, the prior period of adrenarche is also "late" in blooming, which might tend to extend the age norms later than those in western populations (McClintock & Herdt, 1996). If so, that suggestion would provide an intriguing perspective for rethinking what we know from Melanesia. The evidence from Melanesia, nevertheless, suggests the age of 10 has special significance for traditional peoples such as the Sambia. It is at that ritual age, or very shortly before or after, that initiation as a psychosocial intervention is imposed by the society as a means to manipulate the psychosexual changes associated with this developmental pathway (Herdt, 1989). In these societies, in short, where the polarity of the sexes is huge, and the expectations of masculine development are so great, an abrupt and dramatic change is imposed upon the developing boy—typically by age 10, or perhaps a bit later, at 12. This leads us back to the psychobiological developmental literature to rethink the meanings of this age threshold.

Hormones, Adrenarche, and Sexual Attraction

Let us reconsider the interaction between hormones and the development of sexual attraction in order to rethink what might be critical about the age of 10. This exercise is in part an attempt to reconsider the overall role of puberty in the gender and sexual development process. Another goal is to think further about the role of hypothetical intrinsic mechanisms, especially the concept of intrinsic sexual orientation, in the context of cultural regimes of child development in greatly divergent societies like those of the Sambia. Thus I hope to clarify the development of sexual attraction in order to understand the cultural imposition of the age limit of 10 on gender and sexual development among the Sambia. Today, thanks to many new and important studies of sexual development and maturation in the United States, it is possible to rethink the relation between sexual attraction and pubertal processes in general (McClintock & Herdt, 1996). Many prior studies in this area derive their impetus largely from the concept of sexual orientation (reviewed in Bem, 1996; see also Gorman, 1994) and an understanding of the importance of the earliest development of sex, romance, and attraction that begins in childhood and culminates around age 10. Indeed, the absolute age-grading that takes 10 as its divider now looks highly sophisticated and instrumental in light of the evidence which is coming in from a variety of sources.

The relationship between adrenarche and puberty in samples of American men and women has recently been the focus of a major critique (McClintock & Herdt, 1996). While many previous studies of hormones and the development of gender identity and sexual orientation have appeared in recent years (Byne & Parsons, 1993; Meyer-Bahlburg, 1997), such studies have tended to deal far more with the issues of sexual differentiation and gender atypicality rather than with the emergence of sexual desire per se. It is particularly striking that, with the exception of Daryl Bem's (1996) important work on the development of arousability and sexual attraction, little attention has been devoted to the age- and gender-specific mechanisms surrounding the subjectivities of erotic attraction (Stoller, 1976). As Meyer-Bahlburg (1984) has noted, the literature is largely concerned with but one element of this huge developmental area; namely, the brain and genital differentiation of the child, with special consequences when the boy's gender behavior is undermasculinized or feminized (Green, 1987). Typically, these studies tend to take sexual orientation as the implicit object of explanation without taking the effort to explain the outcome of sexual orientation itself. Finally, as pointed out in a previous summary of the literature (McClintock & Herdt, 1996), a general tendency in the older research literature suggests that sexual attraction is synonymous with "puberty" after the age of 11 or 12. In cultural and theoretical terms, this preconception implicitly appeals to the notion that sexuality before "puberty" is "latent," and the development of sexual orientation occurs via unexplained biological forces that take their adult form with the onset of puberty. Clearly, something prior to puberty is transforming the child's body and psyche in the direction of sexual arousal.

What might the precursor of this development be? Adrenarche is a good candidate for the primary (if not the sole) source of the first erotic attraction. First, the adrenals release hormones that are known to be relevant to sexual attraction in adults. Second, there is no difference in the ages at which girls and boys develop. Third, the same hormones continue to rise in concentration during gonadarche.[3] Thus if the gonads provide the bulk of the biological priming for sexual attraction and development of sexuality, then it intuitively follows that the same hormones at earlier ages have a similar effect. Fourth, dehydro-epiandrosterone (DHEA), the primary sex hormone released by the adrenals, is only two metabolic hops away from testosterone and three hops away from estradiol—the major adult sex hormones.

The research literature provides a new picture of these processes, however, at least in samples of heterosexuals and homosexuals in the United States (McClintock & Herdt, 1996). Separate studies of gay-identified males conducted by different investigators from different fields in different parts of the country have pinpointed age 10 as definitive of the onset of first attraction to the same sex. This remembered developmental age is all the more remarkable in that it seems impervious to cultural and historical change. That is, one study has a mean age of 37 years (Hamer, Hu, Magnuson, Hu, & Pattittucci, 1993), while the other has a mean age of 17.9 years (Herdt & Boxer, 1993). The difference of approximately one generation suggests that the developmental onset of first awareness or first attraction to the same sex may be independent of social/historical age cohort differences or simple social learning. In fact, one might have predicted that the sexual revolution in the 1960s and the AIDS epidemic in the 1980s and 1990s would have altered the age of first attraction (Gagnon, 1990). What is even more remarkable is that the age of 9.5 to 10 years is the time when first sexual attraction occurs for heterosexuals as well as homosexuals. A comparable age (10.4 years) has recently been found by Bailey and Oberschneider (1997) in a smaller sample of gay men. These studies thus imply that sexual orientation is independent from the mechanisms governing the onset and manifestation of erotic desire and attraction.

Boys in these studies experienced first remembered attraction at a slightly younger age than did the girls; this difference may itself be significant for understanding subtle but still very powerful micro-mechanisms of the cultural environment that influence the emergence of attraction (Herdt & Boxer, 1993, chap. 5). In fact, sexual attraction before gonadal puberty, erotic fantasy, sexual desire, and perhaps generalized arousability linked to gender differences (Bem, 1996) all suggest that these elements are not dependent upon the biosocial concomitants of the pubertal process in any simple sense. It should be pointed out that the precise identification of pubertal onset in all of these males has not been established (McClintock & Herdt, 1996). Erotic and social precocity may, however, be linked to the observation, although precocity as a distinctive feature of sexual identity development in gay men has long been questioned or denied (Meyer-Bahlburg, 1984). Indeed, there are plenty of reasons to believe that—in developmental and cultural terms—the age of 9.5 to 10 years is a time of critical transition in cognitive, emotional, and social adjustment. It is just that our culture lacks a specific ritual or social marker to signify this critical transition.

As McClintock and Herdt argued in 1996, androgens have developmental effects in adults in a variety of areas, such as aggression, emotions, and sexual development. This is certainly consistent with the important argument of Bem (1996) that biosocial variables do not "code" for sexual orientation as such, but rather for the childhood temperaments that influence a child's preference for gender-typical or gender-atypical preferential practices. Such effects have not been demonstrated in children but are presumed to be causative of the same micro-areas in their developmental systems. Thus androgenization has been regarded as a key effect of sexual development in a continuous sequence from childhood through adulthood, with gonadarche the apex. Previous sexual developmental research has attributed changes in adolescent behavior to changes in hormone levels accompanied by gonadarche. If gonadarche were responsible, however, for these first sexual attractions, then the mean age should be later—around age 12 for girls and age 13 for boys. Clearly, as studies have shown repeatedly, gonadarche happens at an earlier age than this. Since girls experience gonadarche at earlier ages than boys, it should be expected that this sex will be manifested in the mean ages of first attraction (the women recalling an earlier first attraction). Yet evidence from studies attempting to illuminate the sources of sexual orientation have found surprising answers. Herdt and Boxer (1993) studied a group of self-identified gay and lesbian teenagers (ages 14 to 20, with a mean age of 17.9 years). This cohort revealed a sequence of ages of first same-sex attraction, first same-sex fantasy, and first same-sex behavior; the mean age for same-sex attraction was around age 10 for both males and females, but sexual behavior began earlier for boys than for girls. In short, although there appears to be a strong correlation between the age of onset of attraction around 10 and social and psychological pressures, especially those associated with gender roles, all of these factors may influence the earliest desires and the emergence of sexual behavior later on.

The developing hormones of the child between the ages of 5 and 12 are critical for understanding both the physical bodies and the psychological (interpersonal and intrapsychic) development of pre-adolescents (Money & Ehrhardt, 1972). Hormone levels are fairly predict-able across the population. The hormone levels remain low until the maturation of the adrenal glands at ages 6 to 8. Then they begin to climb, in an exponential manner, until reaching adult levels. They begin to plateau after this in both boys and girls. The hormones re-leased during preadolescence are androgens (typically identified as "male" sex hormones). The adrenal glands are small, pyramidal glands located above the kidneys that produce hormones responsible for me-tabolism and the regulation of salt and hormones. Around ages 6 to 8 adrenal glands begin to develop in both males and females. The adre-nal glands (specifically the adrenal cortex) begin to secrete low levels of androgens (typically identified as "male" sex hormones), primarily of DHEA. The specific androgen released by the adrenal glands is in the same metabolic pathways as testosterone and estrogen. There is no sex difference in the rate, onset, or hormone levels until gonadarche. Adult levels of DHEA are reached by age 12 for girls and age 13 for boys (Hopper, 1975). The levels of these hormones begin to steadily climb upward and make a significant increase around age 10. While these levels are low compared to normal adult levels, they are many (10 to 20) times what typical children aged 1 to 4 experience. The hormone levels required for an organizational (long-term, permanent) effect are unknown, but the levels experienced between ages 6 and 10 are with-in activational (short-term, temporary) range (McClintock & Herdt, 1996).

Given the strong possibility that the current popular model of pu-berty and development is incorrect, we must rethink puberty and test the new models in a wide range of fields. Adrenarche clearly increases levels of androgens to significant levels, and if those hormones are responsible for the effects seen in sexual attraction then it also should affect a wide range of behaviors, including aggression, cognition, per-ception, attention, arousal, emotions, and of course, the development of sexual identity and attraction. Even if the hormones released from the adrenal glands are not responsible for the changes in sexual attrac-tion, the concept of "puberty" must now be greatly enlarged and un-packed. The current work suggests that there are two separate matu-rational processes occurring: adrenarche and gonadarche. Any social research that uses puberty as a stage in development will now need to break down the relevant developmental and social behaviors into the two different stages of pubertal formation and maturation. Research-ers will need to take into account that the start of adrenarchal puberty in normal individuals takes place at around ages 6 to 8 and the end of gonadal puberty does not take place until around ages 15 to 17. In between, the age threshold of 10 may mark the average onset of sexual attraction in human populations.

If the onset of sexual attraction is indeed strongly motivated internally by these hormonal developments, and especially the adrenal puberty that seems to reach its peak before the adolescent years, then it is no surprise that nonwestern peoples such as the Sambia have hit upon customs that institutionalize significant life course changes around age 10.

In this view, over generations, the Sambia may have inferred that the micro-events and processes which lead to sexual arousal, attraction, and behavior development in the boy require formal recognition before gonadal puberty. Their effort to impose separation from the mother and siblings and to impose gender segregation, followed by powerful identity changes in the boy through forcible ritual initiations, thus prepare for and anticipate the changes that will occur at age 10. By having placed the child in a new context for learning and perceiving, the Sambia have actively engaged the internal and cultural processes of sex and gender development.

Development of Sexual Attraction in Sambia Males

Issues of sexual culture and sexual nature in explanations of Sambia sexual culture are very well known in the literature; they have been used both to defend and attack "social constructions" and to defend and attack "essentialism" in theories of sexual development. I mean by these paradigms approximately what Carole Vance (1991) has shrewdly said in her remark that an "essence" of a culture is what that culture defines as above and beyond what can be modified or changed. Thus, many anthropologists and other social theorists have argued that the ritual character of Sambia sexuality (reviewed in Herdt, 1993; Westin, 1993), the implementation of homosexual insemination as a universal phase of development among all the males of the tribe (Money, 1987), and the ability of men to halt their inseminations and move on to heterosexual contacts (reviewed by Connell & Dowsett, 1993; Greenberg, 1995; Vance, 1991; and others, noted in Herdt & Boxer, 1995) all attest to the "fluid," changeable, or reversible qualities of sexuality and sexual relations among the Sambia. However, in all of these reviews, the tendency has been to elide the construction of sexual behavior with the development of sexual attraction, so that attraction and behavior are treated as synonymous.

I said above that the Melanesian tradition was based on repudiation of the early developmental period of childhood experience with the mother and the women's world. I expressed the idea that through the ritual initiations, the boys were forced to unlearn what they had known since birth and relearn new concepts and, especially, magical-secret and sacred knowledge which privileged their actions and elected them in the eyes of the men's cult to a superior station in life. I once called this developmental discontinuity based upon ritual—the boy unlearns what he once felt (Herdt, 1990). I still think that that is an accurate description of the situation; however, it does not address the development of sexual attraction.

I believe that for the typical Sambia boy growing up in traditional village social life, the development of sexual attraction remains socially suppressed, and psychologically repressed, until at least middle childhood, if not in fact until his first initiation, which for the age cohort of boys in a village is in the age range of 7 to 10. The evidence for this assertion rests in the corpus of narratives of individual boys, adolescents, and young and middle-aged men, ranging from about 5 years of age to about 70 years of age (Herdt & Stoller, 1990). The evidence for repression remains the most elusive to support, but it can be found in the private statements and narratives of men about their feelings about their mothers and fathers and their playmates (Herdt, 1992). It is indeed remarkable how adult men, even those approaching middle age, express feelings of great longing and grief over their mothers in particular—feelings which they are forbidden by the culture to express in public. These intimate recollections must be understood in very particular contexts of male homosocial bonding (Herdt, 1987b). In growing up, boys and girls sometimes engage in exploratory sex play and, occasionally, sexual intercourse, although these behaviors were seriously sanctioned by their parents and were generally hidden (Herdt & Stoller, 1990). The effect of this prudish developmental regime was the delay of conscious and explicit awareness of sexual desires and attractions until after first-stage initiation.

The Sambia tradition also shielded and justified this sexual repression through a socially structured mechanism of great power which rationalized gender segregation and all the developmental concomitants of such segregation. This mechanism was ritual secrecy. Both the men and the women, in their respective ritual practices and ritual houses, practiced absolute ritual secrecy that made the presence of the opposite sex, and the sharing of any ritual knowledge with the other gender, taboo. In the case of boys, the rite of passage into the men's house marked an abrupt break with the boy's early childhood life with his mother and enjoined him to reject all of that to enter into a secret new world of the men. As I have long remarked, it seems obvious to an outsider that the initiation of the Sambia boy into the men's secret rituals is also their initiation into sexuality and sexual intercourse as it is approved of by the culture (Herdt, 1982a).

In that secret world, the 7- to 10-year-old boy is initiated into sexual intercourse, first as an object of sexual attraction and desire on the part of the older males. By being objectified in this way, he of course is separated from his mother and other women, who are objectified as sexual objects for coitus and the production of children. We should recall that what is "created" in the boy through insemination is his "physical body." This spells growth, strength, and other cultural attributes that are of such importance to his development, masculinity, and reproductive competence that they cannot be left to chance. Instead, they must be ritualized. The use of semen is the key to this process. Sambia cultural tradition values semen as if it has the value of a commodity, such as gold; the value placed on semen in this culture tends toward fetishism. I mean by the fetishistic the collective sense of a religious attachment that goes beyond Freud's (1905/1962) classical sense of a private, eroticized symptom formation; in which the individual derives pleasure from an obsessional-compulsive fixation to an object or body part that unconsciously represents a whole person (Stoller, 1979). Sambia believe—along with a large number of other Melanesian tribes—that semen is not a "natural" male body product, but must rather be introduced externally (as if it were a sex hormone necessary to androgenize the incompetent body, in western discourse) in order to institutionalize ideas of semen transfer, semen depletion, and semen replenishment. This means that as the boy is initiated and comes to share in the belief regarding the power of semen, he acquires a most powerful desire—the desire for semen. This desire, introduced by initiation rituals, is the basis for the development of a physical body that was phenomenologically totally absent in the boy's prior experience. I believe that this serves as the context for the development of his sexual attractions as well.

It is crucial to understand a fundamental aspect of all Melanesian cultural systems and their cosmos. The most highly desired and prized body and being in their world is that of the male. Not only is the male regarded as the most sexy and desired person in the culture, but to desire him is regarded as normal and natural by both genders. As Maurice Godelier (1986) has remarked for the neighboring Baruya culture, the idealized and preferred sexual object and object of beauty and attraction is not the female but the male in these cultures. For the Sambia, the admired and idealized image of the Great Man, a warrior-hunter—strong, powerful, sexual, who can take many wives and kill many men—is prominent in the mythology. What is hidden from the public discourse is the secret ritual understanding that to get this way, he had to be inseminated by many men as he grew up, and he can boast of having had many boys himself when he comes of age.

After initiation, the boys' physical and social distance from their mothers and natal households facilitated the emergence of these erotic and social feelings and the ability to imagine putting these feelings into action for the first time. Here is a critical aspect that involves the join-ing of sexual subjectivity with the development of agency in the grow-ing child (Hostetler & Herdt, 1998). Previously, the Sambia boys had been regarded by their fathers and brothers not as moral and social agents but as appendages of their mothers. The use of sexuality in the men's house when they take the boys as objects is a means of changing this situation, especially their efforts to alter the boys' sexual subjectiv-ity, that is, to transform the link between their own sense of selfhood or sexual being and the social role that they are to take in the society, a developmental pattern I refer to as a "sexual lifeway" (Herdt, 1997). Thus, the homoerotic attraction and the insemination were actually the royal road to creating and teaching the boys to become agents of their own desires, especially masculine agents, for the first time.

But this change, I am claiming, could only be done through gender segregation, and in secrecy, with the string attached that the boys would be treated first as sexual objects before they got to be sexual subjects. These are separable elements of subjective development that in the west are conflated as "sexual orientation." They are also treated as if they are part of the same "biological package" known as sexual orientation. In particular, the ability to locate desire in the person, to be acted upon first as an object and then as a subject—regardless of the same-gender context of the Sambia—suggests that these desires and their expression are being acquired in the micro-context of the men's house and erotically expressed in action more than we previously be-lieved. It is a bit too simple to say that these attractions are learned; nor must we think that they can be "unlearned" in any simple manner without doing violence to the integrity or mental health of the person. Ultimately such subjectivities, when they are lived realities, must be anchored in the social traditions of the community.

The Sambia have a system of boy-inseminating which bears com-parison to the ancient Greeks. As I have long suggested, one can com-pare the Greeks of the Homeric period with the Sambia in New Guinea; even though these cultures are very different in many social and po-litical characteristics, they share a social and mythological devotion to warfare (Herdt, 1984). In the case of ancient Greece, specifically Sparta, I am struck by Sir Kenneth Dover's (1978) image that the Spartan city-state was permanently organized like an army camp. If we make the change in scale, the image fits the Sambia, and indeed, the military character of many precolonial Melanesian cultures, as has been noted by classicists in recent years (reviewed in Herdt, 1993). The dynamics of ritual insemination in both cultural traditions may have been quite similar. The men did not have social and emotional relations with women. The sons were involved in close social and intimate relations with their mothers, and their political relationships to their fathers were thus complicated. Such a cultural world created a kind of sexual lifeway that did not fit into the men's social needs and public practices—not without dramatic ritual and, as it turns out, sexual changes in the younger boys. Indeed, the early Greeks' problem of their budding boys was not only what to do with them but how to bring them into their rightful places as noble warriors and free citizens (Halperin, 1990). Here the Greek emphasis on social citizenship in the later Socratic period becomes helpful in its stipulations about what could be done and what was taboo in sexual and intimate relations (Williams, 1998).

Take note of a striking age similarity that unites the pattern of male sexual development among the Sambia and the Greeks. Here there is a singularly important age parallelism with regard to the commencement of initiation. The Sambia commence initiation beginning at age 7 (up to 10); the ancient Spartans also commenced initiation at 7 years of age. In both cases the boys were separated from their mothers and taken into the men's house or men's camp; they lived for the duration, until well into adulthood, in the homosocial and gender-segregated quarters of the warriors.

However, the respective ages of the onset of sexual interaction were very different, and in one important respect, exactly the opposite. The Sambia begin their sexual careers immediately upon initiation at age 7, and they continue to be the recipients of semen until they achieved physical and social puberty, at approximately ages 13 to 15. The Spartans, however, did not commence sexual interaction until they achieved gonadal puberty, which is believed to have been about age 14 (Williams, 1999). Only after they began to have post-pubertal adolescent traits (especially the presence of some beard on their faces) did they become the object of sexual attraction for Spartan men. Indeed, the American classicist Craig Williams (personal communication) describes that the attractiveness of the Spartan youth reached its peak when he achieved a prominent beard at about age 18. This is, by the way, the very opposite of the Sambia. The boy was sexually attractive and desirable as an object only up to gonadal puberty, around age 15. But when he developed manliness, and the facial beard was considered a key feature of this, he was no longer regarded as an object of desire by older males. In fact, Sambia males find the post-pubertal boy to be sexually unattractive and a culturally inappropriate object of insemination. Hence, puberty can be perceived either as the beginning or the end of regard for the child as a sexual object in the simple sense. What matters is how the child's subjectivity matches the cultural role assigned for a particular sexual lifeway.

The Sambia initiations have two levels of developmental change in store for the boy. At the level of the boy's material body, the practices of ritual initiation, including insemination, are thought to physically "grow" the boy and make his phallus virile. At the level of his personality and subjective states relative to sexual development, the rituals have paved the way for capitalizing on the emergence of sexual attraction by age 9 or 10. Thus, the ritual practices provide for a substitution of desires (the semen practices, the desired role of the male warrior). The concomitant process is the way in which the older boys, now graduated into the adolescent role of bachelors who will inseminate the younger boys, begin to take the latter as their culturally approved sexual objects. There is a replacement, in this way, of the desire to be inseminated and to grow up with the desire to prove that the older adolescent is now "manly" and capable of giving the gift of semen to the younger boy. This desire, on the part of the bachelor, is the necessary step in transforming his own desires en route to adulthood. As he is assigned a woman in marriage and approaches young adulthood, the adolescent begins now to fantasize about procreation with a woman and the culmination of his "growth" process in fathering a child of his own (Herdt, 1989).

Do these changes in sexual desire and behavior occur in this order, and can they be expected to result in transformations both in the material and the subjective state of the Sambia male? This question has often been posed regarding the Sambia studies (Herdt, 1999). As I have shown before, the early developmental changes before age 10, while difficult to document before initiation at age 7, can be demonstrated after the boy enters the men's house. There, boys begin to think about their material bodies, develop plans to "capture" semen and "grow" themselves, and often engage privately in risqué commentaries with their age mates regarding the virtues and values of being inseminated by particular men (Herdt, 1981; Herdt 1987a; Herdt & Stoller, 1990). Likewise, as the boys achieve gonadal puberty, they begin to experience nocturnal emissions and start to fantasize about inseminating younger boys. Typically these youths begin enthusiastic careers as the dominant fellateds. They do not typically require masturbation or mechanical stimulation to be aroused but are fully able and eager to inseminate the boys they select for intercourse at this time. The exceptions to these normative trends, as I have shown before, tend to augment the strong change in desire toward the male body, even to the point of having exclusive interest in sex with boys rather than moving on to sex with women later on (Herdt & Stoller, 1990).

Sexual Lifeways, Not Sexual Orientations

The emphasis the Sambia place upon the physical and mental being of the boy raises the question of their own view and perceptions of these events. The emphasis upon the boy's "being," as in his existential well-being or mental health, all pertain to the process of creating, through cultural events and learning, the state of reality of being (or ontology; Herdt, 1991) which the Sambia embody and institutionalize through their cultural worldview. In an earlier time in theory development it was common to imagine that all or virtually all of this reality conformed to the psychic reality of the unconscious (Freud, 1905/ 1962) or to the universals of cognitive processes everywhere present in human nature (Piaget, 1971). A construct of sexual nature that emerges from such a universalizing paradigm is inevitably insensitive to the cultural environment and predisposed to intrinsic biology. "Sexual orientation" is the child of such a universalizing paradigm. As an ideal type, it still has conceptual value when it is understood to refer to a theory of innate development. But as an empirical pattern of reality, in the simple sense of absolute attractions to a sex object and the scripts implied by such attractions, it is dubious and has outlived its utility.

A theory of sexual development that does not rely upon the conceptual crutch of innate "sexual orientation" needs to rethink "desire" as a heuristic concept for the operation of intimate sexual relationships and cultural institutions. Desire in this developmental cultural model is closer to what anthropologists have called "values," with the additions of the agentic dimension of personal intentionality and the directionality of cultural cognitions (Shweder, 1989). Desires thus include what the actor likes and wants from another person; the general disposition to desire and want to possess a sexual "object" or a culturally valued social role (to be a husband, to be a chief) or goal in life (to be virtuous, to achieve power and influence, etc.). It never has been explained how cultures manage to manufacture desires, like a factory produces paper clips, in the service of simple social learning and social constructionist theories. How do sexual cultures manage to "stimulate" or "produce" desires, in the broad sense of what is "socially valued" and may enter into the symbolic capitol of personhood? This sense of desire is broader than Freud's (1905/1962) aim/instinct complex, even with the open-endedness of the erotic drives that direct fantasy. What current research on human development suggests is that desire can be modified, if not in fact learned; and sexual desires, when bundled together, more nearly resemble what I have called a sexual lifeway, capable of modification and social manipulation, than they do a sexual orientation. Sexual lifeways are cultural models of sexuality and human nature which develop into a level of subjective "realness" that is unquestioned by the person and thus constitute ontological reality. The formation of sexual lifeways is highly dependent upon *developmental and cultural processes* that stipulate preferred sexual subjectivities and approved or tabooed sexual objects.

An ontological fit between the desires of the person and the demands made by Sambia society is registered in the timeworn patterns of their sexual culture. Historically and in material terms, this was overdetermined by warfare, which surrounded them, the emphasis upon warrior roles for men, and the marriage trade that brought the women of hostile villages into intimate relations with men. The long-term solution to the contradictions and human weakness in such institutions was the initiation of boys before age 10—that is, before the sexual attractions of boys could be rooted in the world of women rather than in the men's warriorhood. Which is to say that there is only a loose fit between these traditions and social structures and the development of the sexual behavior of the person.

Consider the more conventional view of the Sambia system by developmentalists who assume the existence of "sexual orientation" as a universal ontology. John Money (1987) has claimed that the Sambia system can inhibit the formation and development of particular sexual habits, such as masturbation or childhood sex play, and stimulate the practice of other habits, such as boy-insemination rituals. But these developments are in line with what he sees to be an intrinsic model of sex-role learning in the direction of masculinity. According to Money's conception of sexual culture, then, sexual development was characterized by significant continuity in gendered objects and sexual desires, with a strong inference that what was felt in childhood (as Freud might have said) would be expressed in adulthood. Sure, there might be interruptions along the way, or lateral movements within the same "dimension" of sexuality (as Kinsey might have said), even with plenty of interruption. Nevertheless, in the end, there would be little change in the main line of sexual orientation and thus of sexual development. It was unnatural to think that desires that were "hardwired" by sexual orientation would exist without the possibility of expression in the social commerce of the local sexual cultures.

Where I differ in conceptualizing the development of sexual attraction is in accepting the force of micro-events and micro-learning in affecting the outcomes of childhood sexual desires. The Sambia sense that if left to his own designs, the boy would fail to make the successful transition into the warrior role. The role requires a kind of social and political ability to manipulate sexual transitions that would not be expected of a boy growing up in a close attachment to his mother. Furthermore, and here I side with Daryl Bem, I believe that the boy and girl in this developmental regime have inhibited their stronger desires, emotions, and cognitions that would aggravate a sense of difference, of being exotic enough, to register desire. It is not the creation of sexual desire itself that may suffer in this case (contra Freud's universal Oedipal complex), but rather the ability of the culture to socially regulate this desire as the boy turns age 7 or 8. Without a major intervention, the boy's micro-learning may not produce the kind of idealized, even essentialized, masculine attachments and warriorhood behaviors that the culture desires. To influence his desires, his father and the men remove him from his mother's world and place him in a homosocial environment. By doing this under the influence of the developing adrenal puberty, they may be able to alter the boy's subjectivities in the direction of male things and men. Thus he is initiated into sexual life and has awakened, for the first time, erotic awareness—even the desire to be a hunter/warrior, the supreme achievement of the men's house.

Thus, to reiterate: In the Sambia boy's sexual development, he begins life in the shadow of his mother in what was a heterosocial environment, with his father somewhere around but not available to him. He is not regarded as an agent in his culture and is regarded as morally inoffensive and without agency. The culture is gender segregated and ritual secrecy divides the society into two parts. This division of developmental subjective being thus pervades the emergence of gender, especially through ritual secret practices, and thus introduces the boy into alternative systems of desires and meanings otherwise never learned in growing up with women and children. By accepting his position as an object of ritual treatment, the Sambia boy's social rank is elevated. By then learning the position of being an object of erotic desire by the adolescent bachelors, the boy gains agency, in that he can begin to refuse, to say yes or no, to their sexual advances. With each of these micro-moments, the boy's sexuality is changed and his desires are enhanced, in the sense that he is moving willy-nilly into the masculine lifeway of his culture. In time, his inseminations enable his growth and manliness, according to the cultural ontology. His learning of the sexual behaviors that come with this territory equip him to become more agentic, and eventually to succeed those who formerly dominated him. Meanwhile, he is learning to take himself as a subject; when this process is complete, his transformation suggests that he has learned the desire to inseminate a younger boy. His sexual agency is not complete, but he is sufficiently differentiated from the women and the women's world that preceded this transition that he can experience them again as totally exotic and dangerous, and thus eligible as sexual objects. Exotic becomes erotic, as Bem (1996) has said. But if a culture wants to ensure the optimal result, it should do it before age 10, and use its full power to change the developmental subjectivities that make a desire worth desiring.

Sexual lifeways are more in keeping with the human realities we know to exist in cultures both strange and familiar. The construct is closer to the human development that enables a match between the personality of the individual and the demands of the society. In this sense, sexual orientation is a very strange construct, ultimately alienating the person from his or her body, and from the desires as well as the demands of their culture. Think about this: Nonwestern sexual cultures are concerned largely or even exclusively with social and sexual production, social regulation, and political outcomes. These outcomes include earning a living and managing the inevitable conflicts of communal life that would impede the ability to sustain oneself; reproduction and the completion of full personhood through social marriage and parenthood, the commerce of social relations and the social continuity of generations, and the ability of the person to operate within roles and collectively work with others in a generally satisfying daily life. It is very hard to alienate desire from sexual lifeway in this regime. By contrast, developmental western psychological theories of the modern period have been concerned with the causes of desires in the biology and family matrix, which have been traced back to ultimate evolutionary or sociobiological causes. Such an imagined model plays out the vicissitudes of sexual history against the backdrop of autobiography, not by virtue of a socially created sexual culture, but rather by virtue of an entity (sexual orientation) that resides in the being of the person and cannot be changed. Such a formula for alienation and social conflict belongs to a society that is totalizing and unable to accept the real diversity of humankind.

REFERENCES

Adkins-Regan, S. (1984). Sex hormones and sexual orientation in animals. *Psychobiology, 16,* 335–347.
Bailey, J. M., & Oberschneider, M. (1997). Sexual orientation and professional dance. *Archives of Sexual Behavior, 26,* 433–444.
Bell, A. P., Weinberg, M. S., & Hammersmith, S. (1981). *Sexual preference.* Bloomington: Indiana University Press.
Bem, D. (1996). Exotic becomes erotic: A developmental theory of sexual orientation. *Psychological Review, 103,* 320–335.
Byne, W., & Parsons, B. (1993). Human sexual orientation. The biologic theories reappraised. *Archives of General Psychiatry, 50,* 228–239.
Connell, J., & Dowsett, G. (Eds.). (1993). *Rethinking sex: Social theory and sexuality.* Philadelphia: Temple University Press.
Dover, K. (1978). *Greek homosexuality.* New York: Cambridge University Press.
Freud, S. (1962) *Three essays on the theory of sexuality.* Trans. J. Strachey. New York: Basic Books. (Original work published 1905)
Gagnon, J. (1990). The explicit and implicit use of the scripting perspective in sex research. *Annual Review of Sex Research, 1,* 1–44.
Gillison, G. (1993). *Between culture and fantasy: A New Guinea Highlands mythology.* Chicago: University of Chicago Press.
Godelier, M. (1986). *The production of great men.* Cambridge: Cambridge University Press.

Gorman, M. R. (1994). Male homosexual desire: Neurological investigations and scientific bias. *Perspectives in Biology and Medicine, 38,* 61–81.

Green, R. (1987). *The "sissy boy syndrome" and the development of homosexuality.* New Haven: Yale University Press.

Greenberg, D. (1995). The pleasures of homosexuality. In P. Abramson & S. Pinkerton (Eds.), *Sexual nature, sexual culture* (pp. 223–256). Chicago: University of Chicago Press.

Halperin, D. (1990). *One hundred years of homosexuality.* New York: Routledge.

Hamer, D. H., Hu, S., Magnuson, V. L., Hu, N., & Pattutucci, A. M. L. (1993). A linkage between DNA markers on the X chromosome and male sexual orientation. *Science, 261,* 321–327.

Herdt, G. (1981). *Guardians of the flutes.* New York: McGraw-Hill.

Herdt, G. (1982a). Fetish and fantasy in Sambia initiation. In G. H. Herdt (Ed.), *Rituals of manhood* (pp. 44–98). Berkeley: University of California Press.

Herdt, G. (1982b). Sambia nose-bleeding rites and male proximity to women. *Ethos, 10*(3), 189–231.

Herdt, G. (1984). Ritualized homosexual behavior in the male cults of Melanesia, 1862–1983: An introduction. In G. Herdt (Ed.), *Ritualized homosexuality in Melanesia* (pp. 1–81). Berkeley: University of California Press.

Herdt, G. (1987a). *The Sambia: Ritual and gender in New Guinea.* New York: Holt, Rinehart and Winston.

Herdt, G. (1987b). Transitional objects in Sambia initiation rites. *Ethos, 15,* 40–57.

Herdt, G. (1989). Father presence and masculine development: The case of paternal deprivation and ritual homosexuality reconsidered. *Ethos, 18,* 326–370.

Herdt, G. (1990). Developmental continuity as a dimension of sexual orientation across cultures. In D. McWhirter, J. Reinisch, & S. Sanders (Eds.), *Homosexuality and heterosexuality: The Kinsey Scale and current research* (pp. 208–238). New York: Oxford University Press.

Herdt, G. (1991). Representations of homosexuality in traditional societies: An essay on cultural ontology and historical comparison, part I. *Journal of the History of Sexuality, 1,* 481–504.

Herdt, G. (1992). Sexual repression, social control, and gender hierarchy in Sambia culture. In B. Miller (Ed.), *Gender hierarchies* (pp. 121–135). New York: Cambridge University Press.

Herdt, G. (1993). Introduction. In G. Herdt (Ed.), *Ritualized homosexuality in Melanesia* (pp. vii–xliv). Berkeley: University of California Press.

Herdt, G. (1997) *Same sex, different cultures: Perspectives on gay and lesbian lives.* New York: Westview Press.

Herdt, G. (1999). *Sambia sexual culture: Essays from the field.* Chicago: University of Chicago Press.

Herdt, G., & Boxer, A. (1993). *Children of horizons.* Boston: Beacon Press.

Herdt, G., & Boxer, A. (1995). Toward a theory of bisexuality. In R. Parker & J. Gagnon (Eds.), *Concerning sexuality: Approaches to sex research in a postmodern world* (pp. 69–84). New York: Routledge.

Herdt, G., & Stoller, R. J. (1990). *Intimate communications: Erotics and the study of culture.* New York: Columbia University Press.

Hopper, B. R., & S. S. C. Y. (1975). Circulating concentrations of dehydroepiandrosterone and dehydroepiandrosterone sulfate during puberty. *Journal of Clinical Endocrinology and Metabolism, 40*(3), 458–61.

Hostetler, A., & Herdt, G. (1998). Culture, sexual lifeways, and developmental subjectivities: Rethinking sexual taxonomies. *Social Research, 65*, 249–290.

Kinsey, A., Pomeroy, W. B., & Martin, C. E. (1948). *Sexual behavior in the human male*. Philadelphia: W. Saunders.

Knauft, B. (1993). *South coast New Guinea cultures*. New York: Cambridge University Press.

Langness, L. L. (1967). Sexual antagonism in the New Guinea Highlands: A Bena Bena example. *Oceania, 37*(3), 161–177.

Lloyd, G. E. R. (1979). *Science, folklore, and ideology*. New York: Cambridge University Press.

Malcolm, L. A. (1968). Determination of the growth curve of the Kukukuku people of New Guinea from dental eruption in children and adult height. *Archives and Physical Anthropology in Oceania, 4*, 72–78.

McClintock, M., & Herdt, G. (1996). Rethinking puberty: The development of sexual attraction. *Current Directions in Psychological Science, 5*, 178–183.

Meyer-Bahlburg, H. (1984). Psychoendocrine research on sexual orientation. Current status and future options. *Progress in Brain Research, 61*, 375–398.

Meyer-Bahlburg, H. (1997). The role of prenatal estrogens in sexual orientation. In L. Ellis & L. Ebertz (Eds.), *Sexual orientation: Toward biological understanding* (pp. 41–51). Westport, CT: Praeger.

Money, J. (1987). Sin, sickness, or society? *American Psychologist, 42*, 384–399.

Money, J., & Ehrhardt, A. (1972). *Man & woman, boy & girl: The differentiation and dimorphism of gender identity from conception to maturity*. Baltimore, MD: Johns Hopkins University Press.

Pattatucci, A., & Hamer, D. (1995). Development and familiality of sexual orientation in females. *Behavior Genetics, 25*, 407–420.

Piaget, J. (1971). *Structuralism*. Trans. C. Maschler. New York: Harper Torchbooks.

Read, K. E. (1954). Cultures of the Central Highlands, New Guinea. *Southwestern Journal of Anthropology, 10*, 1–43.

Shweder, R. A. (1989). Cultural psychology—What is it? In J. W. Stigler, R. A. Shweder, & G. Herdt (Eds.), *Cultural Psychology: Essays on Comparative Human Development* (pp. 1–43). New York: Cambridge University Press.

Stoller, R. J. (1976). Sexual excitement. *Archives of General Psychiatry, 33*, 899–909.

Stoller, R. J. (1979). *Sexual excitement*. New York: Random House.

Stoller, R. J., & Herdt, G. (1982). The development of masculinity: A cross-cultural contribution. *Journal of the American Psychoanalytic Association, 30*, 29–59.

Stoller, R. J., & Herdt, G. (1985). Theories of origins of male homosexuality: A cross-cultural look. *Archives of General Psychiatry, 42*(4), 399–404.

Storms, M. (1981). A theory of erotic orientation development. *Psychological Review, 88*, 340–353.

Strathern, M. (1988). *The gender of the gift*. Berkeley: University of California Press.

Turner, V. (1964). Symbols in Ndembu ritual. In M. Gluckman (Ed.), *Closed systems and open minds* (pp. 20–51). Chicago: Aldine Publishing Co.

Vance, C. S. (1991). Anthropology rediscovers sexuality: A theoretical comment. *Social Science and Medicine, 33*, 875–884.

Weston, K. (1993). Lesbian/gay studies in the house of anthropology. *Annual Review of Anthropology, 22*, 339–367.

Williams, C. (1999). *Roman homosexuality*. New York: Oxford University Press.

NOTES

1. Sambia were forcibly pacified by the Australian colonial government in 1962.

2. A caution regarding the estimation of absolute chronological ages among the Sambia, a people who lack a written language and records: While it is difficult to make age estimates for any individual among the Sambia, their propensity to think in terms of age cohorts for birth, ritual initiation, and major life events, such as menarche, is of great help in placing individuals in absolute chronological sequences within their small communities. As I have noted before in my work, the ability to place individuals in relation to major social and historical events in the region has enabled me, over a period of more than 20 years of fieldwork, to calculate close age approximations (Herdt, 1987a). Within the past 15 years, the presence of a mission station within the Sambia valley and the existence of government birth records have provided different cross-checks for my own guesses, which have usually been borne out by the other records. Finally, in guessing the age of a particular person, the tendency to estimate more or less inclines structurally to the entire cohort, evening out random error. The research literature in New Guinea as a whole has tended for many decades to use age markers which are in keeping with the same age norms claimed for the Sambia (see Read, 1954). I therefore remain convinced that while these figures are based upon estimates, they are relatively accurate for population aggregates.

3. For purposes of this paper, *adrenarche* is defined as maturation of adrenal glands during puberty, while *gonadarche* means menarche in girls and spermarche in boys.

DISCUSSION

Richard Parker: Gil, can you say a bit more about your concept of sexual culture? I agree with you in terms of the centrality of the concept, but when I hear you defining it and talking about the Sambia case, it seems to me to focus very much on normative aspects and to be highly consistent, logical, coherent, a series of things that some postmodern thinking might certainly call us into questioning and that may be associated with a very specific scale of society.

Gilbert Herdt: Obviously this is a large topic. I believe that every community must establish standards for the regulation of sexual behavior within the boundaries of that community. Those standards have to do ultimately with property, with the arrangement of marriage. They have to do with the transmission of power. They also have to do with arrangements between genders or between the alternative categories that are regarded as being gendered within a society. Ultimately what is at stake is the control of sexual behavior which in many communities—including our own in the United States—is ultimately not separable from morality, from moral development. Ultimately what is being politically maintained or created is a moral and social order of things. Now, in the case of the Sambia, I have only very briefly indicated the elements that are important for this piece of my argument: How is the boy being created first as an object and then as a subject of desire? That is my real purpose here. If I were going to explain the female side of things I would have to add a number of other matters. With respect to sexual communities and cultures in the United States or in other complex western societies, obviously we have to take into account the media. We have to take into account various social religious and political forces that may be contesting each other on various matters. Let me give you an idea of something that I regard as very important here with respect to the relationship between the center and margin. If you look as an anthropologist at the cross-cultural record, it can be argued persuasively that all human communities require heterosexual marriage and the creation of children for the completion of full personhood: Personhood is dependent upon marriage and having children to achieve full rights and duties in the community. Such a definitional set of requirements for full personhood obviously places the individual who is attracted to the same gender or, in western communities, an individual who is living an exclusively "gay or lesbian" life, clearly at the margin. Thus, we come to realize that in thinking about the enormously complex and conflictual discussion about legalizing gay and lesbian marriage in the west and having children, adopting children, what is at stake is not the sexual act. What is at stake are the social entitlements, but at a higher level symbolically. What is at stake is the social definition of personhood and whether we are willing to allow persons who are attracted to each other and who are living a long period of time with each other to be constituted as full persons without having children or without being heterosexual or in a marriage blessed by the Church. So in other words, in any one of these components there will always be important stakes involved which I think are partly specific to the community but do have trappings in other cultural settings.

Carolyn Bledsoe: These two papers are very fascinating. But I'm bothered by age 10 and it seems to me that you would have a stronger case if you gave us convincing evidence either that this age is assuredly locked in, in terms of how people calculate when to initiate boys on this basis, or that they're noticing something about the developmental sequence of a particular individual. In other words, some boys mature fast, some mature slow. We could probably safely assume that people are very observant about what's happening around age 6 or 7 so that they can begin to calculate forward in terms of when to initiate.

Gilbert Herdt: The model related to adrenarche comes out of the paper which Martha McClintock and I wrote which argues from three of the most important data sets in the United States that both homosexuals as well as heterosexuals have achieved their first sexual attraction by age 9½ to 10. That's the data that's driving this theory. That's the observation in the United States. There are no comparable data from nonwestern societies to point to. When you look developmentally at the increments that would lead to such an outcome, you find that age 9 probably is a very important boundary marker for reasons that have to do both with cognitive and linguistic change and with hormonal change in the child. There is some slight evidence to suggest that in this particular respect, at least in these three samples, boys have a slightly earlier beginning or onset of first attraction than girls do. But for all intents and purposes, developmentally that difference can be leveled out and treated as irrelevant. With respect then to the Sambia situation, when you interview or interrogate parents, mothers and fathers, and ask them will you initiate your son at this particular time, at least in the case of early initiation in New Guinea societies before the time of late adolescence, it's commonly the case that initiation is for a cohort of boys or girls, although not always. That cohort is based upon a group of boys from a group of villages, typically anywhere from 30 to 50 boys in the age range from 7 to10, who will be brought together and taken through this months-long ordeal. Now a parent in general will be strongly disposed to bring their child to initiate at this time because they don't want their child to be out of sync with their own age mates and age peers in the village any more than children growing up in a neighborhood are going to want to be out of sync in the class level that they have entering grade school. A child will be held back for one reason only; if he is very ill at the time of first initiation. But no other criteria will prevent the child. Children who are blind are initiated. Mentally retarded children are initiated, and so on. There are no exceptions allowed because this is a strong binding system. But if a child is held back because of illness, the parents will attempt as soon as possible after that to have him initiated, even going so far as to carry him into the next neighboring valley, which is a significant distance away, to initiate him, say, in the following year. These cycles of initiation are only done every three or four years for the particular group, therefore they must find a surrogate group. Although that is considered a second-class initiation, it is better than leaving it alone until after the age of 10. So in short, there must be a match between the individual characteristics of the child, the local folk psychology, and the attributions of the society regarding the imperative to be initiated. But I do believe that there is compelling evidence for this being a significant window or threshold.

Caroline Bledsoe: If you followed up on those exceptions and explained that those are really important, that people do notice them, that would be really compelling.

Rafael Diaz: I'm interested in understanding a little bit more about the subjective experience of the inseminated boy and your use of the words sexual object and sexual subject. From that categorization, it looks as though the inseminated boy is simply a passive recipient. He doesn't seem interested, there's no sign of sexual arousal, and there's no sign of some kind of agency in the insemination relationship. How does that differ from being the sexual subject? What drives inseminating boys and the later turn toward women? Do they conceptualize the acts differently? What is the sense of sexual desire in the insemination process?

Gilbert Herdt: You've asked many complex questions, so let me give a very brief overview. You're dealing, in the most extreme case of the age spread, with the range from age 7, when the boy is first initiated, to age 14, when he moves into third stage of initiation, after which he ceases to be a semen recipient. So we've got seven years. In that seven years, he is first an initiate who has been taken out of his mother's home and put in the men's house, where he stays and where a lot of other things are happening. After a period of approximately three years he's then initiated into the second phase, which would be about age 11. That move from first to second stage is the most important developmental marker for the change in sexual subjectivity that you're interested in. Without going into all the particulars, probably two-thirds to three-fourths of all the boys who are brought into the system have what we would call a coercive experience in their sexual subjectivity of the events, particularly in the first year or so. Gradually, over time, as they achieve their own social prominence and status in the men's house, which after all is the ultimate social ladder of importance to them, that subjectivity begins to change and the real transformation occurs after they have been initiated into the second stage. That's when their older brothers, fathers, and grandfathers will begin to really push them and say "You've got to start really masculinizing yourself." An analogy is the idea that each insemination is like a shot of testosterone to masculinize them. They are really getting a huge amount of support, encouragement, reinforcement, and so on from peers. There's a race, they regard it as a race: Who can achieve development fastest? Who will be strongest? and so on. So that once they cross that threshold subjectively, they begin to have wet dreams frequently. Those wet dreams have a culturally patterned content. If you ask about the manifest content, they tell you that the first wet dreams involve the boy inseminating a younger boy. Then toward the end, as he's getting close to his third stage initiation, there's a lot of talk in the air about which girl in the village is going to be marked for his marriage. Then the content of the wet dreams often changes. Obviously I'm glossing over an enormously complex situation, but for the first time those boys will begin to have wet dreams in which the manifest content is focused on women. And that is an enormously complicated, power-laden, shameful, marvelous—you can put all kinds of adjectives on it—experience for them.

Shirley Lindenbaum: You spoke about the ritual experience as a social experiment for the Sambia and I know that other ritual experiments changed in Highland, New Guinea in recent years. Certain rituals dropped out of sight and then they returned again; it was a return to customary behavior. So in these other societies they returned as transformed social experiments. It would be interesting for your argument if you could tell us whether that happened to the Sambia. As what transformed emanation did the ritual experiment come back, and did it focus on the key developmental ages?

Gilbert Herdt: That is another later part of the story, but I think that both for the Baruya and for the Sambia there is evidence that does speak to the issue. In general, as colonial rule became more and more prominent (particularly missionization), ritual secrecy could no longer be maintained, and more and more elements which we regard as central to the initiation and masculinization of the boy would drop out, be suppressed. Beginning in 1981 and 1982, the Sambia self-consciously and explicitly began to hide from the younger boys the practice of insemination primarily because they were afraid they could not control the information, that it would get back to the missionaries and all hell would break loose. That had already been presaged by the dropping of nose-bleeding rites, which was absolutely central, and at the same time, young women were resisting going to the menstrual hut. So that was another piece of the system that was beginning to break down. Today the ritual system as I've described it no longer exists. When there was an "initiation" performed in 1990 and 1993, again when I was present, part of which was filmed in the BBC film *Guardian of the Flutes,* the most secret part was omitted. You see the Sambia saying to the cameramen, "We've decided to open up our system to the world" and on the other hand, out of the other side of their mouths, they're saying "We're not going to show this to them. Do they think we're complete idiots?" Coming back to your absolutely fundamental question about what symbolic substitutes and transformations will ultimately replace this sexual culture on the ground, I believe we do not know the answer yet and the reason for that is simple. This system was of such incredible force in the lives of the Sambia and the Baruya and all their neighbors that it is too soon for an emergent system to have taken its place. The reason for that is some of the elders are still on the scene. They are still strongly contesting that this system has been dropped. They are angry about this and there are powerful countervailing forces, because the young men, who are now 90% missionized, converted, are strongly in opposition to them. I believe in another generation or half generation, let's say 10 years as a marker, then the question becomes meaningful as a new cultural experiment. What transformations could we see taking their place and in the culture?

Discussion Paper: Sexual Orientation—Discussion of Bem and Herdt from a Psychobiological Perspective

HEINO F. L. MEYER-BAHLBURG

Policy Implications

In the psychobiological perspective, sexual orientation is seen as a trait, namely the overall erotic responsiveness to males and females, and the focus of theory is the explanation of why people are located on *some* place on the trait continuum rather than another.

The use of the term "theory" here is different from "theory as a global perspective" or "theory as proven hypothesis," the terms suggested in an earlier discussion section. Instead, "theory" is used for a more or less integrated set of hypotheses that may vary widely in the degree to which they have been tested individually or in combination.

Do etiologic theories of sexual orientation have a bearing on policy in our society? Starting with the first advocates of a biological theory of homosexuality, such as Ulrichs (1868) and Hirschfeld (1920), many theorists hoped—and some still do—that a theory implying biological determinism rather than psychosocial causation would interfere with moral condemnation or criminalization. However, history has shown that a rope can be fashioned out of either theoretical strand.

I think the social process is currently more important for policy than the specific content of etiologic research—the presentation of conflicting theories, scientific conferences, public debate, and media coverage (including the appearance of openly lesbian women and gay men in professional roles). This social process of research contributes to making heterosexuals familiar with homosexual men and women and to breaking down reflexive stereotypes. It thereby facilitates the evolution of public attitudes that affect policy in the long run.

There may, however, be some implications of etiologic theories for the currently contentious issue of psychologic/psychiatric treatment of boys with gender identity disorder. Some proponents of such treatment aim at the prevention of stigmatization and its emotional and educational consequences. Others condemn such therapy because they suspect that it is really directed at suppressing ordinary homosexual development. If sexual orientation in males reflects either a biological predisposition toward behavioral undermasculinization (including diminished gynecophilia and enhanced androphilia in adulthood) or an early childhood social learning phenomenon with long-lasting behavioral consequences, akin to—although not identical with—imprinting, then later therapy that focuses on gender identity issues will have no impact on the emergence of a homosexual orientation. On the other hand, psychosocial intervention may have more impact on the development of homosexuality, if Herdt's (2000) cultural scenario applies.

Psychoendocrine Theories of Sexual Orientation

Historically, the psychobiology of sexual orientation began in the nineteenth century with the interpretation of homosexuality as a form of hermaphroditism (Ulrichs, 1868; Hirschfeld, 1920). Later way stations in theories of sexual orientation were the interpretation of homosexuality as a sex hormone deficiency disorder, the treatment of homosexual men and women with testosterone and estrogens, respectively (which proved unsuccessful in changing sexual orientation), and, when it became possible, the measurement of sex hormones in the blood (which refuted the sex hormone deficiency theory) (Meyer-Bahlburg, 1984).

At roughly the same time, the role of pre- and perinatal sex hormones in the early sex-dimorphic organization of the central nervous system was discovered in animal research (Phoenix, Goy, Gerall, & Young, 1959; Young, Goy, & Phoenix, 1964). This discovery became the basis for a prenatal hormone theory of psychosexual differentiation in humans, of which the differentiation of sexual orientation is one component (Money & Ehrhardt, 1972; Money, 1988). This theory led some to see homosexuality as a form of "central nervous system pseudohermaphroditism," a view that was quite in keeping with the historical trend (Dörner, 1976, p. 217).

A number of arguments support the psychoendocrine theory. One is its similarity to the well-established theory of genital differentiation. In non-human mammals, genital differentiation takes place at specific sensitive periods of tissue organization. It begins with one pair of gonadal anlagen that differentiates into testes or ovaries under the influence of sex-specific genes, followed by the differentiation of two sets—male and female—of internal genital sex anlagen and one set of external genital sex anlagen. This second differentiation is regulated by at least three hormones. The differentiation of the anlagen includes processes of masculinization, feminization, defeminization, and demasculinization. The basic principles appear to apply to all mammals, although there are differences among the species in some particulars, especially with regard to the timing of these differentiation processes relative to other aspects of somatic development and to birth. The essential features of the genital differentiation process apply to the human mammal as well.

Another argument in support of a prenatal hormone theory are the many similarities in brain development and structure and in neuroendocrine features of non-human mammals and humans. Brain differentiation in non-human mammals, which is similar to genital differentiation, also takes place during fairly discrete hormone-sensitive periods of development, and again tends to involve more than one hormone. However, there seems to be more interspecies variability in these factors. We do not fully understand all details of the process in non-human mammals, and we understand less about the process for humans.

The effects of hormones on the sexual differentiation of brain and behavior are wide ranging; that is, a given hormonal condition affects many diverse aspects of behavioral sex differentiation, e.g., juvenile rough-and-tumble play, adult aggression, spatial perception, copulatory behavior, sexual partner preferences, and parenting behavior. The various domains of behavior may differ in the areas of the brain involved as well as in the hormonal mechanisms and the timing of hormone-sensitive periods.

Three specific theories compete to explain the role of sex hormones in the process of sexual differentiation of brain and behavior. One is the classical androgen-only theory in which feminine development is the default development in the absence of androgens (e.g., Dörner, 1976). The second one is the two-pathway theory involving both androgens and estrogens; the latter are intracellularly derived from androgens. In this model, behavioral masculinization is brought about mostly by androgens, and defeminization is brought about by estrogens (Goy & McEwen, 1980). Feminine development is again a default outcome. The third model is the new theory by Fitch and Denenberg (in press). It extends the two-pathway theory by adding to it organizational effects of low-dose estrogens. These have their own estrogen-sensitive differentiation periods which occur somewhat later in development than periods of development that are sensitive to androgens and high-dose estrogens; the additional organizational effects of low-dose estrogens are thought to bring about feminization.

Of the three theories, the androgen-only model has largely been abandoned for non-human mammals as too simplistic. There is much support for the two-pathway model, and considerable support for the newly formulated Fitch-Denenberg theory, although it has not yet been systematically tested by experiments specifically designed for that purpose. There are certainly marked differences between mammalian species, not only with regard to the degree of involvement of the various hormones, but also with regard to the timing of sex-dimorphic differentiation of the brain during the overall course of development.

For the human condition, most of the support for models of this kind comes from the study of intersex conditions. If one sums up the data available across intersex conditions for both 46,XY and 46,XX individuals, one finds considerable support for the androgen-only theory. Some of the major findings include: (1) increased bi- and homosexual orientation in 46,XX individuals with prenatal androgen excess, as it occurs in the syndrome of classical congenital adrenal hyperplasia (CAH) (Money, Schwartz, & Lewis, 1984; Zucker et al., 1996; Meyer-Bahlburg et al., in press); (2) increased bi- and homosexual orientation in 46,XY individuals with presumably normal prenatal male sex hormone exposure but non-hormonal genital abnormalities on the basis of which these individuals were assigned to the female gender and raised as females (e.g., cloacal bladder extrophy [Reiner & Meyer-Bahlburg, 1995] or ablatio penis [Diamond & Sigmundson, 1997; Bradley, Oliver, Chernick, & Zucker, 1998]); (3) increased homosexual orientation in 46,XY intersex individuals with specific enzyme deficiencies who were assigned female at birth and self-reassigned male in later adolescence and adulthood (5-alpha-reductase deficiency [Imperato-McGinley, Peterson, Gautier, & Sturla, 1979] and 17-beta-hydroxysteroid-dehydrogenase deficiency [Rösler & Kohn, 1983]); and (4) absence of bi- and homosexual orientation in 46,XY individuals with complete androgen insensitivity who were raised female (Lewis & Money, 1983; Masica, Money, & Ehrhardt, 1971). There is some suggestive support for the application of the two-pathway model to homosexual orientation, especially from studies involving prenatal diethylstilbestrol (DES) treatment, but overall the interpretation of this evidence is still under debate (Meyer-Bahlburg, 1997). The new Fitch-Denenberg theory has yet to be formally tested in human intersex conditions, but I suspect that the relatively modest increase of bi- and homosexuality in 46,XX females with CAH relative to the strong signs of somatic androgenization finds its explanation in mechanisms suggested by Fitch and Denenberg (Meyer-Bahlburg, in press a).

In any case, overall the limited evidence from intersex syndromes is compatible with the contribution of sex hormones to the development of sexual orientation, along the lines suggested by research on non-human mammals. However, before we make the psychoendocrine hypothesis the cornerstone of a general theory of the development of homosexuality, we have to address a *major* obstacle, namely, that bisexual and homosexual men and women ordinarily do *not* show any evidence of somatic intersexuality. Moreover, homosexual men do not show any discrepancies from heterosexual men in systemic sex-hormone production, release, or metabolism and neither do the majority of lesbian women, although about one-third show increased androgen levels in adulthood that fall in the range of hirsute women, i.e., still way below the male range (Meyer-Bahlburg, 1984). Also, we do not know whether the hormone elevation is limited to adulthood or applies already to the pre- and perinatal stages of development where it might influence central nervous system (CNS) organization. Even if a contribution of these moderately elevated androgens were shown to influence homosexual differentiation during fetal life, it would not account for sexual-orientation development in two-thirds of lesbian women. Moreover, we have to keep in mind that the androgen elevation in the other third of that population is much below the level of what one sees in untreated CAH women whose strong prenatal exposure to excess androgens was usually not sufficient to make them homosexual. Thus, it is doubtful that the modestly increased androgen levels in lesbian women play a significant direct role in the development of a homosexual orientation.

Thus, currently, the support for the theory that endocrine factors cause or co-cause the development of homosexual orientation is limited to categories of individuals with a history of gender-atypical systemic sex hormone levels during pregnancy. None of the diverse conditions with such a history, however, apply to the vast majority of adult homosexuals. What are our options for explaining the development of homosexual orientation in that majority?

One option is a psychoendocrine theory that includes special mechanisms compatible with the empirical findings. The immunological inactivation of testosterone during fetal development might constitute one such mechanism. This mechanism was originally suggested by MacCulloch and Waddington (1981) who proposed that testosterone produced by the fetal gonad might lead to testosterone antibody production in the pregnant mother; these antibodies might pass back to the fetus and reduce the biological activity of the fetal testosterone and thereby yield a behaviorally undermasculinized male fetus. This proposed mechanism is at variance with various other findings however: (1) steroid hormones are not ordinarily antigenic (see Blanchard & Bogaert, 1996), (2) there are no symptoms of prenatal somatic undermasculinization in homosexual men, (3) there are no indicators of somatic undervirilization in adult homosexual men or impairment in libido that would suggest impaired biological activity of testosterone.

An alternative immunologic hypothesis involving H-Y antigen has been proposed by Blanchard and Bogaert (1996; Blanchard, 1997). It suggests a potential explanation for the well-established finding of a birth order effect, according to which homosexual men have a strongly increased probability to come from sibships of multiple and older brothers. But so far this hypothesis lacks an identified hormonal or other mechanism by which psychosexual differentiation would be affected and will therefore not be discussed here any further.

Another option for an endocrine explanation of the development of homosexual orientation in non-intersex individuals is a CNS-restricted hormonal theory. Perhaps human homosexual orientation, in other than somatic intersex conditions, is a form of intersexuality that is limited to the central nervous system and is uncoupled from peripheral intersexuality. That is, it depends on CNS-limited hormonal effects, e.g., in terms of production of hormones or hormone metabolites limited to the CNS, or in terms of CNS-limited changes of steroid receptors. The recently discovered existence of so-called neurosteroids (Baulieu, 1997), i.e., steroids that are produced in the CNS itself, would be a potential explanation of that sort. Moreover, in the last decade, we have learned a lot about tissue specificity of steroid receptors and steroid enzymes (see for instance, the endocrine ontogenesis of 46,XY individuals with 5-alpha-reductase deficiency; Wilson, Griffin, & Russell, 1993). The hypothesis of a CNS-limited neuroendocrine explanation of the development of sexual orientation would still preserve sexual orientation as part of an overall process of psychosexual differentiation to the extent that homosexual orientation, at least in males, is associated with such characteristic features as decreased rough-and-tumble childhood activity, diminished aggression, and lowered spatial perception, all behavioral characteristics shown to be influenced by sex hormones.

On the other hand, it is entirely conceivable that the CNS organization of human homosexuality has more than one developmental pathway, as do many human conditions, e.g., obesity or short stature. One such pathway, as applicable to homosexuality among individuals with intersexuality, may involve systemic endocrine variations. Another may include development independent of hormone effects, based, for instance, on hormone-unrelated genetic factors, or on psychosocial factors.

In the context of this discussion, one has to remember that none of the animal models based on sex hormones constitute a perfect model for human homosexuality. The animal models are primarily developed for the explanation of sex differences in general, not specifically for the explanation of the development of homosexual orientation. In these animal models, the most marked behavioral effects are achieved if gonadectomy is performed early in development and the hormonal milieu is altered during both the early organizational phase and the later activational phase. In human homosexuals, however, the gonads are typically present and as functional as in heterosexuals, and we know from animal research that under such conditions, the behavioral results are much less clear-cut, especially in females.

Other issues raise doubts about the adequacy of the existing animal models for human homosexuality. One is that in the wild, non-human mammals show much homosexual behavior, but no one has demonstrated the development of a homosexual orientation. Even in our nearest mammalian relatives, non-human primates, homosexual orientation has not been observed (Wallen & Parsons, 1997). Experimental manipulations of prenatal sex hormones that bring about marked alterations of sex-dimorphic juvenile play behavior in primates have also not led to the creation of homosexual orientation in adulthood. In fact, there seems to be a marked difference between non-primates and primates. Early manipulation of the sex hormones in rodents, for instance, yield later changes in preferences for the gender of the sex partners, but so far no one has produced a non-human primate homosexual in this way.

One could argue that endocrine or genetic conditions that lead to preferential homosexuality in animals in the wild would quickly be selected out because of failure to produce offspring. If so, such conditions might better survive among domesticated animals. Unfortunately, even in the laboratory, animals that do not perform well heterosexually tend to be selected out and are rarely an object of investigation.

Not all sex differences in CNS function may reflect sex-hormone effects. Recent reports suggest, for instance, that independent of sex hormone effects there are genotype-dependent sex differences in certain aspects of neurotransmitter function (Pilgrim & Reisert, 1992; Sibug et al., 1996). However, the impact of such non-hormonal genetic factors on the psychosexual differentiation of the behavioral domains we are interested in has yet to be investigated.

When we consider non-hormonal mechanisms we also need to take into account that there are well-known phenomena of sexual attraction such as pedophilia and zoophilia for which a specific hormonal basis is implausible and for which learning mechanisms constitute a more likely basis. It seems to me highly probable that the learning mechanisms involved in the development of such patterns of erotic attraction also constitute one of the pathways to homosexual attraction.

Comments on Bem's Paper

Bem (2000, 1996, 1998) suggests another solution to the psycho-endocrine dilemma. He starts with the notion that homosexual men appear to be behaviorally undermasculinized. He combines this notion with data from boys with gender identity disorder (GID)—often labeled pre-homosexual boys, because the majority develop a bisexual or homosexual orientation by late adolescence or adulthood (Green, 1987; Bailey & Zucker, 1995). Boys with GID are typically not only undermasculinized but are also feminized in their behavior and prefer to associate with girls during the process of gender segregation which is so characteristic of middle childhood in this country. Bem postulates that the sex hormones influence the sexual differentiation of temperament, not of sexual orientation itself. He sees the latter as a secondary product of the gender-atypical distance of these boys from the male peer group brought about by their hormone-induced temperament and the putative general arousal caused in the gender-atypical boys by the "exotic" unfamiliarity of gender-typical boys; this arousal becomes eroticized by an unspecified mechanism.

There are a number of difficulties with this theory. First of all, although boys with GID have many signs of behavior that could be interpreted as undermasculinization—such as low levels of rough-and-tumble play, low levels of intermale aggression, increased timidity, low spatial perception ability—there are no reliable indications that their systemic androgens are in any way deficient. There are no symptoms of intersexuality, no problems with the development of secondary sex characteristics, and no signs of decreased androgen or increased estrogen levels. Thus, we are again compelled to look for one of the other mechanisms I discussed before to explain the apparent undermasculinization in the presence of a normal systemic sex hormone milieu.

At this stage of our knowledge, it seems more likely that GID—in boys at least—is not based on abnormalities of androgenization but springs from a not uncommon temperamental pattern (Coates & Wolfe, 1995; Meyer-Bahlburg, in press b) that is known as the inhibited child (Kagan, 1994, 1997) and applies to about 20 percent of the population, both boys and girls. It has also been studied extensively in rhesus monkeys where this temperamental pattern appears to be related to serotonin regulation (as in humans), and is heritable (Higley et al., 1993), but can be enhanced and diminished by specific social stressors such as early separations from the mother (Suomi, 1997). In nonhuman primates, the inhibited temperament has remarkably strong and persistent effects on the lifestyles and fates of the individuals. In their study of boys with GID, Coates and Wolfe (1995) found that about two-thirds had this temperamental pattern. On the other hand, the low prevalence of children with GID suggests that only a small fraction of boys with the inhibited child pattern will develop GID. Such GID development occurs probably under the influence of specific factors in the social environment that facilitate a cross-gender adaptation in an inhibited child (Meyer-Bahlburg, in press b; compare the social learning factors identified by Zucker and Bradley [1995] for GID children in general). In any case, it is doubtful that the temperament of boys with GID can be explained by a systemic sex-hormone theory.

The second major problem with Bem's theory is the separation of sexual orientation from the behavioral domains that are presumably affected by prenatal hormones. Although it is possible in non-human mammals to use very carefully timed manipulations of pre- or perinatal hormone exposure to identify slightly differing sensitive periods for various behavioral domains, there is generally no suggestion that sexual orientation is differently organized than the other domains and not under hormonal control. On the contrary, one would expect that a trait as basic to survival as sexual attraction would depend on biological regulation, if any. Of course, I recognize the fact that nobody so far has come up with a primate model of homosexual orientation. This fact suggests that there may be a major difference between primate and nonprimate mammalian models.

The third issue I find difficult to understand in Bem's theory is the role of arousal. Bem himself acknowledges that it is yet to be established that with generalized arousal gender-atypical boys react to gender-typical males rather than to other people. That general arousal, once it is elicited, can be recruited into existing specifically patterned forms of arousal such as fear, aggression, or sex, is certainly well established. But how does a sexual arousal pattern get established in the first place, and how does it become associated with specific stimuli—in our context with other males as erotic objects—even before there is the experience of homosexual partner sex?

Fourth, why are straight adolescent boys not attracted to noticeably effeminate adolescents? There is certainly unfamiliarity and considerable emotion.

Fifth, even if Bem's theory should turn out to be valid, it would not explain all of homosexuality, because about one-third do not report gender-atypical patterns of childhood behavior. Thus, different explanations would be needed for the homosexual development of that third of the population of homosexual men.

Comments on Herdt's Paper

Herdt comes from a very different intellectual tradition than the quantitative behavioral sciences represented by Bem. I will probably not do him full justice when I try to interpret his essay in the context of the procrustean bed of the preceding discussion.

Herdt's developmental sequence begins with the psychoanalytic notion of the semi-erotic symbiosis of mother and young child. Neither concept—mother-child symbiosis and its semi-eroticism—is part of current animal research or developmental psychology, and their explanatory utility for developmental processes is doubtful, as is the utility of the related concept of "symbiosis anxiety" as a general mechanism of gender development.

Herdt does not address the question of gender-typical behavior patterns of children between two and six years of age and their origins, which figure prominently in the research on sexual differentiation of brain and behavior in both non-human mammals and humans. I think pertinent data on the Sambia for this age group would be of great interest in the context of this discussion.

Between seven and ten years of age, the boys in Sambia culture are inducted into the male initiation rites. They are physically and symbolically segregated from the world of women and small children, and later their insemination by adolescent males is begun. Herdt calls this a "homoerotic period"; the boys become objects of sexual attraction, and now have "for the first time, erotic awareness—but not desire."

When the pubertal/gonadal maturation of the boys is sufficiently progressed, there is another role switch. Now these new adolescents become the ritual insemina*tors* of another generation of middle-childhood boys. This stage ends only when the young men have taken up intercourse with a mature woman and have fathered a child. Herdt uses Bem's ideas to suggest that through the years of ritualistic segregation, the young men have become so distanced from their mothers and other women that they are now sufficiently exotic and dangerous to serve as erotic objects.

These prescribed stages of child and adolescent development among the Sambia certainly have something to do with sexuality and gender, but what specifically do they tell us about the development of sexual orientation in the usual sense of the term, namely overall erotic responsiveness to males and/or females?

Since Sambia culture defines 10 years as the upper age for the start of the initiation rites, Herdt looks for an intrinsic developmental factor that might be the reason. He notes that in some recent studies in industrialized western societies, retrospective dating of first experience of homosexual attraction in both males and females centers on age 10 years, and suggests as the biological/intrinsic factor stimulating the emergence of such first attraction a component of adrenarche, namely the rise of the adrenal androgen dehydroepiandrosterone (DHEA) to an intermediate level between pre-adrenarche and adulthood (McClintock & Herdt, 1996). He seems to imply, but does not make explicit, that it is this allegedly DHEA-triggered development of first erotic attraction that the Sambia want to effect with their ritualistic insemination—an assertion that needs supportive empirical evidence. Many other questions remain open as well.

1. Is the concept of sexual orientation as a trait applicable to Sambia people?

2. What does a "first erotic attraction" at age 10 years mean? Apart from the issue of retrospective dating and the variability encountered in such reports, clinically and anecdotally one certainly sees many episodes of what looks like strong infatuations in children of much younger ages, down to late preschool years, but such early events may be much more difficult to remember in later stages of life.

3. Do we have to assume a hormonal cause of "first attractions" at age 10? There is gradual cognitive maturation, progression in the social rehearsal (including modeling of older siblings and peers), eroticization from sexual initiation by older adolescents and adults (sexual abuse), and early onset of overt sexual interactions with peers—all of which may contribute.

4. If we want to identify a hormonal factor, is DHEA a likely hormone for that purpose? Androgens vary widely in their affinity to androgen receptors and thereby in their biological effectiveness. Although systemic DHEA is abundant, available data indicate that it is primarily systemic testosterone, in particular its free or unbound fraction, that is correlated with aspects of sexual behavior.

5. Is the timing of adrenarche in well-off children from industrialized societies comparable to that in Sambia society? Given the marked relative delay of Sambia children in age at gonadarche, would not one expect a delay of adrenarche as well?

6. Even if DHEA should contribute to the development of sexual desire, how does the desire acquire its direction toward males or females, especially in western adolescents where we know that many experience gendered attraction before overt sexual initiation?

7. Does ritualistic homosexual insemination as practiced by the Sambia instill homosexual orientation in the sense of overall erotic responsiveness? Children of any age can be sexualized by prolonged sexual involvement, especially if it takes place without physical violence, trauma, and pain (at least in the sense that they seek sexual activities that are apparently pleasurable for them), but is that what happens to Sambia boys when they are inseminated? Are they just mouth-fed, or are their bodies caressed and their genitals stimulated to erection and perhaps orgasm? Do they develop really *erotic* attractions to their inseminators or just a liking for older adolescents that give them attention? Do the pre-pubertal boys play sexually with other boys of their peer cohort? And if the boys are indeed eroticized, are they devoid of erotic response to girls or women?

8. Sometimes Herdt's accounts suggest the development of switch-

es in sexual attractions on command. But given the extreme gender-coercive nature of Sambia society, are the reports of the fantasy content, e.g., during wet dreams by male adolescents, really valid or do they just conform to expectations?

9. How do the inseminators induce their own erections for insemination? Do they experience erotic attractions to the boys, or do they masturbate with erotic fantasies and attractions directed toward women?

10. Conversely, when the young men have sex later with women, are their *erotic* attractions—not just their procreative intents—directed toward women, or do they, for instance when they have sex with women, maintain their arousal with erotic fantasies about males, and if so, with males of which age group?

Thus, it seems to me that a lot of empirical fleshing out is needed before we can understand how a cultural theory like the one suggested by Herdt relates to other theories of the development of sexual orientation.

In summary, both Bem and Herdt describe the development of sexual orientation as a multistage process. People are not "born that way"; their sexual orientation emerges over time as a product of multiple factors. Note also that both Bem and Herdt include a biological factor, sex hormones, in their causal model, and consider the irony that someone like me—with "psychoendocrinology" on his professional shingle—has significant doubt about the place of sex hormones in either theory.

As this symposium shows, complex probabilistic theories including multi-stage developmental processes and multiple causal factors—biological, social, and psychological ones—are replacing simple unicausal deterministic models. This evolution of theory building in the area of psychosexual differentiation is the real significance of these two papers.

REFERENCES

Bailey, J. M., & Zucker, K. J. (1995). Childhood sex-typed behavior and sexual orientation: A conceptual analysis and quantitative review. *Developmental Psychology, 31,* 43–55.
Baulieu, E.-E. (1997). Neurosteroids: Of the nervous system, by the nervous system, for the nervous system. *Recent Progress in Hormone Research, 52,* 1–32.
Bem, D. J. (1996). Exotic becomes erotic: A developmental theory of sexual orientation. *Psychological Review, 103,* 320–335.
Bem, D. J. (1998). Is EBE theory supported by the evidence? Is it androcentric? A reply to Peplau et al. (1998). *Psychological Review, 105,* 395–398.
Bem, D. J. (2000). The exotic-becomes-erotic theory of sexual orientation. In

J. Bancroft (Ed.), *The role of theory in sex research* (pp. 67–80). Bloomington: Indiana University Press.

Blanchard, R. (1997). Birth order and sibling sex ratio in homosexual versus heterosexual males and females. *Annual Review of Sex Research, VIII,* 27–67.

Blanchard, R., & Bogaert, A. F. (1996). Homosexuality in men and number of older brothers. *American Journal of Psychiatry, 153,* 27–31.

Bradley, S. J., Oliver, G. D., Chernick, A. B., & Zucker, K. J. (1998). Experiment of nurture: Ablatio penis at two months, sex reassignment at seven months, and a psychosexual follow-up in young adulthood. *Pediatrics, 102,* Article e9. Available on the World Wide Web at http://www.pediatrics.org/cgi/content/full/102/1/e9

Coates, S. W., & Wolfe, S. M. (1995). Gender identity disorder in boys: The interface of constitution and early experience. *Psychoanalytic Inquiry, 15,* 6–38.

Diamond, M., & Sigmundson, H. K. (1997). Sex reassignment at birth: Long-term review and clinical implications. *Archives of Pediatrics and Adolescent Medicine, 151,* 298–304.

Dörner, G. (1976). *Hormones and brain differentiation.* Amsterdam, The Netherlands: Elsevier Scientific Publishing Company.

Fitch, R. H., & Denenberg, V. H. (1998). A role for ovarian hormones in sexual differentiation of the brain. *Behavioral and Brain Sciences, 21.*

Goy, R. W., & McEwen, B. S. (1980). *Sexual differentiation of the brain.* Cambridge: MIT Press.

Green, R. (1987). *The "sissy boy syndrome" and the development of homosexuality.* New Haven, CT: Yale University Press.

Herdt, G. H. (2000). Why the Sambia initiate boys before age 10. In J. Bancroft (Ed.), *The role of theory in sex research* (pp. 82–103). Bloomington: Indiana University Press.

Higley, J. D., Thompson, W. W., Champoux, M., Goldman, D., Hasert, M. F., Kraemer, G. W., Scanlan, J. M., Suomi, J. J., & Linnoila, M. (1993). Paternal and maternal genetic and environmental contributions to cerebrospinal fluid monoamine metabolites in rhesus monkeys (*Macaca mulatta*). *Archives of General Psychiatry, 50,* 15–623.

Hirschfeld, M. (1957). *Die homosexualität des mannes und des weibes.* Berlin: Louis Marcus. (Original work published 1920)

Imperato-McGinley, J., Peterson, R. E., Gautier, T., & Sturla, E. (1979). Androgens and the evolution of male-gender identity among male pseudohermaphrodites with 5a-reductase deficiency. *New England Journal of Medicine, 300,* 1233–1237.

Kagan, J. (1994). *Galen's prophecy.* New York, NY: Basic Books.

Kagan, J. (1997). Temperament and the reaction to unfamiliarity. *Child Development, 68,* 139–143.

Lewis, V. G., & Money, J. (1983). Gender-identity/role: G-I/R Part A: XY (androgen-insensitivity) syndrome and XX (Rokitansky) syndrome of vaginal atresia compared. In L. Dennerstein & G. D. Burrows (Eds.), *Handbook of psychosomatic obstetrics and gynaecology* (p. 51). Amsterdam: Elsevier Biomedical Press.

MacCulloch, M. J., & Waddington, J. L. (1981). Neuroendocrine mechanisms and the aetiology of male and female homosexuality. *British Journal of Psychiatry, 139,* 341–345.

Masica, D. N., Money, J., & Ehrhardt, A. A. (1971). Fetal feminization and female gender identity in the testicular feminizing syndrome of androgen insensitivity. *Archives of Sexual Behavior, 1,* 131–142.

McClintock, M. K., & Herdt, G. (1996). Rethinking puberty: The development of sexual attraction. *Current Directions in Psychological Science, 5,* 178–183.

Meyer-Bahlburg, H. F. L. (1984). Psychoendocrine research on sexual orientation. Current status and future options. *Progress in Brain Research, 61,* 375–398.

Meyer-Bahlburg, H. F. L. (1997). The role of prenatal estrogens in sexual orientation. In L. Ellis & L. Ebertz (Eds.), *Sexual orientation: Toward biological understanding* (pp. 41–51). Westport, CT: Praeger.

Meyer-Bahlburg, H. F. L. (in press a). Estrogens in human psychosexual differentiation. Commentary on "A role for ovarian hormones in sexual differentiation of the brain" by R. H. Fitch & V. H. Denenberg. *Behavioral and Brain Sciences.*

Meyer-Bahlburg, H. F. L. (in press b). Psychosexual disorders: Variants of gender differentiation. In H.-C. Steinhausen & F. Verhulst (Eds.), *Risks and outcomes in developmental psychopathology.* Oxford, UK: Oxford University Press.

Meyer-Bahlburg, H. F. L., Gidwani, S., Dittmann, R. W., Dolezal, C., Baker, S. W., Morishima, A., Bell, J. J., & New, M. I. (in press). Psychosexual quality of life in adult intersexuality: The example of congenital adrenal hyperplasia (CAH). In B. Stabler & B. B. Bercu (Eds.), *Therapeutic outcome of endocrine disorders: Efficacy, innovation and quality of life.* New York: Springer-Verlag.

Money, J. (1988). *Gay, straight, and in-between. The sexology of erotic orientation.* New York: Oxford University Press.

Money, J., & Ehrhardt, A. A. (1972). *Man & woman, boy & girl: The differentiation and dimorphism of gender identity from conception to maturity.* Baltimore: Johns Hopkins University Press.

Money, J., Schwartz, M., & Lewis, V. G.(1984). Adult heterosexual status and fetal hormonal masculinization and demasculinization: 46XX congenital virilizing adrenal hyperplasia (CVAH) and 46XY androgen insensitivity syndrome (AIS) compared. *Psychoneuroendocrinology, 9,* 405–15.

Phoenix, C. H., Goy, R. W., Gerall, A. A., & Young, W. C. (1959). Organizing action of prenatally administered testosterone propionate on the tissues mediating mating behavior in the female guinea pig. *Endocrinology, 65,* 369–382.

Pilgrim, C., & Reisert, I. (1992). Differences between male and female brains—developmental mechanisms and implications. *Hormones and Metabolic Research, 24,* 353–359.

Reiner, W. G., & Meyer-Bahlburg, H. F. L. (1995, October). Psychosexual implications of gender reassignment at birth. Poster session presented at the 42nd Annual Meeting of the American Academy of Child and Adolescent Psychiatry, New Orleans, LA. Scientific Proceedings of the Annual Meeting, p. 115 (NR–102).

Rösler, A., & Kohn, G. (1983). Male pseudohermaphroditism due to 17b-hydroxysteroid dehydrogenase deficiency: Studies on the natural history of the defect and effect of androgens on gender role. *Journal of Steroid Biochemistry, 19,* 663–674.

Sibug, R., Küppers, E., Beyer, C., Maxson, S. C., Pilgrim, C., & Reisert, I. (1996). Genotype-dependent sex differentiation of dopaminergic neurons in primary cultures of embryonic mouse brain. *Developmental Brain Research, 93,* 136–142.

Suomi, S. J. (1997). Early determinants of behaviour: Evidence from primate studies. *British Medical Bulletin, 53,* 170–184.

Ulrichs, K. H. (1868). "Memnon." Die Geschlechtsnatur des mannliebenden Urnings. Eine naturwissenschaftliche Darstellung. Körperlich-seelischer Hermaphroditismus. Anima muliebris virili corpore inclusa. Schleiz: Hübscher. (Cited in Kennedy, H. (1988). *Ulrichs: The life and work of Karl Heinrich Ulrichs, pioneer of the modern gay movement.* Boston: Alyson.)

Wallen, K., & Parsons, W. A. (1997). Sexual behavior in same-sexed non-human primates: Is it relevant to understanding human homosexuality? *Annual Review of Sex Research, VIII,* 195–223.

Wilson, J. D., Griffin, J. E., & Russell, D. W. (1993). Steroid 5a-reductase 2 deficiency. *Endocrine Reviews, 14,* 577–593.

Young, W. C., Goy, R. W., & Phoenix, C. H. (1964). Hormones and sexual behavior. Broad relationships exist between the gonadal hormones and behavior. *Science, 143,* 212–218.

Zucker, K. J., & Bradley, S. J. (1995). *Gender identity disorder and psychosexual problems in children and adolescents.* New York: The Guilford Press.

Zucker, K. J., Bradley, S. J., Oliver, G., Blake, J., Fleming, S., & Hood, J. (1996). Psychosexual development of women with congenital adrenal hyperplasia. *Hormones and Behavior, 30,* 300–318.

Discussion Paper

GARY W. DOWSETT

I want to refer to three important themes in the papers presented in this session. There's no time to raise all the issues I'd like to. These three are: (1) the issue of sexual orientation itself, (2) the contribution of gender, and (3) the biological body. I'd like to do that by introducing a brief report on a pattern of homoeroticism that has yet to be the subject of academic scrutiny. I only recently encountered it in my travels.

These events involve young men performing a ritualized dance for older men, one after the other in sets of three. The dancers often smile at various men lining the arena, occasionally exchanging a word, and dancing to show off their capacities or specialties. At times, some remove parts of their clothing, exposing upper bodies briefly for the audience's approval. Occasionally, a dancer will expose his buttocks to the men for a moment, receiving enhanced approval.

Each dancer then returns for a second short dance, wearing only a genital covering. The dancer quickly removes this, except for footwear, and then proceeds to dance naked and aroused for the men in the audience. He dances quite close to the men at times, stroking his penis and other parts of his body. Many dancers turn around, provocatively swaying their buttocks and then bending over to display their anuses to the audience. Often the dancer will lie down with legs apart on his back and masturbate for a while, or he will lie stomach down and raise his buttocks from the floor.

Each dance lasts only a short while, and this pattern continues from late afternoon until the early hours of the morning, taking twelve hours in all to proceed. The dancers who are not dancing circulate among the drinking and talking audience, stopping for a chat here and there, but never joining the group. At these times, the dancers wear very little, merely covering their genitals and feet.

Occasionally, a dancer and one man will retire a short distance from the main group. The dancer then stands on a small platform so that his genitals are at exactly the height of the seated man's head. The dancer immediately removes all clothing, except the footwear, and proceeds to dance. The man, this time, has direct access to the body of the dancer, and usually begins to caress the dancer's body from the leg upward as the dancer gyrates and moves his body sensuously—but for some reason he never touches the dancer's penis. The dancer will often become erect again without any direct stimulation of his penis, clearly aroused by the adoration, the caressing, and the obvious arousal of the man. Sometimes the dancer will again turn round and bend over, exposing his anus, again never directly touched by the man, and then the dancer will sit, heavily grinding his buttocks into the man's crotch, but never lingering too long. These times mark the most body-to-body contact that happens, but the older man is clothed and does not expose his genitals even if aroused greatly. These single sessions take place alongside each other, each couple but a few feet from the next, so this is a quite public event still. At the end of this dance, which can take from a few minutes to an hour, an exchange of money takes place. The man returns to his peers who have all been watching his pleasure from that short distance, but were also absorbed in the endless parade of nude young men dancing in the full arena.

There are many different kinds of homoerotic dancing in the world. In the Philippines, for example, it is called "snake" or "macho" dancing, and the urban form has begun to merge with a more familiar type of sex work. In Thailand's north, the dancers appear younger, and sometimes one will be chosen to masturbate to orgasm to the wild acclamation of the audience of men and the other boys.

Undoubtedly, boys and young men performing such rituals for men is a long-standing tradition crossing cultures. Think of the gymnasia and the athletics in Ancient Greece, and the explicit sexual contact in Sparta noted in Gilbert Herdt's paper. I am also reminded of the Orientalist Jean-Léon Gérôme's wonderful painting, the Snake Charmer, where a nude prepubescent boy dances with a snake in a bathhouse for an audience of Arab men, the painter capturing the definitive eroticism of moment in a careful but explicit fall of light across the boy's buttocks.

What do these events and their analogues tell us about sexual orientation, apart from the fact that homoeroticism seems to exist in all cultures across time and place? Gilbert Herdt argues for an end to sexual orientation through an experiential progress toward a sexual subject position—a maneuver I find appealing, if incomplete. For different reasons, I would question seriously any a priori invocation of sexual orientation to account for this dancing, for the term depends on that binary opposition, heterosexual/homosexual, at its fundament. In other words, it is a discursive consequence of an earlier discursive conclusion. Many sexuality theorists have cast doubt on that binary opposition, for it is a little more than 100 years old as a post-Enlightenment scientific coding device, one with suspect origins.

On that basis, we must seriously question the reifying of sexual orientation as a meaningful point of departure. If we seek to explain its existence by assuming it, we seriously misunderstand the issue of erotic attraction; the fact of homoeroticism neither proves nor warrants the existence of sexual orientation. Therefore, I must part company with Daryl Bem right at the start, even if I find other aspects of his paper compelling.

This argument about sexual orientation is the most significant difference between these two papers, and I want to examine it further through the example of the dancers. This dancing scene took place recently in Montréal. Yes, this is a contemporary western ritual, and would that we spent more time investigating the erotic forms in our own cultures with the same analytical gaze we so readily bring to more exotic places. For the Sambia are a gift, but their exoticism can allow us to escape our own challenges. The young men dancing in Montréal force us to reckon with something more "proximate" (to borrow Jonathan Dollimore's phrase [1991]) than we are used to.

Like any good ethnographer, I talked with a number of the dancers last week when I was in Montréal, and with members of the Canadian AIDS Society who had taken me there but who did not regard many of the dancers as gay. Indeed, most dancers did not choose that term for themselves, and only one said he was bisexual. Many are in relationships with women and, moreover, two clubs open their doors one night a week to women. Then, the same young men perform both in the arena and one-to-one for women, and have erections for women just as easily as they did for the men. Sexual orientation would seem to fail miserably to account for these young men, just as it fails to account for the Sambia's universal, if periodized, homoeroticism. No explanation that requires fixity in sexual preference, whether based on gender or not, can account for these willful dancing events. Even if we allow for a kind of sexual willfulness permitted boys in the "sow-your-wild-oats" narrative of western masculinity (i.e., a gender role), the notion of a primary object choice as evidence of a sexual orientation remains quite shaky.

If we take Gilbert Herdt's notion of the transfer from sex object to sexual subject as a central cultural process that allows us to supersede sexual orientation in order to produce a field of unfolding possibilities for a sexual career, then we can partly explain these young Canadian men's erotic investment in their dancing for aroused men, irrespective of their reported sexual interests.

These dancers are older than both the Sambian youths and even the young Spartan lovers, and as such beyond the significant periods of development that both Gilbert Herdt and Daryl Bem point to. If there has been a transformation from sex object to sexual subject, it is also clear that remaining an object as well is also possible, and the notion of what I call a "sexual subjectivity" may be required to move beyond subject position (Dowsett, 1996) and might explain both the retention of one's status as both and the processes that might facilitate that double process. How else might we explain the cult of the male body sweeping the west in advertising and sport and the discursive shift of the phallus from active and desiring to passive and desired?

A sexual subjectivity requires more than a developmental capacity to traverse sexual cultures in a linear fashion; it requires an active engagement with the ever-multiplying sexual choreographies of those cultures. Gay male culture, more than any other contemporary western sexual subculture, explicitly plays with these multiplying object/subject possibilities, recognizing the self in the other and thereby threatening the sustainability of the "exotic other" at least in this one regard. But even gay men cannot account for all the homoeroticism in the west: Being homosexually active does not suffice in making one a gay man.

Gay men can tell many tales of scoring so-called straight men, and the evidence from Kinsey and his colleagues would indicate at least considerable potential for experimentation on the part of North American men, most importantly its dramatic argument for social context and historical contingency (Kinsey, Pomeroy, & Martin, 1948). Furthermore, the Australian HIV/AIDS surveys of gay-identified men report high lifetime scores for ever having sex with a woman and a minority population of gay men that had female partners with surprising regularity in the last six months before they were surveyed (Crawford, Kippax, Rodden, Donohoe, & Van de Ven, 1998). Daryl Bem's paper reports even more variability among lesbians. Can we explain these phenomena without the notion of sexual orientation becoming so fluid that it must accommodate the twentieth century's most remarkable transformation of the pathological homosexual into the subcultural gay man of today, and also incorporate the wayward dancers of Montréal, and then deal with the Sambia, let alone Nigerian truck drivers, South African miners, the hijras of India, and sex radicals of Sydney?

It is interesting to note that the two papers in this session on sexual orientation concentrate on homosexuality, even if Daryl Bem's paper offers a model for all sexual interests. This confirms that the century-long desire to explain the causes of homosexuality is never far from our endeavors and reveals that sexual orientation may merely be a politically correct semantic renovation of deviancy. Would that the last century and a half's efforts at trying to explain homosexuality be apportioned appropriately between heterosexuality and homosexuality. Then, at least, some of the mammoth problems facing institutional heteronormativity, such as incest; sexual assault of women and of men; the physical torture of women with corsets, cosmetic surgery, and high heels; systematic misogyny; and various sexual health and population issues might have seen some progress.

The costs to men are clear as well: the phenomenal success of Viagra in the U.S. market, the burgeoning penile implant and extension services, the impotency clinics, the sexual mutilation of boys by circumcision, and the deeply costly mass psychological and legal maintenance of men's anal virginity would seem to indicate that heterosexuality is deeply disoriented. It is clear that the maintenance of institutional heterosexual preference is attended by gigantic social and cultural resources, attesting to its inherent instability.

Our linear fashionings, be they the developmentalism of Daryl Bem's A→F transformation of the codes for gender conformity to the erotic attraction of the exotic other, or Gilbert Herdt's linear cultural evolution that molds desire in an active process of careful additions and transformations, seem then not to be able to account for the end products of their models. While ignoring the decidedly ambiguous nature of heterosexuality, Daryl Bem also cannot account for the universal homosexuality-then-heterosexuality of the Sambia male. Gilbert Herdt cannot explain why the security of exotic object choice in Montréal is not so much in doubt as largely irrelevant to the erotic pleasures of these dancers. And for the rest of us, working any longer with a theory that discursively relegates such behavior to homosexuality would appear no more than sophistry.

Gender—Some Thoughts

If sexual orientation fails to perform, is gender its starting point? How is it that the Sambia produce little conspicuous gender non-conformity in early childhood precisely at the time that biological variables related to such non-conformity in the west would seem to do so? How do we account for the universality of homoeroticism among Sambia men with a model that requires partition along gender lines as its fundamental point of analytical departure?

I suspect that gender as a discursive and conceptual category performs as a conceit here, demanding its privilege because of its well-used claim to account fully for sex differences. That claim is historically powerful, but a conceit no less, because it conceals the possibility that other differences might underpin desire's development that we put in other discursive categories such as personality, physiognomy, aesthetics, and taboos.

Why do the Sambia refuse anal insemination of their boys when some other Melanesian cultures prefer it, and why do the men once married relegate boy insemination to youths and not retain the obvious and universally experienced pleasures of being fellated for themselves, when in other Melanesian cultures the men retain these insemination pleasures for themselves? Are these taboos secure? The ancient Greeks developed an elaborate ethical architecture to encase their relations with youths and one of its purposes was to discourage sodomy—that such efforts were needed attests to their lack of success. Ages of consent perform the same function today—after all, the policing of the pedophile is the policing of us all.

Daryl Bem rightly encourages us to recognize the profoundly culture-driven nature of gender and shies just clear of arguing that an end to gender might see an end to sexual orientation. How could this be in the light of those genes and hormones that code for the behavioral predispositions connected with gender non-conformity? Anyway, the Sambia would seem to say that this will not produce an end to homosexual sex. But my suspicions are that gender has its own interests to protect. The Fa' afafini of Samoa are a case in point. These are last-born males raised deliberately as women to provide care for aged parents. Recently, I was informed that a Fa' afafini member of the Samoan Parliament argued against the introduction of co-educational schooling because it would undermine the traditional female role provided by the Fa' afafini, i.e., providing sexual services to Samoan men. Gender is revealed as performance before our very eyes.

A second example comes from the technological construction of the transsexual—"daughters of the knife" (as termed by R. W. Connell) —which teaches us that the biological body cannot be quarantined from its cyborg future. I'm reminded of John Gagnon's example of the Marines, but what I thought of is that the Marines dramatically change your body too. So I support Gilbert Herdt's demand for a prospective account of desire in production, but would argue that even changes to the physical body itself must be brought into the mix.

But more: I doubt the biological contributions from either a notion of gender non-conformity, already discursively compromised, or from adrenarche as the linchpin to subject formation, in the light of evidence in Anke Ehrhardt's paper of the constructive impact of experience on the body's brain and hormonal systems. Also, her suggestions for reckoning with differences within each gender add weight to the critique of gender itself. Might it be that the gender uniformity of early Sambian childhood precludes the possibility of gender having any biological effect on object choice, a possibility Herdt cautiously approaches in his elaboration of the impact of such dramatic universal homoeroticism being required to achieve the installation of women as at least a reproductive object choice so late in adolescence?

The Body

What kind of biological body are we talking about here? The biological body in these two papers is a very boring body. Where are the smells of crotches and the taste of fresh semen on the tongue? Where is the feel of the frenum and the unique heat of the rectum? Where are the contortions of orgasm and its muscular release of pleasure? What of arousal and its choreography? Where are the cerebral pleasures in skillfully bringing the body of another to gratification?

There is none of this in the bodies we are being asked to consider here. They are merely, and both, narrowly discursive bodies. We cannot logically separate the object of our interrogation from the very linguistic tools we need to apprehend it. The problem then becomes what tools we use: hence, the privileging of particular disciplinary lenses in these papers. The body described here with its hormones, genetic markers, and brain etc., is the body of biology, not the embodied human, not the body-in-sex. Biology's discursive body selectively ignores whole slabs of the embodied engagement with the erotics of sex. We might fruitfully ask How much does the first taste of semen (which is often unpleasant) transform the Sambian boy into an object? How much does his later first orgasm into a younger boy's mouth snap a subject position into place? What are the specular pleasures of another's bared body? What are the erotics of being gazed upon and arousing others, irrespective of object choice?

The body teaches and can do so in a discursive silence. The issue here is which body biology puts into the mix and which holds sway in the argument. The biology of a pre-social body dominates both these accounts at bedrock. No adequate account of the body can refuse the social nature of the body in question: The signifier cannot be separated from its signified. Dare we embark upon the intercourse proposed here between biology and culture, but still refuse the materiality of the body-in-sex itself and, as a consequence, omit yet another part of our sexual subjectivity?

This suggests the need for increased cultural relativism, and again calls into question the utility of universalizing concepts such as sexual orientation. But why also privilege an object-to-subject linearity? And even though there is a significant convergence between these two papers on providing a place for the biological body (albeit a filleted one) and strikingly powerful, if differently hedged, arguments for a central place for the cultural, this marriage between biology and culture still leaves the body quarantined from the debate and sexual subjectivity in exile. It would seem our marriage has yet to be consummated.

Acknowledgment

I would like to thank John Bancroft and the Kinsey Institute for inviting me to this meeting. It is an honor for someone working in a small country to be part of such a consultation and a privilege to be able to provide some of the input.

REFERENCES

Dollimore, J. (1991). *Sexual dissidence: Augustine to Wilde, Freud to Foucault.* Oxford: Clarenden Press.
Dowsett, G. W. (1996). *Practicing desire: Homosexual sex in the era of AIDS.* Stanford, CA: Stanford University Press.
Kinsey, A. C., Pomeroy, W. B., & Martin, C. E. (1948). *Sexual behavior in the human male.* Philadelphia & London: W.B. Saunders.
Crawford, J., Kippax, S., Rodden, P., Donohoe, S., & Van de Ven, P. (1998). *Male call 96: National telephone survey of men who have sex with men.* Sydney: National Centre in HIV Social Research (Macquarie University Unit).

General Discussion

Ken Plummer: I suggest we cluster our discussions around three themes for the moment. The first theme is to establish the theoretical question that we're looking at. The debate here centers on whether the language is one of "orientations and traits" or "preference," or just what it is that we're talking about. My own view is that we cannot disentangle the theory from the terminology. My own favorite versions of "it" concern the question How do sexualities get done? How is desire crafted? How is identity invented, managed, transformed? How is a sexual act given meaning? So what is the theoretical question to which we're trying to direct our attention?

Second, how can we actually connect the different layers of analysis that we're talking about? At one end we obviously have biology; at the other extreme end we have historicized culture, a culture that is very specific within history. We have a new kind of word introduced, "bodies," which is the sociological version of biology and is becoming very popular amongst sociologists. So at one end we have bodies and biology and at the other end historical cultures. What I've felt has been lacking is a sense of what's in the middle, which is sometimes called human subjectivities or "the person." There's been a void here. Foucault has only been mentioned once and Freud has been mentioned little, if at all, which is very interesting. The other thing that's been missing is context. Contexts are the mediums through which these things get done. So you have bodies and subjectivities moving in contexts which are historically and culturally reproduced. And these change over time and space. So how can we connect these things?

Third, how do we speak to each other about doing all that, given that we have very different epistemologies?[1] The papers this morning clearly revealed those different epistemologies. I hope nobody will be offended if I place people in particular kinds of epistemologies. There are clearly some people in the room who believe in strong universalizing general theory, and there are other people who don't believe in that at all and who believe in localized, more specific, changing theory, as well as living with the ambiguities of theory. Some of the papers were in a very strong scientific mould and some of the papers were in an interpretivist cultural mould which are not so strongly scientific but are more concerned with the assembling of cultural meanings. One commentator spoke in a more post-modern mode, which is to say that the old big stories have died and what we're looking for now is the richness of playing around with what we've got, the multiplicity of new local narratives, understanding people's lives on their own terms much more, lives that are always full of ambiguities, contradictions, and changes. One of the things that's happened within lesbian and gay studies recently, which hasn't been mentioned, is the development of this strange phenomena called queer theory[2] which attempts to break down all the existing categories completely. It rejects, for example, the categories of lesbian and gay and they talk about being post-gay and post-lesbian. They don't like those words at all. They sometimes like the word bisexual, but they don't like that word either because it is also too limiting. There's a whole language debate going on about who people are in these post-modern worlds. So that's the third area.

Daryl Bem: When you list all the thousands of things that my theory can't possibly embrace, that to me is the nature of my epistemology and science. I keep breaking down the concept until I have a theory that can handle the phenomena. The term sexual orientation is too broad because it has many components. So among the things you've listed maybe if you were female you would have thought of love before the taste of semen, but love was never mentioned and that's what I can't handle in my theory either. So the problem with sexual orientation as a concept is it doesn't hang together. The components don't hang together especially among people who identify themselves as bisexual. And as someone who myself has a disparity between romantic attraction and homoerotic attraction, I prefer smaller words like sexual attraction or romantic attraction or sexual behavior, which is the one that can be least predicted. So I'm new to this area. That was my first and only publication in 1996 so I am also not that familiar with the literature. I'm a puzzle solver and I say, Isn't it interesting that in the data 70% of gay men and 70% of lesbians said they felt different from other kids on gender dimensions? I wondered if I could account for that in some old-fashioned sense of account and then someone said "Yes, but what about all the biological data?" Oh, yes, I do have to account for that too. The reason I didn't say anything about hormones is because I, too, think the hormone data is the weakest. I thought the genetic data looked a little stronger. I'm welded to the data and if I'm going to be as dogmatic as I am about my theory then by God I'd better be able to say how you account for these data within the narrow con-

fines of what I can do. So what my theory intended to do by implication eliminated most of what you talked about. My view of sexual
orientation is not the Kinsey scale, but I conceive of homoeroticism
and heteroeroticism as two independent dimensions, just as masculinity and femininity have now been treated as separate independent
dimensions. What the relationship is for any particular person is an
empirical question. The more gender polarizing the society, the more
you're going to find the negative relationship empirically between the
two conceptually independent dimensions of homoeroticism and heteroeroticism. So I even think the Kinsey scale is wrong because it assumes a bipolarity. It's also the case that the data for women is not
bimodal, whether you look at the National Opinion Research Center
(NORC) survey or the sexual preference study or virtually every other
study, women are more likely to say they are bisexual than that they
are exclusively homosexual, and with men it is just the reverse.

Colin Williams: I was impressed with what Gary Dowsett had to
say and I think it was good for him that he was the discussant and not
the presenter. I would like to ask him if the position was reversed,
what would a theory look like from his perspective? Would you even
talk about a theory of sexual orientation?

Gary Dowsett: I wouldn't use the words sexual orientation. This
kind of word is atheoretical. The reason why I deliberately used the
example of the Montréal dancers was to demand of myself a kind of
empirical component, because I work empirically with this kind of
theory. That kind of urban anthropology is very similar to what Gil
Herdt has done with the Sambia and his more recent work with young
gay people in the States. Sexuality theory, in the way that I see it in a
post-modern vein, is actually quite eclectic at some points. I don't find
anything that Heino Meyer-Bahlburg said discontinuous with what I
would like to use in thinking about human sexuality. But my demand
would be to stop the quarantining in those bodies of knowledge, and I
think I would argue that the notion of the quarantined body is valid to
the kind of work he was presenting this morning. So I actually think
there is a possibility of mixing our scientific domains and our discursive realms, but that is going to require one major step and that is the
rethinking of the concept of theory in the light of post-modernism.
That will mean rejecting the notion that theory is truth. Theory is
actually about discursive positionings at a moment in time and so any
particular set of positionings is a disciplinary paradigm and they all
have their shortcomings and their blind spots. Our major task is not so
much the development of meta-theory to provide truth, but a recognition of the way in which we can create strategic alliances between
disciplinary forms of theory around the same issue. I actually see no
problems with the marriage between biology and culture—we just

haven't done it yet. So I find nothing discontinuous with what Heino Meyer-Bahlburg was saying, for example, or the other two substantive papers in the session. It's a matter of working on how we learn to make those components mix.

Colin Williams: You seem to be saying that we all tell different stories and we should listen to each other's stories. But nowhere do I hear any sense that one story may be more true than another. So do you reject any notion of validity?

Gary Dowsett: I think I would reject any notion of absolute truth, but not of validity. What I'm trying to argue for here is that the shifts that have already occurred in what I call sexuality theory, which is the way I've been marking it off from sexology, are not discontinuous. Sexuality theory is largely pro-structuralist rather than post-modernist, and by that I mean that it relies very heavily on pre-existing concepts of social structure from social theories such as Marxism or functionalism. Similarly, sexuality theory is enormously dependent on sexology, but it's moved on from it. Our challenge is to recognize the sticky feet of sexuality theory in sexology and the way they relate to each other in some way, but recognize where the shifts have moved to and what they bring with them. I suspect that's the greatest challenge for theory. My reason for arguing this is a policy argument; AIDS has shown us that sexology cannot deal with it and sexuality theory has made a more major contribution to dealing with AIDS than sexology has in terms of public health policy. That alone should require us to keep moving in this direction.

Connie Nathanson: Can you give an example of how sexuality theory has been able to move forward public health policy?

Gary Dowsett: I think all of us in this room who work in HIV in gay communities, for example, would recognize that without the kind of gay and lesbian theory developed over the last 20 years to conceptualize desire inside the cultural framework of "gay," we couldn't have actually created the public health campaigns about HIV prevention on the ground that have produced such a dramatic behavior change in the west in a population that never even needed to contemplate condoms. Gay men took them up with such a huge interest while other men in the world still reject them at such a great rate. That's the way in which I would argue that sexuality theory has had an impact on public policy, whereas behavioral sexology hasn't been able to help at all.

Sarah Hrdy: How do you know that was "sexuality theory" as opposed to being the result of a community with good communication, and they're not dumb?

Gary Dowsett: What is a good community with good communication? This construct of gay community is less than 30 years old and yet it has achieved something that has not been able to be achieved almost anywhere else in the world in that time, in both constructing itself and then dealing with an epidemic. Now it's beginning to come out at the other end. The only way you can start to figure out why that's happened is to try to figure out what constitutes that community as a body of meaning, a body of practice; and I've built on Gil's concept of "sexual culture" here. I throw into the mix not just issues about norms and expectations but also the practices themselves. Safe sex culture is actually built on the bodies of gay men; it's actually built on the interactions of skin and skin and how those things are conceived of and managed. It's not just simply a cerebral exercise. So you actually need to theorize the way in which gay bodies engage each other both with the physicality of those bodies and the meanings in culture that gay men bring to sexual engagement, to figure out how safe sex was invented as an idea and how it was then developed into a health promotion exercise.

Anke Ehrhardt: I want to go back to Ken Plummer's point about what term and then what theory. If we start with sexual orientation as a descriptive term based on the Kinsey scale, which is a way of discussing how people's attraction falls on a continuum of attractions and behavior, I certainly prefer that to sexual preference. Sexual preference seems to imply that we can turn sexual attractions to same sex or opposite sex on and off as a kind of choice and also imply that sexual attraction is not integral enough to a person's life. So seeing sexual orientation, with the Kinsey scale, to be on a continuum rather than any kind of simple dichotomy seems to me to be a very useful paradigm.

John Gagnon: I'd like to resist Anke Ehrhardt's suggestion for the following reason. It seems to me that sexual orientation is such a historically embedded and politicized word. While we may want to use orientation because it connotes a phenomena that appears to be deeper in the organism, harder to change, and more profound than preference, probably neither one of them is particularly good language for the embeddedness of the practices in particular historical social situations. I don't know that actually people are oriented toward each other; the metaphor may not be a good one. I don't like preference a lot, but I think I like it better. Martin Dannecker once made the same argument that you make and I argued that one of the reasons why one chooses orientation is because of the hard-won historical experience of the actor. If I have been persecuted for who I believe I am, who I believe I am can't be merely a preference. It has to have deeper significance than a simple preference.

I think that we may want to abandon that whole body of ideas around the binary opposition, but I don't think there is a continuum to replace it. The Kinsey scale looks continuous, but if you look at the people on the scale, in fact, they are not continuous. It really is sheep and goats at the level of lives lived. It's not that people don't change their practices, but that the cultural biases that constrain the choices or shape the choices have binary qualities to them.

Anke Ehrhardt: We have talked mainly about gay men. I certainly don't think that is true for women. When you describe women's sexuality they are not on Kinsey zero and Kinsey six; they are much more at different points on the continuum. But if we give up both terms, it seems to me that we are just going to have more complicated descriptive terms.

John Bancroft: I would like to link what you've just been saying to Gil Herdt's paper. The main interest in Gil's analysis of the Sambian situation is how the culture determines how the sexual experience is shaped. That needs to be reconciled with what you've just been saying. To what extent is the sense of relative permanence culturally determined or to what extent is it determined at a particular stage in development? That seems to be the question that we're not yet able to answer and for which we need some sort of helpful theoretical approach. In Gil Herdt's case, the cultural picture that he was describing seemed to be very much shaped around the notion of masculinity, to the extent that I couldn't help feeling that the reason why the boys had to be introduced into this before they were age 10 is that if it were any later it would actually conflict with the idea of reinforcing masculinity; it could then be seen to undermine the sense of masculinity. You need to have them when they're still "feminized" by their mothers to masculinize them in that way. So in that case gender seemed to be playing a very powerful role in shaping how sexual experience was used. So what is sexual orientation in the Sambia and how do we conceptualize that?

Anke Ehrhardt: I see that sexual orientation first of all is a descriptive term. Now you are switching to what is the origin of it and what is the etiology of it or what is the developmental course of it.

Leonore Tiefer: I'd like to weigh in on the side of not pursuing sexual orientation as a fundamental term that we need to work really hard on to get into theory. If we do this, it's only because there are some really important political reasons why sexologists, sexuality theorists, or progressives need to offer a theory of sexual orientation at this point in time. If that's our purpose then I'm for it, but here in this sanctuary I want to argue that sexual orientation is a product of a particular historical epoch. As I think radically about what we've been talking about, I'm struck by how much of my original training as a psychologist seems to come up. For example, we should pay more attention to the processes of eroticization as tremendously powerful, explanatory vehicles for understanding the acquisition of feelings and

behavior. Then we have cognitive self-labeling and attribution processes that perpetuate categorical phenomena once they've been set
into action. Plus we have operant and classical conditioning that can
go far in explaining the acquisition of feelings and behaviors over time;
anticipation, conduct, reinforcement. This type of language might help
us communicate and create theory that would be widely useful. But if
theory is for a particular point in time, to create a location for argument or political impact, then it might be better to use the categories.
There are so many components to this sexual orientation. To think of it
as any sort of unified notion of attraction doesn't describe people's
lives in 1998 at all.

Gilbert Herdt: Going back to the issue of should we use sexual
orientation and also the relationship between the development of sexual orientation and development of gender identity, these are strongly
linked historically for a very long time, for a whole variety of reasons.
I mentioned in my paper that the overall historical behavior context of
the culture that I've talked about was warfare. Warfare really was the
main control variable in an objective and ecological sense. That's what
ultimately underlay most of the important social, economic, political,
and psychological features of the system that I've described. Several of
the questions Heino Meyer-Bahlburg raised were very important. He
asked me about the presence of gender-atypical behavior in Sambia
boys between the ages of two and six. I would say that this is an irrelevant question. The presence of this question is a presumption about
the cultural situation of the Sambia. It's not that it is an unimportant
question to raise; and if I were to give you an answer, the standards
that I would have to use would be those of our own culture. Were I to
say that the Sambia boys were mildly or moderately or intensively
feminized, what behaviors or discreet behavioral acts would I have to
point to? And if I were pressed to give an overall global description of
the central tendency, I would say that the kind of gender atypical behavior that Heino seemed to be looking for is absent. However, I can
tell you that there's a sensitivity and softness in Sambia boys which
you would find perfectly understandable and also quite similar to your
own children, which you would not call feminized or gender atypical.
But in the context of Sambia masculinity with its trenchant, phallic
ability to kill, this behavior would be considered "feminine." But is
that gender atypical? No, I would like to say to you that it is not. But
now I just want to join this up with one other piece of the historical
and behavioral situation of the Sambia and cultures like them. In this
set of approximately 60 societies that have implemented these rites of
boy insemination for a period of years, some of them going on until
very old age (although that's unusual, what one might regard as a very
special human experiment), no rule exists for a gender-atypical or

cross-dressing individual. There is no known category or role like the transvestite or the berdache or any of the other categories that exist around the world of third genders. In fact, I could even go further. In Melanesia, which is conservatively estimated to consist of 1,000 cultures and 2,000 different languages and even more dialects, there is no known example of an institutionalized complex of permanent cross-dressing males. Now why is that? It is not an historical accident. It is that the demand requirements of warfare for masculinity are so severe that they will not countenance and will systematically weed out the slightest offenses against the masculine standard. So, in short, what I'm trying to say is that the historical and behavioral complex that produced this system of boy-inseminating rites is the very same one that from the start ultimately rules out the possibility of any institutionalized central tendencies that go against the ability to be aggressive, to wage war, to defend the village, and all of the things that go with that. I believe that that trickles down from the very beginning of development and enters into the first awareness of the child.

Richard Parker: I seem to remember having read something that you wrote some time ago about how your own interpretation of the Sambia over time has switched to categorizing whatever it is they do as sex as boy-inseminating rites and not sex, at least in the terms of our cultural definitions. We've been focusing on the first one of the three challenges that Ken gave us and I would like to leapfrog over the second one of the different levels to the question of universal theories and culturally specific modes of interpretation. Is there any way to interpret that specificity in a way that makes it more universally meaningful, or are we mind-locked into a process of at best translation, which approximates some kind of localized reality?

Gilbert Herdt: I would say first and foremost that in the proximate setting of Sambia culture, which is the setting of my observations and the evidence on which I'm trying to generate an account of what occurs, the practice of what I call boy-inseminating rituals occurs across everyday life, so it's not a practice that takes place at one point in time. Within the meanings of that practice and the doing of that practice are contained most of the components that supply the Sambia with the psychology they need and the social relations they need to make sexuality work, to put it into practice, to produce the things they want. So that the practice provides a conventionalized system of meanings that go along with it, partly folklore, partly beliefs, partly norms, partly roles, what we would call the psychology, as well as the understanding, of "the biology." It also conveys within it, if you wanted to mark off a piece of it, an implicit concept of what is sexual attraction. When we look at the Sambia evidence in the context of the Kinsey study we can see that some of the things that were said there were absolutely valid, but we do have a tendency, as did Kinsey, because he didn't aggregate his observations across time, to think about this behavior as occurring at a fixed point in time. What I think first and foremost is that what is occurring before age 10 and after age 10 should be regarded in some very significant sense as different "basins" of experience with different subjectivities and different consequences. Not just that after 10 and after puberty the social agent is drawn in to all the moral and political consequences of being an adult, which has many weighty things attached to it, including the social consequences of reproductivity; that certainly is implied. But, to come back to your question, the practice itself contains within it some of the elements we need to talk about to do a translation from western culture. But there is something lost in the translation. Conversely, we can't take the Sambia practice or concepts and bring them into a western cultural setting, or certainly into western cultural theorizing, without making important modifications.

John Gagnon: Let me propose some things that people might read. George Steiner, the literary critic, is multilingual; he speaks French, German, and English as a native, and having learned all these languages while very young, he has maintained them. He has a series of essays on translation. One is in a book called *On Difficulty* (1978), in which he talks about the problem of translating from one language to another and the ways in which translation is difficult. He raises the whole issue of what do you mean, for instance, when you call a text difficult? Is Proust difficult? Is Joyce difficult? Now these are textual matters and one can think of them as limited, but the problems that he raises about how you deal with translating discourse are also relevant to the issues about translating performance from one place to another. In a second book called *Real Presences* (1989), he struggles with this problem of the epistemological issue and he raises the concept which is called "texts no longer being understandable because they fall over the horizon of either culture or history." Disciplines in the west are translating machines. Anthropology is a machine for translating the lives of people who live in the Congo into understandable categories that resemble categories that people who live in the United States are familiar with. That's what any discipline is. It's a way of looking at the salient features of complicated alternative situations and making them look alike. Disciplines themselves are historical phenomena. They're translation engines created by westerners. Very often it may be impossible to translate the Sambia into categories relevant to our culture. The original situation is sufficiently alien from your categories of meaning that as a nonmember you are always alien from it. You may have to decide at some point, I just can't make sense out of all of this.

I'll cite Steiner again. He raises the issue of how you read a book or how you receive a work of art. One of Steiner's arguments is that you should receive a work of art courteously, and he means courtesy in the sense of a guest in the house, and as the guest in the house you don't try to tell the host what he or she is about. So when you receive another culture, when you go to another place, you don't go to that culture to interrogate it, but you go with a sense of "I'm a guest here, I don't know why these people do what they do, I'm ignorant. My job is to acquire some sense of meaning of what's going on here," not to take what they do and convert it into my pre-existing system of understanding. It may be that the visitor's understanding machine is actually an act of terrorism and that's what missionaries did to these cultures by destroying indigenous religions. So I'm just raising the issue of translation, membership, the relationship of the observer to the ongoing strange culture and suggesting maybe an attitude, not so much a theory as a stance toward other people's lives, which offers their way of doing things some priority in the interpretation.

Ken Plummer: Let me ask you a question. If you saw that our little lives were also different little academic cultures, different little scientist cultures made up of our own little rituals and our own packages of knowledges and languages, are you also suggesting that we should leave each other alone in the same way? Should we basically just accept each other and accept the fact that we cannot really talk to each other?

John Gagnon: My simple answer would be yes. A more complicated answer would be to refer back to what I said before. The only way that we can become members of a common culture is in fact to become participants in common practices, to do things together. But as long as it stays at the level of "How do I imagine the problem?," as long as the thought style of the disciplines are in opposition, we really can't do much of anything. If we, in fact, work on a problem, if we are in the field and we say "I want to understand this and I have someone who I respect who does this other discipline," we begin to create a community of meaning which is the basis on which interdisciplinarity and a new way of imaging begins to arise. It's not that you can't make ideological statements about interdisciplinarity being a good idea; yes, I think it's a good idea. But, in fact, when you do these kinds of things you have to do them among equals in power. You cannot be an anthropologist who works for a doctor so that you go out and create the categories for the questionnaire which then go into the epidemiology machine which eventually becomes how doctors think. The problem of equality of power in the transactions means there cannot be anybody who is head of the lab. It has to be grassroots up. You cannot create interdisciplinarity from the top down.

Gary Dowsett: I actually think equality and power can't exist in the same space. But my question is to Gil. In your paper, there's a long discussion about the concept of desire, desires and desiring; and the concept of desire as lack of desire, as imagining something else. I don't think it answers our needs here to look for common points of reference that might get us away from sexual orientation, but it seems to me you were gesturing toward that. Yet in your response to Richard, in fact, you withdrew from that possibility in some ways.

Gilbert Herdt: Desire is such a heavily overused term like so many others and it has such a long, thousands of years long, set of meanings that go with it, so that it's easy to use it and it becomes nothing but sophistry. This really comes out of my work with gay and lesbian adolescents. I realize as a result of this that we have a strong tendency, in U.S. culture, to separate off sex acts from other social desires and aims. What I realize, from working with young lesbians more than young gay men, is the presence of a very strong possibility of discrepancy between things. To put it in the simplest form, in the study we did some years ago in Chicago on teenagers ages 14 to 20, the majority of young lesbians had heterosexual experiences, and in the United States in general, I think, there's good evidence to suggest that the majority of lesbians have had heterosexual experiences and the majority of gay men have not. Certainly in younger cohorts there's strong evidence for such a proposition. Lesbians who are 14 and 15 and 16 years old are presented with a very complex situation. They've had prior heterosexual experience, dating, even coitus, and some of them, depending upon their social class background, have a desire to have children. They even have in some cases a desire to be married. They even would like to have a heterosexual marriage although they may not want all the baggage that comes with that. After all, they're only 15. They haven't had to put this in practice. However, their erotic desires are very clear. They're not confused. They desire women and they have every intention of living with a woman and having a life with a female partner. They are therefore presented with two very powerful and compelling possible developmental lines, one leading to a female partner and the other leading to a situation of having children and being heterosexually married. They don't have to deal with the discrepancies between those possibilities at that stage, but ultimately they will by the time they're in their early adult years. I realize because of this the strong tendency in sexuality research to reduce many of these complexities to the question of their sex act.

What is the sex act they want? But that, of course, does not at all cover the full complexity of their lives, nor does it address their future. In my paper, one of the points that I tried to draw attention to is the difference in developmental theory between nonwestern and western cultures. In nonwestern, preliterate cultures, great attention is paid to the question What do these social practices or sexual acts do in leading someone into social relations, into the production of things in society? Whereas in the western tradition development in sexuality theory for at least 100 years has always looked back in time to the origin, to the source, whatever it is. The reason for that is because our ultimate interest is with the individual and not with community or society, and that, I think, is a fundamental point of difference. So, my effort in thinking about desires is really one of trying to provide a language that is somewhat more able to encompass these life course changes with greater flexibility. This is one of the problems I have with the concept of sexual orientation. That encompasses what happens in childhood with what happens in adulthood and also recognizes that the social and the sexual belong in the same package. They should not be put into different packages. Desires, as they come out of social relations, may very powerfully code for what the person wants to be or to have later in development, and they may not necessarily be in concordance.

Anke Ehrhardt: I was encouraged by Gary's comment that it is possible to marry different ways of thinking about different influences. Whether one lives in Sambia or in Montréal, one has a body. So the body might figure in different ways, biological factors may be acting in different ways dependent on the culture and the social context. I wouldn't want a supertheory, but I would like us to think about how we could put these different influences together. How it might work. Not everywhere the same way. Sexual desire and sexual attraction is a good place to start. Both of you think that something happens in the first 10 years. That is not to say that children are just like adolescents and adults. We have to struggle with the critical role that puberty might play. I would totally reject the idea of going to adrenarche, back to a kind of main effect model that because adrenal hormones begin to increase, that's why sexual attraction in a certain way starts. I find that a very outmoded kind of thinking in our biopsychosocial perspective. I do think we need to consider how menarche, how pubertal hormones, may possibly figure into it and how it may in different cultural systems figure into sexual attraction in different ways. That would be a good common ground for us to have a debate rather than issues of sexual orientation or heterosexuality.

John Bancroft: I also wanted to bring us back to the biology-culture interaction and I was struck by one of Gil Herdt's statements. "How can you learn the sexual excitement necessary to create an erection?" is I think how you put it. I think it's also relevant to Daryl Bem's paper. I'm not sure you have to learn how to create an erection; erection occurs. What you learn are the situations which predictably become associated with the occurrence of erection. I'm often taken back to look at the work of Glen Ramsey in the 1940s (Ramsey, 1943) on boys around the age of puberty, which I don't think has ever been replicated mainly because it's very difficult to do and he lost his job doing it in the first place. In his study, boys described how they went through a phase of relatively indiscriminate arousability. They were finding themselves getting erections in a variety of situations which had in common only that they were exciting. Then what appears to have happened over a period of time was that some sort of discriminative learning took place and the erections became associated with more specific and presumably more culturally determined situations. That has always struck me as being an interesting model and possibly one that is relevant to some of the sex differences that we've been talking about, because I'm not sure that anything quite like that happens in girls. Or if it does, it may not have the same impact on learning, because as a boy you have this very clear signal which pops up in front of you, telling you something sexual is happening. This feeds into a sort of conditioning process which may not occur to the same extent in females. This illustrates well how we might think about the psychobiological aspect and its interaction with the cultural context.

Leonore Tiefer: I want to take on this notion of the penis as essentially sexual. I recall that early research as well. Something about excitement causes a genital response. The whole question of general autonomic excitement versus specifically sexual response needs to be reconsidered. Psychophysiological research shows that women are not very good at identifying what's going on in their genitalia. They say they're excited or they're not excited, but it does not bear too close a relationship to genital arousal. Thus, for women, it's confusing to ask are they or are they not sexually excited. They say they are, but nothing's happening in their genitalia, so are they? Are the genitalia the Rosetta stone of sexuality? Men have this component that pops up which also becomes eroticized, but the process is quicker. Again there is laboratory research showing that if men can't see their penis, the correlation between when they say they're excited and what's going on with the penis is not as good. The visual link does seem to be essential. It seems to me that learning sexual excitement is an important concept. Erections occur, yes, but are those erections always sexual? Women provide a useful model where the disjunction is more apparent. There is a disjunction in men; it's just not as well recognized.

Connie Nathanson: I am reminded very much of Howard Becker's work on learning how to get pleasure out of smoking pot. To be totally anecdotal, I can remember my own first exposure to sex and I didn't have any idea what was going on. I got dizzy. I thought "My God, this is terrible, I'm going to faint." I didn't associate this with anything I could interpret. So it seems to me that you learn the meanings of these things and that this is totally learned in social interac-

tions. It is very much like the process of learning how to enjoy mari-
juana, like learning how to enjoy alcohol. These are learned and
they're meanings you learn in social interaction with other people.
They are not given in any sense of the word.

REFERENCES

Benton, T. (1977). *Philosophical foundations of the three sociologies*. London: Rout-
ledge.
Clifford, J., & Marcus, G. E. (Eds.). *Writing culture: The poetics and politics of
ethnography*. Berkeley: University of California Press.
Harding, S. (1991). *Whose science? Whose knowledge? Thinking from women's lives*.
Milton Keynes: Open University Press.
Jagose, A. (1996). *Queer theory: An introduction*. New York: New York Univer-
sity Press.
Outhwaite, W. (1987). *New philosophies of social science: Realism, hermeneutics,
and critical theory*. New York: St. Martin's Press.
Ramsey, G. V. (1943). The sexual development of boys. *American Journal of
Psychiatry, 56,* 217–234.
Sayer, A. (1992). *Method in social science: A realist approach*. London: Routledge.
Sedgwick, E. K. (1990). *Epistemology of the closet*. Berkeley: University of Cali-
fornia Press.
Seldman, S. (Ed.). (1996). *Queer theory/sociology*. London: Routledge.
Steiner, G. (1978). *On difficulty: And other essays*. New York: Oxford University
Press.
Steiner, G. (1989). *Real presences*. Chicago: University of Chicago Press.

NOTES

1. For some contrasting views on epistemology in the social sciences, see
Benton (1977), Harding (1991), Sayer (1992), Clifford and Marcus (1986),
and Outhwaite (1987).
2. For a guide to queer theory, see Jagose (1996). In addition, key statements may be found in Sedgwick (1990) and Seldman (1996).

Part 3

Individual Differences in Sexual Risk Taking

Theorizing Risky Sex

JOHN GAGNON

Introduction

When the two words "sex" and "risk" are used together, as in the phrase "risky sex," they conjure up in most people's minds hazy visions of heedless individuals engaging in sexual practices that will put themselves and others at risk for the transmission of HIV and other STIs (sexually transmitted infections), inappropriate pregnancies among unmarried young people, and the extramarital sexual contacts of politicians. That this view is common in the populace should not be surprising since it has been widely promoted by a number of interested constituencies in cooperation with a pliant mass media, and it conforms with a widely held vernacular theory that sexual problems are caused by out-of-control individuals. One consequence of this promotion of "risky sex" as a cause of disease transmission and adolescent pregnancy has been the granting of a limited license for scientific inquiries into the nature of "risky sex," its causes and consequences, and the development of public policy to reduce its prevalence and thus the prevalence of the health and social problems that are believed to be consequent upon it. Such scientific inquiries are expected to include theories of risky sex to guide the collection and analysis of data, and such theories are expected to be part of the basis for the selection of social policies.

The license that is given to theories, inquiries, and policies based on social science research is limited because other interested constituencies believe that the causes of "risky sex" are already well known and that certain policies, if diligently applied, will eliminate all sex that involves negative health and, more important, moral consequences. Such interested constituencies believe that sexuality does not need to be, indeed should not be, the object of scientific study. The existence of separate and equally important constituencies with quite different methods of theorizing sexual problems and with quite different policy proposals should alert us to the important political and ideological aspects of dealing not only with "risky sex," but with all issues relating to sexuality in the United States.

Contention between various interested groups in sexual matters needs to be understood as the cultural framework inside of which all troubles which seem to be associated with sex are theorized and defined as problems requiring solutions. One set of constituencies, primarily secular in their methods of solving sexual problems, look to the theory-constructing and fact-gathering procedures of various social science disciplines to provide the basis for social policies relevant to sexuality. The other set of groups, primarily religious in their orientation, use various dogmatic texts as the basis for theorizing about and dealing with sexual matters and they pressure the state to conform to these "sacred texts" when public policies about sexual conduct are imposed.

That these groups are in contention about the appropriate ways to theorize and solve sexual problems and about the policies to be applied does not mean that they are not in agreement about various matters related to sexuality. Secular and sacred theorists often share the beliefs that certain sexual troubles are sexual problems and that the solution to those problems resides primarily in changes in individual conduct. Indeed, they share an underlying cultural theory about the nature of sexuality, though they use a somewhat different terminology to describe the origins and expression of sexual conduct.

Sacred and secular conflict about sexuality is rooted in the historical and cultural development of the United States and is present in all contemporary public debates about all aspects of sexual life. That is, it is not possible to have a *public policy* debate about "risky sex"; pornography; child abuse; sex before, outside of, between, and after marriage; sexual techniques; and so forth without this conflict being engaged. This same conflict is also present in discussions of the proper role of women in society and issues of reproduction and family life.[1]

It is possible for a purely secular scientific discussion of the sexual to go forward in the United States only by ignoring or setting aside discussion of the attitudes of dominant religious traditions toward the sexual. Even as such points of view are desacralized by being treated as secular data for purposes of scientific inquiry (i.e., the measure of serious religious belief may be tapped by survey questions that ask about "frequency of church attendance," "devoutness of religious feeling," or whether a respondent has been "born again"), such points of view must be engaged as social realities when public policies are proposed. Indeed, it is the secularization of religious belief as just another belief system by the relativistic social sciences that fundamentally conflicts with notions of a sacred and transcendent realm of sexual meanings and values.

Even though there is a cleavage between the sacred and scientific theorizing of the sexual, the secular traditions themselves cannot be treated as a uniform and coherent body of theories, methods, and findings. It should be recognized that within the secular scientific study of sexuality there are profound conflicts between the disciplinary entities that claim the right to study and, in some cases, manage sexuality. These conflicts are both methodological and theoretical and as a consequence different disciplines treat different sexual troubles as problems and propose different solutions for them. Perhaps the penultimate cleavage in the sciences (the ultimate cleavage is between dogma-based and data-based explanations of the sexual) is between theories of sexual life based on nature or nurture, between the biology of the organism or the social and cultural environment. This contemporary debate has been shaped by the century-long conflict between theorists within biology and medicine who have emphasized the priority of reproduction and the importance of innate sexual drives or impulses in the organization of sexual activity, and theorists who have emphasized the role of non-reproductive purposes in sexuality and the priority of culture and society in determining the organization of sexual conduct. This debate has theoretical aspects, but it is primarily about the historical role of biology and medicine (now biomedicine) in supporting the repression of sexual diversity and in constituting sexuality as illness.[2]

This introduction has offered a number of ideas in a general fashion that are the basis of the remainder of this paper. The paper begins with a consideration of how a sexual *trouble* becomes a sexual *problem;* that is, the ways in which a multipotential and diffuse issue becomes defined as a well-defined problem which has to be ameliorated by changes in individual or collective behavior. This definitional process, which depends on the explicit or implicit use of sexual theory, is usually accompanied by extensive specialized institution building and correlative claims for resource allocation. In this process theoretical work becomes embedded in institutional and disciplinary practice.

Institutional and disciplinary practice are the subject of the second and third sections of the paper, which are concerned with the interaction between institutionally embedded disciplinary theories which are treated as abstractions and the concrete problems at which they are directed. These two sections ask the question What kinds of sex are defined as risky and why? In these sections the historical and ideological situation of sexual theorizing is addressed in terms of the boundaries that are set on theorizing by external forces. In the fourth section, I discuss how specific forms of scientific sexual theorizing are privileged by their similarity to vernacular sexual theories, both those of individual actors and the stories that are told by the media. In the fifth section I propose some alternative sexual theories which direct our attention away from vernacular and media-based theories and away from the individual as the site of sexual theories, sexual problems, and sexual policy. The paper concludes with a cautionary note about the dense social and cultural context in which sexual theorizing goes forward and how this context should be taken into account in explaining sexual conduct, identifying sexual problems, and constructing sexual policies. In this caution I discuss problems of social policy and how policies themselves produce problems.

The *practice of theorizing about sex* exists in an arena of conflict both within a single secular discipline, between secular scientific disciplines, and between the secular scientific tradition and other contenders for the right to manage our sexual lives. Theorizing about sex is not an abstract process, separated in time and space from the messier aspects of social life, but is an ideological practice grounded in the conflicts of particular historical moments and cultural situations. One can act "as if" such theorizing is solely a scientific activity only at the price of increasing the problematic status of sexuality.

Is There a Problem in This Trouble?

What stance should we take toward a *trouble* when it is presented to us as a *problem?* The distinction made here is between something that is *troubling* (we wake up with a pain in our lower back) and our treating our pain in our lower back as the symptom of a identifiable problem (e.g., sciatica or arthritis) which requires that we call a physician to do something about it. The situation of a young girl having a baby out of wedlock is directly *troubling* to her, her family, the young man involved and his family, and perhaps to the baby and others implicated in the event. A young man dies of a new virus after having passive anal sex with a number of male partners. This is directly *troubling* to the young man, his sexual partners, his friends, his family, and a variety of others in his social network. Doing something about these troubles means *identifying* (in the taxonomic sense of classifying) the *trouble* as a *specific type of problem* and calling upon *specific experts with expert knowledge* (persons with theories or theory stories) embedded in *particular social institutions* to *provide a solution.*

Clearly the first issue to be considered is whether this particular *trouble* should rise to the level of a *problem.* This choice is pre-theoretical, at least in the formal sense that theory is used within a disciplinary context. However, a pre-theoretical choice is a necessary step in the process of fully understanding the context in which "disciplinary theorizing" resides. What I am expressing here is a recognition that this pre-theoretical choice is part of a sequence of often unanalyzed decisions that lead to the assignment of "the trouble as problem" to a specific disciplinary matrix. These pre-theoretical choices are essential to understanding the larger social situation in which "theory" is elaborated and applied.

This first choice requires a certain amount of delicacy, perhaps even caution, since deciding that a trouble is a problem of a specific kind will unleash a whole series of theoretical, data-gathering, and policy consequences. This decision is often extra-scientific because it involves asking two sorts of political or ideological questions: the first about individual and collective actors, the second about the cultural climate in which the translation from trouble to problem is made. The first sort of questions are often ruled to be out of court or illegitimate or ad hominum within scientific discourse since they raise questions about the motivations or interests (as individuals, members of social groups, or organizations) of those who have identified this *trouble* as a *problem* that merits a solution. The question of how the promoters of the problem (i.e., problem-identifying entrepreneurs) will profit (and not only in filthy lucre) must always be considered when public attention is called to "a problem that needs solution" (Nathanson, 1991; Becker, 1973).

The second sort of questions are similar, but they focus on the cultural context in which the questions are formulated. A question such as Do individuals vary in their propensities to engage in risky sexual conduct? is already ideological. Why do we start with individuals and propensities? What is it about "individuals," "internal propensities," "risk," and "sex" that seem to go so naturally together? Is there a prejudice in the culture (note here my view that all cultural arrangements are pre-judgments) that links together "individuals," "internal states," "sex," and "risk"? That is, is there a certain way that is *good to think* about these issues in the vernacular culture and the culture as represented by the media? Given the larger cultural prejudice about how to think about a question, is there then a particular "scientific" discipline that is more easily selected to think about this question because its pre-judgments conform to the larger cultural pre-judgments?

The question Is this trouble a problem? cannot be answered without asking *Who* says that this trouble is a problem of a certain kind?, *What* kind of a problem is it said to be? and, if it is an ongoing problem, *Who* has been previously authorized to provide a solution? Any trouble, no matter how novel it appears to be, can be fitted into any previously existing problem-solving apparatus, since as soon as the trouble is assigned to such an apparatus, the apparatus will begin to shape the trouble into the kind of problem that it can manage. Even if a trouble would be better left alone or treated as a different kind of problem, the individuals and institutions which are assigned to deal with the trouble will turn it into a problem for which they have the tools.

The decision that certain kinds of troubles are problems is often taken too quickly; these troubles are usually assigned willy-nilly to individuals and institutions that appear to be appropriate.[3] It is rarely understood that the decision to assign a trouble to a particular problem-solving institution is not a neutral process, but one that ineluctably molds the trouble to conform to whatever problem the selected institution or discipline solves best. To choose whether troubling drug use is a crime problem or a health problem calls into play different social institutions with different problem-solving methods and capacities and different public constituencies and media representations (see the current debate over efficacy of the War on Drugs). Similarly, to decide that a problem is appropriate to one or another scientific discipline elicits the kinds of pre-judgments that constitute the cognitive and material bases for that scientific discipline. The decision that a particular trouble is a psychological, sociological, or an economics problem results in calling forth the appropriate disciplinarian in the expectation that he or she will use their understandings of the world to solve the problem. To those armed with a hammer, the environment has nails in abundance.

This rule-bound response is necessary if there is be a scientific discipline, that is, if advantage is to be taken of what Kenneth Burke once called the "bureaucratization of the imaginative" (Burke, 1973.) The only reason the scientific work of others is trusted is the belief that they have obeyed the rules of their discipline in designing instruments, in making observations, and in grounding their explanations. They must be disciplined members as well as members of a discipline. Shared instrumentation, observations, and explanations are what Thomas Kuhn labeled a paradigm. A paradigm is more than a set of ideas; it is a set of stable social practices that come into play when a trouble is defined as a problem of a given kind appropriate to a certain discipline (Kuhn, 1962). It is thus more than a set of individual practices, it is a set of social practices (which include specific explanatory stories or narratives) that characterize an ongoing collectivity of actors.

Members of a scientific discipline tell disciplined stories (i.e., specific genres of tales) to each other about the problems of their disciplines in seminars, grant applications, peer-reviewed journals, and published books (Plummer, 1995). Out of this constant chattering and scribbling a community of thought is sustained, something Ludwig Fleck called seventy years ago a "thought-collective" with a characteristic "thought-style" (Fleck, 1979). Aspirants to membership in these scientific collectives are "disciplined" to conduct themselves in ways that their ancestors (i.e., mentors) behaved by attending graduate school and writing dissertations. The stories and practices that constitute the disciplines have large areas of agreement and some small areas of difference, what Kuhn labeled normal science (Kuhn, 1962). Across divides of greater or lesser intellectual distance, scientific disciplines reproduce themselves and instruct their members about how to imagine the social world differently (it is the difference that creates the discipline). These disciplines are of course more than "thought-collectives," they are also departments, institutes, and centers with office space, names on doors, persons with differing ranks and honors, laboratories, assistants, grants, budgets—all of the material paraphernalia of job spaces. The "thought" and the stories are embodied in lives, in careers, in getting ahead, even in getting replaced. It is this shared thought and materiality that constitute the resistance to interdisciplinarity and to wild hypotheses.

However necessary these disciplines may be for normal science, they also need to be resisted, primarily because within these disciplines rests the power to construct a specific kind of problem out of a diffuse trouble. Once a trouble is defined as a problem appropriate to a discipline, there is a significant narrowing of the possibilities of thought. Hence in the opening moments, as a trouble is being turned into a problem, there should be a pause. A distinguished theoretician and field researcher in ecology, a field similar to sociology in the fundamentally historical character of its subject matter, once said that the most profitable way to think about troubles was analogous to untangling a knot in a line of rope. He said that, "The best procedure should be pick up the knot and gently shake it, the worst procedure would be pull aggressively on the loose ends" (Slobodkin, 1972, 1999).[4] This metaphor is exactly right; once a tangle has been identified as a potential trouble, then it is best to proceed tentatively, perhaps even agnostically, to determine what kind of tangle you have in hand and how best to comprehend it.

This procedure of problem identification (in the sense of deciding is there a problem and what kind of problem is it) has parallels to the "holism" arguments of Kenneth Burke about essentializing and proportionalizing strategies in literary interpretation. He writes:

> The tendency in Freud is toward [the essentializing strategy]. That is, if one found a complex of, let us say, seven ingredients in a man's motivation, the Freudian tendency would be to take one of these as the essence of the motivation and to consider the other six as sublimated variants. We could imagine, for instance, manifestations of sexual impotence accompanying a conflict in one's relations with his familiars and one's relations at the office. The proportional strategy would involve the study of these three as a cluster. The motivation

would be synonymous with the interrelationships among them. But the essentializing strategy would, in Freud's case, place the emphasis upon the sexual manifestation, as causal ancestor of the other two. The essentializing strategy is linked with a normal ideal of science: "to explain the complex in terms of the simple." (Burke, 1973, pp. 261–262)

Burke goes on to point out that it is actually the complex which needs explaining and it is unclear whether the complex can be reassembled from the simplified scientized bits. The level of organization of the problem may resist interpretations that break it into elementary parts or primitive relations. After we dissect the frog, we should not be surprised that it does not croak.

The process of untangling the knot by gently shaking it or resisting the impulse to interpret a complex problem in simple ways does not produce "theories," but it does express attitudes or stances toward what are offered to us as "problems" that need to be theorized. What these attitudes or stances entail, to use Burke again, is a "tolerance for ambiguity" (Burke, 1984). Thus the first step in a process of theorizing or problem solving is to take a step backward, to disengage from the definition of the problem as first offered. The first questions should not be What kind of a problem is this (according to my expertise) and what is the theory that is appropriate (according to my expertise)? This is the equivalent to pulling vigorously on the free strands of the tangled rope, a choice that may lead to having to cut the resulting knot with a sword. Shaking the tangle gently is equivalent to asking some or all of the following kinds of questions: Is this a problem? Who says so? What are their interests in defining this trouble a problem? What evidence do they provide that this is a problem? What solutions have they put forth? Who will profit from these solutions? Who is praised and who is blamed in the stories they tell about this problem? The first response should be to problematize how the trouble was made a problem.

Disciplinary Theory and Concrete Circumstances

To properly understand the scientific question Why do individuals vary in their propensities to engage in risky sex? requires additional steps backward or, perhaps, sideways. In disciplinary terms this formulation is a psychological question; it concerns the conduct of individuals and will require the measurement of internal states of individuals. It falls directly into the tradition of individual difference research, that is, research which examines the differential response of individuals to what appears to be a common environmental circumstance. As a question in the mainstream of psychological imagining it is highly abstract, ahistorical, and acultural. The question is posed universally and makes a number of assumptions about each of the elements in its question. It assumes that single individuals are proper units of assessment and the locus of agency, that propensities are the basis for conduct, that the calculus of risk can be measured, and that certain forms of sex are risky.

The problem as stated already invites a limited range of solutions, disciplinary and otherwise. It assumes a certain level of analysis; in Burke's terms, individuals and their propensities are the essentialized mode of interpretation, they are the causal agents. Such an individualized interpretation, to use Ken Plummer's recent formulations, demands a certain kind of story in which the outcomes will be based on individual differences, either psychological or moral (Plummer, 1995). Finally, the question conflates two important domains of action, both replete with historical and cultural implications—risk and sex. How immediately we are engaged with this question, in terms of personal biography (Who has not had sex, who has not taken a risk?), career (Do our answers generate grants and promotions?), and the practices of our disciplines (How does what we know digest this problem?), all suggests that we are on dangerous ground. Now is the time to take the step backward or sideways, to count to ten or a hundred, to become tentative.

Questions need to be raised about the question—why do we want to explain or theorize the intersect between risk and sex? What persons have called our attention to the intersect between risk and sex and what are their interests in doing so? The answers to these questions require lowering the level of abstraction, turning our attention away from the "experts" and their theorizing in quiet rooms, disturbed only by the hum of the fluorescent lights and computer fans, to the everyday world in which risk and sex appear to fuse together.

The problem of risk and sex as a secular scientific problem has been primarily generated by experts in public health (and other associated medical researchers), community activists, research funders, and other interested elites worried about the potential transmission of HIV. The concrete problem as specified by the psychologists, epidemiologists, and physicians who dominated the National Institutes of Health Consensus Panel on HIV Prevention is How do we understand and, by implication, prevent *individuals,* both infected and uninfected, from engaging in those forms of sexual conduct that are most likely to transmit HIV (National Institutes of Health, 1997)? The focus on "risk" of transmission or "risky behaviors" is in fact a novel formulation, since it takes the prevalence or incidence of risky behaviors as a proxy for risk of transmission. Given the near-fatality of HIV/AIDS and the lack of treatments for AIDS (prior to the use of the new anti-viral therapies in the 1990s), it is not surprising that the proof of success in prevention has moved away from measuring the reduction in numbers of transmissions to the reduction of risky behaviors.

This decision was also influenced by the realities that new transmissions are rare in most regions in the United States, and to focus on hard-to-measure rare events would reduce the authority of the public health message. Measuring and reporting that reported condom use is rising or declining is far easier than measuring and reporting the rate of new infections that might be the result of that condom use or non-use (or of other unmeasured variables). This represents a movement away from end-state measures of identifiable disease events (how many infections are prevented) to end-state behavioral measures that are often only weakly related to disease transmission. The success of the public health institutions concerned with HIV/AIDS in moving attention toward risky behaviors is part of a more general dependence in health research on the use of behavior change as a proxy for changes in rates of morbidity and mortality. This same question is asked by similar, but not overlapping, interest groups about risk and sexuality in young women (more rarely about young men). How do we prevent young women from engaging in those risky forms of sexual conduct that are likely to result in pregnancy?

This similarity in abstract problem formulation makes it appear that all of the players in these two arenas of problem identification and problem solving (HIV prevention and adolescent pregnancy prevention) have similar theories of why individuals take risks with their sexuality or what might be done to prevent these risky outcomes. However, those who "theorize" risk and sexuality in these two domains do so in the context of an ongoing political struggle about the meaning and value of sexuality itself. The *concrete* question (as opposed to the abstract question) asked by the public health/behavioral science/gay community constituencies in the area of HIV prevention is Why do some men who have sex with men and some injection drug users and their sexual partners differ from other persons in the same class of actors in their propensity to have unprotected penetrative sex (anal or vaginal sex) when they know that the risk of transmission of the HIV virus (and other STIs) is increased? The *concrete* question asked by the parallel public health/population control community in the area of adolescent pregnancy prevention is Why do some young women differ from other young women in their propensity to have un-contracepted penile-vaginal sex when they know that the risk of unwanted pregnancy is increased? (See any issue of the journal *Family Planning Perspectives*.) This concreteness can be increased by specifying that these questions are being asked about specific gendered, raced, and classed sets of actors in the United States in the 1990s whose sexual conduct has already been the subject of years of scientific, political, and ideological dispute.

These two formulations share a common moral presumption: that at least in some cases the sexual conduct is legitimate, that what makes the sex risky is the failure to take precautions. No member of the secular HIV/AIDS prevention constituencies argues that gay men should not have sex at all. While numbers of partners, oral sex, and drug use are often worrisome to certain "absolute zero transmission" constituencies, it is usually not that having sex is thought to be risky; it is the lack of precautions that creates the risk (i.e., driving is not risky, driving without a seatbelt or while drinking is risky). A somewhat different picture emerges among the public health/population control/adolescent health constituencies that are interested in preventing adolescent pregnancy. In this example youthful sex is usually viewed ambivalently, most often as an unpreventable, but rarely virtuous, aspect of young people's growing up. Abstinence would be best, it is often argued, but given that it is unlikely in many cases, successful contraception is better than unwanted births. Practically no one argues that an active sex life is a good in the lives of young people. Even the Sexuality Information and Education Council of the United States (SIECUS) says that it agrees with the idea of abstinence. In this example "risky sex" is both the inability to avoid sex (which is defined as penile-vaginal intercourse) and the inability to use contraception that generates the risk.[5]

The other political and ideological contenders in the HIV and pregnancy prevention domains (i.e., conservative political and religious elites and their constituencies) agree that it is the individual with certain propensities who is at fault in the transmission of HIV and adolescent pregnancy. However, the risk is not the absence of precautions, but the doing of sex. Individuals who are unable to control their sexual impulses, either because they are somehow perverted (i.e., homosexuals) or are simply untutored in proper techniques of restraint (either this-worldly or other-worldly in origin), put themselves at risk of being damned as well as of being vulnerable to disease or pregnancy. Conservative elites, advocates for the traditional family, and members of the religious right (often the same individuals) focus on eliminating "deviant" sexuality. They argue, correctly, that once this goal is accomplished HIV transmission (as well as other STIs) and adolescent pregnancy will simply disappear. Even if those who are HIV positive do not behave safely in all instances, those infections would be eliminated in a generation under such a sexual regime.

To a remarkable degree these two major contenders in the struggles for HIV prevention share a number of theoretical cum ideological commonalities—it is the individual and his or her propensities that are at issue. In the minds of the public and the sexual health establishment it is a question of rational versus irrational action: Do individuals calculate risk properly according to the public health actuarial table and do they act on that calculus? Among the religious conservatives the problem is the issue of moral versus immoral action: Do people properly observe the moral rules that should govern the sexual? Both groups also agree that "sex" is hard to control and is often out of control—they differ, though not as much as one might think, about whether sex itself is a problem or a natural manifestation of human development.

The disciplinary theoretical question Why do individuals differ in their propensities to engage in risky sex? is thus directly abstracted from certain concrete situations involving everyday actors. Why do gay men have unsafe penetrative sex with other men which increases the likelihood of disease transmission? Why do injection drug users have unsafe penetrative sex with their sexual partners which could result in disease transmission? Why do young men and women have un-contracepted sex which could result in pregnancy? What these questions have in common in terms of risk and sex is that the conduct of these individuals can be interpreted as the voluntary outcome of a ratiocinative process. Not conforming to the rational calculus of safe sex can be attributed to failures of learning, the interposition of other values or preferences, or irrationalities induced by sexual desires or behavior-altering chemicals.

Not All Dangerous Sex Is "Risky Sex"

This theoretical connection that is made between "individuals," "propensities," "risk," and "sex" in the domains of HIV/AIDS and adolescent pregnancy cases would be more persuasive if such a connection were applied more generally to other areas of sexuality in which there are easily identified dangers.[6] However, in two other important areas of sexuality a previously held theoretical connection between individual agency and risky sexual conduct has been rejected. The first is in the explanations of sexual violence against women and girls (including sexual harassment) and the second in the explanations of the sexual abuse of children and adolescents. In both of these areas prior explanations of at least some of these occurrences (described as "rape" and "child molestation" in the criminological literature) focused on the role of the woman or child in provoking these events. The question was posed What propensities make a woman or a child put themselves at risk for dangerous sex? The resulting theoretical questions, which directly parallel the questions Why do gay men differ among themselves in their propensity to engage in risky sex that transmits HIV? and Why do adolescent girls differ among themselves in their propensity to engage in risky sex that results in inappropriate pregnancies? can no longer be asked.

Consider the following formulations: Why do women and girls differ among themselves in their propensity to engage in or expose themselves to risky sex? and Why do children differ among themselves in their propensity to engage in sexual contacts with adults?

These are questions that are no longer *good to think,* though they were once thought regularly by scientists who published their research in the scientific literature and remain extant sexual theories in some vernacular cultures. In a recent edition of the *New York Times* there was a report of a gang rape of one 12-year-old and two 13-year-old runaway girls by a group of 20 men in Fresno, California. It appears from the press report that the rape was planned. A young man who promised to drive the girls to their homes delivered them to a motel room where the other men were waiting. After the event reached the press, a rape crisis center reported receiving the following calls:

> [T]he director (of the center) . . . said people had called her office asking if the girls had been wearing sexy clothing or if they had done something to provoke the attack. One man called to say that because the girls had walked into the motel room, it was not fair to call it rape. ("Gang Rape of Three," p. A18)

Not very long ago, the concept of "rape-proneness" or "rape provocation" was a well-accepted concept in the scientific, legal, media, and legal discussions of the causes of rape. How the woman was dressed, whether she was drinking, whether she was alone ("alone" meaning without a male escort) in an inappropriate place, her prior sexual relationship to the person or persons accused, or her entire prior sexual history were elements to be assessed in deciding whether she was a woman who had differential propensities to expose herself to risky sexual situations.

Much of the post-feminist scientific literature about rape has been an attempt to identify these once-respected "scientific" ideas as part of a widely accepted cultural syndrome of rape myths (this exposure of science as ideology is similar to the early feminist critique of "natural" gender differences; Sanday, 1996; Roberts & Mohr, 1994; Baron & Straus, 1989; Holmstrom & Burgess, 1978). Social scientists no longer include the question Does an individual who has been sexually assaulted differ in his or her propensities to engage in risky sex? in the class of questions they ask about sexual violence. It does, however, remain a legitimate question in courts of law where lawyers feel free to theorize in ways that are not permitted in many other venues.

A similar transformation has occurred in the area of adult-child sexual contacts which is now universally labeled child sexual abuse; often with the definition of "child" ranging upward to age 17 in scientific reports (La Fontaine 1990; Driver & Droisen, 1989; Finkelhor,

1986; Li, West, & Woodhouse, 1990).[7] Thus in contemporary media and vernacular versions of child sexual abuse stories the child is conventionally thought of as being "at risk" of abuse by certain classes of adult actors, often persons who are strangers to the child and who have prior records of sexual offenses. The child in these stories is not thought of as capable of "taking risks" as a result of internal propensities. This, of course, has not always been so. From the 1930s to 1950s there was a genre of "expert" stories about adult-child sexual contacts that proposed that children played a significant role by provoking such contacts. The "seductive" or "flirtatious" child might engage in provocative behavior (perhaps not even for sexual motives) that induced a vulnerable adult to act out sexually (see Gagnon, 1965 for a review).

That story was rooted in the psychoanalytic doctrines of the sexualized child and in other elements of middle European high cultural thought about the sexualized pre-adolescent (Werkner, 1994). Such a risk story is no longer possible on primarily ideological or political grounds. The dominant contemporary narrative assumes the child to be entirely reactive and a victim of uncontrolled adult sexual interests. While such a narrative often ignores expert knowledge about the ongoing social relationships that usually exist between abused children and the adults who abuse them, the idea of a more proactive, though not necessarily sexual, role on the part of the child cannot be discussed (Laumann, Gagnon, Michael, & Michaels, 1994).

It is apparent from these examples that only *some* important concrete instances of the intersect between risk and sex can be used to test a theory about how individual differences produce differences in sexual risk taking. Clearly gay men, individuals who are IV drug users, and teenage girls can fall into the imaginary domain of those who are more likely to have "risky sex." The point here is that only certain kinds of actors are assumed to be agentive in sexual matters, to possess propensities that increase their likelihood to put themselves at sexual risk. The instability of what it is possible to think suggests a deep connection between what it is possible to theorize and the cultural and historical context in which the theory is proposed.

At the present moment, although a strong theoretical argument exists that the sexual conduct of adolescent girls (including those who are 18 and 19) can be understood as risk taking, it is clear that recent trends in research and policy making seek to alter this conception. The "discoveries" that pregnant adolescent girls in clinical samples report having been "victims" of child sexual abuse more often than never-pregnant controls or that girls in other studies report that they have more often had sex with considerably older men may undermine the conception that such girls have differential internal propensities to engage in risky sex (unless one wants to argue that they had earlier propensities to be victims of child abuse or to have sex with older men) (Lindberg, Sonenstein, Ku, & Martinez, 1997; Luster and Small, 1997; Stock, Bell, Boyer, & Connell, 1997). The authors of these studies argue that the degree to which the sexual acts of the girls in this social group were voluntary was severely reduced by their prior or contemporary victimization. In this scenario the question becomes Do individuals have prior predisposing experiences that increase the likelihood that they will be unable to prevent exposures to risky sex?

These prior considerations raise an important question about the cultural conception of the sexuality of gay men and adolescent young women (particularly young women of color) that makes them vulnerable to certain kinds of theories about their behavior; theories which argue that they have either some defect in character or possess certain psychological propensities that result in engaging in risky sex. Other persons, women and girls who have been sexually assaulted or children who have had sexual contacts with adults, are exempted from such explanations by virtue of a specific claim to "victim" status. This is not to argue that the latter two groups should not be treated as victims, but rather to suggest that the scientific hypothesis about the relation between individuals, propensities, risk, and sex is a culturally restricted one. One question we could ask about sex and risk in the exploratory phase of our investigations might be Why is it good to think about gay men and adolescent women in this fashion and bad to think in the same way about those who have been sexually assaulted or molested? The answer to such a question would necessarily involve the issue of agency and who has it, whether the propensities to take risks are the same in all groups, whether risks are gauged in the same way by various actors, and whether all sex has similar risks associated with it.

Scientific and Vernacular Theories

It should be clear that the vast majority of theorizing about "risky sex" takes place outside of the domain of scientifically authorized theorizers about risk, sex, and risky sex. These are the vernacular theories and explanations about risky sex which are embedded in the everyday sex-and-risk stories that people tell each other.[8] Such vernacular theories can be found in everyday conversations and gossip as individuals talk to various audiences about what is happening in their personal lives, the lives of persons immediately around them, and the media versions of the stories of the sexually notorious. It is this process of social reproduction through sexual storytelling of all kinds (both within and across generations) which forms the basis for local and ancillary sexual cultures within the dominant culture. Such vernacular sexual stories are not told randomly, but travel through and are conditioned by proximate social networks structured by gender, class, ethnicity, age, and marital status. Who tells what sexual stories to whom is part of scripted nature of social life. Talk shows on the radio and chat rooms on the Internet are modern media formulations of these everyday stories. When such stories are gathered from "respondents" by scientists it is the theories and experiences embedded in these stories which provide the data for the research mills of experts who will fashion their expert theories from the reported grist of everyday life.

It is usually not noted, but all experts on sex and risk were once non-experts on these topics and the personal sex and risk lives of most experts are often not guided by their expertise on these matters. The point is that all experts in a culture were raised with the usual vernacular theories of sex and risk prevalent in their cultures at a given historical moment and had to unlearn or refine these theories in the process of becoming an expert of one sort or another. The vernacular theories known to scientific experts had to be refined or replaced with new theories during their lives as graduate students and as participants in the research process. Few would claim that prior vernacular learning about sex and risk is completely erased by experience with expert representations of sex and risk; indeed, it is probably true that in practice most budding experts on sex and risk have sex-and-risk lives that are much like those who share their educational and social aspirations and experiences. The fact that experts often use their own sex-and-risk autobiographies as ways of understanding the sex-and-risk lives of others (as in the self-stories of risky sexual conduct) suggests that experts are not strangers to the risky sex experiences that others report. Indeed, in order to participate meaningfully with non-expert others in social life, experts may have to act as if they hold the vernacular theories held by their partners in social interaction.

The research mills of experts not only use the stories of risky sex and experiences of everyday folks as "data" to theorize and debate issues of risk and sex with their fellow experts, but these experts also have a variety of opportunities to influence the lives of those who provided the data.

First, the process of higher education influences young people. Previously they were the recipients only of vernacular stories of risky sex (stories which have "theories" of risk and sex embedded in them) that were generated by their parents, their teachers, their religious spokespersons, their peers, and the media; now they are exposed to expert stories of risky sex (and expert theories) in the form of textbooks and lectures. Such expert risky sex theories may even influence (and in certain storytelling situations, replace) various elements of young people's vernacular stories of risky sex and come to be the basis of new vernacular forms.

Second, in the process of policy formation the theories of experts about risky sex are sometimes influential in those social formations that are composed of other experts whose job it is to manage what they view as risky sex and its negative sequelae. Bureaucracies that manage people, e.g., social welfare systems, educational institutions, healthcare corporations, the business community, and the military use some, though not all, of the expert theories about risky sex to support lines of action which are of interest to them. Thus the lives of everyday folks will be impacted by the stories that they have told to experts who have transformed these stories into the basis for social policy.

Third, the stories experts tell about risky sex interface with the media through "science reporting" and interviews with experts and pseudo-experts with varying degrees of storytelling competencies and ideologies. These stories experts tell about risky sex are transmitted through the mass media and may come to influence stories about risky sex in the general public.

In consumer-based infotainment societies stories about risky sex with their embedded theories of sex and risk are retailed each day in all forms of the print and electronic media. Stories about risky sex appear in "news" reports advertisements, advice columns, short stories and novels, talk shows, soap operas (afternoon and evening versions), sitcoms, made-for-TV films, Hollywood movies, and documentaries. No genre is free of the story about risky sex. This massive system of storytelling has an important but complex relationship with the stories of members of the general public and the stories told by experts. In a cheerfully promiscuous and profitable manner the infotainment system calls on the experiences and opinions about risky sex of everyday folks and on the research and talking heads of experts about risky sex and fuses them together with the opinions of news readers and pundits to produce a third force in the telling of stories about risky sex.

What I am describing is a highly conflated storytelling environment with a diverse set of storytellers who tell overlapping, conflicting, and often mendacious stories (usually based on unexamined theories) to serve many different interests. The image of a culture as an ongoing communication machine which is based on producing and reproducing conduct through socially structured storytelling is implicit in the critical work of Kenneth Burke and explicit in some aspects of the sociological work of Nicolas Lumann. Perhaps the most important point is that such a society does not separate "expert" storytelling from vernacular storytelling or media-based storytelling.

This larger context of theorizing has an important implication for theorizing sex and risk within the disciplines. The intimate relationship between individualized explanations of risky sex, explanations of risky sex given in vernacular cultures, and the explanations given by the mass media profoundly influence the content of expert theories. In each of these overlapping domains there is a cultural prejudgment that it is the individual who is the primary causal agent of risk and sex. This overlap means that scientific theory of the relation between risk and sex is not free of bias and prejudgment.

Individual and Social Theories of Risky Sex

It is clear from the foregoing discussion that the formulation of the concrete questions about the sexual conduct of some gay men and some teenage girls—Why do individuals differ in their propensities to engage in risky sex?—carries a good deal of cultural baggage in the United States. This is a culture which treats many forms of conduct, most commonly those that are stigmatized, as matters of successes or failures of individual self-control.[9] The consequence for problem identification and problem solving is that morality tales of internal struggles against temptation are isomorphically mapped over by the scientific categories of individualistic psychology. That individuals who do not succeed in avoiding "risky sexual conduct" differ in some internal characteristics from those who do is a view held by the person in the street, the mass media, religious tradition, medical belief, economic theory, political rhetoric, and individualistic psychology. The fact that there are unexamined exemptions made in this formulation of the relation between risk and sex does not change this nearly hegemonic cultural view of the relation between risk and sex.

Alternative theories of both sex and risk are often hard to propose (and harder to sell) in such an environment. In a recent lecture sociologist-historian Charles Tilly argued that cultural elites and everyday people in most societies support certain kinds of widely held stories (what were once called zeitgeists or worldviews) which justify taken-for-granted courses of action or explanations of conduct (Tilly, forthcoming). Tilly was referring to the stories held and retold by everyday citizens and elites about the origins of their nation (he was referring to Canada) and he argued that sociological stories of a structural sort which contradicted stories of great men and important events were not easily assimilated into national tale telling. So it is with both risk and sexuality in the United States. Pointing to the structural or contextual variables that might create the separate and joint situations of sexuality and risk taking requires explanations that do not implicate the individual or that implicate the differences between individuals only within narrow contexts of action. As a consequence such explanations do not easily fit into the taken-for-granted and dominant explanations of risk and sexuality in the society.

What this suggests is that where an explanation starts in the continuum from gene to individual to small group to the macro-structure of society has important consequences in terms of theory, data gathering, and policy recommendations. The selection of this starting point depends on the cultural perspectives of the society and the theoretical orientations of the specific discipline. In "individual difference" research one starts with the conduct of individuals and works back into the mental life of individuals to identify those internal propensities that might account for the different behavioral outcomes. While some environmental variables, both historical and current, might be included in the analysis (e.g., birth order in the explanation of "homosexuality" or alcohol use in the explanation of unsafe sex) the historical variables are assumed to have been internalized by the individual in such a way that they have become propensities for current actions and the situational variables are treated as evidence of other propensities (e.g., alcohol use is further evidence of risk-taking propensities or disinhibition). The locus of explanation or the potential for behavioral change is internal to the individual. The larger social, cultural, and historical factors are usually treated as relatively constant or primarily operative through the individual. In general the psychologist of individual differences starts with the individual and works her or his way out from the interior of the individual to local contexts of action and assumes that the individual has the ability to choose one line of conduct or another.

Structural and cultural forms of explanation start at the levels of organization that are far removed from the individual level and seek explanations of variations in individual conduct in the constraints and opportunities offered individuals by the world around them. The patterns of conduct (including those of sexuality and risk taking) displayed by individuals are the result of growing up in a specific socially structured milieu in a given historical and cultural situation. The search for explanation often starts at a level distant from the individual (e.g., Is the economy capitalist or socialist? or Is the health care system dominated by fee-for-service or health maintenance organizations or by the state?) and the theorist works his or her way back toward the individual. It is not that individual agency does not count, but that the preexisting social and cultural world constrains forms of sexuality, forms of risk taking, and the relationship between those two factors (Campenhoudt, Cohen, Guizzardi, & Hauser, 1997; Singer, 1998).

Theoretically working from structure and culture to the individual enables us to identify additional sources of "causation" and additional opportunities to change individual conduct by changing elements of the environment rather than propensities of individuals. In the case of risky sex and HIV transmission such sources of policy change can range from providing free needles (thus reducing sexual transmission from injection drug users [IDUs] to their sexual partners and children) to legalizing gay marriage (for needle exchange see Normand, Vlahov, & Moses, 1995). Neither of these policies directly depends on changing the sexual or risk-taking propensities of individuals, though these individual propensities may change in new environments.

Structural and cultural analyses provide alternative environmental explanations of what is considered "risky sexual conduct" in other arenas of sexual conduct. An analysis of the work situation of commercial sex workers suggests that the risks to which women in this industry are exposed in most countries are related to the criminalized and man-dominated contexts in which they work. Many sex workers are harassed and exploited by agents of the criminal justice system, public health workers, clients, pimps and other "managers," and middle-class profiteers who own the work sites in which the trade is practiced. Women who work through escort services are in less danger of exploitation than women who work on the street, in bars, in bordellos, or in most red-light districts. Thus the problem of risk associated with sex is not dependent on the internal propensities of the women to take risks, but is associated with the environments in which sex work takes place. The most recent United Nations recommendations on controlling HIV transmission among sex workers in the third world recognize how important these factors are in exposing sex workers to risk, recommendations that could be extended to sex workers in the first world as well (Joint UN Programme on HIV/AIDS, 1999).

Structural and cultural theories of sexuality provide a movement away from differences among individual actors toward the ways in which the environments for sexual action are organized by the social, economic, and political structures and the cultural meaning systems of the society. This disciplinary perspective moves the attention of the theorist away from the individual to those processes and structures which offer opportunities and constraints on sexual action. Theorizing at this level changes the policy levers that can be pushed and pulled to get the outcomes that are desired. The possibility or impossibility of changing policy at the collective level also teaches us about the actual environments in which sexuality goes forward and how it is associated with risk. If condoms are not easily accessible in the high schools (a structural variable) then the riskiness of sexuality for students in those schools differs from those of students in schools where they are available (Jonson & Stryker, 1993). Similarly, if a society creates opportunities for responsible sexuality for its youth and supports that sexuality structurally, the riskiness of sex for young people is reduced. Propensities to take risks which are attributed to the individual are in fact responses of individuals to the riskiness of the environments in which they operate.

Theorizing sex and risk from a structural or cultural perspective also allows (though it does not guarantee) a more holistic perspective which includes the agentive actor but does not make assumptions about causal priority of the individual. The actions of an individual are examined first from the point of view of the settings in which the actions take place. The problem of risk often resides in the setting and individuals may have little choice about whether to be in such a setting or not. Changing the level of risk may involve changes in the setting rather than changes in the individual. Treating the problem of risky sex as a property of the individual often simply blames the individual for structural conditions about which they can do nothing. In this way the situation is justified by placing the blame for risk taking on the individuals in the situation.[10]

The difficulty of applying structural theories and solutions to identified problems which are supra-individual is more than a question of ideology or cultural beliefs. Ongoing social problems and the ongoing solutions applied to those problems involve important stakeholders who have material interests in the problems, in the solutions, and in the cultural beliefs about the problem. Identifying those who profit from a problem, from its solutions, or from cultural beliefs about the problem means that powerful interest groups are mobilized against such alternative theories. Structural change involves changing ongoing social arrangements which benefit, in a variety of ways, interested individuals and organizations. Treating teen pregnancy as a problem caused by poverty, a lack of jobs, racial inequality in the imprisonment of young men, and the lack of availability of birth control and sex education requires a change in focus to matters of residential segregation (Massey & Denton, 1993), urban poverty (Wilson, 1990; Wilson, 1996), the War on Drugs (Bertram, 1996; Goode, 1997), and political/ideological movements that emphasize absolutist sexual values. Theories that emphasize structure also make poor media stories since they do not focus on praising or blaming individuals. This kind of structural approach does not merely identify "bad guys" but also raises issues about "good guys" whose institutionalized solutions to the problem have become integrated into the problem itself. Thus, in a best-case scenario, incorrect solutions to the problem absorb resources that could be better spent (or left unspent) in other ways; in a worst-case scenario those solutions become self-interested impediments to alternative solutions.

Sexual Theorizing in Social Conte(s/x)t

In the prior sections of this essay I made a number of related arguments that attempt to make the question Why do individuals vary in their propensities to engage in risky sex? problematic in both a pretheoretical and disciplinary theoretical sense. These arguments were:

1. Before a trouble is treated as a problem and assigned to a discipline there is a good deal of pre-theoretical work to be done. This involves an examination of the ideological and political interests of those who propose that this trouble be treated as a problem and the interests of those who are assigned (or volunteer) to deal with it. Since defining a trouble as a problem will nearly always generate proposals to improve the situation by modifying the problem, a cautious approach to problem identification should be taken. This is particularly true since solutions when adopted are rarely evaluated and often become part of a problem. This caution should applied to *all* problem identification, regardless of its social origins or disciplinary orientation.

2. It is important to recognize that when a problem has been defined as belonging to a specific class of problems which are the property of specific disciplines, the problem will become reformulated in the terms routinely available to the specific culture and technology of that discipline. This is true of *all* assignments of a specific problem, or even a general topic (e.g., sexuality, religion, politics), to a specific discipline. Psychologists, sociologists, economists, and anthropologists imagine in different ways and call upon different cultures of explanation both within and outside their disciplines. Theoretical conflicts between disciplines are routine because disciplines are different ways of conceiving and mastering the world.

3. It is necessary to concretize abstract propositions and ask whether the concrete case that is hiding behind the abstract formulation is somehow a *special* case which makes it more amenable to inclusion as an example in the abstract category. Researchers should also seek comparative examples of concrete cases that might be included, but that may be excluded for ideological reasons. It is especially useful if one can find cases that were once included as examples but are no longer so included, or cases that were once excluded but now are included. The changing cultural and historical boundaries and contexts of a theorized category are evidence of the limitations of its claims to universality and generalizability.

4. The selection of what instances can be defined as "risky sex"

from the larger arena of sexual relations that are dangerous to one or another of the participants suggests that there are cultural limitations on theorizing the connection between individual risk taking and sexuality. These constraints on what is good to think in sexual matters demonstrate that the procedures by which disciplines identify problems are not independent of views held by social groups or movements outside of the discipline. Such exogenous influences on scientific choices are of course deeply influential in all social scientific disciplines.

5. The lack of insulation between disciplinary theories of the sexual and the vernacular theories of sexuality held by "the people" in a society and those sexual theories which are represented in the collective culture of modern societies (i.e., the mass media) must be constantly considered. Indeed the everyday sexual stories told by both the "folk," the mass media, and disciplines that are based on individual attributes focus on the lack of self-control exhibited by individuals and the irrationalities of sexual passion as the driving forces for sexual misconduct. In addition, authorized experts about sexuality in a given culture share by reasons of upbringing and sexual histories to a greater or lesser degree the folk beliefs of the culture and are only to a limited extent free of these cultural pre-judgments. These are the cultural underpinnings of the individualistic theories of sexual risk taking, but not necessarily the underpinnings of non-individualistic theories (which are also not free of vernacular and media theories).

Rather than construct local, historically situated, structuralist, or culturalist theories the dominant arguments in this paper have deconstructed individualized, abstract, and universalized theories of sexual conduct. This is because structural or cultural theories, although I prefer them, are often vulnerable in many ways to the same pre-theoretical arguments. A trouble that is defined as a problem appropriate to structuralist theorizing will be reconstituted as a "structural" problem and will be submitted to structuralist explanations and policy making. Structuralists often develop special territorial interests and claims over a problem and become participants in the institutional struggles over resources and rights and honors associated with "solving" the problem. Also structuralists often do not think systematically and comparatively about the historical and cultural situation out of which their theories emerge or their concrete cases are selected. Finally, structuralist and culturalist theorists are often seduced by scientistic claims to the universal applicability of their theories and problem-solving machinery.

Given that structuralist and culturalist theorists of the sexual are vulnerable to many of the ills of individualist theories, why are they preferable? Because such structural and cultural theories *can be* more attentive to the historical and cultural situation of theory building and problem identification and solving. Such theories *can be,* but are not always, more holistic and interactional in their approach. It is also *somewhat* easier for such theories to include more sources of causation. Finally, such theories are preferable because they often go against the grain of accepted theorizing and can offer some resistance to the dominant social, cultural, economic, and political status quo. Once again we are back to a stance which is pre-theoretical.

In sum, science theorizing of sexuality in the social sciences takes place in a contested social and political world with important scientific and non-scientific stakeholders in the outcomes of what theory is chosen to guide what research programs to support what policies. Unlike astronomy, whose starry subject matter is indifferent to the theories of Ptolmey, Galileo, Newton, and Einstein, the people who are the subject matter of sexual theorizing are active, complicit, and resistant participants in the theorizing and policy formation process. Sexual theorizing *is* consequential. It is part of the day-to-day struggle to direct, manage, control and invent human sexuality.

Coda

In this deconstructive exercise readers will note that the focus has been more on sex and less on risk. In part this is a function of what the author knows and what the assignment for the paper was. "Risky sex" represents the overlap in a Venn diagram between the domain of risk and the domain of sex. Most of the argumentation of the paper has addressed this conjunction from the perspective of sexuality. It would be very profitable to approach this conjoint domain from the perspective of risk. For instance, it would be useful to explore how the elite in the society promote and praise risk taking as a useful force in entrepreneurial conduct in the marketplace, in recreational behavior (skiing, surfing, rock climbing, and scuba diving), and in innovative conduct in the arts, science, and technology.

Such an analysis might lead to an assessment of risk management, risk evaluation, and risk allocation in the non-sexual domain and examine how the practices and ideologies involved could provide theoretical and policy alternatives when dealing with risk in sexual matters. For instance, risk is often dealt with in non-sexual domains by insurance or other mechanisms that spread the risk across larger populations. Would it be culturally plausible to "insure" against the negative outcomes of sexual relationships (stalking insurance, divorce insurance, or adultery insurance)? Such considerations may work back toward the sexual, as in the phrase "sexy risk," by asking questions about how the culture makes "risky sex" attractive to various subgroups of the population and how these subgroups are treated when they take such risks (see Vance, 1984).

Acknowledgments

Support for this research was provided by a research leave provided by the College of Arts and Sciences of the State University of New York at Stony Brook and a grant from the Ford Foundation. During the time this work was being completed the author was a consultant at the Center for Health and Policy Research.

REFERENCES

Baron, L., & Straus, M. A. (1989). *Four theories of rape in American society: A state-level analysis.* New Haven, CT: Yale University Press.

Becker, H. S. (1973). *Outsiders: Studies in the sociology of deviance.* New York: Free Press.

Bertram, E. (1996). *Drug war politics: The price of denial.* Berkeley: University of California Press.

Burke, K. (1973). *The philosophy of literary form: Studies in symbolic action.* Berkeley: University of California Press.

Burke, K. (1984). *Permanence and change: An anatomy of purpose.* Berkeley: University of California Press.

Campenhoudt, L. V., Cohen, M., Guizzardi, G., & Hauser, D. (Eds.). (1997). *Sexual interactions and HIV risk: New conceptual perspectives in European research.* London: Taylor and Francis.

Clarke, L. B. (1989). *Acceptable risk? Making decisions in a toxic environment.* Berkeley: University of California Press.

Driver, E., & Droisen, A. (Eds.). (1989). *Child sexual abuse: A feminist reader.* New York: New York University Press.

Finkelhor, D. (1986). *A sourcebook on child sexual abuse.* Beverly Hills: Sage Publications.

Fleck, L. (1979). *Genesis and development of a scientific fact.* Chicago: University of Chicago Press.

Gagnon, J. H. (1965). Female child victims of sex offenses. *Social Problems, 13*(2), 176–192.

Goode, E. (1997). *Between politics and reason: The drug legalization debate.* New York: St. Martin's Press.

Gusfield, J. R. (1996). *Contested meanings: The construction of alcohol problems.* Madison: University of Wisconsin Press.

Gusfield, J. R. (1981). *The culture of public problems: Drinking-driving and the symbolic order.* Chicago: University of Chicago Press.

Heise, L. L. (1995). Violence, sexuality and women's lives. In R. Parker & J. H. Gagnon (Eds.), *Conceiving sexuality: Approaches to sex research in the post modern world* (pp. 109–134). New York: Routledge.

Holmstrom, L. L., & Burgess, A. W. (1978). *The victim of rape: Institutional reactions.* New York: Wiley.

Joint UN Programme on HIV/AIDS. (1999, July). *The UN AIDS Report.*

Jonsen, A. R., & Stryker, J. (Eds.). (1993). *The social impact of AIDS in the United States.* Washington, DC: National Academy Press.

Kuhn, T. S. (1962). *The structure of scientific revolutions.* University of Chicago Press.

La Fontaine, J. S. (1990). *Child sexual abuse.* Cambridge, UK: Polity Press.

Laumann, E. O., Gagnon, J. H., Michael, R., & Michaels, S. (1994). *The social organization of sexuality: Sexual practices in the United States.* Chicago: University of Chicago Press.

Li, C. K., West, D. J., & Woodhouse, T. P. (1990). *Children's sexual encounters with adults.* London: Duckworth.

Lindberg, L. D., Sonenstein, F. L., Ku, L., & Martinez, G. (1997). Age differences between minors who give birth and their adult partners. *Family Planning Perspectives, 29,* 61–66.

Luster, T., & Small, S. A. (1997). Sexual abuse history and number of sex partners among female adolescents. *Family Planning Perspectives, 29,* 204–211.

Massey, D. S., & Denton, N. A. (1993). *American apartheid: Segregation and the making of the underclass.* Cambridge, MA: Harvard University Press.

Nathanson, C. A. (1991). *Dangerous passage: The social control of sexuality in women's adolescence.* Philadelphia: Temple University Press.

National Institutes of Health Consensus Statement. (1997, February 11–13). *Interventions to prevent HIV risk behaviors, 15*(2), 1–41.

Gang Rape of Three Girls Leaves Fresno Shaken, and Questioning. (1998, May 1). *New York Times,* p. A18.

Normand, J., Vlahov, D., & Moses, L. E. (Eds.). (1995). *Preventing HIV transmission: The role of sterile needles and bleach.* Washington, DC: National Academy Press.

Perrow, C. (1984). *Normal accidents.* New York: Basic Books.

Plummer, K. (1995). *Telling sexual stories: Power, change, and social worlds.* London: Routledge.

Roberts, J. V., & Mohr, R. M. (Eds.). (1994). *Confronting sexual assault: A decade of legal and social change.* Toronto: University of Toronto Press.

Sanday, P. R. (1996). *A woman scorned: Acquaintance rape on trial.* New York: Doubleday.

Sanders, S. A., & Reinisch, J. M. (1999). Would you say you had sex if . . . ? *Journal of the American Medical Association, 281*(3), 275–277.

Singer, M. (Ed.). (1998). *The political economy of AIDS.* Amityville, NY: Baywood Publishing Company.

Slobodkin, L. (1972, 1999). Department of Ecology and Evolution, State University of New York at Stony Brook (Personal Communication).

Stock, J. L., Bell, M. A., Boyer, D. K., & Connell, F. A. (1997). Adolescent pregnancy and sexual risk-taking among sexually abused girls. *Family Planning Perspectives, 29,* 200–203, 227.

Tilly, C. (forthcoming). The trouble with stories. In R. Aminzade & B. Pescosolido (Eds.), *Teaching for the 21st Century.* Thousand Oaks, CA: Pine Forge Press.

Vance, C. S. (Ed.). (1984). *Pleasure and danger: Exploring female sexuality.* London: Routledge and Kegan Paul.

Werkner, P. (Ed.). (1994). *Egon Schiele: Art, sexuality, and Viennese modernism.* Palo Alto, CA: Society for the Promotion of Science and Scholarship; Seattle: Distributed by the University of Washington Press.

Wilson, W. J. (1990). *The truly disadvantaged: The inner city, the underclass, and public policy.* Chicago: University of Chicago Press.

Wilson, W. J. (1996). *When work disappears: The world of the new urban poor.* New York: Knopf.

NOTES

1. There is a growing movement in academic circles (primarily in the humanities) to "theorize" sexuality independent of social science fact gathering (which these humanists treat as ideologically suspect). This movement is also anti-dogmatic as well as anti-empirical, which places them in a third intellectual position with reference to sexual theorizing. The existence of postmodernists complicates only the lives of secularists, because of their place in the academy.

2. A deeper and more profound cleavage can be found between the social sciences and sociobiology, a cleavage that is not precisely the same as nurture and nature and lies between an emphasis on *proximate* causes (whether they be biological or social) and an emphasis on what are called *ultimate* causes (which are based on evolutionary principles or the primacy of the gene). A full analysis of the religious character of neo-Darwinian thought in its provision of a guiding principle for human life has not yet been attempted.

3. Lee Clarke points out in his instructive study that a governmental building in New York State in which dioxins (carcinogenic substances) were spread into every nook and cranny by a fire was first assigned to the state agency which was responsible for building cleanliness. The agency promptly sent in unprotected janitors to sweep and dust because the problem was "cleanliness" rather than "decontamination" (Clarke, 1989).

4. Professor Slobodkin (1999) has informed me that the correct quotation is

> To untangle a snarl, loosen all jams or knots and open a hole through the mass at the point where the longest end leaves a snarl. Then proceed to roll or wind through the center exactly as a stocking is rolled up. Keep the snarl open and loose at all times *and* do not pull at the end; permit it to unfold itself. As the process is continued the end gradually emerges. No snarl is too complicated to be solved by this method; only patience is required.

It comes from Clifford W. Ashley, *The Ashley Book of Knots* (NY: Doubleday, 1944); cf. diagram 141 on p. 29, paragraph 141.

5. The systematic use of "sex," "sexually experienced," and "sexually active" to refer only to vaginal intercourse and exclude the repertoire of other sexual techniques used by young people is a conceptual failure that demographers and others who manage teen pregnancy research share with everyday college students. Sanders and Reinisch (1999) report that many contemporary college students do not view oral sex as "real" sex. This emphasis on vaginal intercourse by experts and everyday folks as the primary goal of sexual relationships has unfortunate consequences. By making vaginal intercourse the only form of "real sex" demographers misunderstand the actual complexity of sexual practice in adolescence and they contribute to the simplification of youthful sexuality in the public mind. Finally, by limiting considerations of sex to vaginal intercourse, the pleasures of non-vaginal sex as well as masturbation as alternative appropriate endpoints for sexual pleasure are undermined.

6. In the area of sexuality perhaps the most dangerous sexual practices for women are sexual/affectional and reproductive relationships with men (Heise, 1995). Women are in intermittent danger from men in sexual situations from adolescence to old age. As children and girls they are at risk from heterosexual men who molest them, and as adolescents they are at risk from boys and men who force them to have sex or who have sex with them without protection from pregnancy or disease, and as adolescents and women they are in danger from men who assault them for sexual as well as nonsexual motives. Women are also sexually harassed in the workplace, face the dangers of childbirth as a result of sex with men, and are often left with their children as their spouses leave them to marry younger women. All of these assertions are easily documented, but none of them are interpreted as meaning that "heterosexuality" is a form of risky sex for women.

7. The elasticity of age in these matters is demonstrated by references on the same television news program to Monica Lewinsky as a "girl" of twenty-one, while two boys aged twelve and thirteen, charged with killing four classmates and a teacher, were referred to as "young men." Perhaps news readers do not listen as they speak.

8. How to refer to "the people" is a contentious issue. "The common people" is too archaic and contains the implication that there are "uncommon people" who are somehow better or more knowing than their fellow citizens (recall the phrase: people of the common sort). Folk is not much better and also has the negative racial connotation of *Volk*. In this case the only distinction that is being made is between expert theorists and the theories shared by the "non-expert" people and the mass media. It is clear that the actual *content* of theories held by experts and non-experts is not actually very different except that expert theories are expressed in expert jargon by credentialed speakers.

9. This same prejudice toward blaming the individual can be found in all attributions of cause in accidents. "Human error" is always operator error rather than system designer error, equipment designer or manufacturer error, or errors in the way the system is operated. Such attributions of accident causation to individuals are always profitable in economic and other terms to manufacturers, insurance companies, government regulators, and the like. Attributions of operator error are ways of off-loading the blame and costs of accidents to those who are least able to prevent them. For examples of this practice see Gusfield (1981, 1996) for a discussion of drunken driving and Perrow (1984, pp. 170–231) for discussion of shipping accidents.

10. The argument here is that risk is allocated by social arrangements rather than by individual propensities and that persons at higher risk of nearly all hazards are members of populations who are marginalized in one fashion or another. Such a perspective means that the first recommended policy step would be to change social arrangements and equalize the distribution of risk across the population (to stop red-lining certain social groups). Once this was done it might be appropriate to examine the degree to which there were individual differences in risk taking which could be attributed to "propensities." Examples of the social allocation of risk or the red-lining of certain social groups abound. For instance, in New York City a series of companies that tear down buildings were discovered to have hired homeless men, whom they paid less than minimum wage to tear out asbestos insulation. The men were not informed of the risk, trained to deal with asbestos removal, or provided adequate protective equipment. The problem was only "discovered" when asbestos dust began to threaten non-workers (i.e., the non-homeless or non-marginalized citizens).

Individual Differences in Sexual Risk Taking: A Biopsychosocial Theoretical Approach

JOHN BANCROFT

Introduction

Why is it that some individuals, when faced with a sexual situation which obviously involves risk, continue to engage in the situation whereas others sensibly avoid the risk? This question is central to the current campaigns to change sexual behavior and reduce the likelihood of sexually transmitted diseases, in particular infection with HIV. Intervention programs to prevent HIV risk behavior are proving useful (National Institutes of Health, 1997). A significant proportion of people respond appropriately to them. Others change their behavior without such interventions. However, there remains an important proportion who don't change and who continue with their risky behaviors. What characterizes these individuals, and how can we best conceptualize the processes involved that distinguish between the low risk-taker and the high risk-taker? That is the theoretical objective of this paper. The first part of the paper will focus specifically on sexual risk taking. The second part of the paper presents, briefly, a much broader theoretical framework for understanding human sexuality in an appropriately interdisciplinary fashion in an attempt to convince the reader that the individual-based mechanisms considered in the first part can be situated in the broader socio-cultural context.

Whereas, until now, there has been relatively little relevant behavior change in response to the HIV threat within the heterosexual community, particularly among adolescents (e.g., Poppen & Reisen, 1994), substantial behavioral change has been reported among gay and bisexual men (Becker & Joseph, 1988). In their comprehensive review of longitudinal studies of behavioral change among gay and bisexual men, Becker and Joseph drew the following conclusion: "Even the simplest transmission model suggests that a small group of particularly active individuals may be sufficient to prolong and/or extend the epidemic. The immediate question then becomes why most individuals successfully change their behavior while some others do not. Unfortunately, distressingly little attention has been paid to this central issue. . . . [W]hat is required are vigorous attempts to understand the determinants of AIDS-related behavioral change." Only by increasing such understanding is there likely to be any prospect of designing interventions that will succeed with those whose behavior is particularly resistant to change.

Since Becker and Joseph's article there has been some progress. Factors which have been shown to be associated with resistance to behavioral change include less concern about personal risk (McKusker et al., 1989) and beliefs that vulnerability is due to luck or fate (Kelly et al., 1990). Aspinwall, Kemeny, Taylor, Schneider, and Dudley (1991) identified lower self-efficacy as relevant. They also found that barriers to change of a sexual nature (based on questions such as How hard is it for you to refrain from having a lot of male sexual partners?) predicted increases in unprotected anal intercourse. Two studies have reported on an association between sexual risk taking and the use of sex to reduce tension or cope with stress (McCusker, Stoddard, Zapka, Zorn, & Mayer, 1989; Folkman, Chesney, Pollack, & Phillips, 1992). But so far, close examination of these associations in a way that might lead to appropriate interventions has not been reported.

It is interesting that most intervention programs have been based on theoretical models which emphasize rational appraisal of risk and a consequent commitment to risk reduction. Elements from the Health Belief Model (Rosenstock, 1974), Social Cognitive Theory (Bandura, 1986), the Theory of Reasoned Action (Fishbein & Ajzen, 1975), and the Transtheoretical Model of Behavior Change (Prochaska, DiClemente & Norcross, 1992) are often used, in various combinations, in intervention models aimed specifically at HIV risk behavior (e.g., Three Factor Model of AIDS-Preventive Behavior, Fisher & Fisher, 1992). What is striking about these approaches is that the relevant behavior is assumed to be under voluntary control and virtually no attention is paid to other aspects of the risk-taking context, including the specifically sexual aspects which might make such control more difficult. Ajzen's modification of the Theory of Reasoned Action, which he called the Theory of Planned Behavior, paved the way for such considerations by introducing the concept of perceived behavioral control (Ajzen, 1985). The Health Belief Model also considers barriers to action, which include a wide variety of factors, but, as shown by Aspinwall et al. (1991), these factors can include aspects of sexuality. The AIDS Risk Reduction Model proposed by Catania and colleagues (1990) emphasizes the importance of social networks, the role of the sexual partner in making appropriate change possible, and the willingness of the individual to seek help. Affect is considered in terms of distress about the dangers and how this motivates change. The issue of sexual enjoyment is also considered, though mainly in terms of perception of what will and will not be enjoyable and the impact this might have on commitment to change.

At least two reviews have drawn attention to this neglect of sexuality per se. Kelly and Kalichman state that "HIV prevention efforts must more adequately take into account the complexity of sexual behavior" (1995). They go on to review relevant evidence relating to the nature of the relationship, the social meaning of sex, the pattern of sexual communication, and other aspects and they mention that arousal level may be a risk-triggering factor. In a useful review, Gerrard, Gibbons, and Bushman (1996) address the assumption fundamental to most of the HIV behavioral intervention programs—the assumption that an individual's perceived vulnerability to HIV determines his risk-taking behavior. They point out that perceived vulnerability may be as much a consequence of that individual's risk-relevant behavior as a determinant. On the basis of a meta-analysis of the relevant literature, they conclude that there is more support for the idea that behavior determines the perception of vulnerability than for the idea that the perception of vulnerability determines behavior. They indicate that the evidence is derived mostly from high-risk groups and that their conclusions may not apply to low-risk groups; they also demonstrate differences in these causal relationships which relate to age (the perceived vulnerability of older people is more determined by their behavior) and gender (the same relationship is more evident in women). They also draw attention to four special characteristics of sexual risk taking relevant to HIV which sets it apart from other forms of health-related risks: (1) emotions associated with sex—"the unique nature of the sex drive contributes to the fact that decisions about sex are oftentimes made in the heat of the moment—when the person is emotionally and physically aroused—rather than after careful, or even rational deliberation"; (2) the social nature of precautionary sexual behavior (i.e., the need to negotiate with a partner); (3) the lengthy incubation period for HIV; and (4) the low probability of transmission from contact with HIV. They refer to the growing literature showing that affect can influence judgment and decision-making, and focus attention on how negative feelings about sexuality (e.g., sexual guilt or erotophobia) can adversely effect contraceptive planning (see Gerrard, Gibbons, & McCoy, 1993 for fuller discussion). Interestingly, these effects of negative emotions related to sex were studied in women, and were most apparent with methods of contraception (such as the Pill) "that require prior planning and a consistent daily preventive routine" (Gerrard et al., 1993). In this paper I am focusing on men, and it is quite possible that there are important differences between men and women in these respects. The comparison of men and women in relation to risk taking and the determinants of risk taking in women, both important topics, deserve a paper to themselves.

In recent years there has been an increasing interest in qualitative studies aimed at identifying the key elements in sexual risk taking, particularly in gay men (e.g., Lowy & Ross, 1994; Diaz, 1997; Williams, 1998). These studies illustrate the complexity of sexual scenarios, but three themes recur—the extent to which the individual feels in control of the interaction with the partner, the overwhelming effect of sexual excitement, and the presence of negative mood or low self-esteem. Clearly, socio-cultural factors are important—e.g., the influence of a specific gay subculture on what is appropriate or desirable behavior, cultural influences on the importance of maintaining macho behavior which may include the boldness to take risks or the importance of penetrating one's partner. Gender itself carries certain expectations which are culturally determined. However, even if we accept that socio-cultural influences are very important, we still have to account for the fact that within any specific socio-cultural context, there will be differences between individuals in how they react. One can only go so far in accounting for such differences in socio-cultural terms, and ultimately, individual characteristics independent of culture have to be taken into account. The objective of the first part of this paper is to propose a theoretical model to account for such individual differences.

Other Theoretical Approaches to Sexual Risk Management

Sensation Seeking

The concept of sensation seeking was first introduced by Zuckerman in 1964. Since then there has been an extensive literature that has used the concept (for a recent review see Zuckerman, 1994). In spite of this considerable attention, the concept remains somewhat elusive, and, as yet, has no convincing neurophysiological model underlying it.

Sensation seeking, as measured by Zuckerman's questionnaires, has four components: (1) Thrill and adventure seeking ("I sometimes like to do things that are a little frightening"); (2) Experience seeking—seeking novel sensations or experiences; (3) Disinhibition—seeking sensations through social activities such as parties and sex ("I like to have new and exciting experiences even if they are a little unconventional or illegal"); (4) Boredom susceptibility—an intolerance for repetitive experiences of any kind.

In his more recent theoretical overview, Zuckerman (1994) sees sensation seeking as part of a "broader trait called Impulsive-Sensation-seeking. Underlying this trait, as well as extraversion, is a mechanism that might be called approach. Impulsivity is a style of rapid decision making in deciding to approach." Of the psychophysiological aspects of sensation seeking, one of the more robust findings is that high sensation seekers can tolerate an intensity of stimulation which would lead to inhibition of response in the low sensation seeker.

According to Zuckerman, "Risk taking is a correlate of sensation-seeking, but not an essential part of the definition. The sensation seeker underestimates or accepts risk as the price for the reward provided by the sensation or experience itself" (1994). Further studies focusing on sexual behavior show the relationship between sensation seeking and sexual risk taking to be complex. Horvath and Zuckerman (1993) present evidence suggesting that with most risks, the role of sensation seeking is to modify the individual's appraisal of risk *after* engaging in the risk behavior (i.e., the higher the sensation seeking, the more the behavior would be deemed less risky as a consequence of engaging in it without adverse consequence). This is relevant to the mechanisms addressed by Gerrard et al. (1996), although, in the case of AIDS risk, where the outcome would not be known for some time, this relationship did not apparently apply. White and Johnson (1988) found that sensation seeking predicted the likelihood that teenagers would engage in sexual activity, but not the likelihood of doing so in a risky fashion (e.g., without condoms). Thus, while sensation seeking, and its extensive literature, is of some interest, it does not lend itself clearly to a theoretical model of sexual risk management.

Recent attempts to make Zuckerman's sensation seeking concept more directly relevant to sexual behavior (i.e., sexual sensation seeking; Kalichman & Rompa, 1995; Kalichman, Heckman, & Kelly, 1996) are of uncertain relevance to the basic sensation-seeking concept. Further work to establish these ad hoc measures will be needed before it can be concluded that they are dealing with the same basic theoretical concept as Zuckerman's sensation seeking.

Hypersexuality, Sexual Addiction, Sexual Compulsivity, Sexual Impulsivity, and the Lack of a Coherent Theoretical Model

The concept of sexual behavior that is, in some sense, out of control is relevant to sexual risk taking. The failure to control the desire to engage in sexual activity may result in risk—if it is excessive masturbation or use of pornography, the risk may result from excessive time in the activity that results in failures in work or other commitments; if it is excessive sexual activity with varied partners, the risk may be sexually transmitted disease, social repercussions, or damage to one's primary sexual relationship; if it is illegal sexual activity, the risk is that one will be caught and suffer the legal consequences. One of the best contributions to the literature on this subject is an early paper by Orford (1978) that discusses the concept of hypersexuality and whether it can be meaningfully used to identify certain behavioral patterns as pathological. Orford concludes "our knowledge of drug taking, gambling, television watching, and consuming behavior in general must lead us to expect that the availability of a reinforcing activity will result in the population distributing themselves along a skewed frequency distribution." Orford goes on to point out that since the heaviest use of any such behavior usually carries some cost and the heaviest users are also likely to have the strongest appetites for such behavior, the resulting costs will create conflict and dissonance for those individuals. Orford is reflecting on a concept that Kinsey, Pomeroy, and Martin (1948) developed, the extraordinarily wide variation in the frequency of total sexual outlet in the male population, and is questioning whether one can usefully separate out any particular part of this distribution and categorize it as pathological. In a more recent review, Rinehart and McCabe (1997) remind us that high levels of sexual activity have been labeled in various ways over the past 100 years or so. Labels of nymphomania and satyriasis were commonly used in the past; hypersexuality has been used more recently. Interest in hypersexuality declined during the 1970s, when sexual liberalization was in full swing, and has resurfaced since the 1980s under the labels of "sexual addiction," "sexual compulsion," and "sexual impulse disorder." Rinehart and McCabe (1997) effectively criticize the conceptual inadequacies of each of these categorizations, and it is clear that in each case the conceptualization is based on analogy rather than any meaningful theoretical model. However, while the history of these concepts indicates how medicalization can establish fashions of diagnosis and treatment, one cannot escape the conclusion that there are some individuals who are suffering the consequences of their "out-of-control" sexual behavior, and that some appropriate conceptualization that might guide the professional helper is required. A common but not inevitable finding is the coexistence of other psychological problems such as depression or anxiety (Black, Kehrberg, Flumerfelt, & Schlosser, 1997), and a positive therapeutic response to mood-elevating drugs such as the selective serotonin reuptake inhibitors (SSRIs) (Fedoroff, 1993). Evidence that sexual risk taking is related to maladaptive use of sex when coping with stress or tension (McKusick, Hoff, Stall, & Coates, 1991; Folkman, Chesney, Pollack, & Phillips, 1992) suggests that the relationship between negative mood and problems of sexual control requires particular attention. What has been lacking in the relevant literature is the identification of any measurable personality characteristic (such as sensation seeking) which predictably discriminates between those whose sexual behavior will have problematic consequences and those whose sexual behavior will not.

There have been some attempts to develop instruments for quantifying such problematic uncontrolled sexual behavior (e.g., Perceived Sexual Control Inventory, Exner, Meyer-Bahlburg, & Ehrhardt, 1992; Sexual Compulsivity Scales, Kalichman & Rompa, 1995) but reflecting the background literature, these attempts have been relatively atheoretical and descriptive.

The Kinsey Institute Sexual Risk-Taking Model

This is shown schematically in Figure 1, which distinguishes between risk appraisal (How much risk does this situation involve?) and risk management (Should this risk be avoided?). This distinction is clearly an oversimplification but it is necessary. There will be many situations in which the two processes occur at the same time and it is not always possible to distinguish between factors which influence risk appraisal and those which influence risk management. But the distinction is useful, because the risk appraisal process can and often is carried out before entering the situation where risk is to be taken or avoided. And in addition, the model shows that the individual's appraisal of risk is influenced by his own risk management.

Risk appraisal is influenced by (1) socio-cultural factors, such as norms of behavior (this is of special importance for adolescents who are particularly guided by the norms of their age group; see Poppen & Reisen, 1994); (2) personality characteristics (sensation seeking could be relevant here); and (3) information about the risks, including features such as the immediacy of and odds for risky outcome (this is particularly important for HIV risk, with its uncertain transmission and prolonged latency). Risk appraisal can and often does involve misperception of risks, e.g., the false sense of security felt by many adolescents in "monogamous relationships" (e.g., Hammer, Fisher, Fitzgerald, & Fisher, 1996), or the assumption of low risk when one's sexual partner "looks healthy" (e.g., McKusick, Hoff, Stall, & Coates, 1991; Lowy & Ross, 1994). As part of the risk appraisal process, such misperceptions are not necessarily dependent on the mood of the moment when one engages in sexual activity, but are more enduring. In general, the extensive literature on theoretical models is most relevant to the risk appraisal stage of the sequence. Blanton and Gerrard (1997) reported an interesting experiment in which male subjects were first asked to rate the risk of sexually transmitted diseases (STDs) when interacting with females who had relatively high-risk or low-risk sexual histories. At a later stage, they were asked to carry out the same assessment, this time with the sexual histories of the women accompa-

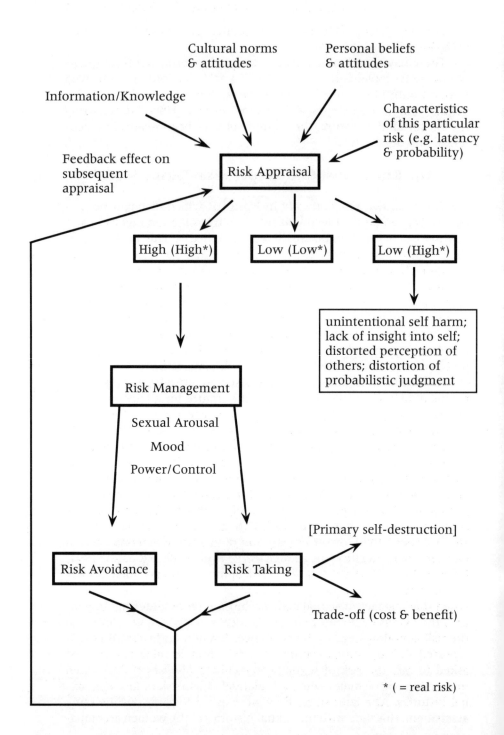

nied by her photograph. This experiment showed that men felt that the more attractive women were lower risks as sexual partners. Although the authors described this finding as a manifestation of behavioral motivation, it seems more appropriate to see it as an aspect of risk appraisal rather than the risk management that would be involved when actively engaged with such a woman in a sexual situation.

The feedback loop in the model is also of potential importance. What are the factors which determine whether engagement in risk-taking behavior increases or reduces that individual's appraisal of risk and vulnerability? Bauman and Siegel (1987) found that gay men who were participating in high-risk sex substantially underestimated the risk they were taking. Is this process determined by some personality characteristic that is as yet unidentified? Is it more a function of the type of risk being taken? Does it reflect the influence of the social group such men identify with? Although these questions are of potential importance, I am not pursuing them further in this paper. My focus is on the *risk management* stage. Given that a level of risk has been appraised, what determines, when the occasion arises, whether risk avoidance behavior results or whether the risks are taken? There are a number of mediating factors that could be relevant here. Some of them, such as alcohol or drug use, have received a fair amount of attention already. I am focusing on three particular mediating factors, each of which has surfaced in the literature I have reviewed above but has received very little research attention. These are (1) sexual arousal, (2) mood, and (3) the sexual relationship, and in particular the individual's power in that relationship to control whether risk avoidance is implemented or not. In each case, when risks are taken rather than avoided, we are looking at a trade-off process between costs and benefits. At that point in time and in that state of mind the benefits of taking the risk are usually immediate. They may therefore outweigh the costs, which are usually to be incurred, if at all, at some time in the future.

(1) *Sexual arousal.* The basic assumption here is that in a state of sexual arousal, normal "rational" decision making is impaired. Sexual arousal and the need to experience orgasmic release determine how the situation is handled. Thus, this factor assumes that a man who recognizes that a particular form of activity is risky and should be avoided when he is not sexually aroused feels less concerned about the risk involved once he is aroused (in a way which might happen with substance use). The immediate payoff has an overriding appeal. Intuitively this theory makes good sense, yet, interestingly, we have been unable to find any attempt to explore this effect in the experimental literature. What is easily demonstrated is the striking difference between how an individual perceives the acceptability of a situa-

tion shortly before orgasm, when he is highly aroused, and shortly after orgasm, when he is in his unaroused refractory period. Yet this effect has not been exploited experimentally either.

However, if high levels of sexual arousal have this disruptive effect on risk management, how would any of us practice safe sex or escape from sexually risky situations? This theoretical model offers an answer to that question. It postulates a dual control from two systems in the brain, one involved in sexual excitation or activation, the other with inhibition of sexual response. When a man is faced with the perception of risk or threat, central inhibition of sexual arousal occurs and it is easier for him to avoid risks. More important, the model postulates that individuals vary in their propensity for both systems, i.e., propensity for sexual activation and propensity for inhibition of sexual response. In the majority of cases, the inhibitory mechanism is assumed to be adaptive, aiding risk management by suppressing sexual response in the face of perceived risk. On the other hand, those with a high propensity for inhibition are assumed to be vulnerable to sexual dysfunctions, and those with a low propensity for inhibition are assumed to be more likely to engage in high-risk sexual behavior.

So here we have one crucial element in our model that explains individual differences in sexual risk taking; the majority of people avoid risk (or respond appropriately to behavioral interventions) because once the risk is appropriately appraised, sexual response is to some extent inhibited and risk avoidance is facilitated. A minority of individuals are lacking in this adaptive mechanism and are more likely to take sexual risks as a result.

This is not the place to explore the evidence for the existence of such systems and their neurophysiological basis, but this has been done elsewhere (Bancroft, 1999). Interestingly, a substantial amount of animal research has explored aspects of the excitatory or activation system, but, at least as far as sexual response is concerned, much less attention has been paid to inhibitory mechanisms. That situation is starting to change. We are considering here a very fundamental mechanism which is likely to be of general significance across species and implemented in a variety of situations where there is an adaptive need to inhibit sexual behavior, whether it be to avoid risk of sexually transmitted infection (of uncertain relevance to other species) or the threat of attack, or whether it is adaptive for the group rather than the individual and is involved in reducing reproductive behavior in the face of population overcrowding (of uncertain relevance to the human). However, there are a number of key questions which need to be answered. Are we talking about an inhibitory system that is specific to sexual response—or one that is non-specific? Is the individual variability in this system genetically determined or learnt or both? And if it is learnt, when does this crucial learning take place? At this stage, in the early development of the model, these questions must remain unanswered.

(2) *Mood.* There is experimental evidence indicating that positive mood is associated with risk avoidance (Isen, Nygren, & Ashby, 1988), and negative mood with risk taking (Baumeister & Scher, 1988). If you are in a good mood you strive to maintain it and don't put it at risk. If you are in a bad mood you are motivated to escape from it and do something *now* to improve it. In addition, as a result of the negative mood, the situation is appraised less rationally. Leith and Baumeister (1996) demonstrated this effect in a series of experiments, which included the induction of general arousal by means of exercise as well as negative mood. The presence of a sad mood on its own, or of general arousal on its own, had little impact on risk taking. When combined, however, risk management was impaired.

Thus we can postulate that in some cases sexual risk taking is increased by the coexistence of negative mood. This, however, confronts us with a paradox. To what extent are sexual arousal and negative mood compatible?

The relationship between mood and sexual arousal. There is a wealth of clinical evidence that depressed mood is typically associated with a loss of sexual interest and impairment of sexual arousability (e.g., Araujo, Durante, Feldman, Goldstein, & McKinlay, 1998; Beck, 1967; Cassidy, Flanagan, Spellman, & Cohen, 1957; Schreiner-Engel & Schiavi, 1986). However, there is also evidence that in a small proportion of men with depressive illness, their interest in sex is not diminished and may even be increased, suggesting a variable relationship between mood and sexual arousability (Mathew & Weinman, 1982; Nofzinger et al., 1993). There is also experimental evidence relevant to more normal reactive mood states. In two studies, induction of depressed mood in the laboratory resulted in an impaired physiological response to erotic stimuli (Wolchik et al., 1980; Mitchell, DiBartolo, Brown, & Barlow, 1998).

The relationship between anxiety and sexual response also appears to be complex. Whereas severe states of anxiety are typically associated with loss of sexual interest and arousability, and anxiety often accompanies failure of sexual response in men with sexual dysfunction, there is evidence that anxiety-inducing situations may enhance sexual response in some men (Bancroft, 1990; Barlow, Sakheim, & Beck, 1983).

How can we account for this apparent confusion? Our theoretical model offers a possible solution. It would postulate that circumstances which induced negative mood (i.e., a reactive mood change) would also be more likely to invoke inhibition of sexual response. However, an individual who has a low propensity for sexual inhibition (particularly if he also has a high propensity for sexual activation) would have minimal inhibition of sexual response, and it is possible that negative mood and sexual arousal could coexist for such an individual. Thus, we would predict that the minority of men who maintain or increase their levels of sexual interest during a depressive illness are men with a low propensity for inhibition of sexual response (a testable prediction). And when we consider the experimental evidence, given the small numbers of subjects in the experimental studies cited above and the lack of any characterization of the subjects beyond whether they were sexually functional or dysfunctional, the varying associations between mood and sexual response could be accounted for in a similar way.

Thus our theory postulates that because of a low propensity for inhibition of sexual response, negative mood and sexual arousal are compatible for a minority of men. This has two relevant consequences. First, if we accept Leith and Baumeister's (1996) conclusion that arousal in general amplifies the tendency for negative mood to disrupt risk management, then we might also accept that sexual arousal could have that same effect. Second, in such circumstances, the development of sexual arousal offers an immediate method for improving mood, i.e., the sexual experience and orgasm, even though immediately after such orgasm the mood might be no better and might even be worse as further evidence of loss of control dawns on the unhappy subject. We can even pursue this relationship further and postulate that, assuming a conditionability of sexual response, particularly in the male, an habitual pattern of sexual arousal associated with low mood could become established, leading to recurrent patterns of sexual behavior which are currently labeled as "compulsive sex."

(3) *Power/control in the relationship.* Whatever the individual's appraisal of risk, his decision to practice safe sex (e.g., use a condom) may be overridden by the partner who insists on having sex without a condom. This is obviously of considerable relevance to heterosexual relationships, although it is important to recognize that the power difference may not be a function of gender but of personality and type of relationship. Similarly, it can be relevant to a sexual relationship between two men. This effect can be manifested at different levels. In its most direct form, one partner wishes to use safe sex but is overridden by the other partner; in that circumstance the choice is not available and to some extent coercion is involved. In a less direct form, the needs of the subject to be accepted and approved of by the partner, who does not want to use safe sex, may result in a weakening of resolve to use safe sex in the subject. It then becomes a trade-off between wanting to avoid risk and wanting to avoid alienating the partner.

The relationship between power/control in the relationship, sexual arous-

al, and mood. An interaction between sexual arousal and power in the relationship also suggests itself. An individual who has a relative lack of control of what happens in the sexual interaction with his partner may have a further loss of control because of persistent sexual arousal. The trade-off tips even further away from risk avoidance. In addition, negative mood, with its increased sensitivity to rejection, may weaken the individual's resolve to assert himself in the relationship.

Evaluating the Model

The dual control theoretical model for sexual response that I described above is the guiding theme in the current research program on males at the Kinsey Institute. We have already developed a questionnaire to measure propensity for sexual inhibition (Sexual Inhibition Scale, or SIS) and propensity for sexual excitation (Sexual Excitation Scale, or SES). The development of this questionnaire was clearly guided by the theoretical model. We set out to formulate questions which would assess both the individual's propensity for sexual activation in non-threatening situations and his propensity for inhibition in potentially threatening situations. The questionnaire also focused on typical physiological response patterns rather than behaviors or attitudes.

This questionnaire has been completed by more than 400 male undergraduates at Indiana University. On the basis of higher-order factor analysis, this has revealed an excitation factor (SES) and two inhibition factors, one that we have labeled "threat of performance failure" (SIS1) and the other "threat of performance consequences" (SIS2). SIS1 is most relevant to sexual dysfunction; SIS2 is most relevant to sexual risk taking. Correlation between SES and SIS1 $r = -0.07$; SES and SIS2 $r = -0.11$; SIS1 and SIS 2, $r = 0.26$. The scores for each of these three factors showed a good and relatively normal distribution in this non-clinical sample. Thus we appear to have three useful, relatively independent measures relevant to our theoretical model.

External validation of these scales is underway in the following manner:

(1) Psychophysiological assessment of response to erotic stimuli. Two groups of subjects, similar in their SES scores, but contrasting in their SIS2 scores (high and low inhibition proneness for threat of consequences), were compared for their responses (genital, subjective, and cardiovascular) to two types of erotic stimuli (a) non-threatening, erotic sequence and (b) erotic sequence with threatening content (i.e., coercion). The two groups did not differ in their response to the non-threatening erotic stimuli. The high SIS2 group showed significantly lower responses to the threatening than the non-threatening stimuli. This was not the case with the low SIS2 group. This study is still in

progress, but this preliminary analysis already shows some validation of our questionnaire measures as relevant to sexual response in threatening situation.

(2) Experimental paradigm of sexual risk taking. This novel study has recently started. Subjects are shown three erotic videos; in one a risk of receiving an unpleasant electric shock is present from the start of the video. The risk increases the longer the video is watched, with the probability of receiving the shock being shown graphically on the video screen. At any point the subject can avoid shock by switching off the film. In the second condition, shock threat does not begin until the video has been running for 1.5 minutes, then the same threat conditions apply. In the third condition no threat of shock is involved at any time. As with the first experiment, high and low inhibition subjects are being recruited to this study. The measure of risk taking will be time watching the video under shock threat. It is predicted that this variable will correlate with the degree of sexual arousal—the higher the degree of arousal, the greater the risk taken—and that the degree of sexual arousal will be predicted best by the SIS2 score.[1]

Before long, we hope to test further the mood–sexual arousal interaction component of the model in two particular ways. First, we want to assess the extent to which individuals typically experience decline in their sexual interest or arousability when depressed. We predict that the majority will report such decline, but a minority will report maintaining their sexual responsiveness and interest when depressed. Our model predicts that those individuals will have low sexual inhibition scores.[2] Second, we hope to assess subjective and physiological response in the laboratory during experimental manipulation of mood. Here we would predict that our normal/high inhibition group would experience a reduction of sexual response in the presence of negative mood, but our low inhibition group would not.

These studies have so far involved heterosexual male undergraduates. Further similar studies are planned for groups of high and low risk-taking gay and heterosexual men recruited in the community.

Assuming that the theoretical model is supported by these studies and the questionnaire method is validated as a means of measuring the propensities for inhibition and activation, then the questionnaire can be used to assess the extent to which propensity for low inhibition of sexual response characterizes those who fail to respond to conventional "rational-based" behavioral interventions. The identification of such a group of intervention-resistant risk-takers, for some of whom mood may be a relevant variable, could then lead to alternative methods of intervention designed to deal with this particular explanatory model. Clearly such an approach would not focus on provision of information about risk (i.e., risk appraisal) but on alternative coping strategies (i.e., risk management).

The Larger Picture: A Comprehensive Theoretical Model of Human Sexuality and Its Determinants

So far the focus on risk taking has involved consideration of sources of individual differences which are less understandable in terms of culture and more understandable in terms of psychological and neurophysiological mechanisms that impact on risk management. If such a model is to have any value, it must be compatible with a more comprehensive theoretical model of human sexuality.

There can be no doubt that the determinants of human sexuality and its behavioral manifestations are many and varied. There is little doubt that the prevailing culture shapes in a powerful way sexual mores and taboos and social expectations of appropriate sexual behavior, which in turn shape sexual behavior itself. There can be little argument that sexual relationships between men and women are determined to a considerable extent by the gender roles and gender power differences that are themselves culturally determined. There can be little doubt that gender power and sexual roles become entangled with political and economic factors.

However, these socio-cultural, political, and economic factors do not shape human sexuality in a biological vacuum. Furthermore, we are not considering a biological "given" either, but rather the potential for considerable individual variation and possibly also for ethnic variation in relevant biological factors. We must take the individual biological variability into account when striving to explain the fact that in a given cultural setting, individuals vary considerably in the extent to which they conform to the cultural pattern.

We therefore need a basic theoretical model which captures the full range and complexity of human sexual expression and its determinants but which also allows us to focus on specific parts of it (as in the first part of this essay) while not losing sight of the whole.

It is fair to say that hitherto a broad theoretical model of human sexuality of this kind has been absent. This reflects the fact that until recently much of sex research has been positivist in its approach. The essence of this approach, to quote Slife and Williams (1997), is that "a method, or logic is the pathway to truth. If someone wants to find out about something accurately, then he or she must turn to a particular process, called 'scientific method,' for doing so." Theorizing in such circumstances is of secondary importance; it serves the scientific method by facilitating the formulation of testable, refutable hypotheses. Up to a point, this approach is defendable. But one crucial consequence is that the field acquires an exceedingly fragmented body of knowledge for which one piece of information is of very uncertain relevance to any other piece. A further consequence has been the failure to take cultural differences sufficiently into account. During the recent upsurge of concern about HIV and AIDS, this became a serious problem when cross-cultural studies of sexual behavior sponsored by the World Health Organization (WHO) were carried out based on a western conceptualization of sexual interactions. WHO researchers quickly ran into difficulties and the resulting research vacuum provided an opportunity for feminist and gay scholars to show their worth, as I saw in 1996 when I attended Richard Parker's international conference in Rio de Janeiro entitled "Reconceiving Sexuality." The epistemological crisis already raging in anthropology, sociology, and the humanities, and increasingly within psychology, has become evident in the field of sex research. The challenge now is to bridge these epistemological divides with a theoretical approach which involves neither biological nor cultural reductionism, and which exploits qualitative, quantitative, and experimental methodologies. The following theoretical exposition is a humble step in that direction.

Cultural Materialism

My starting point is Marvin Harris's account of cultural materialism because, while it is far from perfect, it does provide scope for a broad interactive explanatory model (Harris, 1979).

The cultural materialism model has three parts:

Infrastructure
  a) the mode of production (especially of food and energy)
  b) the mode of reproduction (methods for expanding, limiting, or maintaining population size)
The infrastructure can be seen as the principal interface between culture and nature.

Structure
  a) domestic economy (e.g., family structure, age and sex roles, domestic division of labor, education)
  b) political economy (e.g., division of labor, class system)

Superstructure
  e.g., shared beliefs, symbolism, taboos, religion, epistemologies, and expressions of culture (e.g., music, dance, etc.)

The guiding principle is that of infrastructural determinism, an adaptation of the fundamental Marxist principle; i.e., the modes of production and reproduction probabilistically determine the domestic and political economy which in turn probabilistically determine the superstructure. It is conceded that aspects of the structure and superstructure can achieve a degree of autonomy from the infrastructure, but this should only be considered if the possibility of infrastructural determinism has been thoroughly explored first.

To illustrate how cultural materialism works to explain differences as well as similarities across cultures, let me give a few examples from simple early cultures.

The hunter-gatherer society illustrates a cultural pattern which, while although it has now almost completely disappeared, had the longest history during the very prolonged period before domestication of plants and animals. The mode of production of the hunter-gatherer involved hunting, fishing, and collection of wild seeds, nuts, fruit and so on. This aspect of the infrastructure accounted for their mobile, nomadic existence. Bands of 20 to 50 people were typical. There was intermarriage between neighboring bands which fostered various levels of cooperation among bands. Food production was shared, property was minimal, social stratification was minimal. These were egalitarian groups, with relatively slight sexual dimorphism and relatively equal relationships between men and women. Children were a liability at least for the first few years. They could contribute little to the food foraging activities and imposed considerable restrictions on the mother's activities with the group. Given the impact that diet and nutritional states can have on women's reproductive physiology, long periods of adolescent infertility and later lactational anestrus is assumed to have been secondary to the high-protein low-carbohydrate diet. The birth rate was relatively low and additional methods of controlling population (e.g., infanticide) less necessary.

When social groups turned to agriculture and stock raising, fundamental changes occurred. The change in diet (less protein and more carbohydrates) reduced lactational infertility; the increased birth rate resulted in children who, now growing up in a more home-based lifestyle than the children of hunter-gatherers, could provide useful labor. However, in these circumstances, population pressure became more likely; women's roles were necessarily altered by more child rearing; and warfare between villages increased, which emphasized the importance of male children and led to female infanticide and the establishment of sexual stratification. Polygynous patterns were encouraged by awarding females to dominant senior males, establishing the status of women as property, and reinforcing gender-based differences in power. The acquisition of wealth in the form of land or domestic animals raised issues of inheritance, leading to a variety of devices to ensure appropriate transfer of property and raising the need for the dominant male to protect himself from cuckoldry. An emphasis on virginity resulted, a characteristic of the transfer from father to husband of females as property.

Harris (1979) places considerable emphasis on population density and population growth as a key determining factor in the infrastructure. Harris (1979) points out that prior to 3000 B.C., there was a very long period of relative population stability, although he assumes that with healthy groups there would have been a natural tendency for population size to increase. He therefore concludes that there was a continuing need to suppress population growth by various means, including such negative methods as infanticide or nutritional neglect. He postulates, rather speculatively, that there would have been an ongoing reluctance to use such unpleasant methods so that as soon as the food supply improved, these brakes on population growth were reduced. Once population started to grow, the increased numbers, combined with improvements in agriculture and food production, led to the formation of more marked social hierarchies, development of a powerful elite, incentives for polygyny, protection of property inheritance, and so on. While I am not entirely convinced by this explanation, it is an interesting one, and there is certainly a need to explain the take-off of population after a long period of stability. And it is the emphasis on population control and reproductive behavior that makes cultural materialism of potential relevance to the understanding of human sexuality.

Adapting the Model of Cultural Materialism

Clearly, cultural materialism, as with other models from cultural anthropology, was conceptualized to help explain similarities as well as differences across different cultures, and, by implication, within cultures as they change over time. There is an important difference between establishing a science of culture, which aims to explain differences and similarities between different cultures, and a science of human sexuality, which aims to explain differences and similarities between cultures but also between individuals within those cultures. So how can we use cultural materialism as a foundation for building our theoretical model of human sexuality? The fundamental adjustment to the cultural materialism model that allows this broader objective is the acknowledgement that *the individuals that make up a cultural group, in terms of their innate characteristics and capacities, represent an important element of the infrastructure of that culture.* Obviously, those individuals will be shaped in many respects by the culture in which they live. But each individual has innate or early determined characteristics which may or may not be useful to the process of conforming to or fitting into the culture, or which may be more useful for fitting into one type of culture than another. We can regard such characteristics as the *human resources* within the infrastructure. To take a hypothetical example, a social group which has a high proportion of individuals whose reproductive systems, and hence fertility, are more sensitive for genetic reasons to nutritional factors would have a different infrastructure than a group with a low proportion of such individuals. There would, for example, be a greater reduction of birth rate in the first group in the face of food shortages, and hence a different impact on the resulting structure and superstructure. If certain aspects of sexual responsiveness are genetically or constitutionally determined, then groups with different distributions of such characteristics may well develop different structural and superstructural factors relevant to sexuality and reproductive behavior. So the argument can be made that the individual is relevant to the infrastructure of a culture just as the infrastructure is relevant to the individual. (Harris [1997] regards the "quest for sexual pleasure" as an aspect of infrastructure.)

As I have already mentioned, cultural materialism offers one clear advantage in its consideration of the interaction between reproductive and economic factors. But the mode of reproduction as described by Harris, while relevant and important, needs further elaboration and development for our purposes. Let us therefore examine the reproductive infrastructure more closely, incorporating a notion of human resources which goes beyond simply counting the population.

a) *demographics of population*
   e.g., population density, sex ratios, and age distribution
b) *age-related developmental processes*
   e.g., aspects of cognitive development which delay certain types of learning until the relevant developmental stage has been reached; aspects of emotional development which may be influenced by the developmental stage (both cognitive and neurobiological)
c) *neurobiological basis of sexual responsiveness*
   individual differences genetically determined or acquired, such as:
   —sexual activation (propensity for sexual arousal)
   —sexual inhibition (propensity for central inhibition of sexual response)
   —other relevant physiological mechanisms (e.g., sexual signaling systems)
d) *methods of fertility regulation*
   —inherent (interaction between environment and biology)
   e.g., age at puberty, age when fertile, factors affecting fertility such as STDs, nutrition, and lactation
   —"technology" available for use
   e.g., contraception, sterilization, abortion, infanticide

Let us then consider those aspects of structure of particular relevance to reproduction; i.e., the REPRODUCTIVE STRUCTURE

a) mating patterns (e.g., polygyny, monogamy, incest taboos)
b) levels of sexual stratification
c) levels of sexual segregation
d) age at marriage
e) family structure (matrilinearity or patrilinearity, fatherless families)
f) social management of adolescence and transition to sexual adult
   e.g., induction rituals, separation from parents, teen culture
g) reactions to cultural norms
   i.e., countercultures, sexuality as a form of dissent

And then proceed to the REPRODUCTIVE SUPERSTRUCTURE

a) shared concepts of masculinity, femininity, and male-female relationships
b) shared constructs of sexual identity
c) shared beliefs about appropriate patterns of sexual behavior
d) shared beliefs, attitudes about:
   fertility versus virginity before marriage
   importance of marriage versus family ties
   sex as commodity/exchange
e) importance of sexual conformity
   individual differences in need to conform/rebel
f) identification with sexual countercultures

This leaves us with THE REPRODUCTIVE INDIVIDUAL, who depends in part on innate, genetically determined or early learned characteristics and will show varying degrees of conformity to the sexual mores of his or her culture in terms of gender role, sexual attitudes, and relationship to sexual countercultures.

Fitting the Model to the Modern World

Not surprisingly, this model is most convincingly exemplified using relatively primitive and small cultures. It gets increasingly difficult to apply as we move to complex modern industrial states—but that is a reason to use it with increased rigor rather than abandon it. In the twentieth century, we see pluralist industrial societies composed of a mixture of cultural groups with varying degrees of integration that are also undergoing change at an extraordinary rate. We find other societies that are less developed industrially but are undergoing massive changes as the effects of western societies, both economic and cultural, have impact. Let us consider some of the changes that have happened during the second half of the twentieth century (since Kinsey's initial work) that may be relevant to human sexuality cross-culturally and see to what extent we can use our model to explain changes in the reproductive structure and superstructure that have occurred.

The past 50 years (i.e., the period since the end of the second world war) are quite without precedent in terms of the amount of change that has affected human societies across our planet. These changes have happened most markedly in the developed capitalists countries, but are by no means confined to them. The first 30 of these years have been called the golden age of capitalism (Hobsbawm, 1997).[3] During that time the world economy grew at an explosive rate. World output of manufacturing goods quadrupled and world trade in those goods increased tenfold during the first 20 years. There was a major increase in the standard of living for the large majority in the developed world. Central to this boom was a technological revolution. This utterly transformed everyday life in the developed world and had an appreciable effect elsewhere also. Increasingly the new technologies were capital intensive and labor saving. Increasingly people were needed as consumers rather than as producers. Thus the mode of production has shifted in a major fashion; the move toward production is increasingly less dependent on the workforce, at least in the developed world. Perhaps not surprisingly, this golden age was too good to last and from the mid-1970s onward we have been once again in a period of economic crises.

These major changes in the mode of production represent changes in the infrastructure which, according to our model, we will see reflected in changes in the structure and superstructure. And indeed we see a major social revolution worldwide, evident in massive migration of workers from the country to the town, accompanied by substantial increases in the number of young people going to university for further education. In the 1980s and 1990s we saw a marked decline in the industrial working class in the developed world. Unemployment, a negligible issue during the golden years, became a major problem with huge social impact, accompanied by further labor migration on a massive scale. This has been accompanied by a shift to the left in government of most capitalist countries, together with a substantial move toward the concept of the welfare state. There is thus a move away from the older class structure to one where the main division is between the wealthy (and those in proper employment) and the underclass of the chronically unemployed. In contrast to the 1960s and 1970s, we find from the 1980s onward that a growing proportion of wealth is in the hands of a smaller proportion of the population. These are major changes in "domestic economy" (Hobsbawm, 1997).

The mode of reproduction has changed in terms of the age distribution, complicated by a post-war baby boom and a progressive increase in life expectancy that has resulted in substantial increases in the older age groups. Whereas we have no reason to expect changes in patterns of age-related developmental processes, or neurobiological patterns of sexual responsiveness (much longer time periods would be required before such changes would be apparent), we do see changes in the methods of fertility regulation. The lowering of the age at puberty (and hence age when individuals are first fertile) had probably reached a plateau by the start of this 50-year period, at least in those parts of the world where satisfactory levels of nutrition were established. But the technology of fertility regulation, and its dissemination worldwide, has changed dramatically over those 50 years. This in itself is not a sufficient explanation for the changes in birth rate. Those changes over the past 50 years in countries like the United States illustrate well a basic assumption of cultural materialism theory that productivity drives reproduction. More particularly, the number of children considered desirable reflects the balance of cost and benefit to the parents that children bring. Increasingly in modern industrial societies, or what Harris calls hyperindustrial societies, the economic costs to parents of having children greatly exceed the benefits.

Over the past 50 years we have seen major changes in the role of women in the labor market. In 1940, only 14% of women in the United States were married women who were employed for wages. By 1980, more than 50% of U.S. women fell into this category. There was also a striking increase in the entry of women into higher education. At the end of the second world war, 15–30% of students in the developed countries were women; by 1980, in many of these countries (including the United States), women accounted for more than 50% of students (Hobsbawm, 1997). Having children increasingly posed a major intrusion into the careers and earning potential of women (and to a much lesser extent, men). Such changes were clearly instrumental in the impressive revival of feminist movements from the 1960s on, and from the 1980s onward political consciousness spread beyond educated middle-class women to women in general. The revolt among traditionally faithful women in Roman Catholic countries against unpopular doctrines such as the restrictions on divorce and abortion provides an example. This growing demand by women to improve their rights and to have control over their reproductive lives is now strong worldwide, but still has a fair way to go. The entrenched power structures of patriarchies are slow to respond.

Needless to say, such changes have been associated with a major restructuring of attitudes toward marriage and the family. In particular, there have been dramatic increases in the rates of marital breakdown and divorce worldwide. The United States led the figures at each stage. Between 1960 and 1980, the divorce rate per 1000 population doubled in the United States, though it has since declined to the levels reached in the early 1970s. During the same decades, the proportion of households that consisted of the classical western nuclear family, a married couple with children, fell from 44% to 29% in the United States.

This crisis of the family was associated with dramatic changes in the public standards, both official and unofficial, governing sexual behavior, partnership, and procreation. Again, this was worldwide, though more marked in some countries than others. We see the decriminalization of homosexuality between consenting adults in most developed countries and the legalization of abortion in many. Such laws recognized the new climate of sexual relaxation rather than creating it. This was the recognition that Kinsey wanted to happen when he found the law so out of touch with prevailing patterns of sexual behavior (Kinsey et al., 1948).

Many of these changes reflected what some perceived as a crisis in the relations between the sexes; even more dramatic and revolutionary was the rise of a powerful youth culture, reflecting a profound change in the relations between the generations. The category "youth," stretching from puberty to the middle twenties, became a category with which young people self-consciously aligned. It also became a longer period in the life cycle; puberty itself began several years earlier than had been the case in earlier generations. In the 1960s, the political impact of this youth culture became a force to be reckoned with. This new autonomy of youth as a separate social stratum reverberated throughout the golden years of capitalism; the increasing earning potential of many young people produced a youth culture with major economic impact. Music and fashion were perhaps its most commercial manifestations. The autonomy of this youth culture, and its distancing from the conventions of adulthood, was all the more dramatic because of the international nature of this movement. The music, the dress, the political ideals crossed long-established cultural and language barriers with extraordinary ease, aided by the miracles of modern information technology, themselves very much the domain of the young. The personal liberation of the young from the constraints of their elders became mobilized into social liberation. Inevitably, the most obvious vehicles for liberation were sex and drugs. The rejection of conventional constraints as part of this youth culture became expressed in an openness to the pursuit of sexual pleasure which probably had no parallel, at least in recent history. The historian Eric Hobsbawm (1997) has described this cultural revolution as "the triumph of the individual over society."

The youth culture, and in particular its spread across international boundaries, raises an issue crucial to this theoretical model. Given that a youth culture of this kind, principally rooted in North America and Europe, crosses international boundaries to be so readily taken up by young people in many other cultures, to what extent is it likely to produce fundamental change consistent with the concept of infrastructural determinism? In the case of United States and much of Europe, the infrastructural changes in age distribution and mode of production are such that the youth culture can be seen as a genuine structural change with consequent superstructural changes. In other societies, where the American-style youth culture may be imported, we may see it taken up as part of the expression of adolescent dissent that does not affect the basic structural or superstructural characteristics of that society. While no easy task, that formulation is testable.

We should also consider the role of the sexual counterculture. Here again we see over the past 50 years a gay and lesbian movement which appears to cross international boundaries. Closer examination could well find, however, that cultural contrasts prevail beneath the international facade of the gay movement. Nevertheless, homosexuality as a lifestyle and an organizing fact in sexual identity poses an explanatory challenge to this theoretical model. It would be hard to make the case that the fundamental characteristics which influence whether an individual will engage in exclusively same-sex or opposite-sex sexual relationships are culturally derived. We need to consider the infrastructural characteristics of the reproductive individual to make the evolution of a homosexual or heterosexual identity a possibility.

But given the existence of such individual characteristics, cultural factors will play a powerful role in how they are manifested. They will, for example, influence the likelihood that same-sex behavior will occur during early adolescence, creating a cultural scene in which the propensity of some individuals for same-sex interaction will find an expression that will facilitate the development of a more exclusive same-sex preference. (For individuals without such propensities these early same-sex experiences have no more than an exploratory significance.) Furthermore, the structural inevitability of dissent and counterculture in any culture will provide opportunities to organize structural subcultures, such as the gay subculture, which provide groups and identities for our particular reproductive individual. Important, however, is the idea that particular individuals will, because of individual characteristics related not only to same-sex preference, vary in the readiness with which they embrace or join a particular gay subculture. For example, and returning momentarily to our model of risk taking, the particular style of gay subculture that emerged in the past 50 years in New York or San Francisco, for example, may well have preferentially attracted the high-activation, low-inhibition individuals, leaving the low-activation, high-inhibition men with same-sex preferences to remain in relative isolation or to identify with some other form of group.

At the same time, the more structural and superstructural changes that I referred to earlier, particularly those involving changes in public standards regulating sexual behavior, will have had an enabling effect on the emergence of the gay movement in its various manifestations.

How has our theoretical model fared in this attempt to make sense of this massive change over the past 50 years? Clearly, the model does not provide a "tight" explanation for the changes we have seen. It is unrealistic to expect to be able to account for more than a portion of this broad, highly complex picture. But the above account illustrates an important virtue of the model. Because it assumes the principle of infrastructural determinism, and therefore challenges the evidence to show that structural and superstructural changes can occur independently of infrastructural change, the model requires us to take a broad, interdisciplinary view and avoids any tendency to adopt an overly-focused approach that puts blinders on us.

Clearly, much more work needs to be done to develop the model to establish its full potential. It requires, for example, closer examination of the ways that cultural conflict can add diversity to the culture at both structural and superstructural levels and a greater understanding of the determinants of cultural conflict through the development of countercultures—the rules for breaking rules. Sexuality has been a highly relevant vehicle for expressing social conformity and non-conformity, and it may well be that sexually manifested social non-conformity shows the greatest plasticity or autonomy from the infrastructure. This model also assumes that reproduction and sexuality are closely interdependent, counter to the fashion which has prevailed in the social sciences for some time now, which sees them as essentially separate.

Evaluating the Larger Model

The next challenge is, given this model, how do you evaluate it? How do you decide whether the evidence you obtain reinforces your model, requires it to be modified, or throws its basic value into question? This is the epistemological nub. In the case of the sexual risk-taking model, I was able to propose some fairly specific methods of testing it. It is a model that lends itself to conventional scientific method. When we turn to the larger more embracing model, the situation is very different. There are no clear reasons why we should now abandon scientific method. The crucial point is that it is not sufficient for our task. More often than not rigorous implementation of scientific method requires control of the circumstances—experimentation, in other words—which removes the factor under study from the ordinary world. Interpreting the results in terms relevant to the ordinary world can be difficult. Nevertheless, in my opinion, the rigor of striving to formulate hypotheses that are in some sense refutable is an important and valuable part of scientific discipline. That will take us some of the way.

But there are other, more pragmatic methods of validation to consider, to add to or complement our scientific method. As a clinician, I am concerned with achieving clinical benefits. A theoretical model which results in clinical benefits can be demonstrably useful without necessarily helping us to understand how the beneficial changes were achieved. We can extend this pragmatism to the less individual-oriented, more group-oriented area of social policy. A theoretical model could conceivably be validated by the extent to which it leads to policies which are effective. This is in some respects a radical suggestion. It might cause anxiety in those who fear that science will become modified to sustain a political ideology. But there is no escaping the conclusion that informing the policymaker should be an important part of our objective. The theoretical model that we choose to use may make that task much harder or much easier. It may be the case that the eclectic approach which currently prevails may make it easier for policymakers to pick and choose the pieces of evidence that suit their agendas. That possibility is something we should keep in mind.

Some Conceptual Considerations

There is a conceptual issue which Harris regards as fundamental to cultural materialism—the distinction between "emic" and "etic." This, like Harris's work in general, has been both a controversial and an influential issue in anthropology and to a lesser extent other social sciences. In fact, the distinction goes to the heart of the epistemological crisis in academic thinking. The emic/etic distinction is derived from linguistics. The phoneme is the component of language which conveys meaning (here "emic"). Phonetics are concerned with the production of speech and its use of different sounds (here "etic"). But what started as a linguistic concept that distinguished between the meaning conveyed by spoken language and the mechanisms of speaking has become a metaphor. Thus emic is used to describe meaning as understood by the native user of the language. To quote Harris, "the test of adequacy of emic analysis is its ability to generate statements that the native accepts as real, meaningful and appropriate." The etic operation involves a judgment of the categories and concepts used in description and analysis. Again, to quote Harris, "[T]he test of adequacy of etic accounts is simply their ability to generate scientifically productive theories about the causes of socio-cultural differences and similarities."

Thus, Harris sees infrastructure as an etic concept—something that the ordinary person doesn't need to understand to function effectively within that culture; similarly structure, though to a lesser extent. Superstructure is largely manifested emically, though it can be conceptualized etically, and is of fundamental importance to how an individual functions within a cultural group. This conceptual distinction has arisen in the field of cultural anthropology and in particular the anthropology of primitive cultures, and it captures the distinction between the "native," who has a "primitive" view of the world which is usually incorrect or at best incomplete, and the "scientist" who can, by means of "scientific method" and greater intellectual sophistication, identify the correct view or explanation. Perhaps more important is that the distinction has arisen in the social sciences where there has been a pervasive rejection of any view of human behavior which is not focused on the meanings of the behavior to the actor—the intentions, choices, and motives of the actor. It is rare in the social sciences to study human behavior, particularly behavior which is socially relevant, in terms of how it appears to an observer and how that observer can best make sense of the behavior given the context in which it occurs. Hence, when someone like Harris comes along who wants to do just that, he feels the need to make or attempt to make a clear distinction between the two processes—emic and etic. I suspect that accounts for the emphasis that he has laid on the issue.

When we consider our theoretical model of risk taking, a distinction can be made between the explanations that high-risk actors provide for their patterns of behavior, as illustrated in the qualitative studies (e.g., Lowy & Ross, 1994; Diaz, 1997; Williams, 1998) and those offered in the model. In some respects the differences are not great; the ideas that sexual arousal might interfere with judgment or that mood might alter how we behave surface fairly clearly in the vernacular accounts from these studies. What is clearly different is the theoretical model of individual differences in the propensity for inhibition (and activation) and how that propensity might interact with mood; here we are clearly talking "etic" in Harris's sense. But I am considering my theoretical model from an interdisciplinary perspective with a clear background in behavioral and biological science. I do not see that the emic/etic distinction is necessary for the model to work. There may be a purpose in distinguishing between models which are relevant to what the member of the culture needs to know in order to integrate within the culture and models that represent how the culture works or evolved (which members do not need to know unless they want to develop "specialist knowledge," or more important, change some aspect of the culture). There is also the need to assess the functions of behaviors of cultural relevance in order to make comparisons across cultures. But in general, I prefer to see the issue as one of grappling with complexity. The world is an inherently complex place which to a large extent is too complex to be grasped and comprehended by the human intellect. Faced with this complexity we do the best we can—we formulate models which represent our limited grasp of reality. Sometimes we use the computer to develop such models, which then become usable but again too complex for us to fully comprehend. Thus the person-in-the-street has models of various aspects of his or her world; they may be shared by fellow citizens. The scientist (the outsider) comes along and develops a more sophisticated model, which may prove to be more or less useful. But they are still models of reality. They will always involve some degree of reductionism—sometimes biological, sometimes cultural. What I am seeking is a model where the reductionism is balanced so that both biological and cultural factors have an appropriate role.

Situating the Sexual Risk-Taking Model into the Larger Picture

How do we then situate our theoretical model of sexual risk taking into this larger model, as I promised we would do at the outset? First it needs to be restated that this particular model of risk taking focuses on only one part of the larger picture of sexual risk taking, i.e., the contribution that the individual's constitutional propensities make to the process. It is based on the existence of individual differences in the propensity to respond to sexual stimulation in the presence of risk which, as has already been discussed, may also play a part in determining with which subculture, or set of sexual scripts, an individual identifies. Let us take some examples to illustrate the point.

The varieties of gay scene that exist in an urban center such as San Francisco will attract some individuals more than others, and indeed, there will need to be enough of the right type of individual for any particular scene to establish itself. The individual whose risk management is fairly sound, who can enjoy sex better if it is safe sex, will join the scene where safe sex is taken for granted. We would expect him to have a relatively high propensity for sexual inhibition, although it is quite possible that this individual will also have a high propensity for sexual activation. The individual with poor risk management who periodically engages in high-risk sex (e.g., having anal sex without using a condom with a man he doesn't know because at the time he gets "carried away" by sexual arousal) will tend, as a consequence of such episodes, to reappraise his activities as less risky than they really are and hence see the safe-sex groups as unnecessarily cautious. We would expect him to have a low propensity for sexual inhibition, plus perhaps a personality profile which makes such denial of reality more likely. Another low-inhibition individual may appraise risk more realistically, and usually keep out of high-risk situations, until his mood changes and the negative mood alters his risk management, especially when he is feeling sexually aroused.

An individual who has recently arrived on the scene and who feels relatively alienated (which may perhaps be amplified by ethnic factors) may find himself trading safe sex for the benefits of impressing a member of the in-group. This is more likely to happen if he has a low propensity for inhibition of sexual response.

A "straight" man may find it difficult to negotiate safe sex with a new female partner because his cultural background and his culturally derived sexual scripts require him to assert himself in a macho fashion to maintain his self-esteem. This might preclude negotiation with a woman and favor an assertive, penetrative approach to the sexual interaction. That would be more likely to happen in an individual with a low propensity for sexual inhibition.

In each situation where socio-cultural factors are likely to shape sexual risk taking or risk avoidance, the outcome will be in part a reflection of how the individual's characteristics mesh with the socio-cultural message.

Conclusions

I have presented a theoretical model of risk taking which distinguishes between risk appraisal and risk management. While I have pointed out that our appraisal of risk is influenced as much by how we manage risk as the other way round, the model focuses on three factors which may mediate risk management—(1) sexual arousal, (2) mood, and (3) power/control in the sexual relationship—and on possible interactions between these three factors. Central to the model is the theoretical concept of brain mechanisms which provide dual control of sexual response with individual variability in the propensity for both sexual excitation and sexual inhibition. Individuals with a low propensity for inhibition are more likely to be sexually aroused in risky situations, more likely to be aroused in states of negative mood, and hence more likely to use sex as a mood regulator. Both sexual arousal and mood may in turn influence the individual's sense of power or control in the relationship at the time. This therefore postulates a neurophysiological trait (inhibition proneness) as a crucial individually determined factor that influences risk management.

The essay moves on to propose a broad interdisciplinary theoretical model of human sexuality based on cultural materialism, which recognizes the social infrastructure as the principal determinant of social structure and superstructure. Individual characteristics, such as the postulated propensity for inhibition of sexual response, are seen as part of the infrastructure which interact with structural and superstructural influences (i.e., social scripts) to influence sexual risk taking. While this broad theoretical model is limited in its ability to predict changes and differences in a rapidly changing modern society, it has the particular virtue of requiring consideration of a broad range of psychosocial factors to understand complex patterns of human sexual behavior. This underlines the point that the specific theoretical model of sexual risk taking proposed in this paper is only part of a more complex set of determinants.

REFERENCES

Ajzen, I. (1985). From intentions to actions: A theory of planned behavior. In J. Kuhl & J. Beckmann (Eds.), *Action control: From cognition to behavior* (pp. 11–39). New York: Springer-Verlag.

Araujo, A. B., Durante, R., Feldman, H. A., Goldstein, I., & McKinlay, J. B. (1998). The relationship between depressive symptoms and male erectile dysfunction: Cross-sectional results from the Massachusetts male aging study. *Psychosomatic Medicine, 60,* 458–465.

Aspinwall, L. G., Kemeny, M. E., Taylor, S. E., Schneider, S. G., & Dudley, J. P. (1991). Psychosocial predictors of gay men's AIDS risk-reduction behavior. *Health Psychology, 10*(6), 432–444.

Bancroft, J. (1990). Man and his penis—a relationship under threat? *Journal of Psychology and Human Sexuality, 2,* 7–32.

Bancroft, J. (1999). Central inhibition of sexual response in the male: A theoretical perspective. *Neuroscience and Biobehavioral Reviews, 23,* 763–784.

Bandura, A. (1986). *Social foundations of thought and action: A social cognitive theory.* Englewood Cliffs, NJ: Prentice Hall.

Barlow, D. H., Sakheim, D. K., & Beck, J. G. (1983). Anxiety increases sexual arousal. *Journal of Abnormal Psychology, 92*(1), 49–54.

Bauman, L. J., & Siegel, K. (1987). Misperception among gay men of the risk for AIDS associated with their sexual behavior. *Journal of Applied Social Psychology, 17*(3), 329–350.

Baumeister, R. F., & Scher, S. J. (1988). Self-defeating behavior patterns among normal individuals: Review and analysis of common self-destructive tendencies. *Psychological Bulletin, 104*(1), 3–22.

Beck, A. T. (1967). *Depression: Clinical, experimental and theoretical aspects.* London: Staples Press.

Becker, M. H., & Joseph, J. G. (1988). AIDS and behavioral change to reduce risk: A review. *American Journal of Public Health, 78*(4), 394–410.

Black, D. W., Kehrberg, L. L. D., Flumerfelt, D. L., & Schlosser, S. S. (1997). Characteristics of 36 subjects reporting compulsive sexual behavior. *American Journal of Psychiatry, 154*(2), 243–249.

Blanton, H., & Gerrard, M. (1997). Effect of sexual motivation on men's risk perception for sexually transmitted disease: There must be 50 ways to justify a lover. *Health Psychology, 16*(4), 374–379.

Cassidy, W. L., Flanagan, N. B., Spellman, M., & Cohen, M. E. (1957). Clinical observations in manic depressive disease. *Journal of American Medical Association, 164,* 1535–1546.

Catania, J. A., Kegeles, S. M., & Coates, T. J. (1990). Towards an understanding of risk behavior: An AIDS risk reduction model (ARRM). *Health Education Quarterly, 17*(1), 53–72.

Diaz, R. M. (1997). *Trips to Fantasy Island: Contexts of risky sex for San Francisco gay men.* Unpublished manuscript, San Francisco AIDS Foundation.

Exner, T. M., Meyer-Bahlburg, H. F. L., & Ehrhardt, A. A. (1992). Sexual self control as a mediator of high risk sexual behavior in a New York City cohort of HIV+ and HIV– gay men. *Journal of Sex Research, 29*(3), 389–406.

Fedoroff, J. P. (1993). Serotonergic drug treatment of deviant sexual interests. *Annals of Sex Research, 6,* 105–121.

Fishbein, M., & Ajzen, I. (1975). *Belief, attitude, intention, and behavior: An introduction to theory and research.* Reading, MA: Addison-Wesley.

Fisher, J. D., & Fisher, W. A. (1992). Changing AIDS-risk behavior. *Psychological Bulletin, 111*(3), 455–474.

Folkman, S., Chesney, M. A., Pollack, L., & Phillips, C. (1992). Stress, coping, and high risk sexual behavior. *Health Psychology, 11*(4), 218–222.

Gerrard, M., Gibbons, F. X., & Bushman, B. J. (1996). Relation between perceived vulnerability to HIV and precautionary sexual behavior. *Psychological Bulletin, 119*(3), 390–409.

Gerrard, M., Gibbons, F. X., & McCoy, S. B. (1993). Emotional inhibition of effective contraception. *Anxiety, Stress, and Coping, 6*(2), 73–88.

Hammer, J. C., Fisher, J. D., Fitzgerald, P., & Fisher, W. A. (1996). When two heads aren't better than one: AIDS risk behavior in college-age couples. *Journal of Applied Social Psychology, 26*(5), 375–397.

Harris, M. (1979). *Cultural materialism: The struggle for a science of culture.* New York: Random House.

Harris, M. (1997). *Culture, people, nature: An introduction to general anthropology* (7th Ed.). New York: Addison-Wesley.

Hobsbawm, E. (1997). *Age of extremes: The short twentieth century 1914–1991.* London: Little, Brown and Co.

Horvath, P., & Zuckerman, M. (1993). Sensation seeking, risk appraisal, and risky behavior. *Personality and Individual Differences, 14*(1), 41–52.

Isen, A. M., Nygren, T. E., & Ashby, F. G. (1988). Influence of positive affect on the subjective utility of gains and losses: It is just not worth the risk. *Journal of Personality and Social Psychology, 55,* 10–717.

Kalichman, S. C., Heckman, T., & Kelly, J. A. (1996). Sensation seeking as an explanation for the association between substance use and HIV-related risky sexual behavior. *Archives of Sexual Behavior, 25*(2), 141–154.

Kalichman, S. C., & Rompa, D. (1995). Sexual sensation seeking and sexual compulsivity scales: Reliability, validity, and predicting HIV risk behavior. *Journal of Personality Assessment, 65*(3), 586–601.

Kelly, J. A., & Kalichman, S. C. (1995). Increased attention to human sexuality can improve HIV-AIDS prevention efforts: Key research issues and directions. *Journal of Consulting and Clinical Psychology, 63*(6), 907–918.

Kelly, J. A., St. Lawrence, J. S., Brasfield, T. L., Lemke, A., Amidei, T., Roffman, R. E., Hood, H. V., Smith, J. E., Kilgore, H., & McNeill, C., Jr. (1990). Psychological factors that predict AIDS high-risk versus AIDS precautionary behavior. *Journal of Consulting and Clinical Psychology, 58*(1), 117–120.

Kinsey, A. C., Pomeroy, W. B., & Martin. C. F. (1948). *Sexual behavior in the human male.* Philadelphia: Saunders.

Leith, K. P., & Baumeister, R. F. (1996). Why do bad moods increase self-defeating behavior? Emotion, risk taking and self-regulation. *Journal of Personality and Social Psychology, 71*(6), 1250–1267.

Lowy, E., & Ross, M. W. (1994). "It'll never happen to me": Gay men's beliefs, perceptions and folk constructions of sexual risk. *AIDS Education and Prevention, 6*(6), 467–482.

Mathew, R. J., & Weinman, M. L. (1982). Sexual dysfunction in depression. *Archives of Sexual Behavior, 11,* 323–328.

McCusker, J., Stoddard, A. M., Zapka, J. G., Zorn, M., & Mayer, K. H. (1989). Predictors of AIDS-preventive behavior among homosexually active men: A longitudinal study. *AIDS, 3,* 443–448.

McKusick, L., Hoff, C. C., Stall, R., & Coates, T. J. (1991). Tailoring AIDS prevention: Differences in behavioral strategies among heterosexual and gay bar patrons in San Francisco. *AIDS Education and Prevention, 3*(1), 1–9.

Mitchell, W. B., DiBartolo, P. M., Brown, T. A., & Barlow, D. H. (1998). Effects of positive and negative mood on sexual arousal in sexually functional males. *Archives of Sexual Behavior, 27*(2), 197–208.

National Institutes of Health. (1997). Interventions to prevent HIV risk behavior. *NIH Consensus Statement, 15*(2).

Nofzinger, E. A., Thase, M. E., Reynolds, C. F., Frank, E., Jennings, R., Garamoni, G. L., Fasicaka, A. L., & Kupfer, D. J. (1993). Sexual function in depressed men. *Archives of General Psychiatry, 50,* 24–30.

Orford, J. (1978). Hypersexuality: Implications for a theory of dependence. *British Journal of Addiction, 73,* 299–310.

Poppen, P. J., & Reisen, C. A. (1994). Heterosexual behaviors and risk of exposure to HIV: Current status and prospects for change. *Applied & Preventive Psychology, 3,* 75–90.

Prochaska, J. O., DiClemente, C. C., & Norcross, J. C. (1992). In search of how people change: Applications to addictive behaviors. *American Psychologist, 47,* 102–1114.

Rinehart, N. J., & McCabe, M. P. (1997). Hypersexuality: Psychopathology or normal variant of sexuality? *Sexual and Marital Therapy, 12*(1), 45–60.

Rosenstock, I. M. (1974). The health belief model and preventive health behavior. *Health Education Monographs, 2,* 354–385.

Schreiner-Engel, P., & Schiavi, R. C. (1986). Lifetime psychopathology in individuals with low sexual desire. *Journal of Nervous and Mental Diseases, 174,* 646–651.

Slife, B. D., & Williams, R. N. (1997). Toward a theoretical psychology. *American Psychologist, 52*(2), 117–129.

White, H. R., & Johnson, V. (1988). Risk taking as a predictor of adolescent sexual activity and use of contraception. *Journal of Adolescent Research, 3*(3–4), 317–331.

Williams, A. M. (1998). *The sexual landscapes of middle-class gay men in San Francisco: A white paper on meanings of sex.* Unpublished manuscript.

Wolchik, S. A., Beggs, V. E., Wincze, J. P., Sakheim, D. K., Barlow, D. H., & Mavissakalian, M. (1980). The effect of emotional arousal on subsequent sexual arousal in men. *Journal of Abnormal Psychology, 89*(4), 595–598.

Zuckerman, M. (1994). *Behavioral expressions and biosocial bases of sensation seeking.* Cambridge, UK: Cambridge University Press.

Notes

1. Since writing this paper, preliminary results from this shock-threat procedure have shown it to be complex. While of potential interest, we no longer see it as a simple laboratory model of sexual risk taking.

2. Preliminary results from a non-clinical sample of men, with mean age 47, confirm our first prediction in relation to both depression and anxiety/ stress. For our second prediction, we found that both SES and SIS2 scores predicted the relationship with anxiety/stress, but not with depression. If replicated, this finding would require modification of the theoretical model to distinguish between negative mood states associated with increased arousal (e.g., anxiety) which would conform to our model, and those associated with low arousal (e.g., retarded depression), which may not conform. Studies of a clinical population are now needed.

3. I am indebted to Hobsbawm for much of this brief historical summary of the past 50 years.

Discussion

Anke Ehrhardt: Could you define, in your context in particular, which sexual risk taking you are focusing on with your model?

John Bancroft: That can perhaps be best answered by describing how we approached the development of our questionnaire, which aims to measure traits fundamental to the theoretical model. What makes our questionnaire different from other questionnaires which may correlate with ours is that we designed the questionnaire to specifically look at sexual arousal or lack of sexual arousal. We were specifically looking for questions which on the one hand would assess the likelihood that an individual would get sexually aroused in potentially arousing situations, which would be our measure of sexual excitation proneness, and on the other hand the likelihood of their not being aroused in sexual situations which might contain a threat, which would be our measure for inhibition proneness. So we included a variety of threats; the possibility of getting a sexually transmitted disease is only one of them. A variety of situations which might be construed as threatening were built into our questionnaire, such as finding yourself in a sexual interaction with someone who is under age or having somebody walk into the room and discover you. So our measure of inhibition proneness strives to be fairly nonspecific in that sense. When you come to actually test that inhibition proneness, it gets more difficult. In the laboratory, what we've done so far is to compare and contrast responses of our high- and low-inhibition men in terms of their sexual response to two types of erotic stimuli, one of which is positive and non-threatening and the other which contains a threatening component. So far that has been an element of coercion in the sexual interaction. What we found is that our high- and low-inhibition men are indistinguishable in their response to the positive stimulus, but they are clearly different in their response to the potentially threatening one. But it's quite a challenge to find good ways of really pinning this down in an experimental way. We are interested in studying sexual risk taking in gay and straight men. Our preliminary results, and our reading of the qualitative studies of sexual risk taking in gay men, indicate that while there are a number of contextual variables relevant to sexual risk taking that commonly arise, such as drug or alcohol use, there are three recurring themes which are of direct relevance to this theoretical model: the idea of being overwhelmed by the sexually arousing aspect of the situation, the issue of low mood, and the relationship, in particular the extent to which one has control over the interaction. So that was part of the reason we felt justified to pursue these three particular mediating variables and their interactions with each other.

Lucia O'Sullivan: It's very refreshing to see a model, a decision-making type model, that includes affect as opposed to simply thinking or cognition because I think that's been really neglected in a lot of sexual decision-making models. But I'm curious how much you see affect or mood regulation as being voluntary; how much deliberate affect regulation there might be, how much of it is reflexive.

John Bancroft: I don't know, but it's a very relevant question. We probably need to look at that issue more closely by using qualitative techniques and that's one of the things we're planning to do now that we've got this model. We can use in-depth interviews and actually ask them about these things with a clear focus. But the experimental literature is of potential relevance here because it suggests that in the laboratory if people are in a good mood they are less likely to take risks. They're feeling good and they don't want to spoil it. Whereas with low mood, there's a sense of "I want to change this, I want to change it now." To what extent that is a conscious deliberate sequence of events, I really don't know, but it makes psychological sense.

Bob Michael: John Gagnon, when you and I worked together before you were always concerned about and wanting to avoid medicalizing a problem. In your paper you talk of the propensity to take sexual risk and convert it first into disease and then into gay. Would you defend that statement, that the risk we're most worried about has to do with being gay? The vulnerability of being naked, of being in a vulnerable position with someone, is a sexual risk that is far beyond gay, far beyond disease. Most of what you had to say in your paper applies to those broader issues of exposure to risk as well as this narrower definition or statement that you made. Do you really want to limit it?

John Gagnon: What I was saying is that the interest in this question is primarily provoked by concern about risk among gay men. There is a concrete social concern which lies underneath the theoretical question and it has to do with gay men. There once was a large and respected scientific literature which examined rape proneness, a literature which argued that women differentially have the propensity to put themselves in situations of sexual risk by the way they dress, by where they go. That was a whole conceptual apparatus which feminists spent a great deal of time assaulting as part of the rape myth. Only lawyers say those kinds of things anymore. There was a similar literature which asked why seductive little girls sit on the laps of innocent sex offenders and provoke them into doing bad things. Those questions aren't allowed to be asked anymore. So my concern was about whom is it possible to have certain classes of hypotheses generated. This is a cultural question. There are questions about what is good to think, and it's not good to think those two questions anymore. But it is good to think about gay men as being in control of their own behavior, as taking risks, as not inhibiting their behavior. I'm saying, well maybe there is something else going on here. I don't want to medicalize, I want to anti-medicalize. What you're seeing from John Bancroft and me is that we start imagining from a different place. John starts with the organism and works his way out and I start with this sort of fuzzy stuff out here and try to work my way back toward the individual. That is part of the difference in the way in which we imagine the world.

Dennis Fortenberry: John Bancroft, what do you anticipate the level of measure for the outcome to be? This is a bogus question on my part because I know your questionnaire and I know that you're measuring the sexual behaviors that you're interested in at some aggregate level rather than at event-specific levels. But it seems to me that you must measure the outcomes at an event-specific level and plan your analysis on that basis.

John Bancroft: Well, we are first attempting to do that in an experimental way but using a laboratory procedure as "event-specific," in your terms. Our next step, having measured this propensity with our questionnaire, having looked at how people respond in a laboratory, is to talk individually about specific events, using qualitative methods. That is, of course, still at a fairly early stage. Where we go after that I'm not quite sure. To comment on what John Gagnon has been saying, I must emphasize that we are interested in heterosexual men as well as gay men. We are actually focusing on men, although we have recently modified the questionnaire to apply to women and we're starting to look at this issue in women too. But at the moment we're looking at men, and we're interested in gay and heterosexual men.

Indeed, it could be said that the need to find a useful model is probably more important for heterosexual men than it is for gay men, who are doing a pretty good job already, as Gary Dowsett has indicated.

Ken Plummer: I just wondered, John Bancroft, if you could say a little bit about the whole second part of your paper because you have dealt with the individual part. The interesting or maybe the odd thing about your paper is the way you've evoked Marvin Harris's account. Could you say why you chose Marvin Harris's theory? And the diagram of your specific model of risk taking—how would this connect to the larger picture?

John Bancroft: I've been interested in Harris's ideas for some time and when I came to the United States I started to read him more seriously and I was very impressed. He's an incredible critic of other people's points of view and I had the experience of finding myself in one of the categories that he criticized, the eclectic category I think it was. But he was beating up all and sundry and I thought he was doing it rather effectively. So I found it very stimulating and then I thought, Might this be useful to adapt? He's interested in culture, not in individuals. He's interested in a model which explains differences or similarities across cultures, and maybe that's all it should be used for. But I asked myself the question Can this be adapted to take an individual into account? The way that I have attempted to do that is to see the individual as part of the resources in a society that Harris would regard as part of the infrastructure; part of the raw material that the culture has at its disposal. The individuals involved are going to have various characteristics, some of which are going to be shaped by the culture itself, but some of which they're going to bring with them to that culture because of genetic or early learning factors. So I attempted to expand his notion of reproductive infrastructure and structure to bring the individual and the variability of the individual into account.

Discussion Paper

JAY PHILIP PAUL

It has proved to be a challenge to serve as a discussant for this session.

Perhaps I should acknowledge my own bias in this matter from the outset: Behavior may be a product of forces within an individual, but it is also embedded within—and therefore shaped by—contextual factors, such as interpersonal dynamics, situational factors (e.g., fatigue, drug or alcohol use), and our internal representations or understandings of this emotionally charged realm of behavior.

As with any conference on the role of theory in sexual research, the topics covered have been diverse and dense. Luckily, the "it" (as Ken Plummer put it yesterday) in this afternoon's discussion appears to be reduced in scope from some of the broader topics we have tackled these past two days. Nonetheless, we can only understand sexual risk taking within the context of some of those larger issues, concerns, and ideologies that have been discussed in the course of this conference.

I had understood my task in this capacity as helping to move the discussion along by identifying commonalities and divergencies between these two papers and trying to help us talk about how their different perspectives could in some way enrich the ideas presented by each author. That poses a considerable challenge in some ways, as they have chosen to discuss sexual risk from such different vantage points or ideologies. One has attempted to construct a model of sexual behavior and sexual risk, the other has argued the potential dangers of such models. Luckily, one of the benefits of such divergent arguments is to highlight the areas covered and left unexplored in each thesis.

It appeared to me from my reading of John Gagnon's paper that the very question posed as the topic of this session left him uneasy. I found his reservations to be a very interesting basis for rereading John Bancroft's paper. Given that, I have begun my comments with his paper.

John Gagnon's respectful attitude toward (and concerns about) what is identified as a "problem" appears to be linked to two major concerns: (1) the distortions that may result when one attempts to abstract individual propensities from the concrete everyday scenarios that involve certain sexual behaviors, and (2) the implications such models of behavior can have for the management of such phenomena by "specialists" of a given discipline. Framing the question as stated— revolving around individual differences in the propensity for risky sexual behavior—introduces an inherent ideological bias. To seek determinants within the individual is consistent with our society's individualistic philosophy and much of our explanations of behavior, but to do so limits our approaches to the issue of sexual risk taking. Curiously enough, it leads to interesting parallels in the formulations of risk taking by public health "experts" and those in the conservative religious camp—both of whom are interested in control of individual sexual behavior for different reasons. John Gagnon weaves an interesting picture of how cultural forces can shape the "stories" of sexual risk, and the odd bondings that may occur between divergent movements in promoting certain explanations of risk. The sexual domain holds a peculiar power in our culture, and we have seen how the promotion of social policies in this arena can be based more on ideology than by compelling evidence. Therefore, I believe that his speculations about how little may differentiate the stories of "experts" and a given culture's lay theories should be required reading for all HIV prevention researchers.

This resonates with my own perspective and dual professional experiences of doing AIDS behavioral research and working as a psychotherapist. After all, psychotherapy involves both a process of defining "problems" and working with clients on solutions. The process of defining the problem is very often the basis of defining the process of problem resolution—and it may serve to limit the consideration of possible alternative strategies rather than to generate new problem-solving options. Recognizing the intrusiveness of personal ideologies and perspectives in working with psychotherapy clients is an ongoing learning experience. There is both a tremendous simplicity in conceptualization and a tremendous difficulty in practice of respectfully "shaking the rope to test the knot," as John Gagnon puts it. It appears that we are all struggling with this process of understanding the frames of reference that we each bring to this table.

I will not reiterate John Gagnon's discussion of some of the questions he reviewed about the framing of this topic. Clearly, defining the problem of continuing cases of sexually transmitted HIV infection in individual terms was a key sticking point for him. I appreciate his articulation of some of the problems in viewing risk as determined by individual propensities versus by social arrangements. I also feel that he did a good job at pointing out the way in which narratives about risky sex are embedded in our vernacular theories of "why" and "how."

But when I came away from my reading of this paper, I was left with a question of what is to be done about this pressing concern other than massive social change and redistribution of resources. He has done an excellent job of articulating the problems in maintaining our current frame of reference. I would have liked him to go further in describing either (1) some of the potential benefits to certain shifts in our paradigms, or (2) suggestions for those in the field about how to avoid the rigidity imposed by embracing any single ideology.

Many in AIDS prevention share a tremendous sense of frustration about continued seroconversions. This frustration leads to an eagerness to embrace new ideas and try new methods on the part of those in the trenches of this public health battle. Their capacity to do this is limited by the selectivity of funding sources and the difficulties in evaluating the effects of particular interventions. Policy guidelines that determine prevention programs (especially in the United States) must be carefully tailored to fit two divergent criteria: (1) they must be made acceptable to funding sources, which typically means catering to certain political/economic interests; and (2) they must also be meaningful to and consistent with the ideologies, needs, and frames of reference of the target population. It is easy to see how the articulation of a rationale for prevention programs consistent with the ideologies of prevailing political/economic powers can put it at odds with the second criterion, which measures its utility against the concerns and beliefs of the intended target group.

The practice of defining and targeting "high-risk" subpopulations is strongly entrenched and emerges out of at least two independent sources: economic pressures to put public health funds where they can potentially do the most good (whether "good" is defined in terms of political leverage or public health) and the psychological need to differentiate those "others" who are susceptible to a given health menace from those who are not. It is likely that these forces will remain largely intact, compelling those of us in the field of HIV prevention to devise creative solutions that enable us to work within this paradigm—but not be limited by it.

I am thankful to John Bancroft for the contributions of his paper as well, which include a literature review that pulls from a variety of disciplines. He has approached the question of individual differences in sexual risk taking by making a bold attempt to develop a theory that incorporates some of what we are learning about human sexuality into a model of sexual risk taking. In doing so, he makes a break with the bulk of prior conceptual models of health risk behavior that incorporate or address little that is unique to the realm of sexuality. Much of his argument about the need for a basic theoretical understanding of human sexual expression is key to what led to this conference. Much remains unresolved, but we have covered some intriguing territory. I also appreciate his attempts to not only sketch out a complex model of behavior, but to also identify means of testing components of that theory.

I must further acknowledge that his article was an eye-opener for me. While I accept the proposition that socio-cultural, economic, and political factors do not shape human sexuality in a biological vacuum, I had not considered such factors as those he raised. I found myself challenged, intrigued, but unsure how to evaluate his notions of biological influences on individual propensities toward sexual risk taking. As a psychologist, I am used to considering both proximal determinants of behavior (such as alcohol/drug use, qualities of the relationship with the sexual partner, and life history variables such as developmental experiences and their outcomes in terms of coping strategies, sense of self, worldview, personal meanings, and weights given to various behavioral options). John Bancroft has made one of the most comprehensive attempts I have seen to devise a model of sexuality that incorporates both larger socio-cultural/economic forces, interpersonal factors, situational factors, emotional variables, personality, and biology. I appreciate the distinctions he has made in differentiating risk appraisal and risk management (and the interactions between those processes). His efforts to integrate various disciplines to explain the conceptualization and regulation of human sexuality could stand as a paper in its own right, and perhaps should be treated separately from his efforts to explain sexual risk taking. There is a certain admirable audacity in his attempt at this relatively early stage of our understanding of human sexuality to propose variables that potentially influence sexual risk taking across cultures, social groups, and historical eras.

When we come to consider a question such as that posed by John Bancroft, it helps to be clear about a number of matters, some of which have also been touched on by other discussants. So I would like to pose the following questions, which in many ways follow up on some of the points raised by John Gagnon, but also reflect what I have seen over about a decade of work in the HIV prevention field:

What Is Sexual Risk?

First of all, before we can debate the notion that some people may have a "propensity" toward sexual behavior that puts them at risk for disease, especially HIV, we must be precise. If we are to understand the

underpinnings of this phenomenon, we need to be a little more concrete in identifying what "sexual risk taking" means. There is an interesting tension in his paper that attempts to bridge the divide between
treating sexual behavior as "sex" and sexual behavior as "risk." Although John Bancroft's review of the literature clearly identifies limits
to rationalistic decision-making models of sexual behavior, there were
ways in which his model still seemed to be strongly rooted in that tradition, albeit strengthened in its ability to explain individual variations
by the consideration of neurobiology, power in relationships, and several other variables.

"Sexual risk" has been operationalized in a variety of ways—number of partners, sexual acts (e.g., unprotected anal or penile/vaginal
intercourse), the attributes of the parties engaging in those acts (particularly HIV status), the setting of such acts, and the concomitant
factors (such as substance use, emotional bonds, power differentials in
the relationship) that may enhance or diminish one's sense of risk. The
complexity of defining sexual risk taking is acknowledged in the model
(especially within the discussion of the realm of risk appraisal), but
aspects of the explanation of how the model operates and how to test
it sometimes appeared to take a less sophisticated perspective.

Moving from the explanation of the model to the model-testing
phase, it appears that we may suddenly have shifted to an overly re-
ductionistic conceptualization of sexual risk. In the attempt to test this
arousal/threat component, the operationalization of sexual risk taking
(time watching an erotic video when faced with the potential for an
unpleasant electric shock), although intriguing, so reduces the complexity of this phenomenon that it is unclear how well this experimental manipulation reflects what occurs in sexual interactions. In this
situation, the pairing of the threat of pain with an erotic stimulus is
ongoingly reinforced throughout the experiment, rather than permit-
ting a participant to ignore such ramifications. In real life, there is no
such consistent linkage of sexual choices with unpleasant consequences. Furthermore, the experimental threat involves clear, immediate
negative results, rather than potential—but uncertain—long-term implications. Finally, there is no opportunity for the subject to manipulate the situation to choose a personally acceptable level of erotic stimulation and shock threat—as opposed to simply removing the threat
by removing the stimulus. The propensity for sexual arousal versus
inhibition under threat does not necessarily address the question of
how such sexual arousal leads to various forms of sexual gratification.
High-risk sexual behavior is not the only route to orgasm and "release." The potential for variety in sexual behavior and sexual satisfaction does not appear to be adequately addressed by this operationalization. I would suggest that any measure of "arousal under threat"

first be shown to be related to measures of sexual risk behavior (e.g., self-reported sexual behavior), HIV seroconversion, or even the participant's history of other sexually transmitted diseases. Even finding an association between this measure and sexual risk behavior does not tell us the contribution of this factor as opposed to others in determining risky choices—which is one of the problems in responding to the next question.

How Do We Move from the Act to the Actors in Identifying "Sexual Risk-Takers"?

Once we agree upon our definitions and operationalizations of sexual risk, then we must make some decisions about how to leap across the divide between acts and actors. This has been one of the most problematic issues in most literature on sexual risk taking. Relatively few variables intrinsic to the individual have been consistently found to be related to risk; some of the strongest relationships have been found to be related to such situational variables as having sex under the influence of alcohol or drugs or the nature of the relationship in which sex occurs (e.g., primary vs. casual partners; purported or identified HIV serostatus of the participants). Some descriptive variables of individuals likely to engage in high-risk sexual activity may be markers for some of these situational variables (e.g., relative youth may reflect having fewer sexual risk management resources, less accurate risk appraisal, or a tendency to view sexual relationships—however transient—in "romantic" terms; substance abusers as a group may be more likely to have sex under the influence).

Because neurobiology (the proposed factors of sexual inhibition and sexual activation) is meant to explain only a certain level of "scatter" or individual variation, it is clearly acknowledged that other forces are in operation. Constructing a comprehensive model of sexual risk taking can be tricky, given that so many factors (and their interactive influences) must be considered. Inevitably in this situation, some variables may potentially be irrelevant for some segments of the population but crucial for others. Therefore, testing this model would seem to depend upon having some means of evaluating the relative power of different factors in this model for different subpopulations. For any given sexual encounter, if we view these variations in sexual activation/inhibition under threat situations as key to one person's "decision" to engage in high-risk sexual behavior, how would we explain what has occurred for the other individual in this interaction?

Another consideration that I would like to see dealt with more extensively in this model is the fact that many people are not necessarily consistent in terms of their behavioral choices. Survey data indicate that the proportion of those identified as "sexual risk-takers" is largely dependent upon the time period under inquiry. This fits with the findings on sexual risk "relapse"—despite adequate information, skills at avoiding high-risk behavior, and a history of less risky practices, situations may occur that lead to inconsistencies or departures from usual self-protective behaviors. It is likely that many identified as sexual risk-takers may be only episodic risk-takers. Although John Bancroft acknowledges that these constitutional variables need to be put in the context of the larger picture of factors influencing sexual behavior, I was left unclear about how the proposed model would describe such interactions.

In reviewing the Bancroft model, the focus appears to be on risk management principally within the context of accurately identified high-risk scenarios. There is an implicit presumption that the risk taking of interest is that which is engaged in despite being acknowledged as risky. To what degree do people make such rational evaluations of risk prior to (as opposed to in the aftermath of) a sexual encounter— and how may such risk appraisals be distorted at any given point in time by situational or contextual factors? One of the more interesting underresearched areas is the way in which people can selectively attend to different pieces of information about an event at any given point in time. Emotional states may enhance the salience of particular information or inhibit recall of events associated with other mood states.

This model attempts to incorporate seemingly counterintuitive findings on linkages between negative mood states (anxiety and depression) and sexual arousal. Yet the proposed explanation of particular experimental outcomes does not seem to examine alternate potential explanations for these findings or how well data supports the theorized explanation to the exclusion of other possibilities.

Final Thoughts

Both of these papers have examined the question of sexual risk taking from divergent frames of reference. Whereas Gagnon's paper tolls a warning bell for those who would pursue an overarching theory of individual propensities toward sexual risk taking, Bancroft has tried to elaborate a theory that could explain why individuals with an awareness of sexual risk would engage in such dangerous behavior. Both papers are thought provoking, despite the contradictory nature of their conclusions. Each has attempted to place this issue within a larger perspective of how we derive and attribute meanings to sexual acts and actors. There is much that both papers would seem to share. It would appear that the point at which they diverge most strongly is in the attempt to translate a complex phenomenon, such as sexual behavior, into terms that permit testing and/or validation of a model. The cautionary notes in Gagnon's paper may be most applicable to Bancroft's efforts to formulate an experimental model that can be readily validated by "conventional scientific method." The extrapolations experimental scientists make from real-world situations to simpler scenarios to allow for model testing are possibly those that are most strongly biased by one's discipline or training. This is probably the area of Bancroft's paper that I have treated most critically. I would hope that we can devise a means of promoting the kinds of cross-disciplinary fertilization advocated here by continuing to challenge the formulations of one another's disciplines and a willingness to ask for feedback across our professional areas of specialization.

Discussion Paper

MEG GERRARD

First let me say I find these interdisciplinary discussions very difficult. I think it's very difficult to work to try to understand other people's perspectives when, as John Gagnon has pointed out, we work so hard in graduate school to become enmeshed in the perspectives of our disciplines, to learn the jargon, to learn to think—in my case the way other psychologists think. It's also difficult to keep from dismissing other people's work as irrelevant to yours. In this meeting we've been grappling with those kinds of issues and those kinds of difficulties, some of us better than others. I want to suggest that an analogy that was made earlier today might be appropriate here. And that's that we should receive information from these other disciplines in the same way that we would receive art; that we should do it with courtesy, that we should act as if we are guests, that we should not be interrogating each other, but rather asking questions so we can better understand the other perspective. And having achieved some understanding of what the other perspective is, then decide if that's something that we can take home and whether or not it would fit in our house and we could live with it and be comfortable with it and build on it. Now having said that, I want to move on to talk about the contributions of these two papers and what I see as their commonalities and their points of departure. One outlines an agenda for research, a theory, a framework, a model, about who responds to rational educational interventions and who doesn't, and why these differences occur. The other outlines reasons that it's dangerous to approach problems in this way; that's how I interpreted John Gagnon's paper.

First let me turn to the Bancroft paper. He asks some extremely important questions about the identification of what I would call intervention-resistant individuals. His framework offers several innovations, some of which have been mentioned here in the discussion, some of which may not be obvious to people who haven't done research like this before. First is this distinction between risk appraisal and risk management. I think it's a very important distinction. The vast majority of research on risk has failed to make this kind of distinction and has focused on risk appraisals and assumed that once a risk appraisal is made then the behavior rationally follows. The overwhelming evidence in the risk literature is that people do know when they're taking risks. They do not deny it and they are not ignorant of it and this literature comes from research on adolescents, from research on college students, and from research on adults both in the United States and in Europe. I'm sure there is evidence from other continents; those are the ones that I'm familiar with. That is not to say that they act rationally on this information, but they do know it and they can apply it to themselves in evaluating their own behavior. So I think this distinction between appraisal of the risk and management of the risk is very important. One of the reasons that it's important is that the literature also very clearly says that those risk assessments or risk appraisals have very little to do with our risk behavior. That is not to say that they have nothing to do with it, but they have not been demonstrated to play a large role in our ultimate behavior.

The second contribution that I think this paper makes are the proposals that sexual excitement and sexual inhibition are not only dual processes but orthogonal processes that operate simultaneously and that there are individual differences in which of these processes will dominate in a given person, and, I would add, at a given time perhaps. I embrace the effort to identify these kinds of individual differences in responses in order to try to understand people's risk-taking behavior more. If an individual difference variable moderates the process, then it's very likely to tell us something about the mediating processes that we're looking at. For example, we know that optimism as a personality variable moderates a number of behaviors. We also know that one of the reasons that optimism moderates behaviors as a personality variable is that optimism is one of the mediating processes in those behaviors. The third addition which has been left out of many of the models of risk behavior that we've seen before (and on health behavior in general) is the reciprocal nature here; that what you do changes how you think about a problem. The behaviors you engage in change fundamentally the way you think about the problem. Another contribution that goes without saying is John Bancroft's efforts to go into the laboratory. Not perfect yet, but a step in the right direction. We need to have more experimental research on these kinds of issues.

Let me turn my attention now to John Gagnon's paper. Again, many issues that are very important were raised here. He appropriately warns us against equating unplanned pregnancy and HIV infection, something that we see repeatedly in the literature. There was a large literature from many years on unplanned pregnancy when HIV first became a problem. People borrowed from that literature indiscriminately. I did as well as everyone else. He also makes an implicit warning that the individual difference approach to these problems can lead to blaming the victim, something that he doesn't say explicitly. I think that's something that we need to be aware of and pay attention to. So John Gagnon was talking here about the context and the structure of institutions and how those should be taken into account. I want to raise another kind of possibility. It's not a new issue because it's one that we've talked about for the last couple of days and is another kind of possibility here. I would say that one of the questions we need to ask is not can we create a grand theory—not can we integrate the biological, the genetic, the personality, the evolutionary, the dynamic, the economic, all of these different approaches to these problems—but rather what is the best way to proceed scientifically? What is going to produce the best knowledge for us? Certainly we're getting more sophisticated statistically. Certainly the statistical models and procedures are available that allow me to take all of these other variables and, given a sufficiently large n, feed them into my structured equation models, my latent growth curve modeling, whatever multivariate technique I wanted to pursue. The question is, should I do that and the question is here, specifically I think, should John Bancroft do that? I would argue that it doesn't make sense researchwise, that it doesn't build good theories for us to try to be overinclusive. I would argue that, as Dennis Fortenberry said this morning, being a good researcher is about going through a deliberate process of excluding certain constructs and variables and defining the question in the way in which you can address it. So the goal here in this kind of interdisciplinary meeting is to become aware of the relevant research and ideas from other areas; to pay attention to them; to be informed about them; to have an open dialogue about the differences, the similarities, and the perspectives; to adopt what's useful out of those into your own research and disregard what isn't. I would argue that you need to be aware of the limitations of your theory and your research paradigm, but I would also argue that trying to include everything is likely to lead to frustration and to paralyze you or to dilute your efforts to a point that you won't be making as much of a contribution as you could otherwise. I would argue then, John Bancroft, that you should cut the end off of that paper and stick with the first half where I think you're on the right track and can make a significant contribution to our understanding of that behavior. You dilute your efforts by trying to take in too many other perspectives and fit them into the larger context.

General Discussion

Ed Laumann: Since this is an interdisciplinary group, the topic for this afternoon is on individual differences in sexual risk taking, with the strong implication that there is a predisposition or propensity associated with risk-seeking, risk-neutral, or risk-averse behavior. The economists postulate different types of persons with preferences for these kinds of risk propensities. To my knowledge, however, I know of nobody who has ever demonstrated a generalized disposition to be risk averse or risk seeking or risk neutral. One can readily identify people who are into investments, that may take flyers in the market, but who are very conservative with respect to something else. I would like to hear a discussion of this issue among those of you here who are more familiar with this literature.

Daryl Bem: Ed Laumann asked whether there's a general measure of risk, an individual difference measurement, and the answer is no. The reason for that is virtually all personality traits are usually our constructs that often don't match or map onto that of our subjects, or participants, as we now call them. So, for example, with the old stuff on "need for achievement" it turns out that people who are high in need for achievement love risks if they're in control and hate risks if it's a chance game. They will not play Las Vegas games but they will play poker. So even in this tiny domain of taking risks of that kind, we find no general trait; so subjectively, from the insider's point of view, they don't see those risks as alike at all and that's true of almost every trait. If you pick a trait and measure people across it, you'll never get correlations higher than .3 as you move from one situation to another precisely because most people behave inconsistently with regard to most traits. For each person there are about six traits that they organize their self-identify around and then they're quite consistent on those traits because they monitor themselves to make sure they're consistent on them. But I don't think you're going to find a general risk-taking trait.

John Bancroft: Well, that wasn't what I was referring to. I was saying that I had difficulty finding a measure, a quantification of sexual risk. We actually tried to devise one in a grant application and received a lot of criticism for it. When I discussed it with Joe Catania, for example, his advice to me was don't try to do it, it's too difficult. In fact, what we are attempting to do at the moment is to cover the complexity, which several people have referred to, in various ways in a questionnaire and then see, by using some sort of multivariate technique, whether we can identify categories or types which may be ordinal or rankable in terms of their riskiness. We're considering, for example, the possibility of using latent class analysis for that purpose.

Anke Ehrhardt: I like the idea very much of trying to get at a "risk-taking" predisposition. I think the problem is obviously one of definition, which people you want to start with. I was thinking people with a gambling addiction who go to a casino get taken over, they can't stop. I recently listened to stunt men. Their wives try to stop them but they cannot because of the thrill to jump from higher and higher buildings. So if we could find and define some people who clearly fit that kind of definition of risk-takers, we would find that they know they shouldn't do it but they're doing it because of the kind of thrill that's there. If you wanted to look for a predispositional brain variable, I would go for those people and I would first of all define them by interviews. I would try to put them into simulated situations maybe in a laboratory and then measure what you want to measure. But when it comes to those people who don't use condoms in a situation with a partner, then it all goes wrong because there are many factors which come into that.

John Bancroft: The closest to what you're talking about in the literature is "sensation-seeking" and there is considerable literature on that including psychophysiological parameters. But I think it's been rather elusive and I don't think it's really yet been particularly helpful in understanding sexual risk taking, particularly in relation to HIV.

Leonore Tiefer: Following on Daryl Bem's point about the social-psychological literature on risk taking, I remember reading a book called *Too Much Invested to Quit*. It had a tremendous analysis of a simulated laboratory kind of risk-taking situation that failed to show individual variables dominant in any way over the situational context. When you consider Milgram's work and the whole social psychology of conformity behavior, you again find that situational variables are dominant. It seems to me that meaning of risk in the sexual situation is so genderized that even at this point we should think about different terms that might be used to apply to the situation as experienced by men and women.

Richard Parker: This session, to me, is almost the most crucial or the one I thought would motivate us most because it's the one that most clearly and directly links up to the kind of concrete problem solving and confrontation of real-life dilemmas that John Gagnon quite rightly argued is the place where interdisciplinary collaborations actually happen on the ground. Not as abstract theorizing but in trying to solve problems. I was struck in listening to both of you that for anyone involved in the business of intervening in relation to risk, neither of the two extremes that in some ways are being defended here is a viable option as the basis for the design of a concrete intervention anywhere. Anybody who tries to design an intervention program winds up designing multidimensional interventions. Here I'm talking about real-world interventions, not the kinds of interventions that we sometimes test in research studies, but things we try to put in place on the street. You wind up trying to think of things that will work at an individual level, but also trying to think of things that will work at a collective community level, at the level of collective representations and imagination. Anytime you try to design something that's unidimensional you realize that it's too simplistic in any way, shape, or form to deal with the world in the social context that you're taking on. So this is the most obvious place for integration and yet the way in which we have framed the discussion thus far, we've ignored that. I'd like to ask you both to speak a bit more about how to translate what you're talking about into interventions, even recognizing John Gagnon's understandable resistance to want to do that for all of the reasons that he's made clear. But it seems to me logical to go to the practical consequences of what you're saying to be able to think about its consistency.

John Gagnon: I think when you do a practical intervention, you do everything you can. The psychology department in my university has an extremely good academic experimental clinical program, which means that all the clinical psychologists take the experimental courses. The experiments are always factorial designs in which you keep removing factors, looking for the most important factor that will then generate statistically significant change. In a sense it's a search for the most cost-effective technique. Of the 27 bullets in the gun, which one is going to give us the biggest bang? I think that approach is probably wrong. In the United States we have finally come to understand that what you should do is teach kids to read any damn way they can learn how to read. Some kids learn this way and some kids learn that way and some another way, and you just offer it all. You make a cafeteria out of the learning system, not a single menu. If you're going to design a real-world program, you do as much stuff as you possibly can. Now I think there is some stuff that I would start with, in other words, I would follow my prejudices. My prejudices are to see how the local folks figure out how to deal with the problem before I do any science.

I want to figure out what the vernacular system is. One of the things that happens frequently is everyday people figure out how to do things themselves. Here I'm leaning on Jeffrey Escoffier's work on safer sex. He argues that shared vernacular knowledge produces social solidarity. And social solidarity involves responsible modes of action toward the people you're connected to. You share a common knowledge about the world. If I were trying to inject scientific knowledge into a vernacular set of practices, then I would have to get the local folks to figure out how scientific knowledge, or some alternative version of it, might be acceptable to them and have them see whether it works in the world that they have. The concrete issue that produced this paper which I couldn't come to grips with was I feel that an awful lot of science-based AIDS education is a scorched-earth policy. It's there to replace what local people know, not to add anything to what local people know. My sense is that you have to figure out what the locals want to do and then you do everything you can. If somebody says I've got this flyer I want to put on the wall, that's okay.

One of the things you might want to worry about is whether or not some of the science stuff you want to do may be harmful. The knowledge that we produce for each other inside a discipline is community-based knowledge, but most of that knowledge is constructed to be consumed by that community. So when I talk sociology, I'm talking vernacular knowledge for sociologists, and it creates a lot of solidarity and we promote that knowledge. But that knowledge may not make any sense to anybody out there who's trying to figure out what to do about living their life.

What drives adolescent sexuality from my point of view is not really sexuality but love and romance, and I think that most of the things we try to do with these kids to make them not have babies doesn't have anything to do with why they're doing what they're doing. It's fun to be sexual. It's fun to fall in love. It's fun and painful to have relationships, but it is dramatic. Adults come along and say, well you ought to be rational actors and use condoms. How can we get into their lives in some sensible way which allows them to pick and choose among the things?

John Bancroft: I don't have any illusions about having answers for you guys in the trenches. I'm responding to what I see as a gap in our understanding of what at the moment seems difficult to understand. It remains to be seen whether it will actually result in being able to do anything for people better than you're already doing. It seems appropriate to at least try to understand it and move into that direction if at all possible. On a very obvious commonsense level, it would be a matter of helping people to analyze their own behavioral sequences in such a way that if they were motivated to do so they could identify at what point in a typical sequence they perhaps might do something different. If getting strongly sexually aroused or getting into a low mood is a key factor, then it would be a matter of helping them to develop different coping strategies in those situations. But I have no idea how useful this theoretical approach is going to be in practical terms.

Rafael Diaz: I want to respond to John Bancroft's paper and I have three comments. One of them is very neuropsychologically oriented. The second one is very much about the social context, and the third one is meta-theoretical. I want to draw a little bit on what we know about the development of the physiological arousal/attention system in infants and children. One of the first tasks of the human infant is the ability to sustain a certain homoeostasis of arousal in the absence of the caregiver. A lot of what happens between a young baby and the mother happens to create an interpersonal system of regulation of the baby's arousal, of excitatory and inhibitory mechanisms. So the ability to regulate arousal according to changes in environmental circumstances is first of all an interpersonal variable that only later becomes an intrapersonal variable. So in development what develops is not that we get a better inhibitory system or a better excitatory system, it is that we develop this ability to regulate the system so that our states of arousal/attention are adjusted appropriately according to the circumstances. This ability is associated with the development of the pre-frontal cortex. If that's the way that we develop in terms of our physiological arousal, why should sexual arousal be different? A better model would be to consider the development of sexual self-regulation, or the self-regulation of sexual arousal. What happens to individuals in development that helps them develop this self-regulation of their state of sexual arousal, to adjust appropriately, sometimes demanding excitability, other times demanding inhibition? Because these abilities are derived through experience, through contacts, a better way to talk about individual differences is to talk about how much we need external sources of control to maintain our arousability and how much we can do it on our own. Similar to the baby, who at first depends on the caregiver's input to maintain homeostasis, and later can do it on its own. So it might be that some of the problems you talk about in terms of inhibitory deficiencies might be better postulated in terms of dependence on the context—or external environment. Maybe we have problems with this developmental process because of the sexual silence in our society. Our extreme negative sexual attitudes toward experimentation show how much we're denying children the chance to develop this capacity to regulate sexual arousal. But the most important point is that the regulation of sexual arousal cannot be considered a personal psychological variable; it is a person-context factor. What is important for us for prevention is to help individuals understand in which situations they seem unable to regulate their arousability appropriately, whether it is excitement or inhibition. I think it is a theoretical mistake to understand the regulation of sexuality as something that we bring to a situation. Whether an individual can self-regulate is very much a property not only of what that individual brings but also of the type of partner, the emotions the persons are experiencing, the kinds of substances the persons have ingested or not, the things that are evoked in the situation. So the regulation of the sexual arousal system is also a contextual variable. In your theorizing, it is important to underscore the role of social context in this neuropsychological construct. The meta-theoretical comment that I wanted to make is that I really have trouble with the notion of risk taking, because my sense is that very few individuals recognize that they are actually doing something to take a risk. That's not the discourse that I hear from the men in my studies. What men talk about is being "swept away" by major concerns such as love, social connection, the need for approval, and doubts about their self-worth. The idea that appraisal comes before management is perhaps wrong. I think that people somehow want to feel good and want to feel connected, want to feel approved of and then they may or may not ask themselves, "My god, is this risky or not?" But what is driving the whole situation is not a rational decision making but actually many times a breakdown of this kind of rational processes by which the sexual behavior is regulated by so many other things that have to do with feeling good and feeling connected or feeling flesh-to-flesh contact, which we all want and need from time to time. So I am troubled that an approach to understanding HIV risk or understanding unprotected sex is guided by this idea that people are taking risks in a very rational calculating manner. That doesn't seem to be what the real experience is about, at least for the people I have interviewed.

John Bancroft: The first point you raise is a very interesting one. If you think about the parallel role of excitation and inhibition in the brain, then the models that spring to mind most readily are ones of homeostasis, and there are many. Then the balance of excitation and inhibition is designed to maintain a reasonably stable state, whether it be temperature or body weight or whatever. Interestingly when you come on to sex you move into a different territory in that respect. Sex can't be regarded in the same light as other homeostatic mechanisms. It's a matter of either you go or you don't go. You're not maintaining some steady state of "a little bit sexy" or "very much sexy" and so on. It's different. The only interesting situation where the homeostatic concept may come into play is one where inhibition of sexual behavior can be seen as a population density regulator, which has been proposed in other species. Then with the increase of population density you get inhibitor mechanisms operating in particular individuals within that group to suppress their reproductive behavior. So that's homeostasis for the group rather than for the individual. A novel way of looking at culture for you culture guys. So to respond to your point, I think we have to think about this as being probably fundamentally different. Something happens round about puberty, something called the refractory period comes in which involves central mechanisms of inhibition which are biologically necessary, males being what they are. If that inhibition system wasn't there, they would be having orgasms all the time and nothing would get done. From a simple biological perspective that actually would impair their fertility, apart from anything else. So I think that we are probably justified in thinking of something different in this balance system regarding sexual behavior when compared with other types of arousal mechanisms. On your other point, I don't know that really anything that you say causes me any difficulty for what I'm trying to say. Maybe I didn't make myself adequately clear. I think I would see the social context as central to how the model works because that is what the individual is responding to, and perceiving in that situation some form of a threat. I want this model to be relevant to issues wider than just whether you are at risk for getting HIV. But, as part of that process of responding to the social context, some neurophysiological mechanism is coming into play of which you are unaware, which you have no control over, and that is a fundamental part of my theoretical model. As for the issue that people are not seeing these situations as actually taking risks, that is very much the point I was wanting to make. I think in the cold light of day, when you ask them when they are out of the situation, when they are not actually engaging in these exciting things, they might on the basis of their appraisal of risk say that doing that would involve risk, but when they get caught up in the process then that awareness of risk gets altered. What I'm suggesting is that the effect of being very aroused sexually in that situation could be having a comparable effect to, say, taking a drug or alcohol which in some way alters the way which you manage the situation. So I think what you're saying is right and I think what you're saying is what I also tried to say, that it's what people do in those situations which then feeds back on how they actually appraise their riskiness. There's quite a lot of evidence to suggest that.

Connie Nathanson: On the issue of when we started thinking in terms of risk, the social construction of risk, or "risk talk," long precedes the appearance of HIV. I think Mary Douglas has written very persuasively about risk talk and about the variations in the social construction of risk in relation to social organization. That kind of analysis ought to get in here in some way, because apparently they think about risk in Australia differently than the way that we think about risk. We tend to construct risk in terms of Was it innocently acquired or is the person guilty? Was it voluntary or was it involuntary? Is it universal or is it only you who are at risk or me who is at risk? The shift in our evaluation of smoking came about because it moved from being construed as a risk that you impose on yourself to a risk that was imposed on you by others. So how we think about risk is very socially constructed and changes over time. Thinking of risk management as an intrapersonal process seems to me to be far off the mark. If you're talking about a sexual situation, unless you're talking about masturbation, sexual situations involve two people. In a previous life I have done quite a lot of research on contraceptive risk taking and on risk taking by people who were potentially exposed to sexually transmitted diseases. We found, for example, that condom use is much more likely in casual situations than it is in situations of intimate relationship. The way in which young women decide to use or not to use contraception usually has to do with how they and their boyfriends evaluate side effects. The meaning of contraception or risk is an interpersonal process that happens in the context of a relationship and I don't see how you can think about it apart from the interpersonal context.

John Bancroft: The issue of power and control in our theoretical model, though less well developed than the issues of mood and sexual arousal, does draw attention to the interpersonal aspect. Of course in most situations you are dealing with an interpersonal interaction but that interaction is between two individuals and I don't think it's irrelevant to consider how those two individuals are feeling in that particular situation. One of the things that I wanted to draw attention to was the very important issue of the amount of control that an individual felt he or she had in a relationship. Certainly in relationships between men and women, this is regarded as very important, although a lot of people are now questioning whether this is just a matter of gender or whether it's a matter of the personality characteristics of the individuals involved in that relationship. So I agree it needs to be there, but I think how you deal with that interaction may well be influenced by the extent to which you were sexually aroused at the time and also the mood that you were in. So I can't accept that because two people are involved then what's going on in the individual is irrelevant or inappropriate to consider.

Gary Dowsett: I don't actually think that's what Connie and Rafael are saying. I think it's a philosophical question, an epistemological question, and the model of the individual you're using in this argument can only be conceived of outside of history and context. The way you position everything else that happens to that person, that is, the other person in the interaction, or the place or environment in which things occur becomes simply static and outside the individual in some way that then becomes a backdrop to the individual. I think that that's clearly a philosophical position to take, and I think the argument is being made that that is not the way to come at this issue. One must be taking context as active in the construction of the moment, not simply backdrop to the construct, to the action that happens in the moment. If I can use an example, it's a bit like going swimming. You might think you're doing the swimming, but the water's doing a hell of a lot of the work, and you can't even conceive of the physics of swimming without understanding the properties of water and the way in which bodies and water interact and create action in some way. So context isn't in fact just backdrop or someplace where things might happen with somebody else. It is not denying that there's an individual body that makes individual decisions; it's just that that individual isn't on his or her own ever in the situations. They are only ever interacting with context with which other people engage and that's the issue where risk occurs. As a second comment, I wanted to discourage you from taking the advice of your two well-intentioned discussants to cut off the end of your paper. Do not circumcise your intellect in this way. The struggle that you've engaged in in that paper is a very courageous one, and while many of us could pick holes with either side of it, and many of us could point out the very vast gap in the middle between those two ends of the paper, that intellectual struggle is a very profound and important struggle at this time in the history of western intellectual thought. I would be horrified to see the first half of your paper perfected and then launched upon the world, particularly the developing world struggling with HIV, AIDS, and sexually transmissable diseases, without the second half of your paper continuing to undermine your confidence in the first half of your paper, because the engagement you produced inside yourself is a crucial one for rethinking these issues. If I can just reinforce that point by saying I spent last week in Montréal at a UNAIDS meeting on what are the socio-cultural and economic determinants of HIV infection. The issue that faced us in that meeting is that it's absolutely clear that the psychosocial, behavioral, and individual models of behavior change that have dominated the international effort on HIV have not worked, and they have not produced the results that we need in developing countries or indeed in some developed countries such as this one. It's clear to the people working in UNAIDS and the people they work with that they need to have other models in the socio-cultural and economic area to explain determinants of epidemics. Without those, they can't construct programs. In a sense, your struggle in that paper represents exactly that same kind of struggle. We work with smaller units than you worked with with Harris's model. I think you've used a large company of earth movers there when basically you need a spade at the moment, and I suggest you ditch him for a bit. There are many other sociologists in the room who could give you a few smaller tools to work with, and not make the same mistake sociology makes often, and that is being incapable of dealing with human beings on a human scale some of the time.

John Bancroft: Right now I think the point that you are making could be seen as going to the heart of the epistemological problem that we have here. I have absolutely no problem at all in accepting all that you say about the very dynamic nature of the context. Yet I come from a position where I need to understand how the actors involved in that context behave and what influences their behavior. In a sense we need to be able to do both things and therefore I am perfectly prepared to accept that the model that I presented is focusing on the individual actor, but I do not believe that it precludes or makes difficult the recognition and indeed incorporation of the other person that you're reacting with or the social context in which it is going on. It's simply focusing on some of the potentially relevant characteristics of that individual which may influence that individual's interaction in those situations. We can change our emphasis, but I don't know that we need to throw one out and keep the other. Let's try to keep both. Of course you're right about individually focused intervention programs as largely being a failure, although a document was recently issued in this country saying that they had been useful. Nevertheless, I would be inclined to agree with you. But the point there is that virtually without exception, they have not been looking at these issues of sexuality and mood, and indeed power in the relationship, that I am considering. So I see no reason to just abandon looking at the individual and look only at social groups. Clearly the social groups are very important. I have absolutely no doubts at all about that. You need to influence the social groups that people move in, because that's how they're likely to get influenced in important ways. But I see no justification for abandoning the individual in these situations yet.

Shirley Lindenbaum: I just wanted to underline that last point. I'd be very sorry to see the second part of the paper dropped or divorced from the first half of the paper. I don't think you can understand anything about individual behaviors unless they're contextualized in wide historical shifts. We're seeing this in monumental ways in some of the small-scale societies that we work in with changes of political economy. It's not just in Papua New Guinea but elsewhere that we witness many new forms of desire and some of them are resulting in newly commoditized social forms, social arrangements. Sometimes, as with the example I gave yesterday of newly commoditized ritual forms, we're looking at people venturing into new kinds of sexual behaviors that are associated with many new kinds of risk taking. Some of the risk taking is going to result in STDs and some of it's going to result in death on the highways, because they fulfill two other desires, to buy a truck and drink alcohol at the same time. So people are fulfilling a multitude of new desires that they encounter in this wider context. It would be a shame to try to explain all this new kind of risk taking that we're seeing divorced from the wider political economy, because what we're looking at is not just new forms of sexual behavior but really new regimes of desire. These are tied to new forms of social status and new dangers of various kinds. It's even difficult to separate out the new experimentations in sexual behavior from all these other desires that are tied to it—of money, prestige, and so forth. It's that kind of embeddedness of risk taking in other kinds of overwhelming desires that we're looking at, rather than individual behavior on its own, or rather than just sexual behaviors on their own.

Gilbert Herdt: I think it's very helpful that we're having this conversation toward the end of the session because we really have come back now to the question of scientific worldview and epistemology. I'd just like to pick up on several points that have been addressed to John Bancroft's paper, to which you last responded, John, by talking about the importance of the difference between individual and group. I think individual/group is a very important dimension, but that's not the only dimension that's of relevance here. It's also the difference between what we could call *insider versus outsider perspectives;* that is often what is at issue. The question was put to you Are these men aware of their high risk or not? It seems that what you're attempting to do is to say "We've got to go into the lab and establish the correct procedure and then we're going to examine whether they are aware of the degree of high risk or not." What John Gagnon said, which is probably more the approach of natural history and anthropology, is go into the community and first find out what are their concerns. Then to pick up on a point that both Rafael and Gary made, these points address an issue which you yourself struggled over in the second part of your paper, and which I also applaud. I think it was a very important and courageous attempt to think out the implications of your paradigm. You were struggling with Marvin Harris's distinction between emic and etic, which hasn't been picked up here. Much of Marvin Harris's work in anthropology we would regard as pretty much passé because he wasn't interested in culture, he was really interested in material resources around which cultural and social structure are created. But he popularized this distinction between emic and etic, which actually he mistranslated from linguistics, and should properly be glossed, as Clifford Geertz most persuasively argued it, as the difference between the insider and the outsider perspective. That is to say, what does one individual understand about the sexual encounter? What does the observer to the encounter understand about their meanings of their experiences? So that in an encounter between two individuals, the situation that Gary and Shirley were responding to, one of them could be an insider and the other can be an outsider or they can both be insiders and someone could be observing the dyadic relationship as an outsider, or they can both be outsiders and so on. What I'm trying to draw attention to is this extraordinarily important conceptual as well as operational distinction between understanding the concerns and the meanings of the behaviors themselves on the part of the individuals involved in the situation and on the part of outsiders to the situation.

John Bancroft: I did attempt to discuss this issue of the emic and the etic, which goes to the heart of what we're talking about, although I accept that Harris mistranslated the terms. If I'm going to proceed with trying to develop this theoretical model, I want to test it out with "insiders." And the way I'd want to do that, and indeed the way we're planning to do that, is to carry out in-depth interviews with people who we have identified as being high risk-takers and see whether this conceptualization makes any sense when you talk to them in some detail. I think that would fairly quickly help to decide whether this is going to be useful or not. At present I have an open mind about that, but that's certainly what we intend to do. I'm already doing it in relation to patients that I'm seeing with compulsive sexual behavior and that's proving to be very useful. But the "outsider," as you put it, may be able to bring ideas to bear on this which an insider would not ever consider, and that's basically what Harris means about emic/etic distinction. So the idea of a dual control system in the brain with a variable propensity for central inhibition of sexual response is the outsider's attempt to contribute an explanation to what is happening, which may prove to be helpful or it may not. As I said in the paper, it's still a way of modeling what we're dealing with and the question is whether it proves to be a useful model. But it is a model which is derived from a very different perspective than you would get from talking to the guy engaging in high-risk sex, who would tell you the vernacular stories that John Gagnon talks about, why he takes risk and so on. I think we need to listen to both types of story, to use that metaphor.

Leonore Tiefer: I have a hard time understanding how this risk model applies to women. It occurred to me that maybe that's one way to think about the disjuncture between the two halves of your paper. It's very easy for me to see how the second half of the paper relates to women since the essential concept is reproduction, and the infrastructure, structure, and superstructure concepts are very clearly related to women's lives. When I think about women's risks, risky situations, risky behaviors, there are, of course, disease risk and pregnancy, which might or might not be construed as a risk. We talked about that earlier with regard to adolescence and, depending on where and who defines it, it might or might not be a risk, so that's kind of borderline. But there is an area of risk for women which I think has a profound influence throughout the world, the risk of reputation. Some people have written about this to some extent. Women's reputational loss is a serious risk, never long out of the mind, a risk that relates very directly to these reproductive notions and how they are active in the sexual context, in the interaction of the moment. Of course where I'm going with this is that shame, for women, leads to inhibition and this is important to think about in terms of the risk of the lost sexual opportunity. So in the balance between pleasure and danger, which is where risk lies, we want to think as much about the pressures for excessive inhibition as much as inadequate risk-taking behavior.

John Bancroft: All of us at the Kinsey Institute are very keen to get involved in looking at women as well as men. It raises some very interesting issues. My hunch is that at a physiological level there may be some important differences between men and women in inhibitory mechanisms. There was an interesting review recently, which I cite in my paper, which from an evolutionary perspective suggests that women have a need to have much more marked and more widespread inhibitor mechanisms in place. It goes through a whole lot of literature which suggests that that actually might be so, that there's a lot more inhibition going on in women. If you look at the effect of cultural social processes on female sexuality and the rather more dramatic way that they've changed over the last 50 years in Europe and so on, you can see that as possibly an interaction between social processes focused on women in particular and their propensity for their sexual response being inhibited. So I entirely agree with you, Leonore, and I can't wait to pursue that in one way or another.

John Gagnon: I'm going to make one more attempt to say why the individual model may be a problem using John's terms. It seems to me that what happens is that you have an actor in a sexual situation and he or she has some appraisal or set point, at a given moment in the interaction. The hugging and kissing begins. The pointer goes up and down. It is in the interaction when the set point for appraising the risk begins to change. It's not what the individual's mood is or those kinds of internal processes, but it's actually an interactive process with the thermostat going up and down in the process of doing things with the other person. It is not simply that one estimates where the pointer is and then asks what's the mood and how does that change where the pointer is or how much control is there in the interaction. The feedback is continuously changing each person's appraisal and management at the same time. It's possible analytically to separate appraisal and management. You can give people questionnaires saying appraise this risk and they will perfectly sensibly do that, and put marks on the paper, or answer the questions. But it's in the situation where the appraisal and management go on at the same time. "No, I'm not going to let him touch my breasts." Is that management or appraisal? What is it that these things mean in the process? It's not that I'm against your doing the individual stuff, I can't stop you anyway, but what's happening is that whatever that set point is, is going up and down in the interaction. The individual model may be an ineffective model of the real-world situation. You may be able to make these measurements on the individual but they will probably not be terribly predictive of the situation in which you want to be predictive.

John Bancroft: You may well be right. But I don't know. I am very keen to confess that I have very little experience of dealing with people grappling with the risk of HIV, like Richard Parker, Jay Paul, Gary Dowsett, and Rafael Diaz have, and I respect their experience. But I do have 30 years' experience working with relationships and couples, dealing with sexual interactions, and I do know a reasonable amount about that, and how sexual arousal and mood can play a part in that. And I know very well that although I deal with a dyad, with a relationship, I have to take the individual into account. So I'll be a little bit surprised if that wasn't the case in this other situation too.

Rafael Diaz: I wanted to be sure that you understand, John, that I believe that individuals need to be studied and individuals are important components, but my main point is that the variable that you're interested in—the regulation of sexual arousal—is not an individual variable. For example, we find in Latino homosexual behavior this kind of playing roles of female and male, so the ability to regulate and inhibit depends on what role you're taking. So there's a lot of cultural factors determining what gets regulated, what gets inhibited. I cannot think of regulation of sexual arousal as an individual trait, where you can say this person has a little, or this person has a lot, without reference to the context that provides different degrees of external regulation.

John Bancroft: You say you can't understand what happens to a person in a sexual interaction by studying his individual capacity for sexual arousal. That is a question which is testable. You may be right, although I doubt it. I think that it's distinctly likely that if we have some way of measuring that was relevant to the situation we're concerned about, we will find that there are measurable characteristics, either in the laboratory or in terms of a questionnaire, reproducible reliable characteristics which would predict a reasonable amount of the variance that occurred in interactions. That's testable, so you may prove to be right or wrong in the fullness of time.

Part 4

Adolescent Sexuality

The Impregnable Myth of Teenage Pregnancy: A Case Study of the Gap between Science and Public Policy

CONSTANCE A. NATHANSON

The myth to which I refer in the title of this paper is one in which the metaphor "teen pregnancy" is employed to symbolize everything that is perceived as wrong with American society in general and with black inner-city residents in particular. It is a myth of rampant sexuality, of irresponsible reproduction, and of calculated dependence on "the welfare system." The broad myth is composed of several sub-myths, myths of fact and myths of theory. The myth is impregnable in that it has proved over a period of two and a half decades to be virtually impervious to contrary, or even mildly critical, data and analysis. Indeed, it has not been unusual for these data and analyses to be met with remarkable hostility. By way of background for the ensuing discussion, I begin the paper with a brief review of this work, generated over the past 25 years by a multidisciplinary body of social scientists. I will then go on to examine current public policies in the light of this work, and to suggest some hypotheses to account for the gap between what social science tells us and what policymakers say and do.

Teenage Pregnancy: Data, Theory, and Analysis

My review is organized around the "myths" I refer to in the title, presented in more or less the chronological order in which these myths first appeared.

An "epidemic" of teenage pregnancy was first announced in the mid-1970s. Whether there was, or was not, an "epidemic" depends entirely on the data to which you attend. The adolescent birth *rate,* along with the birth rates of all reproductive-age women in the United States, reached its peak in the mid-1950s at the height of the baby boom. The sheer *number* of births to adolescents reached its height (to date) in 1970 (when baby-boom teens themselves were having babies); and the percent of all births represented by births to adolescents was highest in 1975 (because adolescent fertility was dropping more slowly than the fertility of older women). These data are shown in Table 1.

In the 1980s we were told that "children were having children." In fact, almost two-thirds of births to women under 20 in 1985 were to 18- and 19-year-olds. The proportion of these births to young women under the age of 14, who might fairly be described as "children," was 2%.

Since 1980, teenage pregnancy has been almost universally identified with unmarried black women. Indeed, the percentage of teen births to unmarried teenagers has increased steadily over the last two and one half decades, from 30% in 1970 to 76% in 1996.[1] (And just as the baby boom was common to all women of reproductive age, so has the increase in non-marital births occurred among women of all ages.) However, the *change* in adolescent behavior that this increase represents has been considerably more marked among whites than among blacks: Between 1970 and 1996 the non-marital birth rate to white teens more than tripled, from 10.9 to 34.5 per 1000. Among blacks it increased from 96.9 to 108.5 per 1,000 in 1991 and has since declined to 89.2 per 1,000, considerably lower than the rate in 1970. Nearly two-thirds of teen non-marital births in 1996 were to young white women.

The data I have presented refer, of course, to childbearing, not pregnancy, and some comment on this point is called for. Insofar as "teen pregnancy" has negative social and economic consequences, they are consequences of childbearing, not of pregnancy; a badly timed pregnancy can be terminated. "Teen pregnancy" is a political, not a scientific, label: It has a dual rhetorical function, both as a code phrase for sexual intercourse by adolescent women and as a way of avoiding any consideration of abortion as a solution to the "problem" of early childbearing.

The most deeply entrenched myths about teenage pregnancy—which have generated a veritable industry among scholars—have to do with its causes and consequences. Ever since Charles Murray dazzled the right wing in 1980 with his book *Losing Ground*, it has been accepted wisdom among conservative policymakers that the welfare system "caused" teenagers to have babies for the sake of the welfare check. This assumption has generated a very large social scientific literature employing a wide range of approaches; the majority of these studies have found no or, at best, meager support for the proposition that financial support, or potential financial support, for unmarried women led them to increased fertility (Nathanson, 1991; Moffitt, 1992).[2] The statistical sophistication of these studies is formidable, but there is little evidence that their conclusions have made any difference to the terms of political debate. The same may be said of research on

Table 1
Indices of Adolescent Fertility by Age Category, Selected Years, 1960–1996

Age	Number of Births	Percent of All Births	Birth Rate/1000
10–14 YEARS			
1960	7,462	0.2	0.8
1970	11,752	0.3	1.2
1975	12,642	0.4	1.3
1980	10,169	0.3	1.1
1985	10,220	0.3	1.3
1996	11,148	0.3	1.2
15–17 YEARS			
1960	117,904	4.0	42.7
1970	223,590	6.0	38.8
1975	227,270	7.2	36.1
1980	198,222	5.5	32.5
1985	167,789	4.5	31.1
1990	183,327	4.4	37.5
1996	186,762	4.8	34.0
18–19 YEARS			
1960	423,775	10.0	172.1
1970	421,118	11.3	114.7
1975	354,968	11.3	85.0
1980	353,939	9.8	82.1
1985	299,696	8.0	80.8
1990	338,499	8.1	88.6
1996	307,509	7.9	86.5

the consequences of early childbearing. While a consensus has been reached that early studies overstated these consequences, this consensus appears fragile; the battle over "unobserved heterogeneity" continues, and it appears highly unlikely that victory by one side or the other would have the slightest impact on public policy (Geronimus & Korenman, 1992; Hoffman, Foster, & Furstenberg, 1993a; Geronimus & Korenman, 1993; Hoffman, Foster, & Furstenberg, 1993b).[3]

Over the past two decades, serious scholars have generated a series of reasoned critiques of the teenage pregnancy myth as well as attempts to understand its meaning and importance in American society and culture. The first of these was by an historian, Maris Vinovskis, who had also served as staff director of the Senate Select Committee on Population in the late 1970s (Vinovskis, 1981). Vinovskis questioned the term "epidemic" as applied to adolescent childbearing and described how this and other rhetorical devices were used by advocates to draw attention to what they perceived as a significant social problem. Vinovskis did not, however, question the basic premise that early childbearing had a wide range of negative health, social, and economic consequences, which doubtless spared him the wrath experienced by the next major critic, Arline Geronimus. Geronimus did question, and has continued to question, this premise in a series of studies remarkable for their substantive as well as their statistical originality (Geronimus, 1987, 1991; Geronimus & Korenman, 1992; Geronimus, Korenman, & Hillemeier, 1994). Her fundamental thesis is that early childbearing is an outcome of social deprivation that affects *all* women in deprived circumstances, not just the early childbearers. The "problem" is thus redefined from one of childbearing to one of poverty and deprivation, with concomitant differences in policy implications. The critical perspectives of Vinovskis and Geronimus were extended and expanded in my own monograph, *Dangerous Passage,* published in 1991, and in that of Kristin Luker, *Dubious Conceptions,* published in 1996 (Nathanson, 1991; Luker, 1996.) These books marshal a wide range of statistical and substantive evidence to show that current conceptions about teenagers and their babies are based on a fundamental misunderstanding of the problem: The major cause of future poverty is present poverty, not teen pregnancy.

I have seen little evidence that Luker's restatement of the myths and of their unfortunate effects on public policy had any more impact on policymakers than mine did. Indeed, the evidence is all in the other direction, as demonstrated by the punitive provisions of recent state and federal welfare legislation. My examination of the implicit assumptions—"theories," if you will—underlying current public policy is based on an examination of three sets of documents: the 1996 welfare reform legislation and related programmatic statements from the Department of Health and Human Services, the National Campaign to Prevent Teenage Pregnancy, and recent policy statements of the Alan Guttmacher Institute.

Teenage Sex and Welfare Reform

The "theories" about the sexuality of teenage women that appear to have guided recent congressional policy initiatives are most clearly reflected in the provisions of the Welfare Reform Act for "abstinence education" (U.S. Public Law 104–193, Section 912 [110 Stat. 2353]). These provisions (P.L. 104–193, Section 912) apportion monies (50 million dollars/year for five years) to be allocated among the states for abstinence education. Abstinence education is explicitly and narrowly defined as "an educational or motivational program" which teaches, among other things, "that a mutually faithful monogamous relationship in context of marriage is the expected standard of human sexual activity." The program is required to have as "its exclusive purpose" teaching "the social, psychological, and health gains to be realized by abstaining from sexual activity." It is required to teach that "abstinence from sexual activity is the only certain way to avoid out-of-wedlock pregnancy, sexually transmitted diseases, and other associated health problems," and that "sexual activity outside of the context of marriage is likely to have harmful psychological and physical effects." The program is to "teach young people how to reject sexual advances and how alcohol and drug use increases vulnerability to sexual advances," and, finally, "the importance of attaining self-sufficiency before engaging in sexual activity" (110 Stat. 2354).

Given congressional intent to prevent non-marital births, the omission of contraceptive education from the education provisions may seem surprising. The omission was quite deliberate, reflecting congressional belief that information about birth control undermines the abstinence message (Haskins & Bevan, 1997, p. 5). Lest we continue to be under any illusion as to what Congress had in mind, the legislative purpose is made crystal clear in a document entitled "Implementing the Abstinence Education Provision of the Welfare Reform Legislation," prepared by the National Campaign to Prevent Teenage Pregnancy as guidance for the states. Acknowledging that "there is little evidence . . . that any particular policy or program will reduce the frequency of non-marital births," this document goes on to state that "the congressional attack on illegitimacy is based far more on the value position that birth outside marriage is wrong" than on empirical evidence that abstinence education will be effective. The authors state, based on their talks with the drafters of the abstinence provision as well as the statutory language, that the standard of no sex outside of marriage "was intended to put Congress on the side of social tradition . . . that sex should be confined to married couples. . . . [T]he explicit goal of the abstinence education programs is to change both behavior and community standards for the good of the country" (Haskins & Bevan, 1997, p. 9). The intent of Congress, in other words, is to reforge the links, broken over the last several decades, between sexuality, reproduction, and marriage.

However, Congress is selective in its efforts to reestablish traditional controls: The behavior of some adolescents needs changing more than that of others. The preamble to Congress's list of requirements for abstinence education states that the program's focus is to be "on those groups which are most likely to bear children out-of-wedlock." "Those groups," a small and highly selected subset of all sexually experienced adolescents, are female, economically disadvantaged, and (as shown by the data presented earlier) predominantly white.

The weight attached by the federal government to abstinence education should not be underestimated. A Department of Health and Human Services document published in January 1997 titled "A National Strategy to Prevent Teen Pregnancy" describes a two-pronged approach: (1) "Strengthen the national response to prevent out-of-wedlock teen pregnancies"; (2) "Support and encourage adolescents to remain abstinent." Special attention will be given to "efforts to promote abstinence among 9- to 14-year-old girls" (U.S. Department of Health and Human Services, 1997, p. 1). I remind the reader that the birthrate among 9- to 14-year-old girls has remained virtually unchanged since 1970.

Despite the near-obsessive concern with the sexual and reproductive behavior of adolescents reflected in the Welfare Reform Act, the Act is vague about the causes of the sexual behavior it decries. Congress's theory of adolescent sexuality must be inferred from the solutions it proposes; these "solutions" combine the attempt to legislate a single moral standard of sexual behavior—a standard which is, however, inequitably applied—with a variety of coercive carrots and sticks intended to sanction behavior which deviates from this standard. The vision of sexuality underlying these solutions is in the classic tradition (in this case, perhaps more Hobbesian than Freudian or Kinseyan [cf. Gagnon & Simon, 1973, pp. 10–11]). It assumes a primitive force which the individual is unable or unwilling to control and which, consequently, must be regulated by the state in the interests of social order (and fiscal restraint).[4]

At the same time (and in some contradiction), this vision assumes a rationally calculating individual who has responded to "rewards" (higher welfare benefits) and will respond to sanctions (loss of welfare benefits, among others) by changes in sexual and reproductive behavior. For example, it is suggested that young men who "realize they will wind up paying child support for at least 18 years if they help conceive a child outside marriage" may be less likely to engage in sex (Haskins & Bevan, 1997, p. 3). The congressional theory of adolescent sexuality is a triumph of radical individualism and behaviorism (cf. Naples, 1997).

Abstinence education, as I noted earlier, is to be focused on "high-risk" groups. Congress makes clear its belief that welfare itself is the highest risk; the House report on the welfare reform bill states that "welfare-encouraged out-of-wedlock childbearing increases the probability of teen sexual activity" (U.S. House of Representatives, 1996, p. 4). When it is spelled out, the bill says that welfare causes non-marital births and non-marital births cause teenage sex. Thus, to the congressional theories of declining morals and knee-jerk behaviorism, we may add the inheritance of acquired characteristics: "Bad" behavior by the parent causes "bad" behavior in the child. The racism, sexism, and classism inherent in these "theories" do not need to be spelled out.

The National Campaign to Prevent Teenage Pregnancy

The National Campaign to Prevent Teenage Pregnancy (NCPTP), like the congressional provision for abstinence education, is based on the premise of "a society gone astray" (NCPTP, 1997). An early report, "Whatever Happened to Childhood? The Problem of Teen Pregnancy in the United States," describes teen pregnancy as a "compelling example of how our families, communities, and common culture are under siege" (by what, or whom, is unstated) (NCPTP, 1997, p. 1). The report goes on to describe the consequences of teen pregnancy in ominous terms (apparently on the assumption that all pregnancies lead to births) and to suggest that social norms are at fault: "The consensus that 'teen pregnancy is not OK' is less robust than many imagine" (NCPTP, 1997, p. 11). In line with this belief, the first component of the Campaign's strategy is "taking a strong stand against teen pregnancy and attracting new and powerful voices to this issue."

The Campaign's approach is considerably kinder and gentler than that of Congress. Direct comments about sexuality are limited to the statement that adults need to provide "guidance in accordance with their own values and (encourage) teens to make much clearer choices about when to become sexually active." There is less emphasis on the immorality of early pregnancy and childbearing and more on its potential for interfering with education and preparation to "compete in an increasingly competitive economy" (National Campaign to Prevent Teenage Pregnancy, 1997, p. 1). The tenor of this piece of Campaign literature is, nevertheless, a far cry from the "preventive medicine" approach advocated by teenage pregnancy crusaders in the mid-1970s. The essential problem is defined as a moral one—a problem of "the overall culture"—to be solved by parental guidance, exhortation by celebrities and political leaders, and, presumably, cultural change.

The Alan Guttmacher Institute

The Alan Guttmacher Institute (AGI) has been a powerful advocate for reproductive health services directed toward teenage women since the early 1970s. Indeed, if any single organization can be held responsible for "creating" the problem of teenage pregnancy in the United States, it is AGI (Nathanson, 1991, pp. 46–58). AGI's perspective has changed markedly, however, since 1976 when it published *11 Million Teenagers: What Can Be Done about the Epidemic of Adolescent Pregnancies in the United States.*[5]

In the birth control rhetoric of its first incarnation (in the 1960s as the research and development arm of the Planned Parenthood Federation of America), elimination of unwanted pregnancies was presented as the means of accelerating the "exit from poverty" of poor families. In the 1970s idiom of adolescent pregnancy, the problem was redefined from one of poverty to one of pregnancy itself.

> The specter of *adolescent* pregnancy effectively blurred (earlier) distinctions . . . between poor and nonpoor, black and white . . . , but also between wanted and unwanted, in-wedlock and out-of-wedlock pregnancies: Adolescent pregnancy was defined as "tragic" without qualification. *A central dimension of this shift in emphasis . . . was the designation of sexual and reproductive behavior by adolescent women as a medical rather than a moral problem.* (Nathanson, 1991, p. 48, emphasis added)

11 Million Teenagers has virtually nothing to say about the underlying causes of early sexual and reproductive behaviors. Its focus is on what are characterized as the uniformly devastating consequences of these behaviors and on the solutions advocated by AGI: greatly expanded access to birth control and abortion services.

As I noted seven years ago, AGI's "discovery" of adolescent pregnancy proved to be a double-edged sword; undiscovered, the "facts" of teenage sex could be ignored. Officially sanctioned "facts" (sanctioned in many government venues, including congressional language requiring federally funded family planning clinics to offer "services to adolescents") "demanded the attention not only of humanitarian reformers primarily concerned with the untoward health and social consequences of the behavior in question but also of moral conservatives deeply offended by the behavior itself" (Nathanson, 1991, p. 58). The current hegemony—at least in public discourse—of moral conservative constructions is clearly reflected in the welfare reform bill and in the Campaign to Prevent Teenage Pregnancy.

AGI's institutional response to its loss of control over the terrain represented by adolescent sexuality and its consequences is beyond the scope of this paper. However, its rhetorical response is clearly reflected in its most recent (1994) publication on this topic, openly titled (in contrast to the obfuscation in 1976) *Sex and America's Teenagers*. This document is not only far more nuanced than the two other contemporary documents I have considered; it is also far more nuanced than *11 Million Teenagers*. Several points about AGI's current treatment of adolescent sexuality are striking.

First, like Congress and the Campaign, AGI draws attention to social change: "Over the last century, the transition from childhood to adulthood has been radically, and probably irrevocably, altered" (AGI, 1994, p. 4). The word "irrevocably" is, of course, key. AGI does not wring its hands. It asks, instead, that we "accept the reality of adolescent sexual activity" (p. 5). To this extent, AGI's stance has not altered since the mid-1970s: The "problem" is not sexual activity but its consequences. Emphasizing that "differences in sexual activity between gender, racial, socioeconomic and religious groups have narrowed considerably," AGI says to us, as it did in 1976, everybody (or almost everybody) is doing it.

Second, sexual social change is situated socially and demographically. Sex occurs somewhat earlier; "independence" (or "self-sufficiency" in Congress's language) happens much later as a consequence of structural changes in patterns of education and work—"education and employment have become accepted, almost required, paths to adulthood for young women, as well as for young men" (AGI, 1994, p. 6)— and media-driven social pressures: "Young people are bombarded with sexual images and messages" (AGI, 1994, p. 11). These arguments shift much of the responsibility for non-marital sexual activity from the "irresponsible" individual to impersonal social forces over which the individual has little or no control.

The most remarkable change in AGI's perspective, however, is in its move away from the construction of adolescent sexuality, pregnancy, and childbearing as primarily medical problems with medical solutions (i.e., birth control and, when necessary, abortion), and its renewed emphasis on poverty. While accessible birth control and abortion services are advocated for "sexually experienced teenagers," these and other interventions

> do not address the entrenched poverty that is a major cause of early childbearing among disadvantaged teenage women. Only when their poverty is alleviated, and these young women—and their partners— have access to good schools and jobs and come to believe that their futures can be brighter, is real change *in their sexual behavior* and its outcomes likely to occur. (AGI, 1994, p. 5, emphasis mine)

Reverting, in part, to the rhetoric of the 1960s, the "problem" is, again, defined as one of poverty, not pregnancy; not only social and structural change but poverty itself is a "cause" of (what is here, presumably, defined as) problematic sexual behavior. Thus, AGI turns not only the rhetoric of Congress and the Campaign, but the rhetoric AGI itself espoused in 1976, on its head. From a focus on poverty as the inevitable *consequence* of untimely sexual behavior, AGI identifies poverty as the *cause*. AGI's 1970s advocacy of birth control for teenagers was radical at the time; its current stance is more radical still (but much less well publicized).

Sex and America's Teenagers reviews and draws its policy conclusions from current scholarly research on adolescent sexual activity, pregnancy, and childbearing and, indeed, embraces in large part the critical perspectives I described earlier. However, AGI's influence on public policy is much diminished; neither birth control and abortion *nor* alleviation of poverty are consistent with currently popular definitions of or solutions to the "adolescent pregnancy" problem. Both the imperviousness of current policies to social scientific evidence developed over the last two decades and the intense hostility this evidence has frequently generated raise important questions. I advance three hypotheses to account for these phenomena.

Why the Impregnable Myth?

The first hypothesis is that advocates on all sides, from liberal to conservative, have powerful vested interests in current constructions of teenage pregnancy. The problem from the perspective of the liberals is suggested by the concern expressed by a prominent critic of what he called "revisionist" thinking on teenage pregnancy for "beleaguered policymakers, service providers, and funders who after spending many years and many dollars on the issue of teenage childbearing, now wonder whether the effort has been worthwhile" (Furstenberg, 1991, p. 135). As the same critic points out, "a veritable industry" serving the various teen pregnancy constituencies has developed in the last two decades. My own experience as an occasional speaker to audiences of family planning and social welfare workers attests that chronically underfunded service providers in particular are powerfully committed to the continuing crisis mentality generated by the idea of teenage pregnancy. The Pavlovian effect on donors and politicians of "children having children" is unlikely to be abandoned without a fight. Tidings that the problem is less of a crisis than they have believed and unlikely to respond to the solutions they represent are not well received.

Conservatives are equally committed to the crisis construction, if for different reasons. The combination of moral and fiscal indignation generated by images of sexually irresponsible unmarried teenage females deliberately conceiving to collect a welfare check has worked well for them. This was Charles Murray's vision and it played a major—if not *the* major—role in ending any federal guarantee of income support for poor women with young children.

My second hypothesis has to do with the absence of any effective organized counterattack by or on behalf of the "victims" of constructions of inner-city poverty as a problem of teenage pregnancy. Public policy making in the United States is highly sensitive to organized social movement and/or interest group intervention; in the absence of powerful intervention, policymakers take paths of least resistance. Unlike persons with AIDS or survivors of breast cancer—both recent examples of groups who have made highly consequential public policy interventions—young women who are pregnant and poor have neither the social networks, the resources, nor the incentives to organize on their own behalf. "Rights talk," used so effectively by these and other contemporary social movements, resonates poorly when it comes to early childbearing. Nor do these young women have many powerful friends. Feminists, for example, have been conspicuously silent on the issue of teenage pregnancy. Their dilemma is that while a young unmarried woman's "choice" to reproduce may be inherently suspect on the one hand, on the other, it *is* her choice and one woman does not tell another what to do with her body. More broadly, the maternalist ideology that fueled organization on behalf of mothers and children in the Progressive Era is long dead, children (and most teenage women) do not vote, and no American Association of Retired Persons prowls the halls of Congress to make the case for a construction of reality alternative to the prevailing wisdom.

My final hypothesis is that "teenage pregnancy" functions as a convenient "master frame" (Snow & Benford, 1992), organizing experience and guiding action relevant to a wide range of apparently intractable social problems—"intractable" in part because they are part and parcel of social changes in sexual behavior and family formation and dissolution going on all over the industrialized world, and in part because their solutions are simply unpalatable. Delayed marriage, cohabitation, and non-marital childbearing are contemporary social phenomena we share with virtually every other first-world country except Japan. The emotional charge of these changes is compounded in the United States by the furor over abortion. These are uncomfortable social changes for many people, neatly captured by the symbolism of "teenage pregnancy." Further, it has proved convenient to blame such difficult problems as child abuse, drug addiction, poverty, and an unbalanced federal budget (to name a few) on the behavior of a generalized voiceless "other," outside the bounds of respectability, marginalized by gender, race, and social class. If social problems are caused by untimely childbearing—rather than by institutionalized relationships embedded in American society that distribute power and wealth inequitably—then these problems can be prevented by the selective prevention of childbearing rather than by the redistribution of wealth and power. The inferred relationships are simplistic, but the inferences are easily made, and they lead to policies that call not for institutional change but for the social control of women.

252 | *Constance A. Nathanson*

REFERENCES

Astone, N. M. (1997). Review of the "Personal Responsibility and Work Opportunity Reconciliation Act of 1996." *Contemporary Sociology, 26*(4), 413–415.

Alan Guttmacher Institute. (1976). *11 million teenagers.* New York: Planned Parenthood Federation of America.

Alan Guttmacher Institute. (1994). *Sex and America's teenagers.* New York: Alan Guttmacher Institute.

Furstenberg, F. F., Jr. (1991). As the pendulum swings: Teenage childbearing and social concern. *Family Relations, 40,* 127–138.

Gagnon, J. H., & Simon, W. (1973). *Sexual conduct: The social sources of human sexuality.* Chicago: Aldine Publishing Co.

Geronimus, A. (1987). On teenage childbearing and neonatal mortality in the United States. *Population and Development Review, 13*(2), 245–279.

Geronimus, A. (1991). Teenage childbearing and social and reproductive disadvantage: The evolution of complex questions and the demise of simple answers. *Family Relations, 40*(4), 463–471.

Geronimus, A., & Korenman, S. (1992). The socioeconomic consequences of teen childbearing reconsidered. *Quarterly Journal of Economics, 107,* 1,187–1,214.

Geronimus, A., & Korenman, S. (1993). The socioeconomic costs of teenage childbearing: Evidence and interpretation. *Demography, 30*(2), 281–290.

Geronimus, A., Korenman, S., & Hillemeier, M. M. (1994). Does young maternal age adversely affect child development? Evidence from cousin comparisons in the United States. *Population and Development Review, 20*(3), 585–609.

Haskins, R., & Bevan, C. S. (1997). Implementing the Abstinence Education Provisions of the Welfare Reform Legislation. *Welfare reform resource packet.* Washington, DC: National Campaign to Prevent Teenage Pregnancy.

Hoffman, S. D., Foster, E. M., & Furstenberg, F. F., Jr. (1993a). Re-evaluating the cost of teenage childbearing. *Demography, 30*(1), 1–13.

Hoffman, S. D., Foster, E. M., & Furstenberg, F. F., Jr. (1993b). Re-evaluating the cost of teenage childbearing: Response to Geronimus and Korenman. *Demography, 30*(2), 291–296.

Luker, K. (1996). *Dubious conceptions.* Cambridge: Harvard University Press.

Moffitt, R. (1992). Incentive effects of the United States welfare system: A review. *Journal of Economic Literature, 30*(1), 1–61.

Murray, C. A. (1984). *Losing ground: American social policy, 1950–1980.* New York: Basic Books.

Naples, N. A. (1997). The "new consensus" on the gendered "social contract": The 1987–1988 U.S. congressional hearings on welfare reform. *Signs, 22*(4), 907–945.

Nathanson, C. A. (1991). *Dangerous passage: The social control of sexuality in women's adolescence.* Philadelphia: Temple University Press.

National Campaign to Prevent Teenage Pregnancy. (1997). *Whatever happened to childhood? The problem of teen pregnancy in the United States.* Washington, DC: National Campaign to Prevent Teenage Pregnancy.

Snow, D. A., & Benford, R. D. (1992). Master frames and cycles of protest. In A. E. Morris & C. McClurg (Eds.), *Frontiers in social movement theory* (pp. 133–155). New Haven: Yale University Press.

U.S. Department of Health and Human Services. (1997). *A national strategy to prevent teen pregnancy.* Washington, DC: U.S. Government Printing Office.

U.S. House of Representatives. (1996). *Welfare and Medicaid Reform Act of 1996*. Report of the Committee on the Budget To Accompany H.R. 3734. 104th Congress, 2d Session, Report 104–651. Washington, DC: U.S. Government Printing Office.

Ventura, S. J., Martin, J. A., Curtin, S. C., & Mathews, T. J. (1998). Report of final natality statistics, 1996. *Monthly Vital Statistics Report, 46*(11) (supplement). Hyattsville, Md.: National Center for Health Statistics.

Vinovskis, M. (1981). An "epidemic" of adolescent pregnancy? Some historical considerations. *Journal of Family History, 6* (Summer), 205–230.

NOTES

1. The data in this paragraph are drawn from the following sources: Nathanson (1991, pp. 27–30); Ventura, Martin, Curtin, & Mathews (1998, Tables 1, 17, and 18).

2. Moffitt's detailed review of pertinent economic literature concludes that "the evidence does not support the hypothesis that the welfare system has been responsible for the time-series growth in female headship and illegitimacy" (1992, p. 29).

3. Astone argues that legislative policymakers have paid attention to the *results* of current research—i.e., teenage childbearing is *correlated* with a variety of negative outcomes—just not to their conclusions (1997, p. 413). However, this body of research has long since advanced beyond the stage of simple correlations, and I would argue that conclusions drawn from these more sophisticated analyses also deserve to be called results.

4. There are suggestions in the bill itself, in its exegesis by Haskins and Bevan and in the Department of Health and Human Services "National Strategy" document, of a move toward regarding at least some adolescent women as the victims of "predatory sexual practices" by older men (110 Stat. 2111). DHHS has labeled its program on behalf of 9- to14-year-old girls "Girl Power!"

5. The title of this publication epitomizes—and perhaps initiated—the conflation of "sexually active" with pregnant. Eleven million refers to an estimated number of "sexually active" teenagers, men and women, not to the number of pregnancies (estimated at one million), as the title suggests.

DISCUSSION

Sarah Hrdy: Who are they? The people who are passing this bill presumably are appealing to their constituents, but why do these people care? Help me understand what fuels these positions and underlies this propaganda.

Connie Nathanson: That's a very interesting question. I was reading just the other day a series of essays by Simon Watney in which he was talking about the symbolism of HIV and the relationship between HIV and homosexuality and how that had come to symbolize everything that was wrong with contemporary society. I was thinking to myself, well you could just substitute adolescent pregnancy for homosexuality and HIV and use exactly the same words. In the late 1970s the Alan Guttmacher Institute for humanitarian reasons constructed adolescent pregnancy as a public problem because their agenda was the Planned Parenthood agenda of providing services so that young women could be protected. This was taken up by the right wing and particularly around 1980 there was a book by Charles Murray in which he basically said that welfare is the cause because women are rewarded for having non-marital births. That basically has become the economic conservative appeal. The appeal of this issue to moral conservatives is that this is symbolic of this moral decline. It is both caused by moral decline and symbolic of moral decline. And the problem is that this issue serves the interests of a whole range of people. It serves the interests of "beltway bandit" organizations who want to get money to do research. It serves the interests of researchers because they can start their R01 funding proposal with "Isn't this a terrible problem and therefore shouldn't we be studying it." And it serves the interests of providers because it's very difficult to get money for these kinds of services which are good services. It serves the interest of these providers to say this is a terrible problem, so in addition to having this symbolism for moral conservatives, it became useful to liberal reformers who got on this bandwagon also very early in the 1980s, and so it serves so many purposes. It's amazing that this thing has lasted this long.

Gilbert Herdt: A very simple point about the social component of theorizing sexuality. In the case of both homosexuality and teenage pregnancy, the fundamental challenge is severing sexual behavior from reproduction. So if you tied your set of cultural values to the notion that sexuality should only occur for the purpose of procreation, these are fundamental challenges. So to theorize sexuality here in the social component means to understand the historical, cultural, and psychological reasons why we have coupled sexuality so strongly with reproduction.

Anke Ehrhardt: I think "creating the teenage pregnancy problem" is a little strong. At the same time of course there was internationally a great concern about unwanted pregnancies and the study of different countries including several European countries as well as the United States, with the United States having a problem of lack of coordinated sex education and contraceptive education, etc. And, as we well know, even with the recent decline of teenage births and pregnancies in the United States we are still way above other countries in the industrialized world. But let me address how this bill actually came to pass. It was at the time when many groups were too busy with other things, with Clinton running for reelection, that organized conservative groups within Congress got the bill passed without having the proper debate with groups with opposite views.

Connie Nathanson: On the question of timing, the comparison with other countries was relatively recent. It was in the early 1970s that Fred Jaffe, who at that time was the research director for AGI, wrote a deliberate statement that the issue of directing contraceptive services toward married women and particularly toward women in poverty, which had been part of the war on poverty strategy, had come into disrepute for a whole range of reasons. So the AGI was looking for a new agenda and they hit upon this one, making use of research that was done at Johns Hopkins by Jack Kantner and Melvin Zelnik. And that was done starting in 1971. So this *11 Million Teenagers*, which was the publication that put this issue on the map, which dazzled the Secretary of Health and Human Services, Joe Califano at the time, was published in 1976. So the elaboration of this issue in comparison with other countries, the moving of this issue into developing countries as well so that we now talk about the problem of teenage pregnancy in Africa, and so forth, are all subsequent. The other thing is just a comment that the birth rates among young women have been higher in the United States than they are in Europe for many, many years, long before this issue. They were then more marital than non-marital, but the pattern of higher fertility among women under 20 in the United States as compared with European countries is not recent.

Edward Laumann: I wanted to further comment on the tendency in this discussion to use the passage of the abstinence bill as symbolizing the government position on this issue. Let's bear in mind that this is a 50-million-dollar project and frankly I think you could easily demonstrate that this was simply a political payoff in a situation where we have been investing in excess of seven or eight percent of the National Institutes of Health (NIH) budget, close to a billion dollars, in specialized research for AIDS. We have been investing in a lot of different areas promoted by various other groups with differing viewpoints. So Jesse Helms can never be underestimated as a politician. I think this had to be made as a settlement to allow for other things that were going forward to be approved and supported. It is a "costless" symbolic act and I don't think we want to overinterpret what that really means and where people are really coming from and voting for. It's just tossing a bone to somebody who could make a lot of trouble.

Connie Nathanson: But what tossing a bone did is legitimize abstinence education as the strategy now. When I was writing about this in 1991 this trend was there, but it was not so clear that it was going to become dominant. The first sentence of the welfare bill states that the foundation of society is monogamous marriage. You can dismiss all that as rhetoric and I'm sure there was a lot of bargaining behind the scenes and 50 million dollars is not a lot of money.

Claire Brindis: It's five years of funding, so it's a total of 250 million dollars and for every four dollars of federal funding, the state matches three dollars. So it's a significant amount of money being devoted to the topic of abstinence.

Bob Michael: Connie, could you comment on your table showing trends in births to teenagers?

Connie Nathanson: This shows birth rates for selected age groups 1970–1994. There are several things that are interesting about this. This is birth rate per thousand by age. The pattern for women of all age groups is more or less the same. Second, the birth rates are relatively flat. The birth rate for 10- to 14-year-olds hardly makes the graph. The birthrate for 15- to 17-year-olds doesn't change much. The 18- to 19-year-olds follow the pattern very closely. The epidemic of teenage pregnancy was announced around 1976. These are birthrates. Pregnancy rates are births plus abortions, but abortion is so underreported that I'm not sure that those data are very reliable in terms of change over time.

John Bancroft: But what if there has been a major increase in the rate of abortion?

Connie Nathanson: There are all kinds of different ways of looking at the changes over time and the fertility of women 15 to 19. We can look at them in terms of birth rates. We can look at them in terms of absolute numbers, and we can look at them in terms of percent of the total birth. What people tend to do is to pick the way of looking at the data that is most useful for their particular position. Birth rates were high in the baby boom period for everybody, including 15- to 19-year-olds, and they have basically remained fairly steady since. Last week the *New York Times* reported, I assume from the CDC, that there had been a marked drop in fertility rates since 1996, but I don't have that data. As a percent of the total births, they've been going down. And for non-marital births, which is what most of the fuss is about, the change is primarily among white women and not among black young women, contrary to the usual public perception. So that non-marital rates by race have been converging over this period.

José Barzelatto: Implicit in this philosophy of this legislation is adolescence as a period that goes from menarche to marriage. This is also true from other perspectives. It reminded me of something I experienced in the past with great embarrassment. As we organized a meeting in the middle 1980s about ethics and family planning, a big discussion was going on about adolescent pregnancy and the highest-ranking official of the World Health Organization present (a former minister of Saudi Arabia) said "I don't understand what you're talking about. This is so simple. As soon as girls have their menarche, you marry them. There is no problem of adolescent pregnancy." That's the other way of dealing with it. Instead of proposing abstinence you marry them at the beginning. This was an international conference. So this is not just a U.S. phenomenon. It's seen from different perspectives and it all has to do, in my view, with a much deeper problem, the control of women. This has to do with patriarchal societies, that is what we're talking about.

Sarah Hrdy: I'm assuming that most of the "theys" in this so far are white, so my question is to what extent is there any consensus among black interest groups on issues like teenage pregnancy, abstinence, birth control, sex education? Is there an identifiable position that black groups have taken and do black men and black women agree or do they take different positions?

Connie Nathanson: Very conservative. Church groups, for example, both men and women, are very conservative.

Social Contagion and Adolescent Sexual Behavior: Theoretical and Policy Implications

JOSEPH LEE RODGERS

On Theories and Models

This paper will begin at a meta-level—theorizing about theories. Different disciplines and perspectives can thoughtfully disagree about what theories and models are and the role they serve in science. When we are very clear about our meta-theoretical perspective it sharpens our understanding of the various cross-disciplinary contributions we can make.

The perspective that motivates this introduction and the theoretical model I will present later in this paper is informed by the psychometric tradition as developed in Torgersen (1958) and Lord and Novick (1968). Within that tradition, science involves the interplay between theory and empirical evidence. Models are abstract systems of constructs and the connections between them. When "certain of the constructs are connected to the empirical world by rules of correspondence, the model becomes a *theory*, and, as such, subject to empirical test" (Torgersen, 1958, p. 4). In other words,

A Model + A Measurement Procedure = A Theory.

At the most basic level, a model is an abstract simplification of the real world. It has two basic requirements: (1) It must simplify the world, and (2) it must match reality in some important and fundamental sense. The real world is, presumably, complicated enough that there are any number of ways to simplify it in meaningful ways. Some models can compete with one another about which is more fundamentally correct in matching reality. For example, two theories can be compared to one another to determine whether a religiosity variable or a peer influence variable explains more variance in the age at first intercourse variable among adolescents. Other sets of models—and the theories derived from them—are so completely different in the way they simplify the world that there is no meaningful way to compare them. For example, a theory postulating that dopamine receptor genes influence fertility desires cannot easily be compared to a theory explaining the role that peer influence plays in motivating fertility desires; one theory exists at the physiological/genetic level, the other at a social psychological level. Both approaches appear to match reality in some important senses, but in totally different domains; they simplify reality in such radically different ways as to be practically incomparable.

The point to which the preceding paragraph is directed is, simply, that there is room in science for many, many different models of any particular phenomenon. Further, each model may be operationalized (i.e., turned into a theory with a measurement procedure) in a multiplicity of ways. Within this meta-theoretical context, it is not meaningful to search for *the* "theory of sexuality." There are many ways to simplify the complexities of sexual behavior; physiologists, anthropologists, psychologists, sociologists, economists, and epidemiologists will automatically take the same set of complex behaviors and look at them in different (though often overlapping) fashions.

However, when two theories are comparable, there are two important domains in which they must compete. The first domain is the quality with which they match the empirical phenomena they attempt to model; this match is referred to in the psychometric and statistical tradition as "goodness-of-fit" (or sometimes as the reverse, "badness-of-fit"). The second domain is the simplicity of the theory, or parsimony. This principle, often referred to as Occam's razor, implies that of two theories that fit the world equally well, the simpler one is to be preferred. In the psychometric and statistical tradition, parsimony is usually measured by counting the number of free parameters in the mathematical/statistical statement of competing models and considering the simpler model to be the one with fewer parameters to be estimated (although, it should be added, there are other ways to measure complexity of a theory as well).

Social and behavioral scientists trained in the tradition of linear models are used to the idea that there is an exact trade-off between parsimony and fit. When a model becomes more complex, it necessarily fits the data better; when a model becomes simpler, it necessarily fits the data worse (in each case, assuming the additional complexity is well formulated). Comparison of two statistical models (each representing competing scientific theories) can be done by using standard statistical procedures in the "model comparison framework" (e.g., Maxwell & Delaney, 1990) which originates from the procedures developed by Fisher during the 1920s (including, in particular, the F-test). In this type of statistical test, the fit-parsimony trade-off turns into the question of whether the extra variance accounted for by the more complex model is worth the cost of the complexity of the model. The F-test that provides a statistical answer to this question is, of course, only one way to obtain such an answer, but it is certainly the most widely recognized and often used approach to evaluate this important trade-off.

The model presented in this paper—which has been turned into a theory in a set of articles I have published in collaboration with David Rowe of the University of Arizona over the past decade or so—is one of many different ways to attempt to simplify the complexities of adolescent sexual behavior. Different formulations of our theory can be placed in competition against one another in the two senses described above by asking whether the more complex of the two formulations adds enough increase in the fit of the theory to empirical data to justify the added complexity. Many of our publications have been motivated by the goal of identifying the simplest form of the theory that still fits the data well; that is, by finding the appropriate trade-off between fit and parsimony.

Many social and behavioral scientists work outside the epistemological framework defined in this section. For example, researchers who work in the qualitative tradition assign relatively little importance to measurement, mathematical modeling, and statistical prediction and focus much more attention on description. The use of the terms "theory," "model," and even "science" is fairly different across different traditions. The strengths of the quantitative framework include its careful explication of the assumptions on which it is based, the explicit effort to objectively trade off fit and parsimony, and the ability to use the language of mathematics to help draw scientific conclusions. I hope that those strengths are apparent in the presentation of our theory in this paper. One of the weaknesses of quantitative analysis is the rigidity and inflexibility that a set of "required procedures" can impose on an effort to better understand complex and often mysterious processes. Scientists who are working in relatively unknown and uncharted domains often must discard the rigidity required by stringent measurement and statistical procedures in favor of qualitative methods.[1]

Cross-Disciplinary Applications of Quantitative Methods

Our theory describes how adolescent sexual behavior spreads through an adolescent network through a process of social contagion. The mathematical representation of our model borrows quantitative methodology from the epidemiological literature. These methods can be used to model the spread of disease, the process of social influence, or the diffusion of a marketing innovation like a new laundry detergent. Each involves its own special and different type of contagion, although the same class of mathematical models has been shown to be useful across these domains.

After my presentation at the Kinsey Institute, concern was expressed that we think of the spread of sexual behavior as a disease.[2] This is both true and false. Mathematically, social contagion of sexual behavior (or the use of laundry detergent) *is* similar to the spread of biological diseases. Conceptually, they are totally different. It is fairly typical for different disciplines to borrow quantitative methods from other disciplines. In so doing, they do not necessarily transport the conceptual domain as well. I offer two examples.

Survival analysis models were originally developed in demography and public health as a tool in the study of mortality. These models have their mathematical basis in assumed distributional shapes that fit curves reflecting how many people survive from year to year. Psychologists (and other behavioral scientists) have recently begun to use this type of methodology to study many processes other than mortality. For example, Singer and Willett (1993) used the methodology to study teacher attrition among special education teachers in public school settings. They recognized that an analytic method used for survival versus death could also be applied to other types of survival, including survival in the teaching profession. Their ability to model teacher attrition was enhanced by recognizing an *analogy* between human death and teacher attrition. Nowhere in their writing did they imply that teachers who quit public school jobs actually die; rather, they simply applied a method used by mortality researchers to study a different (but conceptually related) problem.

Item response theory (IRT) is a quantitative method used in statistical test theory to model test-taking behavior. It was developed in the psychometric literature to model the probability that a given test taker would answer a test item correctly. The mathematical basis of IRT is the logistic curve, which suggests that the probability of a correct response is an S-shaped function of the test taker's knowledge about the item's content. Recently, IRT has been applied in many other domains. For example, Rowe, Osgood, and Nicewander (1990) used IRT to model the likelihood of adolescents to engage in delinquent behavior. The "items" the adolescents answered were yes/no responses to questions about having ever performed certain delinquent acts. What emerged from the analysis included measures of each adolescent along an underlying "delinquency continuum." Nowhere in their writing did they suggest that adolescents were trying to pass an actual test when they performed delinquent acts. They simply recognized that the quantitative method used in test theory could be applied usefully to study adolescent delinquency. They recognized an *analogy* between test items and delinquency indicators.

In the same sense, the theory to be developed in this paper takes advantage of a similar analogy to borrow a methodological procedure applied in one domain to an entirely different domain. Along with many other researchers, we have been developing the idea of "social contagion." Social contagion assumes that ideas, opinions, attitudes, and behavior can spread through a social network. The idea of social contagion obviously borrows by analogy from biological contagion, in which viruses and bacteria pass from one organism to another. Further, the quantitative methods used in the epidemiological literature to model biological contagion can be applied fruitfully to model social spread as well.

In all of our writing, we have been careful to include some version of the following disclaimer: We do not propose that sex (or cigarette smoking, or drinking, or delinquency) is a disease in any biological sense of the term. When we discuss the idea of social contagion, we refer completely and only to social influence. Social contagion is a useful idea *by analogy* to biological contagion. Our model is a social influence model, and when we test the theory that derives from our model, we only draw conclusions that apply to social domain. When we use quantitative methods from the epidemiological literature, we do so in the same way that psychologists have borrowed survival models or IRT models and transported them to other research domains.

Theoretical Basis

The theoretical starting point for our theory of the spread of adolescent sexual behavior is the proposition that the most proximate—and among the most important—determinant of a particular adolescent's sexual behavior is the influence of opposite-sex peers with whom that adolescent may (or may not) engage in sexual behavior. Judging from past research, it appears that the "ultimate" model of adolescent sexual behavior contains "social influences like parents, siblings, and peers; it contains sociological institutions like churches, schools, and neighborhoods; it contains biological variables like maturation, pubertal status, and hormones; it contains psychological variables, like intelligence, risk taking, and self-esteem. What it has not previously contained is specific attention to the partners of the adolescents who are contemplating sexual activity" (Rodgers & Rowe, 1993, p. 479).

The methodological starting point for this paper is the belief that considering adolescent sexual partners as an influence on adolescent sexual behavior moves us closer to the actual processes of interest than we have been previously. This point is best made by example. Religion is a distal influence or a correlate of sexual behavior. Researchers have measured the variance in sexual behavior associated with individual differences in religious commitment or have even estimated the proportionate decrease in sexual behavior predicted by an increase in religious devotion. Religious beliefs can have important influences on adolescent sexual behavior, although they are not an integral part of the behavior itself (at least in the modern U.S. culture). But the availability of a partner is a prerequisite for the development of adolescent sexual behavior.

To illustrate this point, consider the movie *The Blue Lagoon*. The basic premise that two adolescents living alone on a desert island could manage to discover sex, become pregnant, and reproduce is not logistically controversial. And they did so, furthermore, without neighborhood influences, parental pressure, sex education, or television. All they had, and all they required, was an available partner. To summarize the point that began this section: Adolescent sexual behavior at a *process level* requires as a starting point two adolescents who potentially might (or might not) engage in sexual behavior. All other potential influences, whether they be societal, sociological, or psychological, emerge from this basic starting point, the couple.

With this motivation, we have proposed a theory and a methodology attached to the theory that has been developed and elaborated in a number of research articles. Our social contagion theory is most completely stated in Rodgers and Rowe (1993). The theory starts with an intact network of interacting adolescents of a given age. Each year, an individual adolescent "pairs up with" or "contacts" an opposite-sex adolescent. If the adolescent is a virgin and is paired with another virgin, they will "discover" sexual intercourse together with some probability (which is usually estimated to be relatively low). This probability is called the "non-epidemic transition" probability (reflecting lack of social contagion), and it corresponds to the premise of *The Blue Lagoon*. On the other hand, if the adolescent is a virgin and is paired with a nonvirgin, then the nonvirgin may "spread sexual behavior" to the virgin with some probability. This probability—called the "epidemic transition" probability—captures the essence of the social contagion process. Social contagion is a type of social influence passed on from one potential sex partner to another. The epidemic transition probability is usually estimated to be higher than the non-epidemic transition probability, and is usually estimated to be higher for a nonvirgin female converting a virgin male than for a nonvirgin male converting a virgin female. This type of transition is reflected in other movies; for example, in the movie *Little Darlings*, Kristy McNichol lost her virginity to a sexually experienced boy at summer camp.

This is a model of how adolescents become sexually experienced—

that is, how they become nonvirgins. Because of the analogy between social contagion and biological contagion, these models have been referred to as "epidemic models" (although, obviously, there is nothing biological that is necessarily spread as an inherent part of the loss of virginity in this process). The name we have given to this class of models is Epidemic Models of the Onset of Social Activities, or EMOSA Models. EMOSA Models are based on the ideas built into the social contagion theory above. Each is captured in a set of equations that can be fit to empirical data to estimate the parameters of the model. Besides the spread of sexual behavior, we have also used the basic social contagion idea to model the spread of smoking, drinking, and criminal behavior (Rowe & Rodgers, 1991; Rowe, Chassin, Presson, Edwards, & Sherman, 1992). The equations that capture each process are a bit different from one another. Each system of equations can be fit to empirical prevalence curves using a nonlinear estimation routine (e.g., SAS software has such a routine called PROC NLIN).

I will not present the EMOSA equations here; those interested in seeing the way these equations are defined can consult Rodgers and Rowe (1993), Rowe and Rodgers (1994), or Rowe, Rodgers, and Meseck-Bushey (1989). Rodgers and Rowe (1993) provided SAS coding to simulate the EMOSA process and to fit the model and estimate parameters using PROC NLIN. Anderson and May (1991) present a broad treatment of this class of mathematical models in an epidemiological framework. These models are the ones we have borrowed heavily from to provide the mathematical basis for our social contagion theory.

Assumptions of EMOSA Sexuality Theories

The conceptual model on which EMOSA theories rest is like all models in that it represents an idealized world based on a number of simplifying assumptions. I will delineate several of those assumptions and discuss how we have investigated their importance. The first sense in which the model is idealized is the assumption that all members of the adolescent network are the same age and progress through subsequent ages together. This assumption also implies another one, that all potential sex partners are of the same age as the adolescent. We have expanded the model to allow for interage mixing with a potential sex partner up to two years older than a given adolescent. This is also an idealized setting, but empirical results suggest that around 80% of first-intercourse experiences occur with a partner within this two-year window (Rodgers, 1996), so that this expanded model does capture most such experiences. However, we have found only slight differences in estimated parameters when this expanded model has been used. Since it requires adding many additional equations to the system to account for all of the possible interage interactions and doesn't appear to affect the estimated parameters, we have typically used the simpler same-age model in most of our work (in the spirit of parsimony). Rowe and Rodgers (1994) present the most complete statement of the inter-cohort contagion model that accounts for cross-age mixing.

Another simplifying assumption of the model presented above is that sexual transition is independent of physical maturity. In other words, there is no mechanism in the model that accounts for physical maturity. Because we felt this to be an important omission, we began adding "maturity filters" to our EMOSA Sexuality Models early in their development (see Rowe, Rodgers, & Meseck-Bushey, 1989). These filters only allow pubertally mature males or females to be eligible to become nonvirgins. When we tested EMOSA theories, they consistently fit better with female maturity filters, but did not respond to the presence of male maturity filters. This finding that emerged from our statistical model-fitting exercise matched several empirical findings that males often report pre-pubertal first intercourse while females almost never do (e.g., Rodgers, 1996, p. 98).

A third simplifying assumption is that the whole population mixes, and that the only important demographic difference between individuals involves their gender. However, we know from considerable past research (e.g., Kahn, Kalsbeek, & Hofferth, 1988; Furstenberg, Morgan, Moore, & Petersen, 1987) that there are substantial racial differences in the sexual prevalence curves that EMOSA Models are designed to reproduce. As a result, we have fit our models assuming unrestricted interactions, and at other times have assumed only within-race interactions. The latter models consistently fit better. Further, an interesting finding that has emerged from these model-fitting analyses is that once differences in pubertal maturity are accounted for, the race differences in age at first intercourse disappear. In other words, the fact that blacks mature on average slightly earlier than whites is almost completely sufficient to account for the differences in the prevalence curves, which are fairly substantial at later ages. Previous research based on linear models could never detect that pubertal maturity differences meant very much. Our nonlinear EMOSA Model shows that even small differences in the ages at which females are pubertally mature (and are therefore eligible to become nonvirgins) can translate into large differences in prevalence rates at later ages (Rowe & Rodgers, 1994).

A fourth simplifying assumption that we have made involves the mechanism by which pairs of adolescents are formed. Most of our models have assumed that opposite-sex adolescents are paired at random each year. This assumption has engendered more concern and criticism from reviewers than all the others put together, for the clear reason that the assumption is so counterintuitive to our experiences. No one feels that their choice of friends, mates, or sexual partners is a random process. Rather, humans choose those partners carefully and purposively. Nevertheless, there are several very good reasons to use random mixing in EMOSA and other models of this type. First, the choice of first sexual partner in adolescent networks may be closer to random than many would expect. Rodgers (1996, p. 101) reported that slightly over one-third of the first intercourse experiences in the ADSEX survey (a study of adolescent sexual behavior) were with a steady partner. The rest were with friends or acquaintances (43%), or individuals who were hardly even known before the sexual experience (19%). Nevertheless, the use of a random mixing assumption need not be based on empirical arguments. In one study (Rowe et al., 1989), we allowed the population to mix in such a way that sexual partners were selected with probability related to their empirical likelihood of sharing virginity status. Parameter estimates were not affected by this adjustment. Finally, Dodd (1955) provided a rationale for why, even if selection is purposive at the individual level, a random mixing assumption works very well at the aggregate level. His argument is based on the fact that processes governed by the combination of many different small features—like partner selection, for example—will behave randomly in the population even with individual-level violations of the random selection assumption. This is exactly the situation we have in our model, and we have consistently used the random mixing assumption in our modeling. It has been shown on both empirical and theoretical grounds to be a reasonable assumption and has the advantage of simplicity in conceptualization and in programming.

A fifth assumption of the basic EMOSA sexuality model is that loss of virginity is the critical (in fact, the only) sexual behavior of interest. A case can be made for this position based on demographic considerations, since sexual intercourse is a (virtual) prerequisite for pregnancy and therefore for childbearing. However, other psychological and health considerations dictate that the development of sexual behavior be viewed as a rather more complex process than the binary transition from virginity to nonvirginity would imply. In one line of research (Rodgers & Rowe, 1993), we expanded the EMOSA sexuality model to include five stages of sexual intimacy, including naïveté, kissing, light petting, heavy petting, and sexual intercourse. Of course this stagewise model is itself a radical simplification compared to reality, but it is certainly closer to a developmental model than the original binary model. We compared the stagewise model to one assuming each of the five processes were independent of the others, and found better fits for a stagewise model (although the ordering of the stages was somewhat ambiguous for blacks). In this analysis, we concluded that the added complexity of the more complicated model was justified because of the improvement in fit that we obtained.

A final adjustment reflects an extension of the model rather than an evaluation of an assumption per se. In a recent article (Rodgers, Rowe, & Buster, 1998), we extended the EMOSA sexuality model to account for pregnancy as well. The social contagion/sexuality part of the model was identical to the original EMOSA sexuality model (Rowe et al., 1989). However, once a girl became a nonvirgin, she became at risk of becoming pregnant with a parameter reflecting the transition probability. By adding a prevalence curve reflecting pregnancy rates, we estimated the likelihood of getting pregnant for girls in several different statuses—those of different ages, those with experienced versus inexperienced first sexual partners, and those who were recent nonvirgins versus those who were more sexually experienced. Surprisingly, the model estimated approximately equivalent pregnancy probabilities across these different categories. We interpreted this result to suggest not that the probability of getting pregnant actually stays fixed, but rather that compensatory processes occur with increasing age and sexual experience. For example, if coital rates increase with age but contraceptive effectiveness does so as well, these factors may approximately compensate in defining the overall probability of pregnancy.

The type of extension developed in Rodgers et al. (1998) could also be applied to modeling sexually transmitted disease (STDs), as well. In these models, the social contagion process is still used to model the spread of sexual behavior. Then, the potential for acquiring an STD is added as an additional component. We have written the equations to estimate STD models, although we have not found STD prevalence curves with sufficient reliability and validity to support a model-fitting exercise. This will be pursued in future research. In particular, such models could be run backward to estimate exposure to and onset of HIV among sexually active adolescents.

Obviously there are many other assumptions that "idealize" our theory in relation to the complexities of the real world. The social contagion process currently has no explicit accounting for religious views, for peer pressure (other than pressure from the potential partner), for media influences, for intelligence or knowledge of sexuality, or for parental influences. (It should be noted that some of these factors are implicitly captured in estimating the transition probabilities.) Methods to account for these types of individual differences are being investigated. In each case, the value of the additional component in fitting empirical data will be evaluated against the cost of a more complex model.

We emphasize that, unlike virtually all other past research on adolescent sexual behavior, our model is a descriptive model that approximates the actual process that occurs within an adolescent network. Researchers using linear models would never propose that an adolescent creates an explicit weighting of religious commitment, tendency toward risk taking, and maturational status in deciding whether to engage in sexual intercourse or not. Such models are predictive, but are certainly not descriptive. EMOSA models are both predictive and descriptive. Because of this, an EMOSA sexuality model can be studied at a process level as one reflecting actual social interactions, and implications of different features of the model can be studied in relation to one another. We can learn a great deal about how different parts of the overall process interact with one another by studying the model's behavior. The example I gave previously of how small differences in maturational age can magnify into large differences in percentage of nonvirgins is only one example of an important finding that has emerged from this type of modeling exercise.

Policy Implications

A number of policy implications emerge from EMOSA modeling, both from theoretical considerations and also from previous empirical analyses. I will discuss three of them in some detail in this section. The assumption throughout this section is that *postponing sexual debut* will produce positive public health benefits in the form of reduced pregnancy and STD rates. Obviously, there are other dynamics—including coital rates after loss of virginity and contraceptive efficacy—that have the same goals and that are not explicitly treated within this discussion. EMOSA models can be applied to such questions, but I will focus here on the more basic premise that intervening at the causal source is an effective prevention strategy.

To set the stage for discussion of these policy implications, I will refer to two different features of the EMOSA model. One is the *probability* of transition to nonvirginity, the other is the dynamic characteristic of the *social contagion process* itself. Most current programs directed toward pregnancy prevention, reduction in the rates of STDs, or reduction in occurrence of adolescent sexual behavior focus on the first, the probability of transition to nonvirginity. "Just Say No" campaigns are explicitly targeted to this goal (and attempt to reduce the probability to zero). Programs that request adolescents to sign virginity pledges have the same goal. A criticism of such programs has to do with selection bias. Presumably, adolescents willing to sign such pledges (or who pay attention to "Just Say No" campaigns) are likely to be those who might well have arrived at the same behavioral outcomes with or without the existence of the program. These programs may in fact be some-what useful at reducing teenage sexual behavior, pregnancy, and STDs, but they fail to capture some important features of the process. Even programs that pay adolescent females not to get pregnant are attempting to reduce the likelihood of unprotected sexual behavior, but they fail to account for important dynamics of the overall process. The EMOSA modeling approach suggests that instead of delivering programs that treat individuals and that attempt to reduce likelihood of certain individual behaviors, educators and policymakers would be better advised to consider the *whole process of the spread of the behavior itself.*

The three specific program/policy implications that will emerge from the following discussion are the following: (1) The individual adolescents who are likely to be sexually precocious (or who are already sexually active) should be targeted for particular attention; (2) program efforts need to begin sooner, at a younger age, with the important goal of postponing nonvirginity even for only a very few adolescents within the social network; (3) more attention should be given to the role of physical/pubertal development. I will discuss each of these suggestions in turn.

The mathematics and demography of biological epidemics have been studied extensively, and we can take advantage of that research and apply it to better understand how socially driven phenomena occur. Technically, contagious biological diseases—like malaria, bubonic plague, AIDS, flu, or the common cold—can occur at low levels in the population for a very long time without ever becoming epidemics. Social or biological epidemics occur when the incidence begins to accelerate geometrically or exponentially. A recent popular science writer termed this phenomenon the "tipping point" phenomenon (Gladwell, 1996). Epidemiologists and public health experts become quite concerned when this type of acceleration occurs. On the other hand, if a contagious process spreads slowly enough, it will slowly die out and disappear. The implication for adolescent sexual behavior—or for smoking or drinking, for that matter—is that a very few individuals can be engaging in these behaviors without an epidemic occurring. Eventually, a high proportion of all adults will become nonvirgins. But the point at which the spread of nonvirginity reaches the "tipping point"—the point at which there is an exponentially exploding acceleration of nonvirgins in an adolescent population—is critical for public health purposes (including designing pregnancy prevention programs and STD treatments). A population in which that explosion occurs at age 18 will have vastly different public health and policy requirements than one in which it occurs at age 14. The fact that a very few 12-year-olds are nonvirgins is not itself a major public health problem. In fact, a few 12-year-olds were undoubtedly sexually active in adolescent networks 50 years ago, when teenage sexuality and pregnancy rates were much lower than they are now.

Rather, it is the potential for these 12-year-olds to "seed the system" at an early age and to spread sexual behavior through their network that is critical. The explosion of 16- and 17-year-olds who are nonvirgins in the United States today is not the result of this age group suddenly one day becoming sexually active en masse. Rather, it is the result of a slow spread of sexual behavior among 12- to 15-year-olds that suddenly passes the tipping point among this older age group. Add to this system the obvious fact that individuals from "outside" the system—much older adolescents or adults—can also "spread" nonvirginity, and the potential for rapid acceleration becomes even more volatile.

Our research suggests that sexuality is primarily spread "contagiously," that is, by a virgin having sex the first time with a nonvirgin. Across a number of different local and national datasets, we have consistently estimated epidemic transition probabilities that are five to ten times greater than the non-epidemic transition probabilities. In other words, there are a lot more adolescents whose first partner is a nonvirgin than those who lose their virginity with another virgin. (Rodgers, 1996, p. 103 gave empirical self-reports of first partner's virginity status as only slightly biased toward epidemic spread, 31% versus 27%, although a large number of these self-reports—42%—indicated uncertainty as to the virginity status of their first partner. Even with this more conservative figure, however, the importance of epidemic spread is critical.)

As I discussed above, most public health efforts are directed at reducing the transition probabilities in the spread of sexual behavior. Additionally, attention should be focused particularly on the adolescents who "seed" the social contagion system. This attention can take two forms. If the age of first intercourse of the first adolescents to become nonvirgins could be delayed even a short period of time, it would have large and magnified effects on nonvirginity prevalence curves at later ages. Or, if sexual behavior among the sexually precocious adolescents did not spread through the network—i.e., if it were contained among the few sexually active adolescents or occurred with individuals outside the network—then the acceleration characteristic of epidemic spread of a behavior would be postponed until later ages. Very little research has been directed at defining the features of (say) 10-year-olds that predict early entry into sexual behavior, and such research could have considerable policy benefits if combined with an EMOSA perspective.

At a very practical level, the considerations above suggest that postponing very young onset may be as effective as reducing the likelihood of sexual behavior at each age, because the second effect will follow naturally from the first. Public health efforts—including parental intervention—directed at pre-adolescents in the age range of 10 to 12 might appear to be failures if they only affected a few children. But, in fact, the EMOSA modeling shows that such small reductions can have important results. Further, the differential transition parameters for males and females suggest that such efforts directed at reducing first intercourse experience of younger boys with older girls could be especially critical.

The third policy consideration is the one already discussed as an example of a finding that emerged from our modeling exercise when we were not looking for it. If a very small difference in pubertal maturation rates can accumulate through the model and create the large race differences in sexual prevalence, then obviously maturation plays an important role in sexual behavior that should be more explicitly accounted for. The age of onset of puberty has been decreasing systematically in the United States among both males and females for many years. Research by Udry and colleagues (e.g., Udry, Billy, Morris, Groff, & Raj, 1985; Udry, Talbert, & Morris, 1986) has demonstrated the relation between adolescent hormones and sexual attitudes/behavior among males and females.

Whatever effectiveness that programs and education have on late childhood and adolescent behavior, they probably need to begin earlier to be effective, simply because adolescence—and sexual maturity—begin sooner now than in previous years (when, for example, adult researchers who study these social processes were themselves adolescents and began to think about normative age-graded processes).

Conclusion

In this paper I have described an idealized descriptive model of how sexual behavior "spreads" through an adolescent social network, I have stated and explored a number of the assumptions built into the model, and I have listed and discussed some policy implications that emerge from the EMOSA approach. Policy suggestions and program interventions are themselves based on models, are themselves full of assumptions, and necessarily vastly simplify the reality they attempt to treat. The EMOSA approach can help us push our modeling—and the policy derived from that modeling—to a higher level, however. Social contagion and the EMOSA implementation of it is closer to an actual descriptive model than previous research has offered and, we believe, therefore has a great deal to say about the processes in which we are interested. This perspective provides one out of many useful theoretical statements about human sexuality.

REFERENCES

Anderson, R. M., & May, R. M. (1991). *Infectious diseases of humans.* New York: Oxford University Press.

Dodd, S. C. (1955). Diffusion if predictable: Testing probability models for laws of interaction. *American Sociological Review, 20,* 392–401.

Furstenberg, F. F., Morgan, S. P., Moore, K. A., & Peterson, J. L. (1987). Race differences in the timing of adolescent intercourse. *American Sociological Review, 52,* 511–518.

Gladwell, M. (June 3, 1996). The tipping point. *The New Yorker, 32*–38.

Kahn, J. R., Kalsbeek, W. D., & Hofferth, S. L. (1988). National estimates of teenage sexual activity: Evaluating the comparability of three national surveys. *Demography, 25,* 189–204.

Lord, F., & Novick, M. (1968). *Statistical theories of mental test scores.* Reading, MA: Addison-Wesley.

Maxwell, S. E., & Delaney, H. D. (1990). *Designing experiments and analyzing data: A model comparison framework.* Belmont, CA: Wadsworth.

Rodgers, J. L. (1996). Sexual transitions in adolescence. In J. A. Graber, J. Brooks-Gunn, & A. C. Peterson (Eds.), *Transitions through adolescence: Interpersonal domains and context.* Mahwah, NJ: Lawrence Erlbaum Associates.

Rodgers, J. L., & Rowe, D. C. (1993). Social contagion and adolescence sexual behavior: A developmental EMOSA model. *Psychological Review, 100,* 479–510.

Rodgers, J. L., Rowe, D. C., & Buster, M. (1998). Social contagion, adolescent sexual behavior, and pregnancy: A nonlinear dynamic EMOSA model. *Developmental Psychology, 34,* 1096–1113.

Rowe, D. C., Chassin, L., Presson, C. C., Edwards, E., & Sherman, S. J. (1992). An "epidemic" model of adolescent cigarette smoking. *Journal of Applied Social Psychology, 2,* 261–285.

Rowe, D. C., Osgood, D. W., & Nicewander, W. A. (1990). A latent trait approach to unifying criminal careers. *Criminology, 28,* 237–270.

Rowe, D. C., & Rodgers, J. L. (1991). Adolescent smoking and drinking: Are they epidemics? *Journal of Studies in Alcohol, 52,* 110–117.

Rowe, D. C., & Rodgers, J. L. (1994). A social contagion model of adolescent sexual behavior: Explaining race differences. *Social Biology, 41,* 1–18.

Rowe, D. C., Rodgers, J. L., & Meseck-Bushey, S. (1989). An "epidemic" model of sexual intercourse prevalences for black and white adolescents. *Social Biology, 36,* 27–145.

Singer, J. D., & Willett, J. B. (1993). It's about time: Using discrete-time survival analysis to study duration and the timing of events. *Journal Educational Statistics, 18,* 155–196.

Torgerson, W. S. (1958). *Theory and method of scaling.* New York: John Wiley & Sons.

Udry, J. R., Billy, J. O. G., Morris, N. M., Groff, T. R., & Raj, M. H. (1985).

Serum androgenic hormones motivate sexual behavior in adolescent boys. *Fertility and Sterility, 43,* 90–94.

Udry, J. R., Talbert, L. M., & Morris, N. M. (1986). Biosocial foundations for adolescent female sexuality. *Demography, 23,* 217–230.

NOTES

1. The conclusion to this meta-theoretical introductory section will make explicit some of the motivation for its inclusion. During my oral presentation of this material at the Kinsey conference, several excellent scholars expressed discomfort with my presentation (while others apparently appreciated the presentation). My sense is that part (but not all) of the discomfort arose from the different epistemological traditions that lie behind qualitative and quantitative methods. The goal of this section was to create a starting point for understanding what the terms "models," "theories," and "science" are intended to mean in this particular paper. In the next section, I turn to what I understand to be a second source of discomfort with my presentation.

2. See editor's comments on page 344.

DISCUSSION

Alex Carballo-Dieguez: I am curious about your choice of vocabulary. You talk about the epidemic spread or conversion of nonvirginity to virgins, which made me think about HIV conversions. Does this choice of infectious disease medical vocabulary denote a theory behind which you pathologize sexual behavior?

Joseph Rodgers: Well, the answer is absolutely not! We're not pathologizing sexual behavior. We're drawing an analogy between a type of mathematical modeling which is epidemiological and which is not typically used in this arena, but which has a language attached to it. You overinterpret the language if you believe that we think of adolescent sexuality as a disease. Certainly it's not. All of these mathematical models came out of the arena of epidemiology, and to appreciate them you need to view this as analogy and not be overinterpretive of the language. If you get bogged down in the verbal language, then you miss the point that it is a mathematical modeling analogy and not one that is to be taken in a literal sense.

Jay Paul: Although you suggest that this language is not meant to be taken literally, you appear to be ignoring the power of the imagery involved. One of the difficulties of using an analogy is the manner in which it can subtly constrain your perspective. The analogy can have at least as much impact as the evidence in shaping your assumptions. Therefore, the concerns raised do not just emerge out of our getting "bogged down in the language"—at issue is the fact that language inevitably limits as well as expresses constructs. I was struck by the policy implications of this model, which apparently includes some sort of "treatment" for those adolescents described as "seeding the system." I would not typically view sexual behavior—even that which might be termed "premature" or "precocious"—as requiring treatment. The use of these terms suggests how influential your use of medical constructs is here and elsewhere in your discussion.

Although the attempt to model what goes on in sexual networks is very important, it is important not to lose the larger context of sexuality for children at these ages. What does it mean to have sex? Although it is relatively easy to classify "virgins" versus "nonvirgins," what meanings and potency do these labels hold? Which of the persons with whom you interact have the most social influence and power as models? What are they doing sexually? This contagion model, which focuses on nonvirgins seemingly "infecting" virgins, does not address any of these considerations. That is what perturbs me most about this paper, although I find the analysis of the networks to be interesting.

Joe Rodgers: I think you're exactly right. The things that you identified are exactly what the model doesn't capture. It doesn't capture religiosity. It doesn't capture individual differences of any type. We've worked some and thought some about how to capture those and we have some ideas. But these are aggregate-level models that identify big broad differences between males and females and blacks and whites and those who are mature versus those who aren't. But individual differences are not things that the model is good at capturing and it wasn't built to do that. We'd like to figure out a way to reformulate it in that direction.

Jay Paul: Nonetheless, you are in some way suggesting implications for policy. It's important to know how this affects all the people involved on an individual as well as an aggregate basis.

Joe Rodgers: Any policy based on research is going to come out of some type of model that may account for individual differences or may not. That model is as much a simplification of reality as is this. What you just said could be applied to all policy that is drawn from research. In that sense, I am very comfortable with what you said. I did want to say something about your concern about the use of the word "treatment." In my part of the psychological arena, the idea of a "treatment effect" is so built into our language that I can't imagine it being misunderstood. A treatment isn't something that is necessarily medical. Nature imposes treatments all the time; for example, we think of gender as a treatment effect that nature has imposed, or we think of treatments that evaluation programs impose. I have a lot of colleagues who work in family planning clinics and they'd be a little surprised at the idea that 12-year-olds shouldn't be "treated" in some way or an intervention program shouldn't be delivered to 12-year-olds who are at risk of having sex. That's exactly who we're talking about. We're talking about 10-, 11-, and 12-year-olds who are, according to the definition of the word, sexually precocious. We in no sense are talking about whether sex is good or bad or indifferent for adults or even 16- to 18-year-olds. But I am prepared to stand up here in front of every-one and say that I'd be happy if 12-year-olds weren't having sex in this country right now. That's a personal moral statement. With the people with whom I come in contact who are working in the field, there are treatments going on and interventions being delivered to try and achieve that goal. That's the background that I'm coming out of when using that term.

John Gagnon: It strikes me that there's not a lot of value added from the model. Nearly every implication of the model is in fact ob-servable without the model. Does the menarche make a difference? In this sense the model is not explanatory but simply descriptive and the model-fitting procedure is interesting, but, for example, I think we already know that girls convert boys faster than boys convert girls. There's nothing in it that surprises me. One of the powers of creating mathematical models is the generation of surprising findings that fall out in a way that I wouldn't have expected them to do, that direct me to different empirical activities. In this case I like the idea, and one thing that I liked about it is that it did have segregation affects on the basis of race which is the argument that Laumann and I made in terms of partner selection using a different set of procedures. It's interesting, but I didn't learn a lot from this one.

Joseph Rodgers: I understand and I appreciate that and I agree. But if it had found something that was highly counterintuitive, then you probably would have said that there's something wrong with the model.

John Gagnon: Only if I disagreed with it.

Daryl Bem: A tactical comment about the use of language. Once you present the abstract model explaining that it came out of epidemi-ology, why not talk about the spread of innovation or early adopters? To take the Internet as an example, that would save you from the notion that Internet users are infecting non-Internet users. I think that different words actually lead you to different policy implications pre-cisely because the language acts as a guide. It has always seemed to me odd that in the school system we hook up sex, alcohol, and drugs. Why not sex and driver education? It seems to me that that's the better model. How can one safely use the machinery, not exploit other people with it, not hurt yourself with it. Sex education has always been paired with alcohol and drugs and you then use that in defense in your use of language.

Joe Rodgers: We've also used the same kind of models to discuss the idea of playing in the school band, which is socially a very positive thing.

Daryl Bem: The language of epidemiology one can see as an abstract system that could impose. As soon as you start on the policy level then I think a shift of vocabulary is needed.

Theo Sandfort: The variables included in the model really limit the kind of potential policy recommendations you can make. By the way you conceive a problem, you also hint at potential solutions for the problem. The problem can be conceived in a lot of ways that are different from your conceptualization here of virginity/nonvirginity. You can think about STDs among adolescents in a lot of different ways and you come up with a lot of different policy recommendations. So I think it's important to look at different variables to include in your model to explore other policy recommendations.

Joe Rodgers: Which ones would you like to add to the model?

Theo Sandfort: It would interest me where the STDs are coming from. Who are giving them to other people? I think that's much more important than to understand why virgins become nonvirgins.

Joe Rodgers: The model can readily be adapted to model the spread of STDs, and we've written the equations. But we don't have good STD prevalence curves for adolescents, for most STDs anyway. We have not yet identified empirical data that we were comfortable fitting our models to. But I agree that that's a very useful extension of this model.

Theo Sandfort: But wouldn't you think that condom use and self-efficacy with regard to condom use and negotiation skills are much more important for teenagers to understand the spread of STDs than the conversion of virgin to nonvirgin?

Joe Rodgers: I'm not sure that's the right language. This is a different type of model than most of the models we come in contact with. The linear models that put predictors in our regression equations are purely predictive models; there's no one who would ever propose that adolescents literally weight these different variable values by some empirical weight and add them up to decide whether to have sex or not. Our model, on the other hand, is trying to capture in an explanatory sense as well as a predictive sense some of the processes that are going on in adolescent networks. So the process of entering into nonvirginity or remaining virgin and pairing up adolescents is the explanatory part of the model that is trying to capture the real world in a simplified idealized fashion, and the presumption is that that happens before pregnancy or STDs are eligible to occur. Before a girl can get pregnant she has to be sexually active; before someone can catch an STD that's transmitted through heterosexual intercourse they have to have heterosexual intercourse. Adding individual differences to these equations is exactly what we'd like to do. We'd like to take the explanatory part of the model and be able to enter into it some predictive variables of the types you're identifying, and then I think it would be—several have implied this and it's absolutely true—a much more powerful modeling approach for both research and policy purposes than it is now.

Theo Sandfort: But the "it" will remain being a virgin or not being a virgin and I think that the "it" that you want to explain with your model should be much broader.

Joe Rodgers: What if the "it" that we explain is the process of becoming a virgin or not a virgin and simultaneously the acquisition of STDs? Isn't that a better model than one that just captures STD transition?

Colin Williams: Again on language. I'm sitting here listening to you speak about "virgins" and "nonvirgins." Do we really have to use those terms? I was wondering if there might be a better term. It sounds like we're at the Vatican or somewhere like that. For example, we could use terms like "sexually experienced" versus "not sexually experienced." I do think that the language we employ not only effects the way that we think but also the message that policymakers receive.

Anke Ehrhardt: I would like to take up a petition to ban the word "virgin." I think "virgin" means pure and it is a religious term and I'm not sure why it has got back into the sexual behavior literature. It would imply that "being sexual" is inferior and not pure.

Joseph Rodgers: I'm very comfortable with both of these suggestions, if we could find better terms.

Anke Ehrhardt: Intercourse inexperienced; that's what you mean by virgin.

Claire Brindis: Theo and I have been considering that instead of "virginity," we could talk about sexual "debut" in a more positive way. I also feel that there's language about secondary virginity that we should also recognize. When someone is sexually active, it doesn't mean that they're always sexually active. I was wondering how your model responds to that because there's definitely a lot of different patterns of sexual behavior among young people.

Joe Rodgers: That, I think, is fundamentally the biggest criticism of this type of modeling approach which we are using and other people are as well. We're all open to criticism on the grounds that we're utilizing what is basically labeled a binary process. Anybody coming to this conference will be more sophisticated than to think that capturing virgin/nonvirgin status is ultimately a good theory of sexuality. It's simply our starting point.

Leonore Tiefer: Labeling people is something that we're trying to get away from in some areas of sexuality theory, moving toward identifying acts rather than identifying people. Think about the entire discourse that exists about the disadvantages of labeling homosexual people as opposed to homosexual acts for example, which might offer new directions for thinking.

Discussion Paper

CAROLINE BLEDSOE

The papers on adolescent sexuality by Joseph Rodgers and Constance Nathanson confront us with the question of baseline assumptions in the framing of a scientific problem. Points of reference of time, place, and circumstance in which social science studies are framed shift rapidly, and with them the assumptions on which we build our views of a "normal" life. Whether we look at the empirical matter through models (Rodgers) or through a social science critique of policy (Nathanson), both papers give unique purchase for understanding the evaluative repertoires or frames from which we write.

Both in subject matter and in theoretical orientation, the papers seem at first glance to come from opposite ends of a very long spectrum. Rodgers writes of adolescent instinct and contagion of risky sexual practices; Nathanson writes in the mode of social science critique: how changing national worries have shaped the history of attempts at control. Rodgers asks how we learn more about adolescent behavior in order to place closer controls over it; Nathanson seeks to discover the source of our own bias in order to free up control over adolescents.

Rodgers presents a model of social contagion of the transition to nonvirginity among adolescents in the United States that searches for the dynamics underlying multiple events in the adolescent pathway to adult sexual life. Focusing on the initiation into sexuality of a virgin by a nonvirgin, it takes as a key assumption the possibility that delaying the onset of sexuality will slow the rate of contagion. In this epidemiological model of social contagion, taken to a figurative extreme, the problem is not sexually transmitted disease, but disease-transmitted sexuality.

Reservations about the model loom large. In its stark behaviorism, with little attention to context or history, it can do little more than portray sexuality, once it infects an adolescent population, as an unfettered force; what Nathanson alludes to as a Hobbesian "primitive force" that an individual cannot, or will not, control, and which the state must therefore attempt to regulate. We are also given a thin sense of the edges of the model; how to decide when sexuality is acceptable, how controls (institutions, policies, practices) might offset the spread of the contagion. Certainly, for example, marriage and habitation should figure importantly in mitigating the negative connotations of some teens who engage in sex. We do see a hint of such a connection. The fact that the risk of pregnancy is somewhat independent of sexuality is accompanied by a speculation that as age and sexual experience accumulate, compensatory strategies such as contraception and abortion are taken up. Yet if a modeling strategy of research is pursued, the complexities of social life need systematic incorporation.

While it is easy to object to the austere objectivity of Rodgers's model in its attempt to strip culture and context from a set of "brute" empirical facts (Searle, 1969), this same characteristic is also its strength. The model attempts to take nothing for granted. We see, therefore, a nonlinear relationship that might have eluded our usual cultural logic of time and physical and social development; e.g., puberty does not necessarily precede sexual experience for boys. While this relationship could certainly be observed in other ways, the logic of the model brings it to light quickly. Some other examples of empirical findings that the model highlights in this way:

•Once differences in pubertal maturation are accounted for, race is not a significant predictor of the onset of sexuality

•Small differences in the age of puberty for girls are associated with large differences in later sexual activity

•Two-thirds of first sexual encounters are not with a steady partner

Constance Nathanson's interest in adolescent sexuality uses an entirely different approach. Her paper presents a textual analysis of the recent history of ideological filters of several major research and policy documents in the United States over the last two decades: congressional provision for abstinence education, growing out of concerns for welfare reform; the National Campaign to Prevent Teenage Pregnancy; and various statements by the Alan Guttmacher Institute. Nathanson points out that over the last two decades, moral convictions about sex, pregnancy, marriage, economics, morality, and disease have shifted dramatically in the national consciousness of worries about adolescent sexuality. On the basis of previous research with Robert Schoen, for example, she argues that while adolescent women have some room to maneuver in the bargaining over sexuality, young women's calculus remains subject to shifts in societal values which now makes it difficult for them to refrain from sex.

Her analysis also offers enticing clues to changes in American cultural views of marriage and gender roles. In the discussion of the congressional provision, for example, we see a panoply of cultural terms by which Americans express their worries about the tide of dangerous adolescent sexuality: alcohol, drug use, not yet attaining self-sufficiency, etc. We also see important terms for factors that Americans believe might control this sexuality: self-sufficiency, education, motivation, punitive measures. Perhaps the most promising example in the set for future research of this nature, however, is that of the Alan Guttmacher Institute. As Nathanson notes, this institution, best known for creating the image of "the problem" of adolescent fertility in the United States, shifted its perspective almost completely in policy statements issued less than two decades apart.

Despite their vastly divergent approaches, these two papers find common ground in their efforts to achieve distance from this volatile issue of adolescent sexuality. Indeed, one might argue that the interest in this case here should be less in reconciling the views than in appreciating the variant insights their differences bring to light. Both reflect the fact that adolescent pregnancy or sexuality continues to evoke impassioned emotions in adults, as witnessed in their studies, their speeches, and their policies. We might best describe the results as policies of ambivalence that, on the one hand, condemn adolescent sexuality as a blight on the national character and, on the other, celebrate it as a human right in which all people, including adolescents, should be permitted to engage.

REFERENCE

Searle, J. R. (1969). *Speech acts: An essay in the philosophy of language.* Cambridge: Cambridge University Press.

Discussion Paper

DENNIS FORTENBERRY

I was asked to comment on the papers by Rodgers and by Nathanson and on adolescent sex from a research perspective. The authors of these papers have used somewhat divergent approaches to their assigned task of discussing theory and adolescent sex research. However, the marked differences in the two papers offer some opportunity to examine larger issues raised by both.

I took as my beginning assumption the idea that successful research—like good art or music or literature—is a process that is as much one of deliberate exclusion as one of intentional inclusion. And as I thought about myself from the perspective of a research consumer and a research producer, it occurred to me that one of the things that distinguishes us from all but the most insane of artists is the fact that we must confess to our peers what we don't do and don't know and be judged on that basis. It's with an eye then on both what is included and what is excluded that I will make a few comments on some of the things that we've heard.

Some key elements are excluded from each of the papers, although perhaps with different effects. The sexual dyad, for example: the individuals paired by sexual contact. How did the pair come together? Under what circumstances? What is the meaning of their "coupleness" beyond two individuals who are conjoining certain spans of epithelia? What are the long-term meanings and influences? In many cases, they appear to be negligible. In others, where the dyad's sexuality is marked by circumstance (for example, the "first time") or by consequences such as infection or pregnancy, a dyad's sexuality may reverberate through lifespans and (sometimes) into the genetic memory of our species.

The dyad is made up of two individuals. But a dyad implies something more. Relatively little research addresses potential influences of an adolescent dyad's relationship on its sexuality. In part, this is true because of very thorny problems associated with defining the true domain of the dyad rather than the isolated contributions of the individuals. A similar issue bedevils much family research: defining what a family is, who represents it, and who has the appropriate authority to report for the family.

Clearly, dealing with the issue of dyads in adolescent sex research remains a theoretical and empirical challenge. One way of getting around this is simply to treat the sex partner as if it were a discrete quantity. Establish the number of partners during a specified period of time. One can even translate those numbers into culturally meaningful designations: "abstinence" for those with no sex partners; "monogamy" for those with one; "promiscuity" for those with more than one partner. Treating the sexual partnerships as a quantity thus provides a means for judging the sexual behavior of adolescents (abstinence is best, monogamy is good, promiscuity is bad) as well as providing a point of public health intervention. So if one "reduces" the number of partners, risk for adverse consequences such as STD or HIV is reduced. It's like passing up on a bowl of ice cream because the cholesterol budget for the day has been expended. Although this does not seem to be sound logic when applied to sexual partnerships, without a means of understanding adolescent sexual dyads, this is about the extent to which anything can be said or done.

Each of the papers does raise issues of an exchange or transfer occurring with an adolescent sexual dyad. In the Rodgers paper, the exchange is apparently unilateral and defined by the researcher simply as a change of status, from virgin to nonvirgin. From this model's perspective, this status change is most likely to occur in conjunction with a sexually experienced partner. Rodgers's epidemiological metaphor is that nonvirgin status spreads within an adolescent population by this status "transmission" from nonvirgins to virgins. More important, the model has considerable explanatory power and stands up to a variety of assumptions about other influences on the traditionally important status change from virgin to nonvirgin. It is important to note, however, that this model gives only implicit attention to sexual dyads.

The Nathanson paper also incorporates a concept of exchange into its theory of adolescent sexual behavior. In this instance, sexuality is a resource exchanged for social or economic benefits. The model also works well empirically in explaining sexual activity, but again only implicitly incorporates the sexual dyad.

The Nathanson paper also asks the question of why adolescent sexuality is treated as if it were inherently problematic, as if adolescent sex were only of relevance in terms of pregnancy and sexually transmitted diseases. For the most part, research interest on adolescent sex and sexuality is primarily concerned about these presumably negative consequences of sexual behavior. With the exception of an eloquent editorial by Anke Ehrhardt in the *American Journal of Public Health* (1996), very little has been said about how little is known about the importance of sex (not just sexuality) in the development of both interpersonal and sexual competence. Focus on negative consequences leads to perspectives on adolescent sexuality largely focused on coitus. Very little else gets much theoretical or empirical attention. The sexual repertoire of teenagers (and its development) is given scant attention. The potential importance of that sexual development for later development is given even less attention. This replacement of attention to adolescent sexuality by almost obsessive attention to adolescent coitus has gotten worse during the era of HIV because of the focus on condoms and the necessity for an erect penis to use one.

What are some other elements of importance not addressed in the two papers? What about the social and sexual networks of adolescents? What are those networks? How do they overlap? How do they exist in geographic space? And—during the past half decade or so—how do they exist in cyberspace? The influence of computer-linked communications on adolescent sexuality is receiving a lot of anecdotal attention. Systematic attention in the near future may be necessary to keep our theoretical models in touch with social reality.

Each of the papers under discussion uses some specific words to talk about adolescent sex. I want to say a few things about these words and what meanings they have in terms of operationalization and measurement. When one looks at most of the literature on adolescent sexuality, one finds that its focus is really on a single issue: Has coitus ever happened? The answer is treated as a "no" or a "yes" and translated to a status of virgin or nonvirgin. Nonvirgins are also called "sexually experienced" even if they only have sex once and haven't much experience at all and—for reasons that never make sense to me—this status change is translated to "being sexually active." So an adolescent with one coital experience is as sexually active as one with a thousand experiences. The condition of "sexual experience" is apparently permanent, even though 10% to 30% of adolescents with any lifetime coital experience report no coitus within the previous ninety days or so. From an epidemiological perspective, this conflation of prevalence measures with incidence measures leads at best to imprecision and confusion and at worst to badly misguided inferences.

An example of this type of problem can be seen in much of the literature about alcohol or drugs as causal factors for adolescent sexual activity, especially sexual activity that is risky for STD or pregnancy. You can't make the judgments about causal relationships between alcohol and drugs and coitus on the basis of prevalence measures. You just can't do it. It doesn't work. It's illogical and yet it's done and in fact social policy has been derived from it despite the fact that the few event-level measures in studies that have been done for the most part have had difficulty showing that causal relationship.

This suggests that we need to expand the repertoire of measures and measurement strategies. We have to keep in mind that answers usually depend on how the questions are asked and in what context. One recent development in this area is the use of computer-assisted audio self-interviews (Turner et al., 1998). This may be an important technology to consider as a means of understanding sex and sexuality among young people. The technology could be used in several different ways. You can take the computer to them. You set it in from of them, put earphones on them, and let them go. You can do it over the telephone. This offers the possibility of achieving a much clearer understanding of sex and sexuality within an adolescent's daily life.

The final issue to address in terms of adolescent sex research is implicit in all research: consent and research permission and research participation by teenagers. This is partly but not entirely an ethical and legal issue. After all, our theories are of little use without data by which to test them. Very little is known of factors associated with the willingness of adolescents to participate in sexuality-related research. Even less is known of factors associated with the willingness of their parents to grant permission. This is a perennially contentious area that must be addressed every time adolescent sex research is proposed. We certainly can't guarantee that better data will improve the ethical and legal debates. Nonetheless, there are currently some real challenges to even the most basic kinds of sexuality-related research with adolescents.

REFERENCES

Ehrhardt, A. A. (1996). Our view of adolescent sexuality—A focus on risk behavior without the developmental context. *American Journal of Public Health, 86,* 1523–1525.

Turner, C. F., Ku, L., Rogers, S. M., Lindberg, L. D., Pleck, J. H., & Sonenstein, F. L. (1998). Adolescent sexual behavior, drug use, and violence: Increased reporting with computer survey technology. *Science, 280,* 867–873.

Discussion Paper

CLAIRE BRINDIS

What I would like to talk about really has to do with the disconnect between policy and theory. This disconnect reflects both the disconnect between policy and research and the disconnect between policy and logic. There are three areas that I would like to spend some time on. One is to think about what drives policy. Why should policymakers care about today's meeting and the work that you are putting forth in your papers? The second area that I want to discuss has to do with the question of what factors interfere with successful policy formulation. Finally I'd like to talk a little bit about the challenges of translating research into policy.

What I've been struck about in today's discussion around the "abstinence" dollars and "abstinence" focus is the "dis-ease" that this country has around sexuality. In discussions between sessions the schizophrenia that this country has around sexuality and particularly adolescence sexuality has been commented on. This has largely occurred because I think that adolescents have been marginalized in this society and so their sexuality is confrontational to us in a number of different ways and when they play out their sexuality there is a discomfort among adults. Sometimes people also comment that adolescents actually mirror adult behavior because I don't think of adolescents living their sexual lives isolated from all the messages that they receive and, in fact, the countermessages that they receive. Sex sells every single product that they've ever been exposed to—videotapes, films, music, television, etc. They also do receive some protective messages about how to access contraceptives and how to be responsible. However, these messages are relatively brief in light of a multibillion-dollar media industry that avoids the theme of responsibility. We don't spend the same kind of energy and time in preparing and equipping young people with the kinds of skills that they need to be effective in their sexual negotiation skills.

The whole area of policy formulation in adolescent sexuality is symbolized by welfare reform and its emphasis on reducing welfare dependence by abstaining from sex. I agree we should think of that as just one piece of policy that is going on right now, but to me it's very powerful because it brings up a number of what I call "policy hierarchy" issues. When policymakers think about making decisions, they're mostly affected by whether it's related to death or cost. Perhaps the third area is frustration. I think of adolescent sexuality in some respects as forcing both the second issue of cost and the third issue of frustration. We know that even when you have the best research available, as was very evident recently with the data on needle exchange (where we have scientific evidence that documents that having access to clean needles does not increase the number of people who engage in drug use nor does it create additional AIDS problems) it is not sufficient to formulate policy. Even the best scientific research can be too threatening to policymakers because underlying this theme is the theme of a society that feels that it is out of control. As a result, what I find now are tremendous efforts by policymakers to develop ways to dictate social control. Second, as reflected in welfare reform, there is an incredible punitive spirit in the development of new social policy. We must recognize that the passage of welfare reform did not occur as a result of a sneaky stealth approach to policy development. What got that legislation passed is that there was widely held frustration among both the right and the left about the fact that welfare doesn't seem to work. The concern I have is that policymakers as a whole tend to think about issues in a very simplistic manner. They'd have a very hard time sitting in this room with you all. Data and research and theory have to be translated into one single piece of paper. The concern I have about the punitive spirit of welfare reform is that we're throwing the baby out with the bath water. We are focusing on abstinence and getting out the message that not only do we know what's best for you—how you should behave and the implications of that paternalistic kind of image—but also that we want to police your behavior. I think that's very threatening from a social engineering perspective and actually goes very much counter to the philosophy that drives a society that believes in individualism. Third, in welfare reform policy there is tremendous effort to reduce the number of non-marital births, whether they're teenagers or adults. Policymakers are concerned about the fact that it's costing society so much money when people who are not in marriages bear children. Policymakers, I must say, not only blame the victim, but they also fail to acknowledge how previously established policies have helped to create the negative repercussions that we're now trying to deal with. So let me give you a few examples of what I mean by that because I don't think that there's total malicious intent on the part of Congress. Although I agree that there is a very strong religious right who does have a sense of wanting to imprint human behavior and have social control, for the most part people who come to Washington have generally good intentions. Good intentions established programs like Aid to Families with Dependent Children (AFDC). Good intentions started Title X, which is the federal family planning program. Good intentions started Section 8 (federal housing vouchers for poor people). Let me briefly comment. Ironically AFDC, Title X, and Section 8 have had both positive and negative repercussions in our communities. AFDC is oftentimes seen as the incentive for people to get pregnant. It is seen as the incentive for women not to get married. But if you look at the amount of money provided by AFDC and the high teen birth rates in Mississippi (where the reimbursement for AFDC is much lower than it is in states like California, for example), you see that the stereotypical image of AFDC payments as an incentive to bear children out of wedlock does not explain what happens in that state. What I wanted to comment on is that the presence of AFDC is seen as having created the issue of non-marital births. What we need to point out to policymakers is how AFDC policies contributed significantly to pushing men out of the picture. We need to recognize the impact of policies that encouraged social workers to come into people's homes to see if there was a man in the house and how social policy has contributed to the creation of negative aspects and restrictions on the creation of families. Look at Title X's family planning program. Both the women's health movement and feminism and the availability of the technology of the birth control pill paved the way to public policy to pay for subsidized family planning services, which I applaud. At the same time, as a result, we changed the power dynamics among both men and women because no longer was contraceptive decision making seen as the responsibility of the man as well as the responsibility of the woman. As a result, many of the services have been directed toward women with little recognition of the role of men. What I see now is a tremendous desire to "reinvent" men and to bring them back into the fold, and how do you do that in a comfortable way? How do you bring them back to the "responsibilities" that many men want to have? Let me share a couple of experiences I've had with evaluations of teen pregnancy prevention programs where some of these issues emerge. There's a program in San Francisco where they've received federal dollars to do a parenting education program for young fathers. In order to enroll men, they've decided to offer incentives. We know now that there's a tremendous amount of controversy about what are the incentives that you need to bring people in for programs, but in this program, they decided that if a young man came in for eight sessions of parenting that they would get a pair of Nike shoes at the end of the final session. Well, needless to say, I can tell you that that was a phenomenal way to get young men into the program, but at the end of the eight sessions, three or four of the twelve young men went up to the director and said, "You know what, I don't want those shoes anymore. Could I have the money to pay for diapers and food for my baby?" So I think we need to recognize that as we have pushed men out of the picture, we have created a vacuum and created negative stereotypical images of the idea that these men don't want to be responsible for their children. We must also question whether we have created the economic opportunities they need to be responsible fathers, because I think in many respects it's the fact that we have shifted our economics from a manufacturing base to a high-technology base that has created the unemployment and inequality that we see now. Dr. Julius Wilson, a sociologist at Harvard, has written extensively (Wilson, 1996) of the negative repercussions of the Section 8 housing vouchers which were supposed to allow low-income families access to better housing. However, because of segregated housing, Section 8 housing did not afford the types of housing opportunities originally envisioned. As a result, greater numbers of young children grew up in environments where all that they saw were poor unemployed individuals. I think that social imprinting and modeling has great implications, so a point I want to make here and now is that we have to be very careful about the policies that we recommend and to think through in an anticipatory way what are both the potential positive and the negative repercussions of introducing any kind of policy change. Another point to consider in what drives policy is the concept of simplistic morality that I see over and over again, not just in Washington, but throughout our whole country. I think of the morality interwoven with a lot of the policy decisions that are happening right now as strands that resemble the strands of a DNA model. There appears to be a great deal of magical thinking which occurs among adults. We think of adolescents as having magical thinking from a cognitive perspective, but the reality is that adults have magical thinking about wanting to return to a golden era, a golden period when Ozzie and Harriet were around. Others believe that if we condone sexual activity by allowing sexually active adolescents access to contraceptives, we will be giving them the wrong message. Contraceptive services become symbolic of that sexual activity. The whole effort about abstinence is also representative of morality through social policy. The whole effort that Nancy Reagan attempted with the "Just Say No" campaign around drugs has to do with the sense and the fear that we have a society that is totally out of control. It's interesting to me that the concern about "more sex equals more welfare" comes, I think, in some part because we have a distrust of young people. We have a loathing of young people; we are marginalizing them and in some way making them the enemy. I agree that, as

Connie has commented, a number of different power groups helped create this problem because it allowed for the identification of funding streams and research streams to apply to the issue of teenage child-bearing. But the reality is that adolescents and children are not valued in our society, and as soon as we can get clear on that I think we can make more movement. I think it's problematic. We have failed children and adolescents in a number of ways—for example, we do not even pay for adequate contraceptive services for young people. Only about a third of the teens who are at risk of a pregnancy actually have access to subsidized care. It's been fascinating to me to see the arguments about the need to fund Viagra pills because I can bet you a lot of money that reimbursement for Viagra use is going to be subsidized far earlier than contraceptives in managed care plans. As managed care gobbles up much more of our systems and as teenagers have less access to our safety net providers, I fear very much for them about where they're going to turn for contraceptive protection. Adolescents, given the right access to care and services, certainly are capable of acting in a responsible manner. We did an analysis in California of how many pregnancies are averted by responsible teenagers and demonstrated that a great number of sexually active adolescents are responsible and that in California approximately 200,000 pregnancies are prevented by adolescents' effective use of birth control. That finding has been used as a part of a public campaign in trying to reframe the issue of adolescent pregnancy.

Let me also comment on the fact that as we think about the factors that interfere with policy formulation, we need to recognize that in our American culture we put the sense of community as secondary to the role of the individual and I think that we need to ask at what cost that is happening. The private sector certainly dominates; we are in a capitalist society. There are a lot of payoffs for the activity that we see here. We struggle with what the role of government should be in this whole area. We also have this image that people can succeed in this very pluralistic competitive environment and if they fail to succeed it's their fault, without a recognition of the structural and economic factors that interfere. We also have a lack of clear consensus about what we should be doing in this area. We fear that the answer for young adolescents versus middle adolescents versus late adolescents should be different and the lack of consensus is a very difficult factor. Finally, another factor that I think interferes is this very narrow segmented policy perspective that we bring to the issue. I think it's very important to bring drug and alcohol policy along with sexual activity because we know that approximately a third of the kids are engaging in drug and alcohol use before they engage in sexual activity. From my vantage point, of course, I wonder why so many kids have to use alcohol and drugs to have sex. What's the message that we have given to young people about their bodies so that they have to use the crutch of alcohol or drugs to feel comfortable about engaging in sexual activity? We also have to think about what are the incentives we provide very young people. In her paper Connie talks about poverty and the fact that poverty is seen by policymakers as a consequence of teenage pregnancy. The data also shows that five out of six girls who end up giving birth (note that I'm saying giving birth versus getting pregnant) are already poor before they become pregnant. No one is talking about economics and very few people are talking about income incentives and I think until policymakers recognize the complexity of adolescent pregnancy and the necessity of combining adolescent pregnancy with economic development, youth development, school-to-work activities, we will not make a dent.

The last area that I want to touch on has to do with the challenges of translating research into policy. What will it take to build a consensus on policy regarding adolescents in our society? I think it's important to learn from other public health campaigns. I want to focus on just one. I think I have to say that the AIDS campaign is very successful. I recognize that we're not there totally yet, but it's a very, very important model for public policy action. Today I want to focus on the SADD (Students Against Drunk Drivers) and the MADD (Mothers Against Drunk Drivers) campaigns. Why have we created a social norm around not drinking and driving? If we think about that social change, we see that it's a very powerful public health message in which social norms have been developed; part of the answer for me is that it wasn't just one sector that created the answer. We required both formal policy from the perspective of government policy and informal policy—for example, insurance companies giving a video film to new drivers and a 5% reduction in insurance premiums. I can tell you that for a 17-year-old that's a very important incentive. Thus, we had insurance policies, government policy, and neighborhood bars (and other locations where people sell drinks) engaged and involved. Also a very significant private and public sector marriage between the people who actually are selling you alcohol who came on board with the importance of the message of a designated driver. The media are involved, as well as a number of other major stakeholders engaged in community-wide campaigns that have one unified message. One consensus message. Let me also say that youth themselves were at the forefront of the success of the SADD campaign and, in fact, there are one million adolescents involved in SADD campaigns across the country. Recently they've expanded their efforts from drunk driving to other socially challenging issues like drugs and other behaviors that compromise health. In fact, at the National Campaign to Prevent Teenage Pregnancy awards about three weeks ago, the SADD campaign won an award for moving into the area of sexuality.

A second challenge is how to translate the data that we already have. Just the fact that we do have data is not enough to be convincing, as I commented earlier. Even when we have good data, we don't always find the key to market the information successfully. Here I would like to argue that we need to be thinking about what policymakers care about in the way that we translate data for them. I can tell you that money and costs drive a lot of their decision, along with morality. When I dealt with a number of private foundations and I was trying to encourage them to deal with some research in the area of sexually transmitted diseases, it wasn't until I spoke to these elderly gentleman (members of the board) about the fact that they may not have grandchildren that I finally got their attention regarding the importance of the research. The sense that I was trying to sell to them was, your daughter may have chlamydia, she may not know about it, and at the time that she's ready to have your grandchild, your legacy, she may be infertile. So it's a challenge for me and for all of us to figure out what's the key to make that policymaker listen.

A third area is to find stealth solutions. By stealth solutions in the area of adolescent pregnancy I refer to the many efforts underway across the country that have to do with school-to-work programs, academic remediation, mentoring programs, economic opportunities, and the availability of technology. The whole concept that school and education provides a sense of future can be seen as one of the best contraceptives. It's not the only contraceptive, but it's an important contraceptive. As an advocate for adolescents, when I see efforts underway in Congress or in California (or wherever I am), I applaud those efforts because I think a sense of the future is such an important ingredient in efforts to reduce the incidence of adolescent childbearing. I'm hoping that other advocates who are trying to get money for these programs eventually will join me in my work. Another area is the need to recognize that polarization and ideology has totally prevented us from creating those compromises and unless we understand the ideology of the very far right, as well as the ideology of the left, we're not going to find common ground. It may be that youth development is the common ground. It's the compromise for the 1990s, even though I would like to have condoms and other contraceptives much more readily available. Finally, I think it's important for us to recognize that adolescents are a part of the larger society. Today we're focusing on adolescents. I think about the fact that while 85% of youngsters will say "I didn't intend to have this pregnancy," I find that adult women are not all that different! If you ask an adult woman, "Did you plan to have this baby?" between 50 and 66% of women will say, "I did not plan to have this pregnancy." Teenage behavior mirrors adult behavior. Why aren't adult women and adult men planning their babies? I think it has to do again with the discomfort and "dis-ease" that we have with sexuality and how that gets translated into our discomfort with the use of contraceptives.

REFERENCE

Wilson, W. J. (1996). *When work disappears: The world of the new urban poor.* New York: Vintage Books.

General Discussion

Gary Dowsett: I'll use my foreignness to start doing the cross-cultural perspective here. This is actually a conference about the role of theory in sex research, not a conference about the role of theory in sex research in the United States alone, I assume. The first point I wanted to make is that some of the generalizations about young people that I've been hearing this afternoon are very North American specific. Some of the political context in which the modeling and the research designs and the reporting has happened are very United States specific. That's not a bad thing; that's where we are at the moment. But I don't want it to be forgotten, because there is a tendency in this literature and in discussions about young people in general to assume that what applies in North America will apply in the rest of the world; and, in fact, it doesn't. That's my first point.

My second point is that this comes out of a fairly strong registration of culture shock on my part. Not the first time I've experienced it here in the States so far, I might say, but certainly culture shock at hearing things about national legislation that promotes abstinence. That is politically impossible to conceive of in Australia and would be regarded as abhorrent. And we don't have a democratic system of individual rights as you do here. But it would be culturally totally inappropriate and unachievable in any public health program in my country.

The next point I'd like to make is about the nomenclature that we've been using throughout the afternoon. I don't think I've been at a conference for a long time where I've heard the words "teenager" and "adolescents" used. Yet these words have been used interchangeably in this particular session. Certainly in the kinds of work I've been doing with WHO and UNAIDS since 1993 on young people and sexual risk taking in developing countries in relation to HIV and AIDS, the words "adolescent" and "teenager" have been completely expunged from the vocabulary that we've used for a number of reasons: the first being that both of those categories are semantic maneuvers that have been developed only very recently in fact, "teenagers" much more recently than "adolescents." This relates quite specifically to changes in thinking about age cohorts that have developed since the early eighteenth century. Many of you will know about some of the social research or cultural work on the invention of childhood that describes the period of change in Europe at the end of the eighteenth and the beginning of the nineteenth century. The invention of "childhood," in fact, relates quite distinctly to the development of modern societies, particularly to the development of industrial societies. The consequence of that for an international perspective is that the idea or category "teenagers" does not occur in some countries. That's not to say that the cohort of 13-, 14-, or 15-year-olds is not there, but rather that the concept of an extended childhood, which delays the acceptance of adult responsibilities both in the workplace and in relation to the family and to childbearing and childrearing, does not exist in some countries to this day. "Teenagers" is a very western and very recent concept, and we shouldn't reify it, believing that because it exists here we haven't in fact merely invented it. We've extended the life of childhood through extended schooling for 12 years now and I've seen papers which still define young people as being younger than 25. Now in many countries some people might have three- or four-year-old kids when they're 25. I think we should think seriously about this problematization of young people as if they are a problem by definition rather than simply a category that we are creating and constructing in our own industrial and post-industrial societies in more problematic ways. In the work that we've been doing with WHO and UNAIDS—qualitative and ethnographic studies across seven countries and three continents which will be coming out in *Critical Public Health* soon and also in a UNAIDS report—it's absolutely clear that young people have not just simply a legitimate sexual culture but that they actively create legitimate sexual cultures of their own. It's extremely hard for adults to recognize that this is not just premature adult behavior or copying, mirroring adult behavior. Young people actually construct from their own bodies and their own subcultures active, legitimate, owned, and talked-about sexual cultures in places like streets, schools, behind trees, when parents aren't home. Unless we can recognize that element of legitimacy somewhere in young people's sexual activity, we can only ever cast their sexual experience as problematic and unfortunate. And we will be caught then in a trap about how we develop public health policy and public health interventions to deal with supporting their rightfully constructed and legitimately owned sexual experience.

Connie Nathanson: Well, you took away my first question which was why are we problematizing adolescent sexuality in the first place. So you've said all that needs to be said about that. I want to raise the

Foucaultian question which certainly was brought to my mind even more powerfully by an article in *Science*, "Adolescent Sexual Behavior, Drug Use and Violence: Increased Reporting with Computer Surveyed Technology." It was reinforced in my mind by Dennis Fortenberry's comments; the notion that you make things visible in order to control them. And this passion for making visible more and more refined details of adolescent sexual behavior to the exclusion of most other things about adolescence (if I may use that categorization for the time being) seems to me to raise questions. Many of the consequences of the making of greater and greater detail, making visible greater proliferation of "knowledge" about this period of life, have in fact been quite negative from the standpoint of public policy. I suppose this calls the whole research enterprise into question in some sense, but I think it needs to be called into question. I think what we have done has been misused, and Foucault would have predicted that.

John Gagnon: Let me follow on from Gary Dowsett's position because I think it's a very important one. I want to argue that young people are more insulated from us adults than we usually think. They are bombarded by large amounts of sexual material. One of our problems is that we actually don't know in any adequate way whether or not they're responding to it. As a matter of fact, my sense is that there's a very active vernacular culture of the sexual among young people which is highly protected from most of the kinds of things adults do. Adult versions, scientized versions, of sexuality have very little purchase on what happens among young people. Young people talk about love. They talk about all kinds of things we never talk about when we talk about their lives. They're living inside schools and inside streets and malls and making a life. We adults try to manage that life from the outside and we spend lots of money having very little effect on their behavior. It's not because we have somehow not found the way in, it may be that we can't find the way in. There's no easy way to take the "health belief model" and put it in the lives of young people. It doesn't make any sense in the day-to-day worlds in which they live. I share Connie's view on this, that the attempt to make troubles more visible, more public, not to leave alone vast areas of vernacular culture, in fact is destructive of those cultures. There's been a long history of criticism of the fact that young people are romantic. If you read marriage and family textbooks, they're constantly arguing that "Young people just shouldn't be so romantic, they should think carefully about the consequences of their behavior." In fact, being romantic is what drives much of adolescent life. Emotional attachments and passionate caring are how adolescents experience some aspects of their world and at the same time we adults are busy saying be rational, calculate what's going to happen to you. Adults are working absolutely against what flourishes among young people. So I have a sense that much of the science enterprise about adolescence is largely for us and not for them.

John Bancroft: I sense there's a feeling in the room that we are making a problem out of adolescent sexuality which doesn't exist. I accept many of the points that have been made and I think the point that John Gagnon has just made about youth having its own culture is one of increasing importance that carries with it considerable implications for their own welfare. It seems to me that there are certain aspects of the situation which are culturally determined, and here in the United States we're talking about a very different cultural context than the one that Caroline Bledsoe has been studying in Africa. We need to consider the following: We are in a situation in which young people, compared with the past, are reaching puberty at an earlier age, they are becoming fertile at an earlier age. They are living in a society which has become more individualistic and less family oriented. With the certainly desirable moves toward better equality between men and women, women need to have much longer periods of education in order for them to be able to get the best out of their subsequent lives. Generally speaking, for both men and women in our culture, the optimum time for marriage has been delayed from what it was in the past. Yet here we are with young people who are at their maximum sexual responsiveness at this very early stage. Whatever else you want to say about it, it is important for them to recognize that they are now capable of creating new human beings. As a father of five children, I'm painfully aware of the awesome responsibility having children carries. I think that we have a responsibility as a culture to do whatever we can to enable young people who, as I've already said, are now living in a more youth-oriented culture of their own to be able to recognize and implement that responsibility. Unfortunately, although the youth culture can do quite a lot, it can't provide young people with contraceptive services. We may be boiling it down to something as simple as that. Certainly one of the contrasts between the United States and Europe, which was convincingly demonstrated by the cross-cultural study carried out by the Alan Guttmacher Institute, points very much in that direction. The context that we're hearing about, with the objective of denying that young people should be sexual until they are married, whatever else it might be doing, is making it more difficult for these young people to recognize that they have these responsibilities and that there are sensible ways of exercising their responsibilities, which would allow them to do the very positive things that John Gagnon is talking about, being romantic and learning to form intimate relationships. There seems to be a trend at this meeting to deny that there is a problem to be dealt with. Maybe the issue is not whether there is a problem, but what type of problem it is.

Dennis Fortenberry: I am astounded actually by the comments of Connie Nathanson and John Gagnon. It sounds as though you're proposing to create a behavioral natural park where intrusion is not only not welcome but not permitted. That this is an area that is so naturally good that we shouldn't study it and that there's nothing to be gained by studying it. I don't understand that.

Connie Nathanson: I simply was raising the question. We need to be responsible about and to think about the potential consequences of our own research. And as far as a Disney World for adolescents, I don't think that was exactly what I had in mind.

Dennis Fortenberry: This reminds me of the arguments about the Manhattan Project; should this be investigated and what will be the good and evil uses of the knowledge? I think we're incapable of making that judgment.

Connie Nathanson: That's a reasonable argument.

John Gagnon: For a long time, we in the social sciences have meddled in people's lives out of our own interest. Every problem doesn't have to be studied. Every trouble doesn't have to be a problem. That is, social scientists are part of the process of constructing the problem. The knowledge production industry of which we are a major part is not a passive instrument. We ought to ask ourselves whether or not we should bother thinking about this as a problem or whether or not we should just let it work itself out. Benign neglect may not be a bad solution for certain problems. My position is not that it's naturally good out there. But our job is to not make it worse. Not to build housing projects which we then have to blow up 30 years later. Not to create pseudo-AIDS programs which replace the naturally occurring AIDS programs of gay people. Not to create institutes and organizations which in fact absorb money before it ever gets to the poor. Social workers profit, researchers profit, but the money never gets to anybody who needs it. So do we really need to know within one and a half percent how many adolescent young men have had casual sex with other men? I've done that kind of research. But I raise the question, do we need that level of precision? Do the young people need it? Is sensible human policy going to be created for the young people by what we do? If not, we should start saying to ourselves "Study something else."

Connie Nathanson: I want to respond to John Bancroft's comments. There is an increasing body of research that suggests that if there is a problem, it is not sex. The problem is presumably too early childbearing which then interferes with success in the marketplace or something like that. That seems to be the general view. There is increasing evidence that the negative outcomes that researchers and policymakers have been most concerned about, such as high school drop out, negative health consequences, are largely the results of the fact that women are poor who have these children, not because they had them when they were young. It is poverty that accounts for the negative outcomes and there has been some very sophisticated research suggesting that not all, but a large portion of the variation in outcomes is due to "unobserved heterogeneity"—that is, variation due to poverty that pre-existed. So if you take an older women from the same circumstances, she's going to have the same kind of negative outcomes. So it's not the fact that the person is adolescent, it is the fact they that those who have children are more likely to be poor, and that's very clear if you look at the data. Differences between the more and less advantaged in terms of sexual activity are getting less and less. There are greater differences in contraceptive use and the greatest difference in terms of childbearing.

John Bancroft: Yes, in terms of childbearing, because the adolescents who come from more affluent families get abortions. Maybe that's not a cause of concern for some people, but I think abortion is a traumatic experience and there are better ways to deal with one's reproductive capacity than getting pregnant and having the pregnancy aborted. I quite agree with you that if you are only looking at the birth rate then poverty becomes a major issue.

Anke Ehrhardt: While I agree that research done on adolescents in this country is very biased and often very problematic, as a clinician working with adolescents, I'm also very much with John Bancroft and Dennis Fortenberry. The idea to leave adolescents totally alone seems to me out of the question. Apart from childbirth. Adolescents have the right to sex education, they have the right to access to contraception and to disease prevention. So sexual behavior is not the problem; the problem is that we adults do not provide adequate information and adequate services. When you talk to adolescents you learn that they certainly want input. And we have a generation of parents who also haven't had any sex education, who have a very distorted view of sexuality, and who can't talk to their children. And teachers who are not trained to talk about it. I get invited to schools to talk to parents. Parents for the most part feel very incapacitated and want to learn how to talk to their adolescent children about sex. Of course, as John Gagnon said, there is the whole culture of adolescent sexuality which is quite different. And the decisions which adolescents make have to do with romance and with love. But when adolescent groups interact with our people at the HIV center, they say "Why don't you help us to make decisions about what we should do? Should I have sex with this girl or with this boy?" Adolescents would like input as long as it is not punitive or irrelevant to their lives—"Just say no," "Don't have any sex," etc. So while much of the research which has been done is very problematic, focusing only on teenage pregnancy or disease prevention, we also need to find ways to have appropriate interaction, provide appropriate education, and give access to appropriate services

Leonore Tiefer: I don't think that it's an option not to get involved in the policy debate or the research in this area. If we just abdicate, the field will be taken over by those whose interests are clearly antithetical to any progressive vision of adolescent sexuality. That would be derelict in the extreme. In terms of our theory, I think we have an obligation to think about, as Michelle Fine put it, the missing discourse of desire of adolescent girl sexuality. We have become hung up on policy in this discussion and the theory has gone. But we need to think about theory in a comprehensive way that will entail positive, comprehensive components. I agree with Anke that young people want to talk about sex, are eager to talk about sex, and of course that makes the utmost sense because sex is everywhere and it needs to be made sense of. It comes out of every newsstand and out of every television and out of every news interview with the president. We have to talk to young people about it often because they can't talk to their parents. It's our obligation to have something to say to them based on research. There are ways that we can be proactive in our research. For example, the issue of young people having children brings up right away the notion of childcare. Not that it is only young people's children who need childcare, but the current debate focuses on the dangers of childcare in terms of early development, social development, sexual dangers, cognitive development, so on. I was around during that entire first wave of thinking: Krech and Rosensweig and the enriched environment. Do you remember how rats' cortexes got thicker with all those toys? Whatever happened to that? It seemed like the benefits of childcare was once a proven issue, but here it is back again. These things don't get solved. Activism is an ongoing commitment. It seems like there's plenty for people to do in terms of research and policy. What has been said today that is relevant to the theory of young people's sexuality? I was taken aback by Gary's international perspective implying we didn't even know who we were talking about much less what we were talking about. So it seems to me that the theory in this area is extremely undeveloped and requires a great deal more discussion before we can even lay out the terrain, do research, and recommend policy.

Gary Dowsett: I don't think the question is whether we do research or not on young people. I think that's irrelevant. The question is how we do it and how we conceive of the research object that we're examining. The classic example is the way in which almost all of our policy-related work on young people by definition considers them "at risk." That phrase is so common now that almost every young person is at risk of something somewhere sometime. What I would argue for is a research approach very similar to what we now do with indigenous people in my country. Social science and medical science cannot do research on indigenous people unless indigenous people have a say in that research, in the design of that research, in the way in which the research questions are set up and established, so the cultural nuances of their lives are taken into account in the conceiving of the research. That doesn't compromise scientific objectivity. What it does do is ensure that any scientist working with that population is deeply sensitive to the cultural and social concerns of the people for whom the research is being done. There's an issue here about how we conceive of young people, and whether we conceive of them as being human beings in their own right, how we respectfully include their behaviors and their culture in the research questions that we think are important to pursue.

Richard Parker: I want to call our attention to what seems to me to be a relatively simplistic and unproblematized view that we as researchers tend to have about what is policy and what policymakers supposedly need to make the policies that they make. I assume there are a few of us here who have experience not only as researchers but also as program people, particularly in relation to the sorts of research findings and theoretical approaches that can provide the foundation for the development of programs. The cultural issues that are left out of many of these models are absolutely central; that's clearly the major conclusion from 15 years of work in relation to HIV, and I suspect in relation to most of the other kinds of so-called problems that we associate with adolescent sexuality. There are places were we can find that kind of work. There are huge research literatures about the sexual cultures and the youth cultures that exist in different settings. Yet we haven't drawn on that work in looking at sexuality in any way, shape, or form.

Sarah Hrdy: The chances that any of our Pleistocene ancestors were living a healthy life, as we define healthy and wholesome, are probably zero. The reason that sex among young hominids was going on and yet the females were not getting pregnant younger than would be healthy for them was of course the very long period of adolescent sterility that characterizes humans living in foraging environments, where they're nomadic. Also the food constraints make for a delayed onset of menarche. A !Kung girl reached menarche around 16 or 17, and would not give birth for the first time until 19 or so. So they have a long period of adolescent sterility just as do all of the great apes. Girls are able to get pregnant at such early ages because the period of adolescent sub-fertility is cut short. If we were living like our ancestors, we wouldn't have a teenage pregnancy problem. We have changed the conditions of life for young girls. We need sex education and birth control to compensate for what we have altered. Teenage pregnancy can be viewed as an unintended consequence of sedentary lifestyles and richer diets.

Bob Michael: I wanted to respond to Leonore Tiefer's question, "Where's the theory in all of this policy discussion?" I want to suggest that there is an implicit theory that's out there that I like very much. It has to do with the fact that these young people are making choices. This is the science of economics; that study of making decisions under scarce resources. Much of their sexual behavior is very purposive and they are sexual, even those who are not sexually active. They are making choices about their sexuality all the time and there are probably few periods in life when one's sexual choices or the decisions about sexuality are more purposive than in that period. They may not be quite what we think of as wholly rational and they may indeed be romantic, but they are purposive. There's wonderful evidence of increased condom use in response to higher risks of disease. There are all kinds of purposive behavior, from the way they comb their hair to which street they walk down on their way to school. That leads me to the issue of why do we do research and it is in part because of this implicit theory or paradigm or perspective. We do the research not because their behavior is pathological, but because the choices they make have import. It is important to them and it's important to us. There are very important long-term consequences of romantic sexual decisions and actions that young people, just like older people, do or make. There are those implications for disease, for fertility, for skill acquisition, and they affect well-being in the long run. To find out better what the implications are of one kind of behavior, one kind of choice, what the options are for this or that, seems to me to be respectful to them in understanding they have purpose in their behavior. They're receptive to a sense of responsibility if in fact they are given the opportunity to know what the facts are and the opportunity to access the resources. That may mean condoms in this case or something else in that case, to effect and achieve that responsibility.

Anke Ehrhardt: I just wanted to add to Bob Michael's theory or model, which I liked, the access to information and education for sexual pleasure—how to become proficient in giving and receiving sexual pleasure, how not to engage in abusive relationships, positive learning about sexuality and gender relations.

John Gagnon: There is a theoretical question in this discussion having to do with whether you think that sexuality emerges organically from the life of the untutored child or whether you believe that the responsibility for the sexuality of members of a culture depends upon how it is elicited by adults and peers. One of the results of having an isolated youth culture is that we can let the young self-educate, we can let the sexual world of youth operate pretty much on its own. On the other hand, if you have a model of adult sexuality that you want youth to conform to, you would involve actively, self-consciously engage in the elicitation of desire as opposed to passively letting it happen. I'm not sure that anybody here is ready for that one.

John Bancroft: John Gagnon's point reminded me that Alfred Kinsey had the view 50 years ago that the most important transmitters of sexual knowledge and values to young people were other young people and that was how change in society was implemented. I don't know whether or not we can still say that because obviously the media for communicating about sexuality are very different than they were 50 years ago. But it underlines the point that the youth culture, the peer-group culture, is still profoundly important in terms of sexual development. I'd like to have a theory to help me to explain why the age of onset of sexual activity has gotten younger. I think it's particularly important to have that explanatory model because what we're finding now is additional evidence that negative experiences during childhood may be contributing to an earlier age of onset (Browning & Laumann, 1997). That leaves attempting to reconcile the apparently negative effects of childhood sexual experiences with what appears to be a general tendency for earlier onset of sexual activity. We seem to be lacking a sufficiently comprehensive explanatory model to help us with that.

Gary Dowsett: One word—"culture." The WHO's Knowledge, Attitudes, Beliefs, and Practices studies that were done by WHO's Global Program on AIDS in the late 1980s in 16 developing countries found remarkably diverse median ages for onset of sexual activity, as low as 15 and 16 in some countries in East Africa and as high as 26 and 27 for females and males in Singapore, for example. The later study we did in Zimbabwe found the earliest age of onset reported was nine for girls in some parts of rural Zimbabwe. That disparity between nine in Zimbabwe for young women and 27 for young men in Singapore tells us that the concept of the age of onset is useless, because it is such a decontextualized and abstract term that it is unable to explain almost anything that is going on at that first sexual encounter. So, in our attempts to make a meeting between biology and culture, it's in those moments when we actually look at a concept like "age of onset" that the paradigms just cannot meet in any way. That is when we actually ought to start doing some talking. That's when we start to have the real theoretical debates, because then we're no longer just talking about explanatory models of something, which are more like paradigms; we're actually starting to talk about the way knowledge is produced, and how we understand the knowledge that we produce.

REFERENCE

Browning, C. R., & Laumann, E. O. (1997). Sexual contact between children and adults: A life course perspective. *American Sociological Review, 62*(4), 540–560.

Part 5
Policy and Culture

Sexuality and Culture

RICHARD G. PARKER

Bob Michael and I have the rather daunting task of summarizing our impressions of what has emerged during the meeting—in my case, in relation to culture, and in his case, in relation to policy.

My aim is to highlight a number of the issues that have drawn my own attention and to underline some of the insights that I think have emerged here as well as some of the major remaining problems or dilemmas that I see. I will try to focus my discussion around three major issues or areas: (1) the search for theoretical integration; (2) the interpretation of sexual cultures; and (3) the relationship between culture and structure. (I should add that I am going to valiantly resist Ken Plummer's challenge to me from yesterday afternoon's coffee break—much as I would love to, I am not going to offer a grand synthesis and an overarching theory which will resolve all of our dilemmas. On the contrary, I'll probably leave us with more unsolved dilemmas than I started with. Such is life!)

The Search for Integration

Over the course of this meeting, we have struggled to come to terms with our apparent desire for integration—though at times it has not been clear if we want to integrate disciplines, to integrate theoretical perspectives, or to integrate, quite simply, disparate dimensions of human experience.

I am somewhat tempted to wonder if this burning desire for theoretical integration may be itself at least partially culturally specific—peculiar especially to the United States where, after having constructed an entire society around notions of segregation and social exclusion, a strange desire to compensate in other ways seems to exist, through other quests for more integrated worlds. Whether or not this integration is really necessary—or whether it is *always* necessary—is a point which I will come back to. For the time being, however, I want to take it at face value as our apparent goal and to ask what such integration would imply for the concept of culture.

Indeed, throughout this conference, beginning with Anke Ehrhardt's presentation two days ago and her call for the development of a biopsychosocial model to understand gender and sexuality, on through the debate between the two Johns (Bancroft and Gagnon) yesterday afternoon, I have been repeatedly reminded of the classic article published more than 30 years ago by the anthropologist Clifford Geertz, "The Impact of the Concept of Culture on the Concept of Man" (Geertz, 1973). (The same article, published today, would no doubt refer to the concept of "humankind" rather than "man.") In this article, by opposing the view of human *nature* that emerged from the European Enlightenment to the scientific understanding of human *evolution* developed in the twentieth century, Geertz quite compellingly focused our attention on the symbolic dimensions of cultural forms. The Enlightenment view of human beings, he argued, was as "wholly of a piece with nature" and shared "in the general uniformity of composition which natural science, under Bacon's urging and Newton's guidance, had discovered there" (p. 34). An underlying human nature "as regularly organized, as thoroughly invariant, and as marvelously simple" as Newton's mechanistic universe was therefore thought to exist (p. 34). And this notion of a universal human nature gave rise, in turn, to what Geertz described as a "stratigraphic conception of the relations between biological, psychological, social and cultural" phenomena, a conception in which human beings were understood as a "composite" of analytically reducible levels:

> Strip off the motley forms of culture and one finds the structural and functional regularities of social organization. Peel off these in turn and one finds the underlying psychological factors—basic needs or what-have-you—that support and make them possible. Peel off psychological factors and one is left with the biological foundations "anatomical, psychological, neurological" of the whole edifice of human life. (p. 37)

This same stratigraphic analytic strategy Geertz identified as part of the heritage of the Enlightenment that is still with us in the twentieth century would appear to be very much alive—perhaps more in the study of sexuality than in many other areas. Indeed, the dominant tendency in sex research generally, and in a number of the papers presented at this conference, has quite clearly been to strip away cultural (and often social) phenomena as if they were somehow insignificant epiphenomena that need not be accounted for—or that actually inhibit us from encountering some kind of enduring truth—a "cultureless" model.

As Geertz pointed out more than 30 years ago, however, the very evolution of *Homo sapiens* has come to be understood as an interactive process in which physical transformation and cultural development overlap in a kind of feedback relationship—a relationship in which simple protocultural activity (such as tool use) stimulates anatomical development (the opposable thumb, for example) and above all neurological transformation, which, in turn, leads to further cultural elaboration. The point of this concern with evolutionary process is quite explicitly not to suggest evolution as a grand explanatory theory, as Anthony Walsh argued in his paper, but to suggest that because of evolution, human beings are "unfinished animals"—totally dependent for their completion, as Geertz puts it, on extrasomatic cultural forms (Geertz, 1973). The individual realities of human subjectivity depend fundamentally on the collective, intersubjective, cultural constructs that are, of course, our most distinctive mark as a species. And what all of this suggests is that there exists no such thing as a human nature independent of culture. Strip away culture, and one finds not an underlying universal reality but simply protoplasm that is not viable.

At one level this argument would certainly lead us in the direction pointed to by a number of speakers at this conference (perhaps most forcefully by Anke Ehrhardt and Gil Herdt)—that seeks to replace the stratigraphic approach with a more synthetic one "in which biological, psychological, sociological, and cultural factors can be treated as variables within unitary systems of analysis" (Geertz, 1973, p. 44). Yet, while I am in some ways sympathetic to this relatively catholic position, I also worry that the overly narrow pursuit of such interactive models should not divert attention from the equally important need to attend, with sufficient sophistication and complexity, to the phenomena of any specific aspect of this system. In short, mindful of Ken Plummer's warning from the first day of discussions about the potential dangers of grand theory, I would also caution us to beware of the potential oversimplifications of the quest for integration (which often camouflages what is actually a return to stratigraphic reductionism). Indeed, I confess that my own position tends to be more similar to what Jeffrey Weeks, in a very different context, described as "radical pluralism" (see Weeks, 1991)—what a number of commentators at this conference have described as the establishment of respectful dialogue across disciplines—in which the search for theoretical synthesis is understood as one among a large number of quite legitimate and fundamentally important options for theoretical development and research activity (though recognizing, as John Gagnon reminded us, how very difficult it will be, within existing structures of power, to truly realize such a radical pluralism on the ground).

Sexual Cultures

The discussion of sexual cultures emerged as a second major theme here at this conference—especially in Gil Herdt's paper, but also, I think, in John Gagnon's paper and in comments by Gary Dowsett, Leonore Tiefer, and others. Here I would like to emphasize the important distinction, which we often ignore in our discussions, between the singular, *culture*, and the plural, *cultures*.

Culture has, of course, been notoriously difficult to define (witness Kroeber and Kluckhohn, who, in their classic review, found well over 100 definitions of culture in use in the field of cultural anthropology [see Kroeber & Kluckhohn, 1952]). While I share Gil's understanding of culture as a system of norms, values, and meanings which regulates sexual conduct, I would want to take a somewhat more Foucaultian turn and emphasize the extent to which culture quite literally *produces* whatever it is that we think we can call sexuality in any given setting (Foucault, 1978). Culture not only regulates desire, it incites it!

I would also want to place a somewhat more post-modern (there's that word again) emphasis not on the systematic and coherent dimensions of culture, but on its often incoherent, inconsistent, and contradictory character. We must remember that there are also rules for breaking the rules of sexual conduct, and that in the midst of rapid social change (as Shirley Lindenbaum and Gil Herdt both pointed out) things often fall apart.

In practice, however, our focus must always necessarily be on sexual cultures rather than sexual culture. Empirically, what disciplines such as anthropology are about is the translation between cultures— from the exotic to the familiar (as Gil Herdt pointed out) and from the vernacular to the specialized (as John Gagnon pointed out). Picking up on the discussion from yesterday afternoon, this implies a transposition from "etic" to "emic" signification, or from outsider to insider meanings. Or, to use Geertz's already appropriated terms, from the "experience-near" categories of specific cultures to the "experience-distant" language and categories of interpretive social science (Geertz, 1983). And I want to emphasize interpretive here in order to recognize (remember, I am arguing in favor of radical pluralism in theory as well as in practice) the quite legitimate epistemological status of interpretive disciplines in search of explication rather than explanation—in this case, a kind of cultural hermeneutics in which the interpretation of cultures is not fundamentally different from the interpretation of texts, and in which the investigation of sexual identities and sexual communities is not really unlike the interpretation of other domains such as religious beliefs or political ideologies (see Parker, 1991).

That said, however, it seems to me to be a very open question whether or not it will ever be possible, out of the interpretation of a cacophony of different voices, diverse sexual cultures, to construct a more general theory of sexual culture (let alone its relation to those other strata—social, psychological, biological).

Culture and Structure

Finally, a few words about culture and structure. It is strange (well, perhaps not strange, but worrisome) that structural issues have been largely absent these past two days. They did come up in Connie Nathanson's very compelling paper, but were lost in our discussion of the eminently cultural assumptions of Joe Rodger's so-called cultureless model. Perhaps surprising, they come up as well in John Bancroft's attempt to interpret variations in individual risk behavior—though most commentators seem to agree that the way such issues are posed by Marvin Harris's theory of cultural materialism is fundamentally problematic.

If Connie Nathanson got first prize (from Gary Dowsett) for being the first person at this conference to mention Foucault's name, Shirley Lindenbaum gets *my* first prize for being the *only* person here to have called attention to the political economy of desire. Again, it is important to emphasize that political economy, as Shirley uses it certainly, or as I would like to use it, does not imply the grand narrative of orthodox Marxism, much less Marvin Harris's cultural materialism. It *does* imply, however, the fundamental need to attend to the complex political and economic structures and forces within which sexual cultures are situated. Such forces impinge as much on the lives of Gil Herdt's Sambia (Herdt, 1981, 1987) as they do my Brazilians (Parker, 1991, 1999) or Gary Dowsett's dancers in Montréal (Dowsett, this volume, pp. 125–132), and we can clearly no longer continue to treat sexual cultures as if they existed outside of history, as if they were unique or disconnected.

Globalization is hardly a new phenomenon but it has taken place with unprecedented speed in the closing decades of the twentieth century, as Fordist regimes of production have been replaced by regimes of flexible accumulation and industrialization and as post-industrial society, urban networks, and world cities have increasingly displaced the importance of nation-states, demographic transitions have taken place (often in quite unexpected settings), and new or changing sexualities have emerged with a force that has largely escaped our capacity for interpretation and analysis (see Appadurai, 1996; Harvey, 1990; Parker, 1999). As Shirley pointed out yesterday afternoon, the result of such changes in political economic structures has been the emergence of new forms of desire, newly commodified and ritualized sexualities, new types of sexual behavior and risk taking, and so on. (I should also add that new forms of fundamentalism, Islamic and otherwise, are also the product of these same forces.)

My own sense is that while we have made headway these last few days in opening up lines of communication between different disciplinary perspectives and in breaking down at least some of the boundaries that would otherwise limit the horizons of our diverse perspectives, we have nonetheless only brushed the surface of these broader political and economic issues as they impinge upon the sexual field. In the long run, and as something of a transition to Bob Michael's comments, I would suggest that these political and economic factors may be more crucial than any other to the question of policy and the policy relevance of our work. As Leonore Tiefer cautioned us in her comments in the opening session, we meet here in a specific historical moment which necessarily conditions the possibilities for both theory and practice, and we would ignore this only at our own peril.

Acknowledgment

I would like to thank John Bancroft and his colleagues at the Kinsey Institute for the invitation to be here—and particularly a special thanks for all that has been done in recent years to restore the Kinsey and to make it a respected, safe, and welcoming environment both for those who come from a more classical sexological tradition and for those of us whose work has been framed by more sociological or social science approaches to sexuality theory.

REFERENCES

Appadurai, A. (1996). *Modernity at large: Cultural dimensions of globalization.* Minneapolis and London: University of Minnesota Press.
Foucault, M. (1978). *The history of sexuality, volume 1: An introduction.* New York: Random House.
Geertz, C. (1973). *The interpretation of cultures.* New York: Basic Books.
Geertz, C. (1983). *Local knowledge.* New York: Basic Books.
Harvey, D. (1990). *The condition of postmodernity.* Cambridge, MA and Oxford: Blackwell.
Herdt, G. (1981). *Guardians of the flutes: Idioms of masculinity.* New York: McGraw-Hill.
Herdt, G. (1987). *The Sambia: Ritual and gender in New Guinea.* New York: Holt, Rinehart, and Winston.
Kroeber, A. L., & Kluckhohn, C. (1952). *Culture: A critical review of concepts and definitions.* Cambridge, MA: Harvard University Press.
Parker, R. G. (1991). *Bodies, pleasures and passions: Sexual culture in contemporary Brazil.* Boston: Beacon Press.

Parker, R. G. (1999). *Beneath the equator: Cultures of desire, male homosexuality, and emerging gay communities in Brazil*. New York and London: Routledge.
Weeks, J. (1991). *Against nature: Essays on history, sexuality and identity*. London: Rivers Oram Press.

DISCUSSION

Gilbert Herdt: You deserve accolades for that valiant effort to draw themes and insights into what's happened the last three days. I'm very intrigued by what you said about sexual cultures. The thought is this; we have present here multidisciplinary perspectives and, if I were going to lump many things together, I would say what's represented here are two very different modes of understanding and explanation, one having to do with social differences and the other having to do with individual differences. What you said about sexual culture lends itself to thinking about these two quite interestingly different but actually complementary ways of lumping the world and dissecting the world. I'm very sympathetic to your point about adding the additional awareness of meanings and inscriptions on bodies as a level or dimension of analysis of sexual culture. However, I have personally come to believe, and this is rather remarkable for a reconstituted Freudian to say, that the social regulatory dimensions of sexual culture are the more preeminent. That is to say what really should be given emphasis in a hierarchical study of Sambia culture, organizations, structure, and lives is a model in which the regulation of behaviors takes precedence over the inscriptions of meanings on individual lives. However, I would say that that is only because of the attention that I'm placing on the structural and the cultural or, if you like, the political economy. From an entirely different standpoint, that of individual differences, the meanings which are inscribed on the individual across the course of life as the person moves through different social status positions and occupies different power positions, some of which are in contest with each other, some of which may differ and create chaos and the kind of fuzziness to which you were referring, are also very, very interesting, but may not give us the same power of explanation about this cultural system.

Richard Parker: I certainly understand and share your concern about the regulatory characteristics and I think that reframing the issue of culture as always linked to the issue of power is absolutely essential, but again with a Foucaultian notion of power as both regulatory but also productive; productive of systems of resistance as much as systems of oppression that opens up possibilities for movement in a variety of different ways. I also think we might move away from that traditional anthropological concept of culture as somehow coherent and systematic, and move toward a more open-ended attention to incoherences in culture, the contradictions and inconsistencies. In that way, we may begin to find ways of merging that interface that you mentioned between cultures and individuals because ultimately it is those inconsistencies that make agency possible. It makes it possible to have choices, to have options. I see it in some ways as the social constructionist's dilemma: If one takes a social constructionist position, how does one account for the possibility that individuals make choices? It's because they operate in a field that does give them options, so we really have to pay a good deal of attention to that. In part I think that because of the traditional evolution of the discipline of anthropology through work in very small-scale settings we have not been as conscious of interconnections as we might otherwise be, and that's one of the real changing areas of work in the field right now.

Gil Herdt: Here's a different twist on it. Suppose we grant that there are always going to be scholars interested in both social differences and individual differences using the same body of data and suppose I say to you, if you want to understand desire, or sexual desire, social desire, are you willing to cede the study of individual differences to a perspective that's entirely outside of anthropology? Let's say that one begins with an ideology of inherent properties, internal traits, and so on, how would you frame the problem of individual differences, granted the concerns of our colleagues here who are involved with measurement and individual behavior and development?

Richard Parker: The answer is no, I'm not at all willing to cede. On the contrary, I think that cultural perspectives when properly framed offer in some respects the most compelling way of accounting for individual differences.

John Bancroft: So how do you use cultural differences to account for the fact that if you remove a man's testosterone he loses sexual desire and if you give it back to him he regains it?

Richard Parker: That's a loaded question.

Gary Dowsett: To take your challenge, irrespective of the testosterone going in and out, how that body with the testosterone going in and out understands what's happening to it at that very moment is vastly culturally determined. If you give a shot of testosterone to someone in Latin America, the notion of where you stick that penis is going to be entirely different than what the Sambian elder will do with that shot of testosterone, than what someone in Spain will do, and what someone in the cold north of England will do with that testosterone. You can't divorce the fact that the effect of that testosterone will be immediately instantaneously read within the subjectivity of sexuality.

Anke Ehrhardt: This is at the core of the debate. It is exactly correct that it gets interpreted differently, it would have different effects. But can we talk about that variable, that testosterone, in this kind of nctwork of effects, or would you ignore it totally because it is so integrated and not even take that into consideration?

Gary Dowsett: I don't want to ignore the testosterone. In fact, that is why I actually took you at your word in your paper, Anke—that the differences between gender could literally be an end to gender as a concept. You cannot conceive of the testosterone without the language that created the word to describe the thing from the cultural form that investigated it. What John Bancroft was trying to show is that you can in fact only examine the testosterone and pretend that all the rest might not be happening. That's the challenge that Richard Parker set up for us.

John Bancroft: What you said is absolutely right. The way the testosterone effect would be experienced would be socially deter-mined. But if the culture involves fellating small boys or whatever the culture determines, if you take the testosterone away, it won't happen. The biological basis of the sexual desire will have gone, whatever the culture. How the sexual desire is shaped and manifested is culturally determined, but the fact that there is sexual desire there is biological determined.

Gary Dowsett: But they might still fellate little boys for entirely different reasons.

John Bancroft: I don't think they will unless they have powerful monetary or political incentives to do so.

Gary Dowsett: That's the same thing.

Leonore Tiefer: What you are saying is that when you take away the testosterone you'll still do the behavior but it won't be sexual. This is precisely the point; we are not all in agreement. You can establish the set of variables and decide which ones are and aren't sexual. But those decisions come out of a place and are made for a purpose so the fact that you agree that the behavior might continue is, I think, ex-traordinarily important.

John Bancroft: There is a debate here about how you define sexuality or sexualities and where it comes from, and those of us that come from a biological perspective understand or believe that we are creatures that are built around a process of sexual reproduction. The testosterone is there or it has been programmed to react in the way it does to serve sexual reproductive needs. That's what I mean. Now how sexuality is interpreted in a cultural sense obviously is an additional very complicated layer. Below that there is a very fundamental bio-logical process of sexual reproduction and we are divided into males and females because of that.

Leonore Tiefer: Well I don't want to sound crazy, but I used to think that and I don't anymore. My own work with men in urology departments over the years was enormously illuminating for me when I realized that the biomedical system by which they were coming in, being evaluated, being tested, and so on and then given injections into the penis (now they would be given pills) was all based on one system of understanding that had nothing to do with these guys who were operating out of a system of masculinity. What they were coming in for was damage to their masculinity, which was extremely diverse. So I've come to see Viagra, for example, as an antidepressant and that's how I understand how it works. Whatever it does, phosphodiesterase to the contrary notwithstanding, I understand how it's being used by men in a different way than how the medical establishment has legitimized and developed it. These things are coexisting.

Sarah Hrdy: I'd like to address a question to Gil Herdt because he's brought up this related issue of regulation of behavior taking precedence over the meaning of lives, and I think that gets to the core of what Richard Parker is saying. When you were talking yesterday about the Sambia and saying the Sambia cannot abide such and such and the Sambia do this, when you said the Sambia, what I read into what you were saying was the power-holding older men in Sambia culture. Would you agree with that? It comes to what we're talking about when we talk about culture; you were talking about inconsistencies and the incoherence of it all. I have to say I don't find it helpful to think about the incoherence of it all.

Gilbert Herdt: Yes, thinking about this as a hierarchical social system, at the top there are elders, there are war leaders, and then a little bit further down are full adult men married with many children, hunters, and shamans. A little bit further down are young married men and then you go down further and you're at the adolescent men who are in the position of inseminating. Then at the bottom are the boys who are just climbing up the ladder and starting their careers. Outside of that system of course are women, who are also, by the way, socially ranked as higher and lower status based primarily upon the number of children they have and their marriage to senior men. In this pyramidal view, power and authority can indeed be traced up. But not wanting to give away entirely the importance of the point that Richard has made, I would add to that a problem which I mentioned in my paper but I didn't emphasize yesterday. How can we explain that this system, this culture, in its genius, has created the notion that the male is the desired object? It is the male, not the female, that is the sex object, the object of beauty, the object of attraction, the object of social interest. And many New Guinea cultures have done this. It is not a coincidence or accident that that powerful cultural image and methodology rests alongside this system of institutionalized homoerotic relations.

Sarah Hrdy: To me, men may *seem* like the objects of desire in this system, if young boys basically buy the propaganda that's being fed to them. But the older men in the system seem to be getting just what they want out of it: removing young men from sexual competition with them. The older men don't seem to be mistaken about what they desire and they seem to be using the system with extraordinary psychological insight to manipulate it in ways that enable them to get what they want. So Richard Parker, what's wrong with the hypothesis that these guys have self-interests and use culture to pursue them, creating traditions along the way? Culture in some respects takes on a life of its own, but underneath it all lies human nature, organisms with motives and goals. In this case, older men exercise control over younger men or boys in order to get what the older men in Sambia culture would like to have.

Richard Parker: As I said, the stratigraphic approach is alive and well in the twentieth century.

Sarah Hrdy: I own to the stratigraphic approach, I do.

Gary Dowsett: I actually think we're creating a straw man here in this separation between culture and individual differences. There's no way in the world that analysis of culture leaves out concepts of the individual and individual differences. The dilemma for the culturalist perspective that Richard Parker announced today is that very often the individual differences perspective does in fact leave out culture. We saw a very good example in Joe Rodgers's model yesterday, and he quite clearly admitted that it was a cultureless model. I think culturalists can't leave out individuals and that's part of our dilemma. But I wanted to say that that has already been bypassed. Foucault bypassed that issue and I think Foucault actually showed us a way in which sexuality as a structure of knowledge and power literally inscribes itself in the subjectivity of individuals. It is not the case that culture is out there and individuals are here and they interact somewhere in the middle. In Foucault's model, sexuality as a system of power is literally inside our bodies. It is historically and literally in our bones and our genes and our cells and it has been built there over time as a structure of power. The only way it exists as a culture is literally through our bodies and our consciousness, our subjectivity of our bodies as sexual things. That is present even in Foucault's model, translated to the very disciplines of science that we use to know that subjectivity. So in his model, he would look at all of our disciplines and read them as already inscribed within the system historically. So the linguistic turn that comes out of Foucault is about the relationship between the sign and the signified, that you cannot separate them. There is literally no objective object out there that can preexist its knowing, because it's a system of power rather than simply a system of knowledge. I think it's a straw man to set up this difference between culture and individual differences. It literally cannot exist in the culturalist model.

Richard Parker: I wanted to go back to something that I said early on in my comments, particularly for folks who come from a more biological or biomedical perspective. I want them to get a feel for what it would imply for them to truly integrate a culturalist perspective into what they do. It's more of a turning upside down of the world than I think people might at first imagine.

Anke Ehrhardt: Or the other way round.

John Gagnon: My argument is that it is probably easier for sociologists to do individual differences than it is for individual differences people to go the other way. I think that it's easier for me to accommodate John Bancroft than for John to accommodate my perspective. There are good fundamental reasons why that's true and it's just the way it is. My comment goes back to Gil Herdt. Gil's tension between Freud and Durkheim raised an interesting problem, which is that when he first went to the Sambia he was much more strongly psychoanalytic. But what simple societies call forth in us are Durkheimian solutions or ideas about social regulation. I have a whole shelf of books that emerged out of the nineteenth century which talk about the way in which societies regulate behavior and the focus is on societies as coercive mechanisms that regulate the lives of individuals inside of them. The dilemma of the field of sociology often has been the degree to which we have oversocialized individuals, leaving no room for agency. Sociology often does not leave any room for people who are making choices. Gary Dowsett's notion was that social life generates individual differences and one of the mechanisms happens to be errors of transmission. Social reproduction is not cloning. If your parents always reproduced the people they wanted to reproduce there would be no variation either by class or by a whole series of other "variables." So there must be errors in the reproduction system and there has to be a world in which people are freed up from the immediate coerciveness of structure in order to live lives. You can think about mechanisms by which that would work, but I'm not sure that the individual/social distinction really is forceful anymore.

Anke Ehrhardt: I'd like us to stay on the ground. I'd like us to stay with testosterone for a moment. I would like to know whether indeed we can consider that in a dialogue. You are saying that how somebody experiences a lack of testosterone is culturally determined, but I recently worked with a couple in the United States where the man had a problem with testosterone from birth. He could not penetrate, so clearly while there was sexuality in the widest sense going on in that relationship, there was not penetration because of lack of testosterone. This had an enormous effect on the couple's interactions, and with testosterone injections that changed. So I completely understand that the reasons that that was a problem for that couple were culturally determined by our society. If we are to have a dialogue, testosterone is a variable to be considered. But from what you say, you would ignore it, it would not be something which you would take into account.

John Bancroft: Can I put this into a practical context? John Gagnon has very effectively said that the real test of our ability to work together is if we're tackling common practical problems. Let me put a problem to you into which we can bring both testosterone and culture. This is the research we're doing on the effects of oral contraceptives. We initially did a study of sterilized women so they didn't need contraception, they volunteered. We studied women in Scotland and we studied women in the Philippines, and we compared oral contraceptives with a placebo (Graham et al., 1995). We found in the Scottish women that there was a clear negative effect of the contraceptive on the sexual interest of a significant proportion of the women. This was not apparent in the Filipino women and our interpretation of that was that they seemed to have low levels of sexual interest to begin with. But we were left thinking that we didn't have an adequate understanding of the cultural difference to know how best to have done the study in the Filipino women in the first place and certainly how best to interpret results. So we are now working with Family Health International toward doing studies of the effects of steroidal contraceptives in women in different cultures. This raises the question of how we evaluate the effect of an oral contraceptive on the woman's quality of sexual life and we're very conscious of the fact that we may need to conceptualize that in a very different way for women in a different culture. The direct effect of an oral contraceptive, however, may be to lower the woman's level of free testosterone. How do we conceptualize what effect that's going to have in different cultural contexts? That's an example of where there is a need to integrate our disciplines.

Gary Dowsett: I don't see any problem with that. What I'm concerned about is that almost all of the work on sexuality, and the history of sexuality as I understand it post-Foucault, has not been like that. We only have to go back to the work in this country on homosexuality up until the 1950s that was done on people already incarcerated in jails. There the very phenomenon that was being examined in that biomedical model was already a damaged species of people because of their environment in jails. It's precisely the issue about contextualizing the production of knowledge, the understanding that knowledge systems themselves are culture specific. The very tools we work with in science are products of the history as languages, as words, as accumulations of ideas and we know that those scientific accumulations of ideas at times go down the wrong track and get things wrong. Now it's actually understanding the cultural relativity of our own scientific tools that is the essence of the science/culture knowledge question. The application of that, which is what you're talking about, John, is about the politics of how knowledge is produced. It's about how knowledge claims are made by certain knowledge systems; it's about the ownership of the understanding of the human being. The culturalist perspective is a challenge to that concept of the right to ownership that any discipline, including our own, makes to say that this is the only way to understand. That one can produce a piece of knowledge about testosterone and claim that it is *the* knowledge about testosterone. Kuhn would tell you straightaway that's only the paradigm you've got so far. The paradigm will change when someone else disapproves the current theory. So that cultural relativity of knowledge itself is the real essence here. The application is a question of politics.

John Bancroft: I think you should grant us that, Gary. The fact that we have organized this meeting and brought you all in is recognition of that fact and the need to communicate about those issues. I sense that there is this perfectly correct feeling among many of you that essentialist science has made a lot of mistakes over the years. But it's time to start to accept that some of the people in that field are thinking differently about it.

Connie Nathanson: I think that everybody here is more positivist than I am, because what you seem to be interested in is explaining, in some fashion or other, individual behavior. That is not what I'm interested in explaining, which has to do with the politics of sexuality in some sense. I'm interested in accounting for the ways in which different political and social organizations, societies, think about the issue of sexuality, think about what to do about it. I've been reading a book called *La santé publique: La liberté individuelle* which is a publication of a French symposium on public health. It brings intellectuals and ministers of health together. That is one huge difference from what we're able to do in this country. You would never get Jesse Helms or even Donna Shalala in this room to talk to us, and they got Claude Evin and Simone Veil in with Alain Touraine and so on, and they were able to talk to each other. But the problematic, with the United States, of course, as the bête noir, is the notion that prevention and concern about individual risk is totalitarianism. Is public health a totalitarian kind of project? What does our concern with prevention really mean? Where does individual autonomy fit in? I think of the wonderful discussions in the French symposium of the cigarette and the symbolism of cigarette (and we Americans laugh at the fact that they all smoke), but this is a very serious ideological, philosophical difference between the two countries. Their discussion highlights differences in terms of how they think about inclusion and exclusion. It uses words that we don't use. It expresses all the issues that we're concerned with in a completely different way, with completely different consequences for public policy and for the way in which policies are made. I feel as if this way of thinking has profound consequences for what policies get made and I'm not sure how to fit it in with the way in which the discourse has been going. Or is it just something so completely outside of it? I'll go off and do my thing and you all go off and do your thing and they don't have any connection with each other.

REFERENCE

Graham, C. A., Ramos, R., Bancroft, J., Maglaya, C., & Farley, T. M. M. (1995). The effects of steroidal contraceptives on the well-being and sexuality of women: A double-blind, placebo-controlled, two-center study of combined and progestogen-only methods. *Contraception, 52,* 363–369.

Comments on Policy Issues

ROBERT T. MICHAEL

My assignment in this segment was to reflect on what has emerged during our discussions over the past several sessions as it relates to policy. Since we have had several discussions about the meaning of words, I suppose I should begin by suggesting a definition for what "policy" might mean in terms of sexuality. I suggest that in general a "policy" is simply a plan of action or a set of rules to guide actions. Notice that this definition is quite different from Claire Brindis's statement earlier in the conference that policymakers dictate social control. I don't think policymakers typically have that much clout. They only stipulate a few costs or gains from one action or another and thereby attempt to influence behavior; they don't actually control very much. It is not clear that we should wish policymakers to have more control than they have in the area of sexual behavior, but it is clear, I think, that they do not have much. The instruments by which policy might have influence about sex are not controlling ones, fortunately.

A policy is also specific to time and place, unlike some of the other focuses we have explored during the conference. Gary Dowsett commented earlier with a critical tone that much of the discussion here has been "North America bound." While some sexual matters may be universal and while it might be interesting to explore the similarities and differences in institutions, meanings, and behaviors from one culture to another, in the policy arena the context and interpretation are always of great relevance.

While I will have a few remarks about the policy relevance of some of our discussion over the past day or so, it seems to me I may have more to contribute by offering a description of how an economist like myself thinks about the rationale for policy intervention. So before reflecting on the discussion we have enjoyed at this conference, I will indicate what I think is the justification for our having policies about a matter as private as sexuality and sexual behavior.

There are at least three levels at which we might consider there being policy: these are (1) personal or private policy, (2) group expectations or social "norms" that act as guidelines for behavior and might be thought of as informal policy, and (3) the most common context of governmental policy that directly or indirectly promotes or discourages some behavior or other. Typically when we talk about policy we mean these actions by government that set the rules of behavior or purposely or inadvertently affect behavior by taxes or subsidies, by privileging some behaviors and making other behaviors more difficult or more costly or less attractive in some way. My first point is that an awful lot of sexual policy is private policy or informal policy; that is, decisions and actions by individuals or couples or by social groups that are not particularly related to any government action. We too often overlook these most important policy decisions.

When we consider governmental policy that affects behavior, I am reminded of the important point made by Gil Steiner and implied by the title of his book, *The Futility of Family Policy* (1981). The complexity of crafting a policy that has the intended effects, and of avoiding policies that have quite unintended effects, is surely as true about sexual behavior as it is about family policy and family behavior.

When governments do set out to have an influence on behavior by an explicit policy, it is important that they be clear about the rationale for having any particular collective policy about that matter. Is that matter a legitimate domain for government intervention, and if so, why? That is a prior question to the issue of just what that particular policy should be. First, I want to argue, one should consider whether there is a good rationale for any policy on that matter. After all, most of the private actions we take and most of the behaviors we engage in are not subject to direct policy attention by governments, and you probably agree with me that this is surely the way we like it. If the government is going to set forth some guidelines or some rules, or impose some tax or give some subsidy to encourage some action, the first question that needs to be addressed is why. In my discipline of economics there are a few strong justifications for government policies, but in the absence of any justification there is a widespread consensus that governments can and often do do more harm than good by attempts to impose rules or incentives, so in the absence of one of these strong justifications, no policy is probably the best policy.

Those justifications for government actions include cases where the decisions and actions of one person or group have direct impact on the well-being of others who were not involved in that decision. These impacts are described as "externalities"; common examples include the impact of air pollution from driving a car. That pollution adversely affects others so we collectively, through governments, pass laws and impose penalties on those who drive cars that emit excess pollutants.

There are several such "externalities" from sexual behavior and it is reasonable and proper for governments to set policies to discourage those externalities that are harmful (i.e., diseases transmitted sexually) and to encourage those externalities that are beneficial (i.e., the efficacy of contraceptives).

A second class of cases in which government policy is called for are those instances in which, like it or not, we must all share the same circumstance. These are called "public goods," defined as nonexcludable and nonexhaustible, meaning that if the good is available to one of us it must be available to all of us since we can't exclude someone from having use of it if it exists, but its use by one of us doesn't diminish its availability to others. National defense is the quintessential "public good" since whatever level of defense it provides to you is also available to me, but then your enjoyment of that security doesn't diminish my use of it either. With regard to public goods, we must collectively decide how much to have, since we must all have the same amount of it. Our collective decision about the potholes in our local streets or the lighting of our streets at night are good examples of local "public goods" since we all drive those streets and the wealthy and the poor among us all must endure the same quality of roadbeds and lighting.

Now, that description may seem to you rather far removed from anything having to do with sexuality. But consider the fact that laws are public goods in that they apply to all of us equally. So if you consider the laws we have about access to RU486, about the availability of abortion, about discrimination on the basis of sexual preference, or about public nudity at the local beaches, and so forth, then sexually related "public goods" are in fact quite ubiquitous.

While there are good justifications other than externalities and public goods for establishing public policies, these seem to me to be the two most pertinent in terms of policies about sexual behavior. My next point is this: If we consider public policies as governmental rules (laws or regulations) that guide or restrict behavior, or as government taxes or subsidies that change the costs of doing one thing or another, then it seems that there should be a rather high burden of evidence on government, or on ourselves collectively as we govern ourselves, before we attempt to alter behavior by setting a policy. If we are to intrude in each other's lives by having governmental or formal social policies, there should be a good reason. Private policies are our own concern and responsibility and informal social norms may be disregarded if we are willing to incur the disapproval of our peers or social network, but formal governmental policies are not so easily disregarded. The two justifications suggested here can meet that high standard for imposing governmental policy. If the externality is substantial, then there is a good justification for government influencing the behavior; if there is a true public good involved in the matter, governmental policy or collective decision on the matter may be unavoidable.

But often the allegation of an externality is not well founded, and many alleged public goods need not be so. Consider the issue of what two consenting adults do with each other in private that does not produce a pregnancy or does not transmit a disease or harm either partner in ways that impose costs on others of us. Then their actions have no externalities and by the logic of my argument, there is no justification for our having a policy about that behavior, whatever it is.

Another rationale for public policy in sexual matters that we often encounter is that of moral authority, an assertion that this or that is categorically right or wrong. Disagreements about these judgments are difficult to resolve and I suggest that moral authority is not a good justification for policy formation for just that reason. If I can show observable or objective evidence that your behavior harms me in some way, then I have shown an externality from your behavior, and I may have the right to affect your behavior or to raise its cost to you to reflect that adverse effect on me. But if I argue that your behavior is inappropriate or wrong (as I judge right and wrong) or that it simply offends my sensibilities, then I do not have the justification to impose my judgment on you because I do not have objective evidence of an externality. This is an application of that high burden of evidence before a policy intervention is warranted. We can each probably find examples in which we think this standard is too demanding, but I argue that to use that high standard will prevent much strife. Much of the contentious dispute about sexual behavior in our nation revolves around an inappropriate attempt to influence sexual behavior by government policy that is not warranted. We as a country have widely varying opinions and deeply held judgments about what sexual behavior is appropriate, but these differences need not be resolved by government policy; indeed, they often cannot successfully be so, as is sadly evident.

But so that I do not take us too far afield, I will turn to the discussions we have had at this conference as related to topics in social policy. If you are interested in an elaboration of these points about public policy as applied to sexual behavior, I refer you to an essay on the topic (Michael, 1999). I turn now to the discussions we have enjoyed during this conference; the presentation by Connie Nathanson was directly related to policies, and she emphasized the importance of implicit theories as they guide policy debates. In her excellent discussion of the "policy mush" surrounding adolescent pregnancy, sex, and childbearing, she emphasized the fact that those with a political agenda frame the issue to their advantage. Here is an instance in which insisting on the high standard of evidence that there is a justification for a policy might reduce the range of the debate. Is there a justification for a policy about adolescent sex, per se? About adolescent pregnancy? About adolescent childbearing? The three would not have the same justification and there may be no valid reason for a policy about one of these but a strong justification for a policy about another.

This case of adolescent sex and reproductive health can bring my discussion back to the taxonomy I suggested earlier about private policy as distinct from governmental policy. Perhaps the information about the effects of childrearing on the well-being of the infant and the mother should be more energetically presented to adolescents as they formulate their private policies and plans of action and as they and their peers formulate their informal policies. This does not necessarily, however, justify public policy that imposes additional costs on those adolescents who take risks or behave imprudently.

John Gagnon's discussion of the sexiness of risk per se, and his contention that teenage sex is driven by romance and the search for the dramatic life and excitement, challenges and may undermine the implicit theory of rationality I hold here. Similarly, I think Meg Gerrard's point is very important that individuals may cognitively know they are taking a risk but do not act on that knowledge if it is not psychologically transformed into relevance to their lives. That too may challenge my presumption of rational choices being made. But there is surely a lot of evidence of strategic behavior by teenagers in their sexual behavior; indeed they spend an awful lot of their time and attention on that strategy! So if they seem unimpressed by the "information" they are given, then perhaps, as Gagnon advises, we would do well to first look at what the locals do and attempt to understand why they do it before jumping to conclusions that they are not strategic or rational in their private policies and actions.

It may be in the area of risk taking in sexual behavior that the role of policy in sexuality is most important. One clearly defensible policy position is the promotion and dissemination of information so that the private policies of individuals and couples can be better informed. And the information that comes from good research has a clear public goods attribute—information about the adverse effects on a fetus from a pregnant woman smoking is a public good, for example, and the policies that produce convincing evidence about that effect from research and the policies that promote the widespread sharing of that information have clear rationales and real value. Clarity about the risks from sexual behavior—all those risks of pregnancy, of disease, of physical harm in some circumstances, of social disapproval in others—deserve to be documented and shared. Similarly, as Anke Ehrhardt suggested, the information about successful sexual behavior and how to be effective in providing sexual satisfaction and the associated "risks" of joy and pleasure just as surely need to be documented and disseminated.

One final point. I am struck by the fact that this conference on the role of theory in sex research has a parallel in the role of theory in sex policy. The role of theory is quite similar and powerful in both. As our host said, human sexual conduct is too complex to be grasped in reality, so the best we can do is to develop models which are simplified versions of it and come to understand them well. Theory, implicit or explicit, guides policy thinking just as influentially as it guides research. It provides the ideas, suggests the associations, attempts to help establish the causal linkages or indicates the levers or instruments by which social policy might have effects. It leads to ways of looking for evidence and ways of looking at evidence. Theory is as essential, as influential, and as challenging in sexual policy making as it is in sexual research. The wide range of topics and issues raised in this conference on the role of theory can usefully be applied to considerations of sex policy just as it can be a guide in sex research.

Acknowledgments

As the final speaker at our conference, let me express the thanks of all of us to John Bancroft and his staff for organizing a stimulating and provocative conference here at the Kinsey Institute. I am sure we all believe that the discussions we have had and the insights we have gained during this conference will affect our own research. The wide range of perspectives and the diverse interests that have been shared here have been of great value. We appreciate the opportunity to have been a part of this fine event. I am sure, as well, that we all applaud John Bancroft for the leadership he has brought to the Kinsey Institute. In renewing its stature as an important contributor to sex research in our country, all of us who are engaged in research on this interesting subject share in the benefits and for this too we thank you, John.

REFERENCES

Michael, R. T. (1999, forthcoming). Private sex and public policy. In E .O. Laumann & R. T. Michael (Eds.), *Social organization of sexuality: Further studies.*

Steiner, G. (1981). *The futility of family policy.* Washington: Brookings Institution.

General Discussion

Leonore Tiefer: This was too neutral for me. When you say things like, "policy is simply an action plan," the apparent objectivity of your discussion doesn't relate to the way I understand policy, which is integrally related to the exercise of power. Richard Parker reminds us that the Enlightenment ushered in an era with assumptions about some unitary underlying human nature. The biopsychosocial model we use seemed to be a way to analyze underlying human nature giving equal time to equally powerful interests—psychological, biological, and social. The replacement of that stratigraphic model by the current one in which the idea of unitary human nature has given way to the notion of a world divided by gender, race, class, sexual orientation, and disability shows us another way of attempting to represent diverse interests. But in this new way, power is integral to the conceptualization of interests in theory, research, and policy. The assumption in the neutral model of policy that we can discuss our subject in a purely scientific way is one that I as a sexologist have long ago abandoned. I think it was Connie Nathanson who said that there was this disjuncture between data and logic in the area of policy. There is irrationality in the area of policy and as a scientist, as a sexologist, I long ago abandoned any notion of being able to discuss policy without regard to the fact that sexuality drives people nuts.

Jay Paul: I appreciated Bob Michael's neutral stance in his attempt to outline a framework which we could then debate. I would like to hear more about the interplay between the different levels of policy which were identified. Your focus appeared to primarily be on personal policy and on formal institutional policy. It appeared that we ended up hearing very little about that middle level of informal group policy. If there's anything that has been emphasized and "overlearned" in these past two days, it is that individuals must be seen in the context of their own groups. An important area for further exploration is really to seek to understand how formal policy affects not only individuals, but groups.

Connie Nathanson: I want to point out that the hierarchy of what were good and relatively good reasons for having some rules, some sort of regulation, is itself an ethical moral judgment. The notion that the best reason for regulation, the only possible reason, is that it is some kind of externality comes right out of utilitarian philosophy. This has indeed become, in the form of what has been called rights talk, the major argument so that everything becomes an externality because costs to taxpayers are an externality. So the fact that philosophically we believe that that's such a good argument means that every argument gets framed in those terms. That's why, as I was arguing the other day, the nonsmokers' rights movement was so successful; the individual harm that I do myself is not so important, but the harm that I do others is dreadful. So everything gets framed in terms of "the harm I do others." Now, the French have a very different notion of priority. The French would at least begin rhetorically, though I think there's a relationship between rhetoric and what actually can be legitimated in terms of policy, that smoking is a social act, a way of relating to somebody else and an act of inclusion. This is in itself an ethical and moral judgment, and policymakers select arguments that will fly from the tool kit of culture. They select the argument that will fly in their particular social and cultural contexts and the policies that they have the organizational apparatus to implement. Ours is a regulatory society; that is, the regulation of the market society. The French have a much more statused kind of culture. All of those things, those issues, go into what policies are made.

Bob Michael: From my perspective, the picture I live with is one in which property rights are awfully important and if you start with them then these externalities are in fact an essential and legitimate ground for creating public controls. I don't disagree with what Leonore Tiefer said on the influence of power in effecting policy. I'm talking about the rules of engagement, how in fact we go about setting up what should or shouldn't be engaged in as public policy. My own instinct is there's a lot of stuff dealt with as public policy for which there's no rationale. So I would put a very high standard on what it is we're going to set as rules that prevent one of us from doing something that another of us doesn't like. Within those rules we should be relatively explicit about what would permit the public policy to be made or not, and then within that, quite explicit about our priorities about where to place those weights. That strikes me as the right thing to do. Let's set some rules. We can argue about what goes in and what goes out of these rules but it really gets subtle. Take something like the externalities of a traditional marriage; it's argued there are some. It's argued that it is beneficial to all of us that we live in a society with stable traditional marriages and therefore we are going to privilege that form of family structure over and above another. Now we're into an area where we say, "Hey, wait a minute, maybe we don't want to draw the line right there. Some other form of nontraditional family relationship, which was not either common or even conceived of at the time the traditional forms were privileged, also deserves these same encouragements." That's where the debate probably should take place, but it's in a context in which we're only going to set these policies after they have passed the high standard of externalities. If you have another set of criteria by which you want to establish that it's relevant to policy, be explicit, put it out there. I'm quite happy with mine. If you're not, take issue with that.

John Gagnon: I think what's interesting about Bob Michael's argument is the question How does a trouble become a problem? What you're really arguing is here we have troubles and the question is What are the criteria by which we now decide that this trouble is worth becoming a problem? Now, I agree with Connie Nathanson that the framework for this derives from utilitarian liberalism in the nineteenth century—the notion that Bob Michael's approach is a strategy for managing how troubles become problems. I think there is a certain mechanistic quality about it but I think that you're quite right. You can probably get anybody who has more than four children into an externality argument which says their fifth child is too high a cost to others. For instance if I were an Indian from South Asia I could argue that every American child costs a great deal more to world resources than an Indian child; therefore it's an externality cost to us Indians. The externalities argument plays in a lot of ways.

Daryl Bem: Within our society we tend to use the utilitarian argument for setting policy because that's where we have the most consensus, whether it's articulated consciously or not. So if we're going to make policy changes in the United States, that allows us to start with a larger consensus. On the other hand, if I were a religious fundamentalist, I would feel totally disempowered, whether I realized it or not, because the tool kit that I'm allowed to argue with is exactly the one that you people who want data and logic have decided that I must use. So the reason I want creationism to be taught in the public schools is because religiously I believe that, but I'm not allowed to use that argument in the public forum. I must use the tools that you have provided. I must argue, for example, that there's empirical evidence for creationism. Well, that's not why I believe it and I don't care whether there is empirical evidence or not, but you have not permitted me to use the tools that really animate my belief in the public forum. So I've lost. But the reason the progressives have the upper hand is precisely because I must argue on their playing field, not on mine.

Leonore Tiefer: I would propose we discuss this question: How should sex research and theory be used and what is the role of sex researchers and sex theorists in either ensuring that our research is used in some way, preventing our research and theory from being used in other ways, or preparing the way for our research and theory to be used? In other words, how can sex research and theory become a player? We're not going to decide this philosophical matter so I say let's get down and dirty and figure out how should we play this!

Dennis Fortenberry: One of the things that we have to do with our theory and with the work that the theory generates is to not only anticipate how that will help inform what the policy should be and can be, but also to help us begin to think about who will be damaged by it. There will always be failures of any policy and we will always then have to deal with an increasingly evident number of individuals or groups who have failed. Part of what I think our theory begins to let us do is anticipate who they may be, what proportion of that group may not benefit from the policy or may in fact be damaged by it, and then anticipate alternatives, at least in an ideal sense.

Gary Dowsett: I get the sense that apart from Connie Nathanson, we haven't been specifically talking about which nation plays with policy in this way. I'd like to reinforce the point that other nations do not conceive of policy in the same way Bob Michael has conceived of it. That goes without saying. My concern, however, is, that the way in which sex research informs or doesn't inform public policy in the United States doesn't affect the United States only. Because of the hegemonic position of the United States in the rest of the world with regard to international policy, issues of reproductive health, and issues of HIV and AIDS and STDs, the ways in which sex research done on people in the United States affects the rest of us is absolutely crucial to your considerations here. So it's not in fact that you can only play in your own backyard; you play in everybody's backyard when you do research in this country and when you make public policy in this country. So we find in Australia, with a very small research establishment working on sexuality for example, that American data on teenage pregnancy, on homosexuality, will always be used in the policy debates, whether or not it has any impact or meaning in Australian culture. The same is often done with issues of indigenous people, for example; the situation of indigenous people in North America tends to dominate the debate in the Western Pacific about the situation for indigenous people and their lives. This is a plea for recognizing that we are no longer playing simply inside the boundaries of nation-states.

Jay Paul: Just one brief example relevant to Dennis Fortenberry's comments on anticipating the potential negative consequences or failures of any implemented policy. This is a positive example, as it demonstrates a collaboration between different points of view and among different disciplines that are examining the issue of postexposure prophylaxis (PEP). Health care workers exposed to blood products through needle sticks have a reduced likelihood of HIV seroconversion if they immediately go on anti-retrovirals for a brief time period after exposure to HIV (Cardo et al., 1997). Similarly, pregnant mothers who are HIV positive have reduced the likelihood of vertical transmission to their offspring if they take anti-retrovirals (Centers for Disease Control and Prevention, 1998b). In July 1997, the Centers for Disease Control and Prevention (CDC) sponsored a meeting to review the issues of providing antiretroviral therapy for those who might have been exposed to HIV through unprotected intercourse or sharing injection needles. This meeting brought together a broad spectrum of scientists, health experts, clinicians, and members of affected groups to discuss the concerns related to providing anti-retrovirals after such a risk exposure (Centers for Disease Control and Prevention, 1998a), because many issues arise in the provision of such services (Katz & Gerberding, 1997) and the existing needs demand more than simply providing pills.

In a collaborative project, San Francisco General Hospital, University of California–San Francisco's Center for AIDS Prevention Studies, and the San Francisco Department of Public Health are running a study whereby anti-retrovirals are offered to those who come to the recruitment sites within 72 hours after possible sexual exposure to HIV. This should provide data on the efficacy of this treatment in reducing HIV seroconversions, but built into this study was the question of the understandings of respondents about PEP treatment, the sense of threat attached to HIV seroconversion, and the impact of such services on risk behavior. The availability of other local study samples also permits examination of the impact of PEP availability on the attitudes and behaviors of the broader San Francisco gay community.

John Bancroft: Are you yet able to say what sort of impact it has had on the attitudes in the gay community?

Jay Paul: As far as I know, it is too early for that, but there have been a good number of anecdotal reports of people who described themselves as being less concerned about being exposed to HIV sexually, either because of the potential of postexposure prophylaxis or because of current treatments that seem to have a stronger impact on HIV. Although this is likely to be a minority of men who have sex with men (Dilley et al., 1998), it nevertheless represents an important consideration in ensuring redoubled primary prevention efforts at a time of increasing efficacy of secondary prevention efforts. Ekstrand and my colleagues (1998) will be presenting data at the International Conference on AIDS from the San Francisco Young Men's Study that indicates that the likelihood of engaging in unprotected anal intercourse has greatly increased in this cohort over the past few years. Dilley and his colleagues (1997) studied 54 men who had sex with men (recruited as part of an intervention counseling study) and documented that 15% already had taken "a chance of getting infected when having sex" because of the availability of new treatments. Because of the way in which the question was asked, we cannot know whether this reported increase in risk behavior was a response to the existence of antiretroviral postexposure prophylaxis or a decreased fear of HIV disease because of the enhanced effectiveness of current combination drug therapies. But this represents a situation where the implications of a medical policy have been of concern to a broad range of professionals and members of the affected communities, and thus incorporated into research in this area.

Connie Nathanson: I know that many of you have been involved in trying to bring about social change in various domains related to sexuality. Probably many of you have had occasion to address policymakers. I would be very interested in knowing what kinds of arguments you have used. I would like to get the people who are more directly involved in sexuality research into this discussion about policy. The people who are on the ground who are involved in this kind of research who have confronted policymakers, who have tried to bring about change, what kinds of arguments have they used? What arguments have been successful? What have not been successful?

John Gagnon: Since there is no sexual left in America, we have a sexual middle and a sexual right, so the rhetoric the center uses with policymakers is health, health, and more health, not pleasure, pleasure, pleasure. Our goals are to improve their health and that's what scientific researchers say to policy elites over and over again. It's the mantra in front of every NIH grant proposal. It is, after all, the National Institutes of *Health* who fund this research. The health mantra is central to policymakers. If you make the argument, "I am doing this in order that people can have better sex lives, so that they have better orgasms and more orgasms and with more people," at that moment you have probably stepped outside the edge of social toleration. It's not that some people haven't made those arguments. It's not that in some school here, some school there, some sex education teacher hasn't said that. But if you look at the constituted ideology of the sexual center, that is not what we say. That's why we work in medical schools, because we're in the health business. So if you're going to make an argument to a policymaker, you better be talking about reducing some kind of problem and replacing it with health.

John Bancroft: Your position may be post-modern, but it's certainly pre-Viagra.

John Gagnon: We've now discovered a way that general practice physicians can deal with impotence in the same way we did with the pill in the treatment of birth control.

John Bancroft: Yes, and it raises quite interesting questions relating to what you've been saying; whether this is promoting health or promoting something else. It will be interesting to see this issue followed through.

Anke Ehrhardt: I think that John Gagnon is correct on that level of policy making, but there are lots of different policymakers and I think among those of us who are concerned about more liberal attitudes toward sexuality, we argue perhaps too much on that level. And while we were not looking, the school boards were invaded by people with very conservative notions. So I would say we should look again at how European countries manage to get better policies in terms of sex education. In terms of changing policy beyond health, we need different arguments and we might be quite successful in the consumer movement, just as the religioius right has been in schools, since we are at a time where consumer movements are important. There I think we can use different arguments than health.

REFERENCES

Cardo, D. M., Culver, D. H., Ciesielski, C. A., Srivastava, P. V., Marcus, R., Abiteboul, D., Heptonstall, J., Ippolito, G., Lot, F., McKibben, P., Bell, D. M., & Centers for Disease Control Prevention Needlestick Surveillance Group. (1997). A case-control study of HIV seroconversion in health care workers after percutaneous exposure. *New England Journal of Medicine, 337,* 1485–1490.

Centers for Disease Control & Prevention. (1998a). Management of possible sexual, injecting-drug use, or other non-occupational exposure to HIV, including considerations related to antiretroviral therapy. Public Health Service Statement. *Morbidity and Mortality Weekly Report,* 47(RR–17), 1–14.

Centers for Disease Control & Prevention. (1998b). Public Health Service Task Force recommendations for the use of antiretroviral drugs in pregnant women infected with HIV-1 for maternal health and for reducing perinatal HIV-1 transmission in the United States. *Morbidity and Mortality Weekly Report,* 47(RR-2), 1–30.

Dilley, J. W., Woods, W. J., & McFarland, W. (1997). Are advances in treatment changing views about high-risk sex? [Letter]. *New England Journal of Medicine, 337,* 501–502.

Dilley, J. W., Woods, W. J., McFarland, W., Sabatino, J., Rinaldi, J., Adler, B., & Lihatsh, T. (1998, June). Improved antiretroviral treatment does not affect sexual decision-making among the majority of men who have high-risk sex with men. [Poster 23130]. Poster session presented at the 12th International Conference on AIDS, Geneva, Switzerland.

Ekstrand, M. L., Stall, R. D., Paul, J. P., Osmond, D. H., & Coates, T. J. (1998, June). Increasing rates of unprotected anal intercourse among San Francisco gay men include high UAI rates with a partner of unknown or different serostatus. [Poster 23116]. Poster session presented at the 12th International Conference on AIDS, Geneva, Switzerland.

Katz, M. H., & Gerberding, J. L. (1997). Post exposure treatment of people exposed to the HIV virus through sexual contact or injection-drug use. *New England Journal of Medicine, 336*(15), 1097–2000.

Some Conclusions and a Few Afterthoughts

JOHN BANCROFT

As we approach the end of this millennium, many of us in academic life find ourselves at a troubled but extraordinarily interesting and potentially very important time in the history of ideas. Put briefly, though not necessarily simply, this is the crisis between positivism and post-modernism. For most researchers in the natural sciences, this crisis may impinge very little on their day-to-day work. For those in anthropology, sociology, history, many departments of psychology, and some of the humanities (such as English), this is a time when faculty departments are being split asunder. And in the biomedical sciences, there is growing awareness that many health issues can only be properly comprehended if socio-cultural factors are taken into consideration, usually in ways for which biomedical scientists are ill prepared. For those of us concerned with human sexuality, there is a particular challenge. While few will argue that either biology or culture is irrelevant to human sexuality, the epistemologies that prevail in grappling with biology and culture are peculiarly irreconcilable. How do you deal with biology if you are a post-modern culturalist concerned with sexuality? How do you deal with culture, in its post-modern sense, if you are a reproductive biologist? The answer is that in the majority of cases, you deal with it by ignoring it or writing it off in some fashion. And there is another reason why the field of sex research is in this kind of turmoil; a large part of the intellectual rebellion comes from feminist, gay, and lesbian scholarship, where there has been a political as well as an intellectual motive for challenging the status quo. That rebellion has brought into the field a wealth of intellectual talent that previously was in relatively short supply.

A key objective of the workshop that led to this book was to explore how these two contrasting elements of current sexual scholarship might start to build bridges which would lead to fruitful, creative collaboration, facilitating the dialectic process so that a more mature, improved field of scholarship could emerge. To what extent did we succeed? To a limited extent. The discourse (in its conventional sense) remained civil (with one or two exceptions). The issues, the gaps over which bridges might be built, came into sharper focus. The bridge building, however, remains to be done.

Since the conference and the editing of the discussions and the receipt of the revised papers by the participants, I have had the opportunity to reflect on the meeting and to consider its strengths and weaknesses more closely. Let me summarize my impressions and organize my reflections around four particular themes: the use of theory, the issue of the individual versus the culture, the issue of insiders versus outsiders, and the relationship between theory and policy (or politics). There were a number of other equally interesting themes that emerged through the meeting. I have selected those which were both relevant to the objectives of the meeting and of particular interest to me as its organizer. This is therefore a personal statement. I will be drawing attention to comments by some of the participants, but not all. I hope that those whom I cite will not be offended by my taking this opportunity to have the last word and, also, that those whom I have not cited will not conclude that their contribution was considered unimportant or insufficiently provocative.

The Use of Theory

Clearly, and not surprisingly, people came to this meeting with a variety of definitions and uses of the idea of "theory." For Sarah Hrdy, a theory is "a hypothesis that has been tested, and tests have been confirmed and replicated" (p. 57). She cited "natural selection" as an example of a theory and "kin selection" as a tested and proven example of a subset of natural selection. In her view, evolutionary theory in its general sense is not a theory but a perspective. Robert Michael took a comparable view; he feels confident with "200 years of economic theory" which has clearly stood the test of time (e.g., "as prices fall, quantities rise; as incomes go up people want more" [p. 60]). Daryl Bem insisted that his theory should have the possibility of being wrong. All Joe Rodgers requires of a theory is that it is a useful simplification of reality; for him "a model + a measurement procedure = a theory" (p. 258). He endorsed my formulation of the need for "simplified models" that had been part of my letter of invitation to all participants.

Joe Rodgers would almost certainly say, in addition, that such simplified models are used to generate testable hypotheses. In other words, the theory leads to the testable hypothesis, not the other way round, as Sara Hrdy would have it. The main issue of contention is how they are tested. Interestingly, the most telling critique of Anthony Walsh's use of life history theory came from Sarah Hrdy, a sociobiologist and evolutionary anthropologist. She reminded us, at least by implication, that a theoretical model (or perspective as she would call it) requires intellectual rigor to be good. Clearly she does not see the idea of "genes switched on and off by the environment" as an example of such rigor (p. 35).[1] In addition, she raised the crucial issue of how you test a hypothesis. "Confirming prediction is not enough," she asserts (even replication of such confirmation), when that same prediction could be derived from a variety of other explanatory theoretical models. This is a problem many of us have with much of evolutionary theory, which, as Joe Rodgers said, is "not a very interesting theory because it is so facile at explaining everything . . . non-falsifiable" (p. 62). So this brings us to the Popperian standard of "falsifiability" which is regarded by many positivist scientists as the hallmark of the scientific method. Thomas Kuhn (1970) has pointed out, effectively, that a great deal (he would say most) of modern science does not meet that standard, and the work of many evolutionary theorists would support his conclusion. But the fact that positivist scientists vary in the extent to which they maintain Popper's standard does not, in my opinion, detract from the value of striving to achieve it. I have been brought up to aim for refutability of hypotheses, and even though in my own research I have achieved that to a variable extent, depending on the issue being examined, I have not been persuaded that this is other than good intellectual discipline for any scientist. Having said that, as I tried to point out in my paper, there are only certain aspects of what we struggle to explain and understand in sex research which lend themselves to such hypothesis testing, and for other aspects of research we must look for other ways to increase the validity of our conclusions.

Ken Plummer pointed to the demise of "grand theory." "In the academic circles I generally move in these days, the idea of any kind of unitary, integrative, monolithic theory that brings everything together is simply out of court. . . . the time has arrived for a multiplicity of much more localized specific theories" (p. 54). This was of particular relevance to me, having attempted to formulate for this conference not what I would call a grand or, for that matter, a monolithic theory, but certainly a broad and integrative theoretical model. And, as I explained during the discussion, I embarked on this project late in my career precisely because a lifetime of a multiplicity of much more localized specific theories in the natural sciences was becoming increasingly untenable simply because of the rapidly increasing complexity of biological knowledge. It was becoming more and more difficult to relate the wealth of new knowledge about very specific parts to the whole. Ken Plummer would perhaps say that we should be content to deal with a multitude of parts and forget about the whole. With society, that may make sense; it is a more difficult strategy to sustain when one's interest is the person. And maybe the change that Ken Plummer described is, indeed, of particular relevance to the circles in which he generally moves. In his introduction to *The Return of Grand Theory in the Human Sciences* (Skinner, 1985), Quentin Skinner writes of an "unashamed return to the deliberate construction of . . . grand theories of human nature and conduct," although he notes that this trend is most noticeable in the fields of moral and political philosophy. And he also points out that the iconoclasts, such as Foucault, could be regarded, paradoxically, as "grand theorists." I shall not, therefore, prematurely abandon my "broad integrative scheme" and, interestingly, I was encouraged by several of the less positivist participants to persevere with it (with, needless to say, heavy qualifications!).

But apart from Ken Plummer's interesting and highly relevant comments about theory, we heard much more about theory, in explicit terms, from the positivist members of this group. Of the postmodernists Gary Dowsett had the most to say: "Theory is about discursive positionings at a moment in time and so any particular set of positionings is a disciplinary paradigm and they all have their shortcomings and their blind spots" (p. 135). "[C]ertainly in my area of post-structuralism contemporary sexuality theory doesn't look anything like the sexuality that I'm hearing coming out of papers this morning" (p. 56). He marked off sexuality theory from sexology, seeing it as "largely pro-structuralist rather than post-modernist (because) . . . it relies very heavily on pre-existing concepts of social structure from social theories such as Marxism or functionalism." In explaining its relevance to safer sex for gay men, he commented, "You actually need to theorize the way in which gay bodies engage each other both with the physicality of those bodies and the meanings in culture that gay men bring to sexual engagement, to figure out how safe sex was invented as an idea"(p. 137). It seems clear that more time should have been given at this meeting to obtaining a more comprehensive description of "contemporary sexuality theory" and the role of such theory in practical approaches.

Both Leonore Tiefer and John Gagnon reminded us that we build theories in response to particular historical contexts, in response to particular issues of the time. As Gagnon put it "Theorizing about sex is not an abstract process . . . but an ideological practice grounded in the conflicts of particular historical moments and cultural situations" (p. 152).

The Individual versus Culture

The issue of whether one can usefully consider the individual as one strives to explain or understand human sexuality (or sexualities) recurred at various points through the meeting. In the session on sexual orientation, Daryl Bem considered how varying patterns of development might lead to contrasting forms of interaction with culture (by determining which scenario, same-sex or opposite-sex, became exotic and then erotic). His model was clearly built on the notion of individual differences. Gil Herdt also focused on the individual in the sense that he focused on a particular stage of psychobiological development in interaction with his very specific cultural scenario. But it is noteworthy that he implied a standard form of individual at that stage; his real emphasis was on the peculiar characteristics of the cultural pattern that was imposed. He did not consider the extent to which individuals might respond or not respond to this interactive process.

Not surprisingly it was in the session on "Individual Differences in Sexual Risk Taking" that this issue came into sharpest focus. The participants at the meeting could probably be divided (with no doubt a proportion remaining unclassified) into those whose bread and butter was to consider individual differences and how they contribute to explaining varying interactions with the cultural environment, and those who considered the individual to be of limited relevance when considering the sexual interaction of two people. Somehow the dyadic process, in their minds, invalidates the individual as a source of explanation, even a partial one. So we heard from Rafael Diaz that "the regulation of sexual arousal cannot be considered a personal psychological variable; it is a person-context situation" (p. 228); Connie Nathanson argued that "[t]hinking of risk management as an intrapersonal process seems to be far off the mark. . . . [S]exual situations involve two people" (p. 231); and Gary Dowsett, with his characteristic eloquence, reminded me that it's like swimming—you can't understand swimming "without understanding the properties of water and the way in which bodies and water interact" (p. 232)—(I wish I had thought at the time to comment that when using his metaphor and striving to explain why some people were good swimmers and others were bad swimmers, it would be appropriate to hold the properties of water constant!). I found all this strange and surprising, even though I have absolutely no difficulty in accepting that you can't predict a sexual interaction between two individuals by considering one of the individuals in isolation. On the other hand, you may well improve your prediction by considering the characteristics of both individuals. I will return to this issue later, when considering policy and politics and the issue of political correctness, which I may have transgressed.

But it was in the final session, while discussing Richard Parker's summary comments on cultural factors, that the individual versus culture and biology versus culture issues exploded into the discussion. Gil Herdt asked whether, in attempting to understand sexual desire, Richard Parker was "willing to cede the study of individual differences to a perspective . . . entirely outside anthropology?" To which Richard replied that "cultural perspectives when properly framed offer in some respects the most compelling way of accounting for individual differences" (p. 314). At that point I provocatively asked how he would account for the effects on sexual desire of replacing and withdrawing testosterone in a hypogonadal man. Gary Dowsett was prepared to answer: "[T]he effect of the testosterone will be immediately, instantaneously read within the subjectivity of sexuality"—and that is culturally determined (p. 314).

The idea that a hormone might have biological effects relevant to sexual and reproductive behavior, regardless of how one's culture shapes sexuality, seemed to be a crucial issue which polarized the debate. Ironically, a short time after the meeting I received the results of a study of testosterone replacement I had been involved in. This study compared a new non-reducable androgen (MENT) with testosterone in hypogonadal men, who were withdrawn from their previous androgen regime and after a period put on either one or the other of these two androgens (Anderson et al., in press). The relevant point is that, of the 20 hypogonadal men studied, 10 were from Scotland and 10 were from Hong Kong. The predicted and highly characteristic effect of testosterone on sleep erections, manifested by erections on first waking, was observed in both groups. But there were some interesting differences between the two centers. First, the Hong Kong men did not report a decline in their general mood during the withdrawal period and hence did not show the typical improvement in mood when the androgens were replaced. Secondly, the effects on sexual interest were less striking in the Hong Kong men. All previous studies of this kind, mainly double-blind placebo controlled studies, have been carried out in Europe or North America and have shown consistent results (more so for sexual desire and sleep erections than for mood). There are a number of possible explanations for the apparent cultural difference in this recent study, some less interesting from the point of view of this debate. But without doubt we should examine carefully how men in these two contrasting cultures experience androgen withdrawal and replacement. My expectation is that we will find a clear biological effect, essential to the maintenance of normal levels of sexual desire, but one that will be experienced in subtly different ways in the two settings. In addition to that there will be cultural differences in how best to find out about these experiences. I am prepared to concede that culture will shape the effects of testosterone, but as a reproductive biologist who is familiar with the almost universal role of testosterone as necessary for normal male mammalian sexual behavior, I have difficulty in accepting that direct effects of testosterone are not fundamental to the establishment of human male sexuality, however it might be culturally crafted. I accept Leonore Tiefer's observation that men seeking Viagra are "operating out of a system of masculinity"(p. 316), but I would assert that such culturally reinforced focus on erectile "potency," which is very much alive in the modern United States, will only be manifested in men who have adequate levels of testosterone to fuel their sexuality. Another example of the need to distinguish the human from other species that arose during the meeting was the need to conceptualize human sexuality as distinct from human reproduction. Here again, I remain committed to the idea that to understand human sexuality we need to understand its relationship to reproduction. I entirely accept that there are many sexualities which are divorced from reproduction and which are important aspects of human sexuality, but I would argue that we need to consider and understand the reasons for divorcing sex from reproduction rather than see reproduction simply as a red herring which until recently obscured our understanding of sexuality.

Insider versus Outsider Knowledge

This is an issue, central to much of the epistemological debate, which received surprisingly little attention. It is of particular interest to me, as I tried to convey in my discussion of "emic" versus "etic" in my paper (pp. 202–204). Gil Herdt picked this up, stressed the importance and expressed his preference for Clifford Geertz's terminology of "insider" versus "outsider" knowledge (p. 234). It was an underlying theme for some of those who questioned my theoretical approach to risk taking, the theme being that unless the people concerned think in such terms, what relevance does a particular model have to real life? On a larger scale, it reflects the post-modern prioritizing of reality as experienced, however that may be conceptualized, rather than a more objective, intellectual conceptualization of reality. The first has validity, it might be argued, the second does not. The distinction is at its simplest when considering relatively primitive cultures, as both Harris and Geertz did, where there is a very large gap between models of reality held by the insider or "native" and those held by the expert, sophisticated outsider, the cultural anthropologist. Since writing my paper, I read Jeffrey Escoffier's paper on the invention of safer sex (in press). I particularly liked his approach to this issue; he referred to vernacular knowledge, commonsense, everyday knowledge and Clifford Geertz's "local knowledge" as alternative terms for the concept of "insider knowledge." But he pointed out that the difference between insider and outsider is much more blurred in a modern industrial society. He quotes Gramsci: "Every philosophical current leaves behind a sedimentation of 'common sense': this is the documentation of its historical effectiveness. . . . Common sense is not something rigid or immobile, but is continually transforming itself, enriching itself with scientific ideas and philosophical opinions that have entered everyday life" (1971, p. 316). So where does the insider end and the outsider begin? This blurring of the two is a cause of concern for John Gagnon, who worries in his paper, and in its call to inaction, that the "stories about risky sex" experts construct will contaminate vernacular knowledge.

The conclusion I draw from all this is that we should certainly seek insider ideas about sexuality and sexual risk taking and we should listen to them, but we should not restrict our attention to them. At the same time, as Richard Parker points out, any new expert ideas that may come forward which might prove to be helpful in combating epidemics in the community need to be translated into real-world interventions that are thought about at both an individual and a collective community level.

Relationship between Theory and Policy

As we planned this meeting it was our intention, and the intention of the Ford Foundation (which funded the meeting), to pay some attention to policy. In particular, we wanted to consider how different theoretical approaches might facilitate the development of good effective social policy, the extent to which some theoretical approaches were perhaps more comprehensible to policy makers, and hence more influential than others, and so on. This issue was addressed at three levels. First, all contributors and discussants were asked to keep policy issues in mind as they prepared their comments; second, in session four, on adolescent sexual behavior, presenters were specifically asked to address policy issues in relation to their theoretical perspective. Third, we asked Robert Michael to summarize the meeting from the perspective of policy.

Clearly, our initial hopes and expectations were naïve and unrealistic. Robert Michael, both in his summing up and in his contributions to the discussions, displayed a rational approach to a benign concept of policy. For the rest, the issues were not so much about policy as about politics.

This became clear in the session on adolescent sexuality. First Joe Rodgers offended several participants by being "politically incorrect." He used a terminology which was seen to be politically loaded. He was so attacked for his terminology that his theoretical approach that relied on mathematical modeling derived from epidemiology received scant attention. I believe this was unfortunate; he could have avoided much of the problem by using different terms, and that may have allowed us to look more seriously at the pros and cons of his modeling approach, albeit one with a "cultureless" content. But he was attacked because it was felt that conceptualizing the problem in that way might lead to his model being used for undesirable purposes that pathologize adolescent sexuality and medicalize possible interventions that might derive from his model, even though, as he stresses in his paper, which he modified after the conference as a result of these attacks, this was not his intention. This reaction reminded me of the political opposition to a variety of theoretical approaches that could conceivably be used to support undesirable causes (e.g., research into brain differences between men and women). Political opposition of this kind can become extreme, and disturbingly so, as has been well documented by Morton Hunt (1999).

Connie Nathanson's contribution to the adolescent sexuality session was clearly focused on the issue of teenage pregnancy. Insofar as she focused on theory, it was the theory of the policymaker, ranging from the well-intentioned but misguided policy of the Alan Guttmacher Institute to use teenage pregnancy statistics to justify greater access to contraceptive services to the right-wing attempt to interpret those same statistics as evidence that the country's welfare system was making the situation worse by "rewarding" young women for getting pregnant. Nathanson's presentation, based on her book *Dangerous Passage* (Nathanson, 1991), was a compelling account of how statistics can be used or misused for a variety of political purposes. Perhaps her main political message was that all of these approaches focused on the individual teenager (who either needed contraceptives or should be denied the financial incentive to get pregnant) and ignored the real explanation for the teenage pregnancy statistics—poverty. Ipso facto, the politically correct approach was to concentrate on the elimination of poverty. I was disappointed that we seemed to be unable to get beyond that point to examine theoretically how, for example, poverty impacted on adolescent sexuality. Kristin Luker's (1996) book on teenage pregnancy, most of which was making the same point as Connie Nathanson, nevertheless has a section in which she examined why and how young women affected by poverty do what they do to get and stay pregnant. Such a theoretical analysis could be used to consider ways of helping these young women make the best choice in their given circumstances (which sometimes might be "get pregnant"). Such a use might also be interpreted as meaning that one was discriminating between those who were capable of making the right choices and those who weren't; i.e., again putting the blame on the individual rather than on society. So the prevailing message from this session is that focusing on the individual woman simply detracts from the larger and more important issue of ending poverty. As someone who has held a distinctly left-of-center political position throughout my life, I have absolutely no difficulty identifying passionately with the politics of ending poverty. But I have been a practicing physician who, like many others with various types of community-based roles, has spent all his adult life striving to work with individuals and families to help them help themselves. Maybe for that reason, the idea that focusing on the individual is unacceptable because it detracts from the larger task, and even worse, justifies the social status quo is anathema to me. Both tasks are important and necessary.

This theme also emerged, even more explicitly, in John Gagnon's paper. I had naïvely assumed when I invited John to participate that he would respond to the issue of "Individual Differences in Sexual Risk Taking" by invoking his sexual scripting approach. I was wrong. Instead he elaborated his view that even considering the individual in relation to sexual risk was inappropriate, politically unacceptable. "Treating the problem of risky sex as a property of the individual often simply blames the individual for structural conditions about which they can do nothing. In this way the situation is justified by placing the blame for risk taking on the individuals in the situation" (p. 169). He appears to be occupying a moral high ground which puts him above the need to intervene in the lives of individuals or social groups and hence removes him from a situation where he might conceivably make things worse, and certainly protects him from any accusation that his career or research program might have benefited from such interventions. Although the participants of this meeting were predominantly committed to active intervention at one level or another, I was left wondering whether some of the discomfort with my individual-oriented theoretical approach stemmed from recognizing it as politically incorrect in this same way.

If we were to follow John Gagnon's lead, we would remain extremely cautious about presenting any new theoretical ideas for fear that they might be ill used by policymakers or, alternatively, attacked on political grounds. Anke Ehrhardt made the important point that while we agonize over what we might put into the gap, others with "very conservative notions" will waste no time in filling it (p. 334).

On one side of the epistemological divide, the influence of Foucault was not hard to find. Gary Dowsett even awarded a prize for first mention of him. And the Foucaultian message that was perhaps most evident, even if implicitly, was that scientific endeavor to understand human sexual behavior is driven by a desire for social control and hence fundamentally morally suspect. This was a friendly, congenial group, selected in part for that reason, and the debate was stimulating and enjoyable. But the efforts to build bridges seemed to be one-sided, starting with Anke Ehrhardt's opening, clear statement of commitment to this cause. I was left wondering whether we positivists who were striving to make contact were in some sense stigmatized by our associations with traditional science.

This may read more negatively than I feel. I believe John Gagnon may have made the most relevant, constructive statement on the whole issue. "The only way you can create interdisciplinary theory is by doing concrete interdisciplinary projects. You have to work with somebody else who's doing empirical research, measuring something else in a concrete way. There are no theoretical ways to construct interdisciplinary theories. All you get is talk about talk. . . . [I]nterdisciplinary work is emergent" (p. 59). On that point I'm inclined to agree with him. One lesson we may learn from this meeting is that in order to obtain the sort of effective cross-disciplinary cooperation that we were searching for, we might have structured the meeting differently. We could have chosen one specific theme of practical and political importance, identified some practical real-world objectives in tackling that theme, and then asked people with different theoretical perspectives to make practical suggestions how they would tackle those objectives, explaining in the process how their theoretical approach informed their proposals. Maybe next time!

REFERENCES

Anderson, R. A., Martin, C. W., Kung, A., Everington, D., Pun, T. C., Tan, K. C. B., Bancroft, J., Sundaram, K., Moo-Young, A. J., & Baird, D. T. (in press). 7alpha-methyl-19-nortestosterone (MENT) maintains sexual behavior and mood in hypogonadal men. *Journal of Clinical Endocrinology and Metabolism.*

Escoffier, J. (in press). The invention of safer sex: Vernacular knowledge, gay politics and HIV prevention. *Berkeley Journal of Sociology.*

Gramsci, A. (1971). *Selections from the prison notes.* New York: International Publishers.

Hunt, M. M. (1999). *The new know-nothings: The political foes of the scientific study of human nature.* New Brunswick: Transaction Publishers.

Kuhn, T. S. (1970). Th*e structure of scientific revolutions* (2nd ed.). Chicago: University of Chicago Press.

Luker, K. (1996). *Dubious conceptions: The politics of teenage pregnancy.* Cambridge, MA: Harvard University Press.

Nathanson, C. (1991). *Dangerous passage: The social control of sexuality in woman's adolescence.* Philadelphia: Temple University Press.

Skinner, Q. (Ed.). (1985). *The return of grand theory in the human sciences.* Cambridge: Cambridge University Press.

Wilson, E. O. (1975). *Sociobiology: The new synthesis.* Cambridge: Harvard University Press.

NOTE

1. Sociobiology, for all its controversy, was based on a rigorous theoretical approach by E. O. Wilson (1975) and others. Unfortunately, not all of their followers have maintained this standard.

Conference Participants

TOMAS ALMAGUER is with the Department of Sociology at the University of Michigan in Ann Arbor.

JOHN BANCROFT was trained in medicine at Cambridge University and in psychiatry at the Institute of Psychiatry, London. He has been Director of the Kinsey Institute for Research in Sex, Gender, and Reproduction and Professor of Psychiatry at Indiana University since May 1995. For the previous 19 years he was Clinical Scientist at the Medical Research Council's Reproductive Biology Unit in Edinburgh, Scotland. He has extensive research and clinical experience in the relationship of reproductive hormones to sexuality and well-being, psychophysiology and pharmacology of sexual response, and the management of sexual problems. He is author of *Human Sexuality and Its Problems* (2nd edition, 1989), was founding editor of the *Annual Review of Sex Research,* and is a past president of the International Academy of Sex Research.

JOSÉ BARZELATTO received his medical degree from the University of Chile and did postgraduate studies in endocrinology at Massachusetts General Hospital. He worked at the World Health Organization in Geneva, Switzerland, from 1975 to 1989. From 1989 to 1996 he was Director of Reproductive Health and Population for The Ford Foundation in New York City. He is currently Vice President of The Center for Health and Social Policy.

DARYL BEM, Professor of Psychology at Cornell University, obtained his Ph.D. in social psychology from the University of Michigan. He taught at Carnegie-Mellon University and Stanford before joining the faculty at Cornell in 1978.

CAROLINE BLEDSOE is Professor of Anthropology at Northwestern University.

CLAIRE BRINDIS is Director of the Center for Reproductive Health Policy at the University of California, San Francisco, and a researcher in the fields of adolescent pregnancy prevention, women's health, and health policy.

ALEX CARBALLO-DIÉGUEZ was born in Argentina and migrated to the United States in 1982. He received his Ph.D. in Clinical Psychology from the New School for Social Research in 1986. During his initial years in New York, Dr. Carballo-Diéguez provided psychotherapeutic services to individuals afflicted with AIDS and HIV. In 1988 he joined the HIV Center for Clinical and Behavioral Studies at New York State Psychiatric Institute and Columbia University, and his professional activity progressively switched to a full-time involvement in research. His area of inquiry is sexual risk behavior among men who have sex with men, particularly those of Latin American background. His work, published in peer-reviewed journals, discusses issues of sexual identity, childhood sexual abuse and its association with adult HIV-risk behavior, perceived barriers to condom use, and cultural issues to be considered in HIV prevention.

DIANE DI MAURO has worked more than 15 years in the field of human sexuality, specializing in the areas of sexuality education and sexuality research. She is currently the Program Director of the Sexuality Research Fellowship Program at the Social Science Research Council, which provides dissertation and postdoctorate support for sexuality research in the social and behavioral sciences. Dr. di Mauro is the author of *Sexuality Research in the United States: An Assessment of the Social and Behavioral Sciences* and the co-author of *Winning the Battle: Developing Support for Sexuality and HIV Education* and *Communication Strategies for HIV/AIDS and Sexuality.*

RAFAEL M. DIAZ is by training a social worker (MSW, New York University 1977) and a developmental psychologist (Ph.D., Yale University 1982). In 1955, after 13 years as a professor of psychology and education at the University of New Mexico and Stanford University, he joined the faculty of the Center for AIDS Prevention Studies at the University of California, San Francisco. Rafael's current research is aimed at identifying socio-cultural barriers to safer sex practices in Latino gay/bisexual men, and in developing culturally relevant risk-reduction interventions in this community. He is Principal Investigator of an NIH project entitled "A Sociocultural Model of HIV Risk in Latino Gay Men." The project involves qualitative, quantitative, and intervention design studies in the cities of Los Angeles, Miami, and New York. Dr. Diaz is also Principal Investigator of a four-year study recently funded by the National Institute on Drug Abuse entitled "Drug Use and Risky Sexual Behavior in Latino Gay Men."

GARY W. DOWSETT is Associate Professor and Deputy Director of the Australian Research Centre in Sex, Health, and Society at La Trobe University in Melbourne. A sociologist by trade, he has long been interested in sexuality, particularly in relation to the rise of modern gay communities. Since 1986, he has been researching the nature and impact of the HIV epidemic on Australia's gay communities. He has also worked as a consultant to WHO's Global Programme on AIDS in Geneva, and as an adviser to the United Nations Development Programme and the Joint United Nations Programme on AIDS (UNAIDS). His international work includes designing a seven-country study of young people and contexts of risk in relation to HIV/AIDS. He has recently been developing training programs in community-based research and qualitative research design. His most recent book is *Practicing Desire: Homosexual Sex in the Era of AIDS,* published by Stanford University Press in 1996.

ANKE A. EHRHARDT, Director of the HIV Center for Clinical and Behavioral Studies at the New York State Psychiatric Institute and Columbia University since 1987, has done extensive research in the area of sex and gender for the last 30 years. She is co-author (with John Money) of *Man & Woman, Boy & Girl* and has written more than 160 scientific publications. Her research has included a range of studies involving the interaction between sex hormones, social/environmental factors, sexual behavior, and mental health, including the long-term effects of prenatal diethylstilbestrol (DES) exposure on gender, sexuality, and mental health in female and male offspring; the psychosexual development of adolescents with early puberty; sex hormones and sexual orientation in lesbians and heterosexual women; and the effects of antidepressants on sexual functioning.

DENNIS FORTENBERRY is Associate Professor of Pediatrics at Indiana University–Purdue University Indianapolis.

JOHN GAGNON, Distinguished Professor Emeritus of Sociology at the State University at Stony Brook, received his undergraduate and graduate degrees from the University of Chicago. He is author or co-author of *Sex Offenders* (1965), *Sexual Conduct* (1973), *Human Sexualities* (1977), and *The Social Organization of Sexuality* (1994). In addition he is co-editor of a number of books, most recently *Conceiving Sexuality* (1995) and *Encounters with AIDS: Gay Men and Lesbians Confront the AIDS Epidemic* (1997). He is now a Senior Scientist at the Center for Health and Policy Research.

MEG GERRARD is Professor of Psychology at Iowa State University.

CYNTHIA ANN GRAHAM is Assistant Professor, Department of Psychiatry, and Adjunct Assistant Professor, Department of Psychology, at Indiana University. She received her M App Sci in Clinical Psychology from the University of Glasgow, Scotland, and her Ph.D. in Clinical Psychology from McGill University, Canada. Her research has focused on female sexuality.

GILBERT HERDT is Professor of Human Sexuality and Anthropology, and Director of Human Sexuality Studies at San Francisco State University. He has published more than 50 papers and 20 books.

SARAH BLAFFER HRDY, Professor Emeritus of Anthropology, is author of *The Langurs of Abu: Female and Male Strategies of Reproduction; The Woman That Never Evolved;* and *Mother Nature: A History of Mothers, Infants, and Natural Selection.*

EDWARD O. LAUMANN, Professor of Sociology at the University of Chicago, is co-author of *The Social Organization of Sexuality: Sexual Practices in the United States.*

ERICK JANSSEN is Associate Scientist at the Kinsey Institute for Research in Sex, Gender, and Reproduction. He received his Ph.D. at the University of Amsterdam, the Netherlands, in 1995. He has published on the psychophysiology of sexual response and on sexual dysfunction. His current research interests include the study of (gender differences in) inhibition and activation of sexual arousal and of the determinants of high-risk sexual behavior. He is a member of the Editorial Board of the *Dutch Journal of Sexology* and reviewer for several journals, including the *Journal of Sex Research* and the *Archives of Sexual Behavior.*

SHIRLEY LINDENBAUM is Professor of Anthropology at the Graduate Center, City University of New York. Her fieldwork in Papua New Guinea (on kuru) and in Bangladesh (on cholera) was a prelude to more recent work on AIDS in the United States. She is author of *Kuru Sorcery: Disease and Danger in the New Guinea Highlands* (1979); co-editor (with Gilbert Herdt) of *The Time of AIDS* (1992); and co-editor (with Margaret Lock) of *Knowledge, Power, and Practice: The Anthropology of Medicine and Everyday Life* (1993).

HEINO F. L. MEYER-BAHLBURG is a Research Scientist at the New York State Psychiatric Institute and Professor of Clinical Psychology in the Department of Psychiatry of the College of Physicians and Surgeons of Columbia University. He is also the Co-Director of a psychoendocrine clinic and a research program on developmental psychoendocrinology with a focus on psychosexual differentiation. He also conducts research on the development of sexual behavior in the HIV Center for Clinical and Behavioral Studies.

ROBERT T. MICHAEL is the Eliakim Hastings Moor Distinguished Service Professor and Dean of the Irving B. Harris Graduate School of public policy studies at the University of Chicago. He is co-author of *Sex in America* (1994) and *The Social Organization of Sexuality* (1994). An economist, he writes on topics in family economics, including cohabitation, investments in children, and measuring poverty, as well as on adult sexuality.

CONSTANCE A. NATHANSON received her doctoral degree in Sociology from the University of Chicago in 1967. She is a professor in the Department of Population and Family Health Sciences at the Johns Hopkins University School of Hygiene and Public Health, and during 1998–1999 was a visiting scholar at the Russell Sage Foundation in New York City. Dr. Nathanson has published on a wide range of population issues, including gender differences in mortality, abortion, contraceptive use, and teenage pregnancy. Her most recent book, *Dangerous Passage: The Social Control of Sexuality in Women's Adolescence,* analyzed changing U.S. policies toward the management of women's transition from child- to womanhood. Nathanson's present research interests are in the social and political forces that govern decisions in public health policy. She is working on a manuscript based on a comparative study of policy decision processes in four countries.

LUCIA O'SULLIVAN is a social psychologist and research scientist at the HIV Center for Clinical and Behavioral Studies in the Department of Psychiatry at Columbia University. She is author or co-author of numerous articles and chapters on sexual coercion and influence, communication, and gender roles in dating relationships. She also studies social cognition, focusing on dating relationships of urban adolescents. She recently received a Your Researcher Award from the Society for Sex Therapy and Research and a Career Development Award from the National Institutes of Health.

RICHARD G. PARKER is a professor in the Sociomedical Sciences Division of the Joseph L. Mallman School of Public Health at Columbia University and the Department of Health Policies and Institutions in the Institute of Social Medicine at the State University of Rio de Janeiro. He has published extensively on issues related to gender, sexuality, and the politics of health and has carried out long-term ethnographic research in Brazil. His most recent book is *Beneath the Equator: Cultures of Desire, Male Homosexuality, and Emerging Gay Communities in Brazil.*

JAY PHILIP PAUL was trained as a clinical psychologist and has published numerous articles on sexual orientation, HIV risk reduction among gay/bisexual men, and substance use among gay/bisexual men. He has worked at the University of California, San Francisco's Center for AIDS Prevention Studies for the past decade.

KEN PLUMMER is Professor of Sociology at the University of Essex, U.K. He is author of *Sexual Stigma* (1975), *Document of Life* (1983), and *Telling Sexual Stories* (1995), editor of various collections, and author of numerous articles. He is currently editor of the journal *Sexualities.*

CHRISTOPHER PORTELLI is Director of Information of the Sex Information and Education Council of the United States (SIECUS) in New York City.

JOSEPH LEE RODGERS is Professor of Psychology at the University of Oklahoma. He does research in the areas of quantitative, developmental, and social psychology. He has been developing conceptual and mathematical models of adolescent transition behaviors (including smoking, drinking, and delinquency, as well as sexual behavior) for around two decades. He is co-editor of *Genetic Influences on Human Fertility and Sexuality* (forthcoming from Kluwer). Rodgers has held visiting appointments at Ohio State University, the University of North Carolina, Duke University, and Odense University in Denmark, and has won a number of teaching and research awards from the University of Oklahoma.

STEPHANIE SANDERS is Associate Director of the Kinsey Institute for Research in Sex, Gender, and Reproduction and Associate Professor of Gender Studies at Indiana University.

THEO SANDFORT is a social-sexologist and directs research at both the Department of Clinical Psychology (Utrecht University) and the Netherlands Institute of Social Sexological Research (Utrech, Netherlands). He is editor of *The Dutch Response to HIV: Pragmatism and Consensus* (1988) and co-editor (with Michel Hubert and Nathalie Bajos) of *Sexual Behaviour and HIV/AIDS in Europe* (1998).

LEONORE TIEFER was originally trained as a comparative and experimental psychologist. She re-specialized as a clinical psychologist, and currently holds Clinical Associate appointments in the Departments of Psychiatry at Albert Einstein College of Medicine and New York University School of Medicine. Her most recent book is *Sex Is Not a Natural Act and Other Essays* (1995).

ANTHONY WALSH is Professor of Criminal Justice at Boise State University, Idaho. A former police officer and probation officer, he has published books on love, sexuality, counseling, law, statistics, criminology, juvenile delinquency, and biosociology. His primary interest is criminology from the perspectives of behavior, genetics, and evolution.

MARTIN WEINBERG is Professor of Sociology at Indiana University.

Index

Aborigines, Australian, 44, 86
abortion, 199, 242, 248, 249, 250, 251, 256, 280, 299, 324
abstinence, 47, 159, 268–69, 283, 286, 289, 294, 297, 299–300; and welfare reform, 244–47, 255–57, 280, 287
adolescents, female: age at first intercourse, 23, 24t, 39, 43–44, 258, 263–64, 265, 266, 268–71, 274–75, 276–78, 283, 284, 303; expectations concerning relationships, 37, 42; homosexuality among, 143; menarche in, 35–40, 42–44; relations with adults, 247, 267, 296–97, 299, 302–303; sexual behavior among, 20, 183, 227, 242, 258–72, 273–78, 279–81, 282–85, 343; sexual expectations, 9, 11, 14. *See also* adolescents, male; children, female; pregnancy, adolescent; women
adolescents, male: age at first intercourse, 24, 25t, 26, 43, 258, 263–64, 265, 266, 268–71, 274–75, 276, 278, 280, 283, 284, 303; homosexuality among, 143, 183; sexual behavior among, 227, 258–72, 273–78, 279–81, 282–85, 343; sexual expectations, 9, 11, 14. *See also* adolescents, female; children, male; men
adrenarche, 87, 88, 104n3, 130; and sexual attraction, 84, 89–92, 100, 105–106, 119–20, 144. *See also* androgens
aggressive/dominance behavior in males, 9, 11, 12, 14, 31, 75, 76, 115, 117
Aid to Families with Dependent Children (AFDC), 288
AIDS. *See* HIV/AIDS
AIDS Risk Reduction Model, 178–79
Ajzen, I., 178
Alan Guttmacher Institute, 247–50, 254, 255, 280, 281, 297, 344

alcohol use and sexual risk taking, 167, 210, 218, 230, 245, 275–76, 281, 284–85, 290–91
Alexander, Richard, 35
Altmann, Jeanne, 42
anal intercourse, 130, 158, 160, 217, 332–33
Anderson, Roy M., 264
androgens: and gender differences, 9–10, 31, 33, 112–13, 117; testosterone, 89, 91, 111, 114, 120, 314–15, 318–20, 341–42. *See also* adrenarche
anthropology, 44, 53–54, 63, 194, 202–203, 234, 310, 313–14, 341
anxiety, 187, 209n2, 219
Australia, 44, 86, 230–31, 294, 331

Bailey, J. M., 27, 72
Bancroft, John: comments by, 30, 43, 51, 58–59, 138, 144–45, 209–10, 211–12, 225, 227–28, 229, 231, 233, 235, 236, 237, 256, 297, 299, 303, 314, 315, 319, 320, 332, 333, 334, 336–46; comments on, 54, 62, 63, 211, 212, 213, 215–16, 217, 219–20, 221–22, 223, 228–29, 234–35, 236–37, 298–99, 308, 315, 318, 327
Barkow, Jerome, 18
Baruya, 94, 108
Barzelatto, José, comments by, 256–57
Bauman, L. J., 185
Baumeister, R. F., 187, 188
Becker, Howard, 145
Becker, M. H., 177–78
Belsky, Jay, 20, 39
Bem, Daryl, 89, 90; comments by, 61, 80–81, 134–35, 224, 275–76, 330; comments on, 99, 100, 116–18, 119, 121, 127–29, 130, 144, 225, 337, 340
Bem, Sandra, 48–49
Bem Sex Role Inventory, 20
berdache, 63, 140
Berscheid, E., 73

cultural materialism, 192–206, 311
cultural variables, 42, 97–101, 152, 167–
72, 191–206, 303–304, 316–20,
336; vs. individual differences, 167–
70, 180, 212, 307–12, 313–15, 317–
18, 337, 340–42. *See also* social
constructionism; social variables

Dangerous Passage, 244, 344
Dannecker, Martin, 137
Darwin, Charles, 57
date rape, 12
dehydroepiandrosterone (DHEA), 89, 91,
119–20
Denenberg, V. H., 112–13
Department of Health and Human
Services, 246
depression, 187–88, 190, 209*n*2, 219
DHEA (dehydroepiandrosterone), 89, 91,
119–20
Diaz, Raphael: comments by, 31, 107,
228–29, 237, 340; comments on,
234, 237, 340
diethylstilbestrol (DES), 113
Dilley, J. W., 333
divorce, 14, 25, 198–99; among females,
22, 23, 27; among parents of
females, 20, 22, 23, 24*t*, 26, 27, 28,
39; among parents of males, 24, 25*t*,
26. *See also* marriage
Dodd, S. C., 266
dominance/aggressive behavior in males,
9, 11, 12, 14, 31, 75, 76, 115, 117
Dörner, G., 112
Douglas, Mary, 230
Dover, Kenneth, 95
Dowsett, Gary: comments by, 31, 56–57,
135–37, 142–43, 231–33, 294–95,
300–301, 303–304, 314, 315, 317–
18, 319–20, 331, 339, 340, 341;
comments on, 135, 144, 234, 235,
237, 296, 300, 310, 311, 318, 322,
339, 340, 341, 345–46
Draper, Patricia, 20, 37
Drickamer, Lee, 42
drug use: and adolescent sexuality, 245,
251, 281, 284–85, 289, 290–91; and
HIV/AIDS, 154, 158, 160, 162, 168,
210, 218, 230, 275–76, 287, 332
Dubious Conceptions, 244
Durkheim, Émil, 318
Dzur, C., 9

Eberhard, Mary Jane West, 34, 35
economics, 323, 337
Ehrhardt, Anke: comments by, 30–32,
42, 51–52, 60, 137, 138, 144, 209,
225, 254, 277, 299, 302, 314–15,
318–19, 334; comments on, 30–31,
33, 35, 51, 130, 284, 300, 308, 309,
326–27, 345, 346
Ekstrand, M. L., 332
*11 Million Teenagers: What Can Be Done
about the Epidemic of Adolescent
Pregnancies in the United States,* 248,
253*n*5, 255
Ellis, Albert, 7
Ellison, Peter, 36
"Emancipation and the Change of
Heterosexual Relationships," 13
emic vs. etic, 202–203, 234–35, 310,
342–43
The Enlightenment, 308, 328
environmental variables. *See* cultural
variables; social variables
Epidemic Models of the Onset of Social
Activities (EMOSA), 264–72, 273–
77, 344
Escoffier, Jeffrey, 227, 342–43
essentialism, biological. *See* biological
essentialism
estrogens, 9–11, 89, 91, 111, 112–13,
117
Evin, Claude, 320
evolutionary theory, 57–58, 61–62, 309,
337, 338; and sexuality, 17, 19, 26,
36, 39–40, 56, 76, 81. *See also* life
history theory
exotic-becomes-erotic theory, 67–78, 90,
100, 119, 340; criticism of, 116–18,
127, 128–29, 130; evidence for, 70–
74, 80, 81; features of, 67–70, 74,
80–81, 121, 134–35

family relationships, 196, 198–99, 323
feminism, 49, 52, 57, 161, 192, 198, 211,
251, 288, 336
Fine, Michelle, 300
Fisher, H., 18
Fitch, R. H., 112–13
Fleck, Ludwig, 154
Ford Foundation, 343
Fortenberry, Dennis: comments by, 211,
298, 331; comments on, 223, 296,
299, 331